ANNUAL EDITIONS

United States History

Volume 2—Through the Present Reconstruction
Twentieth Edition

D0073940

EDITOR

Robert James Maddox (Emeritus)
Pennsylvania State University
University Park

Robert James Maddox, distinguished historian and professor emeritus of American history at Pennsylvania State University, received a BS from Fairleigh Dickinson University in 1957, an M.S. from the University of Wisconsin in 1958, and a PhD from Rutgers in 1964. He has written, reviewed, and lectured extensively, and is widely respected for his interpretations of presidential character and policy.

Higher Education

Boston   Burr Ridge, IL   Dubuque, IA   New York   San Francisco   St. Louis
Bangkok   Bogotá   Caracas   Kuala Lumpur   Lisbon   London   Madrid   Mexico City
Milan   Montreal   New Delhi   Santiago   Seoul   Singapore   Sydney   Taipei   Toronto

ANNUAL EDITIONS: UNITED STATES HISTORY, VOLUME 2, TWENTIETH EDITION

1 2 3 4 5 6 7 8 9 0 QPD/QPD 0 9 8

ISBN 978-0-07-339762-7
MHID 0-07-339762-8
ISSN 0733–3560

Managing Editor: *Larry Loeppke*
Senior Managing Editor: *Faye Schilling*
Developmental Editor: *Jade Benedict*
Editorial Assistant: *Nancy Meissner*
Production Service Assistant: *Rita Hingtgen*
Permissions Coordinator: *Shirley Lanners*
Senior Marketing Manager: *Julie Keck*
Marketing Communications Specialist: *Mary Klein*
Marketing Coordinator: *Alice Link*
Project Manager: *Sandy Wille*
Design Specialist: *Tara McDermott*
Senior Administrative Assistant: *DeAnna Dausener*
Senior Production Supervisor: *Laura Fuller*
Cover Design: *Kristine Jubeck*

Compositor: Laserwords Private Limited
Cover Image: Library of Congress (foreground) and Comstock/Corbis (background)

Library in Congress Cataloging-in-Publication Data
Main entry under title: United States History Vol. 2: Reconstruction Through the Present. 20e.
  1. United States—History—Periodicals. 2. United States—Historiography—Periodicals. 3. United States—Civilization—Periodicals.I.1. Maddox, Robert James, *comp*. II Title: United States History, Vol. 2: Reconstruction Through the Present
658'.05

www.mhhe.com

Editors/Advisory Board

Members of the Advisory Board are instrumental in the final selection of articles for each edition of ANNUAL EDITIONS. Their review of articles for content, level, currentness, and appropriateness provides critical direction to the editor and staff. We think that you will find their careful consideration well reflected in this volume.

Preface

In publishing ANNUAL EDITIONS we recognize the enormous role played by the magazines, newspapers, and journals of the public press in providing current, first-rate educational information in a broad spectrum of interest areas. Many of these articles are appropriate for students, researchers, and professionals seeking accurate, current material to help bridge the gap between principles and theories and the real world. These articles, however, become more useful for study when those of lasting value are carefully collected, organized, indexed, and reproduced in a low-cost format, which provides easy and permanent access when the material is needed. That is the role played by ANNUAL EDITIONS.

This volume begins with an article on post-Civil War Reconstruction, a period that ended in 1877. It was a very different world from the one we are living in today. The United States remained primarily a rural, agricultural nation. People for the most part lived much the same as they had 100 years earlier. They read by candle, lantern, or gaslight at night, they traveled by foot or by wagon, and they rarely ventured far from their home towns.

The following decades brought vast changes in all aspects of American life. Automobiles, expanding railroad systems, and airplanes enabled people to routinely travel to places they would only have dreamed about earlier. Massive population shifts, from farms and small towns to cities and suburbs, and from one section of the nation to another, radically altered the face of the nation. Immigration brought with it a host of opportunities and problems. At home, people could listen to the radio, watch television, or, more recently, explore new worlds of information via their computers. Diseases that once were almost certainly fatal or at least debilitating have now been virtually eliminated, resulting in life expectancies unheard of in the past.

With all of these "improvements," one would be hard put to argue that people in modern society are happier or more content than they were in the past. Extreme poverty is still with us in a land of untold wealth. Television and motion pictures, furthermore, encourage frustration by allowing even the poorest souls to glimpse those with lifestyles that only the wealthiest few would have enjoyed a century earlier. Other issues we face today also have echoes in the past: race relations, gender roles, domestic terrorism, and environmental problems, to name just a few. Some people fear that we are destroying the very planet on which we live. At least one new epidemic—AIDs—has become a scourge just as smallpox once was. Some fear that a pandemic of Avian Flu might break out that could be as devastating as the flu epidemic of 1918–1919 that cost as many as 40 million lives. Studying history will provide no "answers" to our modern troubles, but perhaps can provide some helpful guidelines.

Someone once said that historians wrote about "chaps," meaning white males who enjoyed positions of power or influence. Older history books tended to concentrate on presidents, titans of industry or finance, and military leaders. Women usually were mentioned only in passing, and then primarily as the wives or lovers of important men. Minority groups were treated, if at all, as passive objects of social customs or legislation. Mention of sexual orientation was simply out of the question.

Now virtually everything that has happened is considered fit for study. Books and articles tell us about the lives of ordinary people, about groups previously ignored or mentioned only in passing, and about subjects considered too trivial or commonplace to warrant examination. History "from the bottom up," once considered innovative, has become commonplace. Welcome as

these innovations are, they often are encumbered by two unfortunate tendencies: many are freighted down with incomprehensible prose (one of the criterion for inclusion in this volume is that articles be written in standard English), and many are produced to advance agendas the authors try to fob off as scholarship.

Traditional history is still being written. For better or worse, there *have* been men and women who have exercised great power or influence over the lives and deaths of others. They continue to fascinate. Presidents such as Franklin D. Roosevelt and Harry S. Truman had to make decisions that affected enormous numbers of people at home and abroad. Thomas Alva Edison changed millions of lives with his inventions, one of which, the incandescent light bulb, is treated in this volume. Rosa Parks never held any official position of power, but she deeply affected the way thought about segregation in the South during the 1950s.

Annual Editions: American History, Volume II, constitutes an effort to provide a balanced collection of articles that deal with great leaders and great decisions, as well as with ordinary people, at work, at leisure, and at war. Practically everyone who uses the volume will think of one or more articles he or she considers would have been preferable to the ones actually included. Some readers will wish more attention had been paid to one or another subject, others will regret the attention devoted to matters they regard as marginal. That is why we encourage teachers and students to let us know what they believe to be the strengths and weaknesses of this edition.

Annual Editions contains a number of features designed to make the volume "user friendly." These include a *topic guide* to help locate articles on specific individuals or subjects; the *table of contents extracts* that summarize each article with key concepts in boldface; and a comprehensive index. The essays are organized into six units. Each unit is preceded by an overview that provides background for informed reading of the articles, briefly introduces each one, and presents challenge questions. Please let us know if you have any suggestions for improving the format.

There will be a new edition of this volume in two years, with approximately half the readings being replaced by new ones. By completing and mailing the postpaid article rating form included in the back of the book, you will help us determine which articles should be retained and which should be dropped. You can also help to improve the next edition by recommending (or better yet, sending along a copy of) articles that you think should be included. A number of essays included in this edition have come to our attention in this way.

Robert James Maddox
Editor

Contents

UNIT 1
Reconstruction and the Gilded Age

The concepts in bold italics are developed in the article. For further expansion, please refer to the Topic Guide.

UNIT 2
The Emergence of Modern America

UNIT 3
From Progressivism to the 1920s

The concepts in bold italics are developed in the article. For further expansion, please refer to the Topic Guide.

UNIT 4
From the Great Depression to World War II

The concepts in bold italics are developed in the article. For further expansion, please refer to the Topic Guide.

UNIT 5
From the Cold War to 2007

The concepts in bold italics are developed in the article. For further expansion, please refer to the Topic Guide.

UNIT 6
New Directions for American History

The concepts in bold italics are developed in the article. For further expansion, please refer to the Topic Guide.

The concepts in bold italics are developed in the article. For further expansion, please refer to the Topic Guide.

Correlation Guide

The *Annual Editions* series provides students with convenient, inexpensive access to current, carefully selected articles from the public press. **Annual Editions: United States History, Volume 2: Reconstruction through the Present, 20/e** is an easy-to-use reader that presents articles on important topics in the study of United States History. For more information on *Annual Editions* and other *McGraw-Hill Contemporary Learning Series* titles, visit www.mhcls.com.

This convenient guide matches the units in **Annual Editions: United States History, Volume 2, 20/e** with the corresponding chapters in one of our best-selling McGraw-Hill History textbooks by Davidson et al.

Annual Editions: United States History, Vol. 2, 20/e	Nation of Nations, Volume II: Since 1865, 6/e by Davidson et al.
Unit 1: Reconstruction and the Gilded Age	**Chapter 17:** Reconstructing the Union (1865–1877)
Unit 2: The Emergence of Modern America	**Chapter 18:** The New South and the Trans-Mississippi West (1870–1896)
	Chapter 19: The New Industrial Order (1870–1900)
	Chapter 20: The Rise of an Urban Order (1870–1900)
	Chapter 21: The Political System under Strain (1877–1900)
Unit 3: From Progressivism to the 1920's	**Chapter 22:** The Progressive Era (1890–1920)
	Chapter 23: The United States and the Old World Order (1901–1920)
	Chapter 24: The New Era (1920–1929)
Unit 4: From the Great Depression to World War II	**Chapter 25:** The Great Depression and the New Deal (1929–1939)
	Chapter 26: America's Rise to Globalism (1927–1945)
Unit 5: From the Cold War to 2007	**Chapter 27:** Cold War America (1945–1954)
	Chapter 28: The Suburban Era (1945–1963)
	Chapter 29: Civil Rights and the Crisis of Liberalism (1947–1969)
	Chapter 30: The Vietnam Era (1963–1975)
	Chapter 31: The Age of Limits (1965–1980)
	Chapter 32: The Conservative Challenge (1980–1992)
	Chapter 33: Nation of Nations in a Global Community (1980–2000)
Unit 6: New Directions for American History	**Epilogue:** Fighting Terrorism in a Global Age (2000–2003)

Topic Guide

This topic guide suggests how the selections in this book relate to the subjects covered in your course. You may want to use the topics listed on these pages to search the Web more easily.

On the following pages a number of Web sites have been gathered specifically for this book. They are arranged to reflect the units of this *Annual Edition*. You can link to these sites by going to the student online support site at *http://www.mhcls.com/online/*.

ALL THE ARTICLES THAT RELATE TO EACH TOPIC ARE LISTED BELOW THE BOLD-FACED TERM.

Internet References

The following Internet sites have been carefully researched and selected to support the articles found in this reader. The easiest way to access these selected sites is to go to our student online support site at *http://www.mhcls.com/online/.*

AE: United States History, Volume 2

The following sites were available at the time of publication. Visit our Web site—we update our student online support site regularly to reflect any changes.

General Sources

American Historical Association
www.historians.org

This is the logical first visitation site for someone interested in virtually any topic in American history. All affiliated societies and publications are noted, and AHA links present material related to myriad fields of history and for students with different levels of education.

Harvard's John F. Kennedy School of Government
http://www.ksg.harvard.edu/

Starting from this home page, click on a huge variety of links to information about American history, ranging from data about political parties to general debates of enduring issues.

History Net
http://www.thehistorynet.com/

Supported by the National Historical Society, this frequently updated site provides information on a wide range of topics. The articles are of excellent quality, and the site has book reviews and even special interviews.

Library of Congress
http://www.loc.gov/

Examine this Web site to learn about the extensive resource tools, library services/resources, exhibitions, and databases available through the Library of Congress in many different subfields that are related to American history.

Smithsonian Institution
http://www.si.edu/

This site provides access to the enormous resources of the Smithsonian, which holds some 140 million artifacts and specimens in its trust for "the increase and diffusion of knowledge." Here you can learn about American social, cultural, economic, and political history from a variety of viewpoints.

The White House
http://www.whitehouse.gov/

Visit the home page of the White House for direct access to information about commonly requested federal services, the White House Briefing Room, and the presidents and vice presidents. The "Virtual Library" allows you to search White House documents, listen to speeches, and view photos.

UNIT 1: Reconstruction and the Gilded Age

Anacostia Museum/Smithsonian Institution
http://www.si.edu/archives/historic/anacost.htm

This is the home page of the Center for African American History and Culture of the Smithsonian Institution. Explore its many avenues. This is expected to become a major repository of information.

American Memory
http://memory.loc.gov/ammem/ammemhome.html

American Memory is a gateway to rich primary source materials relating to the history and culture of the United States. The site offers more than 7 million digital items from more than 100 historical collections.

UNIT 2: The Emergence of Modern America

The Age of Imperialism
http://www.smplanet.com/imperialism/toc.html

During the late nineteenth and early twentieth centuries, the United States pursued an aggressive policy of expansionism, extending its political and economic influence around the globe. That pivotal era in the nation's history is the subject of this interactive site. Maps and photographs are provided.

William McKinley 1843–1901
http://lcweb.loc.gov/rr/hispanic/1898/mckinley.html

Browse through this Library of Congress site for insight into the era of William McKinley, including discussion of the Spanish-American War.

American Diplomacy: Editor's Corner—If Two By Sea
http://www.unc.edu/depts/diplomat/AD_Issues/amdipl_15/edit_15.html

This essay provides a brief biography of Alfred Thayer Mahan and reviews his contributions and influence towards expansionism in American foreign policy.

Great Chicago Fire and the Web of Memory
http://www.chicagohs.org/fire/

This site, created by the Academic Technologies unit of Northwestern University and the Chicago Historical Society, is interesting and well constructed. Besides discussing the Great Chicago Fire at length, the materials provide insight into the era in which the event took place.

UNIT 3: From Progressivism to the 1920s

International Channel
http://www.i-channel.com/

Immigrants helped to create modern America. Visit this interesting site to experience "the memories, sounds, even tastes of Ellis Island. Hear immigrants describe in their own words their experiences upon entering the gateway to America."

World War I—Trenches on the Web
http://www.worldwar1.com/

Mike Lawrence's interesting site supplies extensive resources about the Great War and is the appropriate place to begin exploration of this topic as regards the American experience in World War I. There are "virtual tours" on certain topics, such as "Life on the Homefront."

www.mhcls.com/online/

World Wide Web Virtual Library
http://www.iisg.nl/~w3vl/

This site focuses on labor and business history. As an index site, this is a good place to start exploring these two vast topics.

The Roaring 20's and the Great Depression
http://www.snowcrest.net/jmike/20sdep.html

An extensive anthology of Web links to sites on the Roaring 20's and the Great Depression.

UNIT 4: From the Great Depression to World War II

Works Progress Administration/Folklore Project
http://lcweb2.loc.gov/ammem/wpaintro/wpalife.html

Open this home page of the Folklore Project of the Works Progress Administration (WPA) Federal Writers' Project to gain access to thousands of documents on the life histories of ordinary Americans from all walks of life during the Great Depression.

Hiroshima Archive
http://www.lclark.edu/~history/HIROSHIMA/

The Hiroshima Archive was originally set up to join the on-line effort made by many people all over the world to commemorate the 50th anniversary of the atomic bombing. It is intended to serve as a research and educational guide to those who want to gain and expand their knowledge of the atomic bombing.

The Enola Gay
http://www.theenolagay.com/index.html

The official Web site of Brigadier General Paul W. Tibbets, Jr. (Ret.) Offers a wealth of historical analysis and photographs of the events surrounding the use of atomic weapons on Japan in 1945.

UNIT 5: From the Cold War to 2006

Coldwar
http://www.cnn.com/SPECIALS/cold.war

This site presents U.S. government policies during the cold war. Navigate interactive maps, see rare archival footage online, learn more about the key players, read recently declassified documents and tour Cold War capitals through 3-D images.

The American Experience: Vietnam Online
http://www.pbs.org/wgbh/amex/vietnam/

Vietnam Online was developed to accompany Vietnam: A Television History, the award-winning television series produced by WGBH Boston.

The Gallup Organization
http://www.gallup.com/

Open this Gallup Organization home page to access an extensive archive of public opinion poll results and special reports on a huge variety of topics related to American society, politics, and government.

STAT-USA
http://www.stat-usa.gov/stat-usa.html

This site, a service of the Department of Commerce, contains daily economic news, frequently requested statistical releases, information on export and international trade, domestic economic news and statistical series and databases.

U.S. Department of State
http://www.state.gov/

View this site for an understanding into the workings of what has become a major U.S. executive-branch department. Links explain what exactly the department does, what services it provides, what it says about U.S. interests around the world, and much more.

UNIT 6: New Directions for American History

American Studies Web
http://www.georgetown.edu/crossroads/asw/

This eclectic site provides links to a wealth of Internet resources for research in American studies, from agriculture and rural development, to history and government, to race and ethnicity.

National Center for Policy Analysis
http://www.public-policy.org/web.public-policy.org/index.php

Through this site, click onto links to read discussions of an array of topics that are of major interest in the study of American history, from regulatory policy and privatization to economy and income.

The National Network for Immigrant and Refugee Rights (NNIRR)
http://www.nnirr.org/

The NNIRR serves as a forum to share information and analysis, to educate communities and the general public, and to develop and coordinate plans of action on important immigrant and refugee issues. Visit this site and its many links to explore these issues.

STANDARDS: An International Journal of Multicultural Studies
http://www.colorado.edu/journals/standards

This fascinating site provides access to the *Standards* archives and a seemingly infinite number of links to topics of interest in the study of cultural pluralism.

Supreme Court/Legal Information Institute
http://supct.law.cornell.edu/supct/index.html

Open this site for current and historical information about the Supreme Court. The archive contains many opinions issued since May 1990 as well as a collection of nearly 600 of the most historic decisions of the Court.

We highly recommend that you review our Web site for expanded information and our other product lines. We are continually updating and adding links to our Web site in order to offer you the most usable and useful information that will support and expand the value of your Annual Editions. You can reach us at: *http://www.mhcls.com/annualeditions/*.

UNIT 1

Reconstruction and the Gilded Age

Unit Selections

1. **The American Civil War, Emancipation, and Reconstruction on the World Stage,** Edward L. Ayers
2. **1871 War on Terror,** David Everitt
3. **Little Bighorn Reborn,** Tony Perrottet
4. **Gifts of the "Robber Barons",** James Nuechterlein
5. **The Spark of Genius,** Harold Evans
6. **Global Cooling,** Mark Bernstein
7. **Lockwood in '84,** Jill Norgren
8. **A Day to Remember: December 29, 1890,** Charles Phillips

Key Points to Consider

- Discuss "The American Civil War, Emancipation, and Reconstruction on the World Stage." How did these events influence people in other nations?

- What practices did industrial leaders use that earned them the name "Robber Barons." What, if any, were their positive contributions?

- Why was ice of such great value during the 20th Century? How did technological advances involving the use of ice alter the distribution and consumption of perishable goods?

- Discuss events leading to the Wounded Knee Massacre? Who were the "Ghost Dancers," and what were they trying to achieve?

Student Web Site

www.mhcls.com/online

Internet References

Further information regarding these Web sites may be found in this book's preface or online.

Anacostia Museum/Smithsonian Institution
http://www.si.edu/archives/historic/anacost.htm

This is the home page of the Center for African American History and Culture of the Smithsonian Institution. Explore its many avenues. This is expected to become a major repository of information.

American Memory
http://memory.loc.gov/ammem/ammemhome.html

Abraham Lincoln had wanted to reunite the nation as quickly as possible after four years of war. During the last months of his life, he had instituted simple procedures through which Southern states could resume their positions within the union. Only a few high-ranking Confederate officials were prohibited from participating. But what about the former slaves? Lincoln's version of reconstruction would result in the South being ruled by essentially the same people who had brought about secession. Those who became known as "Radical" or "Extreme" Republicans refused to abandon Freedpeople to their former masters. They wished to use the power of the federal government to ensure that blacks enjoyed full civil and legal rights. At first they thought they had an ally in Vice President Andrew Johnson, who assumed the presidency after Lincoln's assassination. When this proved untrue, a grueling struggle ensued which resulted in Johnson's impeachment and the Radicals in command of reconstruction. The South was divided into five military districts and federal troops were sent to protect the rights of Freedpeople. White Southerners used every means possible to keep blacks "in their place." As discussed in the article "1871 War on Terror," these methods included terrorist organizations such as the Ku Klux Klan and the Knights of the White Camelia. "The American Civil War, Emancipation, and Reconstruction," among other things, analyzes the ultimate failure of Radical Reconstruction.

Historians used to debate whether business leaders during the latter part of the 19th Century should be regarded as "industrial statesmen" or "robber barons." Most of them were both. "Gifts of the Robber Barons" examines two such individuals, Andrew Carnegie and Andrew Mellon. Without denying the shady business practices these men often employed, the author concludes that they, and others like them, did much to create a modern industrial society.

Thomas Alva Edison's invention of the incandescent light bulb during the 1870s was a boon to millions of people who previously had to read by candle, lantern, or gaslight. He took out nearly 1,100 patents during his lifetime, many of which wrought enduring changes in the way people lived. "The Spark of Genius" goes beyond Edison's prowess in the laboratory to emphasize his abilities to bring his inventions to practical use.

Today the most common means of refrigeration is based on electrical power. During the 19th Century ice taken from rivers and lakes provided virtually the only means of preserving perish-

Library of Congress

able goods. "Global Cooling" examines the history of what was once a worldwide enterprise. During the post Civil War period the increasing use of ice to refrigerate warehouses and railroad cars revolutionized the distribution and consumption of meats and produce.

The treatment of American Indians constitutes a sordid chapter in this nation's history. Time after time tribes were pushed off their ancestral lands, often with violence or the threat of violence. Many times they were promised that if only they moved to this or that area they would be permitted to live in peace thereafter. Such promises usually lasted only until whites decided they wanted those lands too. "A Day to Remember: December 29, 1890" describes that massacre of Sioux Indians at Wounded Knee Creek in South Dakota.

The American Civil War, Emancipation, and Reconstruction on the World Stage

EDWARD L. AYERS

Americans demanded the world's attention during their Civil War and Reconstruction. Newspapers around the globe reported the latest news from the United States as one vast battle followed another, as the largest system of slavery in the world crashed into pieces, as American democracy expanded to include people who had been enslaved only a few years before.[1]

Both the North and the South appealed to the global audience. Abraham Lincoln argued that his nation's Civil War "embraces more than the fate of these United States. It presents to the whole family of man, the question, whether a constitutional republic, or a democracy . . . can, or cannot, maintain its territorial integrity." The struggle. Lincoln said, was for "a vast future," a struggle to give all men "a fair chance in the race of life."[2] Confederates claimed that they were also fighting for a cause of world-wide significance: self-determination. Playing down the centrality of slavery to their new nation, white Southerners built their case for independence on the right of free citizens to determine their political future.[3]

People in other nations could see that the massive struggle in the United States embodied conflicts that had been appearing in different forms throughout the world. Defining nationhood, deciding the future of slavery, reinventing warfare for an industrial age, reconstructing a former slave society—all these played out in the American Civil War.

By no means a major power, the United States was nevertheless woven into the life of the world. The young nation touched, directly and indirectly, India and Egypt, Hawaii and Japan, Russia and Canada, Mexico and Cuba, the Caribbean and Brazil, Britain and France. The country was still very much an experiment in 1860, a representative government stretched over an enormous space, held together by law rather than by memory, religion, or monarch. The American Civil War, played out on the brightly lit stage of a new country, would be a drama of world history. How that experiment fared in its great crisis—regardless of what happened—would eventually matter to people everywhere.

More obviously than most nations, the United States was the product of global history. Created from European ideas, involvement in Atlantic trade, African slavery, conquest of land from American Indians and European powers, and massive migration from Europe, the United States took shape as the world watched. Long before the Civil War, the United States embodied the possibilities and contradictions of modern western history.

Slavery was the first, most powerful, and most widespread kind of globalization in the first three centuries after Columbus. While colonies came and went, while economies boomed and crashed, slavery relentlessly grew—and nowhere more than in the United States. By the middle of the nineteenth century, the slave South had assumed a central role on the world stage. Cotton emerged as the great global commodity, driving factories in the most advanced economies of the world. The slaves of the South were worth more than all the railroads and factories of the North and South combined; slavery was good business and shrewd investment.

While most other slave societies in the hemisphere gradually moved toward freedom, the American South moved toward the permanence of slavery. Southerners and their Northern allies, eager to expand, led the United States in a war to seize large parts of Mexico and looked hungrily upon the Caribbean and Central America. Of all the slave powers—including the giants of Brazil and Cuba, which continued to import slaves legally long after the United States—only the South and its Confederacy fought a war to maintain bondage.[4]

Ideas of justice circulated in global intercourse just as commodities did and those ideas made the American South increasingly anomalous as a modern society built on slavery. Demands for universal freedom came into conflict with ancient traditions of subordination. European nations, frightened by revolt in Haiti and elsewhere and confident of their empires' ability to prosper without slavery, dismantled slavery in their colonies in the western hemisphere while Russia dismantled serfdom.

Black and white abolitionists in the American North, though a tiny despised minority, worked with British allies to fight the acceptance of slavery in the United States. A vision of the South as backward, cruel, and power-hungry gained credence in many places in the North and took political force in the Republican party. The global economy of commodities and ideology, demanding cotton while attacking slavery, put enormous and contradictory strains on the young American nation.[5]

Meanwhile, a new urge to define national identity flowed through the western world in the first half of the nineteenth century. That determination took quite different forms. While some people still spoke of the universal dreams of the French and American Revolutions, of inalienable attributes of humankind, others spoke of historical grievance, ethnic unity, and economic self-interest. Many longed for new nations built around bonds of heritage, imagined and real.[6]

White Southerners, while building their case for secession with the language of constitutions and rights, presented themselves as a people profoundly different from white Northerners. They sought sanction for secession in the recent histories of Italy, Poland, Mexico, and Greece, where rebels rose up against central powers to declare their suppressed nationhood, where native elites led a "natural, necessary protest and revolt" against a "crushing, killing union with another nationality and form of society".[7]

As the South threatened to secede, the Republicans, a regional party themselves, emphasized the importance of Union for its own sake, the necessity of maintaining the integrity of a nation created by legal compact. It fell to the United States, the Republicans said, to show that large democracies could survive internal struggles and play a role in world affairs alongside monarchies and aristocracies.[8]

Once it became clear that war would come, the North and the South seized upon the latest war-making strategies and technologies. From the outset, both sides innovated at a rapid pace and imported ideas from abroad. Railroads and telegraphs extended supply lines, sped troop reinforcements, and permitted the mobilization of vast armies. Observers from Europe and other nations watched carefully to see how the Americans would use these new possibilities. The results were mixed. Ironclad ships, hurriedly constructed, made a difference in some Southern ports and rivers, but were not seaworthy enough to play the role some had envisioned for them. Submarines and balloons proved disappointments, unable to deliver significant advantages. Military leaders, rather than being subordinated by anonymous machinery, as some expected, actually became more important than before, their decisions amplified by the size of their armies and the speed of communication and transport.[9]

The scale and drama of the Civil War that ravaged America for four years, across an area larger than the European continent, fascinated and appalled a jaded world. A proportion of the population equal to five million people today died and the South suffered casualties at a rate equal to those who would be decimated in Europe's mechanized wars of the twentieth century.

The size, innovation, and destructiveness of the American Civil War have led some, looking back, to describe it as the first total war, the first truly modern war. Despite new technologies and strategies, however, much of the Civil War remained old-fashioned. The armies in the American Civil War still moved vast distances on foot or with animals. The food soldiers ate and the medical care they received showed little advance over previous generations of armies. The military history of the Civil War grew incrementally from world history and offered incremental changes to what would follow. Although, late in the war, continuous campaigning and extensive earthen entrenchments foreshadowed World War I, Europeans did not grasp the deadly lesson of the American Civil War: combining the tactics of Napoleon with rapid-fire weapons and trenches would culminate in horrors unanticipated at Shiloh and Antietam.[10]

Diplomacy proved challenging for all sides in the American crisis. The fragile balance of power on the Continent and in the empires centered there limited the range of movement of even the most powerful nations. The Confederacy's diplomatic strategy depended on gaining recognition from Great Britain and France, using cotton as a sort of blackmail, but European manufacturers had stockpiled large supplies of cotton in anticipation of the American war. British cartoonists, sympathetic to the Confederacy, ridiculed Abraham Lincoln at every opportunity, portraying him as an inept bumpkin—until his assassination, when Lincoln suddenly became sainted. Overall, the North benefited from the inaction of the British and the French, who could have changed the outcome and consequences of the war by their involvement.[11]

Inside the United States, the change unleashed by the war was as profound as it was unexpected. Even those who hated slavery had not believed in 1861 that generations of captivity could be ended overnight and former slaves and former slaveholders left to live together. The role of slavery in sustaining the Confederacy through humbling victories over the Union created the conditions in which Abraham Lincoln felt driven and empowered to issue the Emancipation Proclamation. The Union, briefly and precariously balanced between despair and hope, between defeat and victory, was willing in 1862 to accept that bold decision as a strategy of war and to enlist volunteers from among black Americans.[12]

The nearly 200,000 African Americans who came into the war as soldiers and sailors for the Union transformed the struggle. The addition of those men, greater in number than all the forces at Gettysburg, allowed the Union to build its advantage in manpower without pushing reluctant Northern whites into the draft. The enlistment of African Americans in the struggle for their own freedom ennobled the Union cause and promised to set a new global standard for the empowerment of formerly enslaved people. The world paid admiring attention to the brave and disciplined black troops in blue uniforms.[13]

The destruction of American slavery, a growing system of bondage of nearly four million people in one of the world's most powerful economies and most dynamic nation-states, was a consequence of world importance. Nowhere else besides Haiti did slavery end so suddenly, so completely, and with so little compensation for former slaveholders.[14] Had the United States failed to end slavery in the 1860s the world would have felt the difference. An independent Confederate States of America would certainly have put its enslaved population to effective use in coal mines, steel mills, and railroad building, since industrial slavery had been employed before secession and became more common during wartime. Though such a Confederacy might have found itself stigmatized, its survival would have meant the evolution of slavery into a new world of industrialization. The triumph of a major autonomous state built around slavery would have set a devastating example for the rest of the world, an encouragement to forces of reaction. It would have marked the repudiation of much that was liberating in Western thought and practice over the preceding two hundred years.[15]

Driven by the exigencies of war, Northern ideals of color-blind freedom and justice, so often latent and suppressed, suddenly if briefly bloomed in the mid-1860s. The Radical Republicans sought to create a black male American freedom based on the same basis as white male American freedom: property, citizenship, dignity, and equality before the law. They launched a bold Reconstruction to make those ideals a reality, their effort far surpassing those of emancipation anywhere else in the world. The white South resisted with vicious vehemence, however, and the Republicans, always ambivalent about black autonomy and eager to maintain their partisan power, lost heart after a decade of bitter, violent, and costly struggle in Reconstruction. Northern Democrats, opposing Reconstruction from the outset, hastened and celebrated its passing.[16]

If former slaves had been permitted to sustain the enduring political power they tried to build, if they had gone before juries and judges with a chance of fair treatment, if they had been granted homesteads to serve as a first step toward economic freedom, then Reconstruction could be hailed as a turning point in world history equal to any revolution. Those things did not happen, however. The white South claimed the mantle of victim, of a people forced to endure an unjust and unnatural subordination. They won international sympathy for generations to follow in films such as *Birth of a Nation* (1915) and *Gone With the Wind* (1939), which viewed events through the eyes of sympathetic white Southerners. Reconstruction came to be seen around the world not as the culmination of freedom but as a mistake, a story of the dangers of unrealistic expectations and failed social engineering. Though former slaves in the American South quietly made more progress in landholding and general prosperity than former slaves elsewhere, the public failures of Reconstruction obscured the progress black Southerners wrenched from the postwar decades.[17]

When the South lost its global monopoly of cotton production during the Civil War, governments, agents, and merchants around the world responded quickly to take the South's place and to build an efficient global machinery to supply an ever-growing demand in the world market. As a result, generations of black and white sharecroppers would compete with Indian, Brazilian, and Egyptian counterparts in a glutted market in which hard work often brought impoverishment. The South adapted its economy after the war as well. By the 1880s, the South's rates of urban growth, manufacturing, and population movement kept pace with the North—a remarkable shift for only twenty years after losing slavery and the Civil War—but black Southerners were excluded from much of the new prosperity.[18]

As the Civil War generation aged, younger men looked with longing on possible territorial acquisitions in their own hemisphere and farther afield. They talked openly of proving themselves, as their fathers and grandfathers had, on the battlefield. Some welcomed the fight against the Spanish and the Filipinos in 1898 as a test of American manhood and nationalism. The generation that came of age in 1900 built monuments to the heroes of the Civil War but seldom paused to listen to their stories of war's horror and costs.

The destruction of slavery, a major moral accomplishment of the United States Army, of Abraham Lincoln, and of the enslaved people themselves, would be overshadowed by the injustice and poverty that followed in the rapidly changing South, a mockery of American claims of moral leadership in the world. Black Southerners would struggle, largely on their own, for the next one hundred years. Their status, bound in an ever-tightening segregation, would stand as a rebuke to the United States in world opinion. The postwar South and its new system of segregation, in fact, became an explicit model for South Africa. That country created apartheid as it, like the American South, developed a more urban and industrial economy based on racial subordination.

Americans read about foreign affairs on the same pages that carried news of Reconstruction in the South. Even as the Southern states struggled to write new constitutions. Secretary of State William Henry Seward purchased Alaska in 1867 as a step toward the possible purchase of British Columbia. President Grant considered annexation of Santo Domingo, partly as a base for black Southern emigration; he won the support of black abolitionist Frederick Douglass, who wanted to help the Santo Domingans, but was opposed by Radical Republican Senator Charles Sumner.

Americans paid close attention to Hawaii in these same years. Mark Twain visited the islands in 1866, and Samuel Armstrong—the white founder of Hampton Institute, where Booker T. Washington was educated—argued that Hawaiians and former slaves in the South needed similar discipline to become industrious. At the same time, Seward signed a treaty with China to help supply laborers to the American West, a treaty that laid the foundation for a large migration in the next few decades. In 1871, American forces intervened militarily in Korea, killing 250 Korean soldiers. The leaders of the Americans admitted they knew little about their opponents, but brought the same assumptions about race to the conflict that they brought to their dealings with all non-Europeans everywhere, Koreans—like Hawaiians, Chinese, American Indians, and African Americans—needed to be disciplined, taught, and controlled.

4

No master plan guided Americans in their dealings with other peoples. In all of these places, the interests of American businessmen, the distortions of racial ideology, and hopes for partisan political advantage at home jostled with one another. As a result, the consequences of these involvements were often unclear and sometimes took generations to play out. Nevertheless, they remind us that Americans paid close attention to what was happening elsewhere, whether in the Franco-Prussian War (1870–1871), where the evolution of warfare continued to become more mechanized and lethal, or the Paris Commune (1871), where some thought they saw the result of unbridled democracy in chaos and violence—and wondered if Reconstruction did not represent a similar path.

Some people around the world were surprised that the United States did not use its enormous armies after the Civil War to seize Mexico from the French, Canada from the English, or Cuba from the Spanish. Conflict among the great powers on the European Continent certainly opened an opportunity and the United States had expanded relentlessly and opportunistically throughout its history. Few Americans, though, had the stomach for new adventures in the wake of the Civil War. The fighting against the American Indians on the Plains proved warfare enough for most white Americans in the 1870s and 1880s.[19]

The United States focused its postwar energies instead on commerce. Consolidated under Northern control, the nation's economy proved more formidable than ever before. The United States, its economic might growing with each passing year, its railroad network and financial systems consolidated, its cities and towns booming, its population surging westward, its mines turning out massive amounts of coal and precious minerals, its farms remarkably productive, and its corporations adopting new means of expansion and administration, became a force throughout the world. American engineers oversaw projects in Asia, Africa, and Latin America. American investors bought stock in railroads, factories, and mines around the globe. American companies came to dominate the economies of nations in Latin America.[20]

Americans became famous as rich, energetic, and somewhat reckless players amid the complexity of the world. As the Civil War generation aged, younger men looked with longing on possible territorial acquisitions in their own hemisphere and farther afield. They talked openly of proving themselves, as their fathers and grandfathers had, on the battlefield. Some welcomed the fight against the Spanish and the Filipinos in 1898 as a test of American manhood and nationalism. The generation that came of age in 1900 built monuments to the heroes of the Civil War but seldom paused to listen to their stories of war's horror and costs.

T he American Civil War has carried a different meaning for every generation of Americans. In the 1920s and 1930s leading historians in a largely isolationist United States considered the Civil War a terrible mistake, the product of a "blundering generation." After the triumph of World War II

and in the glow of the Cold War's end, leading historians interpreted the Civil War as a chapter in the relentless destruction of slavery and the spread of democracy by the forces of modernization over the forces of reaction. Recently, living through more confusing times, some historians have begun to question straightforward stories of the war, emphasizing its contradictory meanings, unfulfilled promises, and unintended outcomes.[21]

The story of the American Civil War changes as world history lurches in unanticipated directions and as people ask different questions of the past. Things that once seemed settled now seem less so. The massive ranks, fortified trenches, heavy machinery, and broadened targets of the American Civil War once seemed to mark a step toward the culmination of "total" war. But the wars of the twenty-first century, often fought without formal battles, are proving relentless and boundless, "total" in ways the disciplined armies of the Union and Confederacy never imagined.[22] Nations continue to come apart over ancient grievances and modern geopolitics, the example of the United States notwithstanding. Coerced labor did not end in the nineteenth century, but instead has mutated and adapted to changes in the global economy. "A fair chance in the race of life" has yet to arrive for much of the world.

The great American trial of war, emancipation, and reconstruction mattered to the world. It embodied struggles that would confront people on every continent and it accelerated the emergence of a new global power. The American crisis, it was true, might have altered the course of world history more dramatically, in ways both worse and better, than what actually transpired. The war could have brought forth a powerful and independent Confederacy based on slavery or it could have established with its Reconstruction a new global standard of justice for people who had been enslaved. As it was, the events of the 1860s and 1870s in the United States proved both powerful and contradictory in their meaning for world history.

Notes

1. For other portrayals of the Civil War in international context, see David M. Potter, "Civil War," in C. Vann Woodward, ed., *The Comparative Approach to American History* (New York: Basic Books, 1968), pp. 135–451 Carl N. Degler, *One Among Many: The Civil War in Comparative Perspective*, 29th Annual Robert Fortenbaugh Memorial Lecture (Gettysburg, PA: Gettysburg College, 1990); Robert E. May, ed., *The Union, the Confederacy, and the Atlantic Rim* (West Lafayette, IN; Purdue University Press, 1995); Peter Kolchin, *A Sphinx on the American Land: The Nineteenth-Century South in Comparative Perspective* (Baton Rouge: Louisiana State University Press, 2003). My view of the workings of world history has been influenced by C. A. Bayly, *The Birth of the Modern World, 1780–1914: Global Connections and Comparisons* (Malden, MA: Blackwell, 2004). Bayly emphasizes that "in the nineteenth century, nation-states and contending territorial empires took on sharper lineaments and became more antagonistic to each other at the very same time as the similarities, connections, and linkages between them proliferated." (p. 2). By showing the "complex

interaction between political organization, political ideas, and economic activity," Bayly avoids the teleologial models of modernization, nationalism, and liberalism that have dominated our understanding of the American Civil War.

2. Lincoln quoted in James M. McPherson, *Abraham Lincoln and the Second American Revolution,* reprint (New York: Oxford University Press: 1992, 1991), p. 28.

3. The seminal work is Drew Gilpin Faust, *The Creation of Confederate Nationalism: Ideology and Identity in the Civil War South* (Baton Rouge: Louisiana State University Press, 1988). For an excellent synthesis of the large literature on this topic, see Anne S. Rubin, *A Shattered Nation: The Rise and Fall of the Confederacy, 1861–1868* (Chapel Hill: University of North Carolina Press, 2005).

4. For a useful overview, see Robert W. Fogel, *Without Consent or Contract: The Rise and Fall of American Slavery* (New York: W. W. Norton, 1989).

5. David Brion Davis, *Slavery and Human Progress* (New York: Oxford University Press, 1984); Davis, The Problem of Slavery in the Age of Revolution, 1770–1823 (Ithaca, NY: Cornell University Press, 1975), and Davis, *Inhuman Bondage: The Rise and Fall of Slavery in the New World* (Oxford University Press, 2006).

6. For helpful overviews of the global situation, see Steven Hahn, "Class and State in Postemancipation Societies: Southern Planters in Comparative Perspective," *American Historical Review* 95 (February 1990): 75–98, and Hahn, *A Nation Under Our Feet: Black Political Struggles in the Rural South From Slavery to the Great Migration* (Cambridge, MA: Belknap Press of Harvard University Press, 2003).

7. Quoted in Faust, *Creation of Confederate Nationalism,* p. 13.

8. There is a large literature on this subject, not surprisingly. A useful recent treatment is Susan-Mary Grant, *North Over South: Northern Nationalism and American Identity in the Antebellum Era* (Lawrence: University of Kansas Press, 2000). Peter Kolchin also offers penetrating comments on nationalism in *A Sphinx on the American Land,* 89–92.

9. Brian Holden Reid, *The American Civil War and the Wars of the Industrial Revolution* (London: Cassell, 1999), 211–13; John E. Clark Jr., *Railroads in the Civil War: The Impact of Management on Victory and Defeat* (Baton Rouge: Louisiana State University Press, 2001); Robert G. Angevine, *The Railroad and the State: War, Politics, and Technology in Nineteenth-Century America* (Stanford, CA: Stanford University Press, 2004).

10. For a range of interesting essays on this subject, see Stig Forster and Jorg Nagler, eds., *On the Road to Total War: The American Civil War and the German Wars of Unification, 1861–1871* (Washington, DC: The German Historical Institute, 1997).

11. See D. P. Crook, *The North, the South, and the Powers, 1861–1865* (New York: Wiley, 1974), R. J. M. Blackett, *Divided Hearts: Britain and the American Civil War* (Baton Rouge: Louisiana State University Press, 2001), James M. McPherson, *Crossroads of Freedom: Antietam* (Oxford: Oxford University Press, 2002), May, ed., *The Union, the Confederacy, and the Atlantic Rim,* and Charles M. Hubbard, *The Burden of Confederate Diplomacy* (Knoxville: University of Tennessee Press, 1998).

12. See Allen C. Guelzo, *Lincoln's Emancipation Proclamation: The End of Slavery in America* (New York: Simon and Schuster. 2004).

13. See Joseph T. Glatthaar, *Forged in Battle: The Civil War Alliance of Black Soldiers and White Officers* (New York: Free Press, 1990).

14. See Leon Litwack, *Been in the Storm So Long: The Aftermath of Slavery,* 1st Vintage ed. (New York: Vintage, 1980, 1979) and the major documentary collection edited by Ira Berlin, Leslie S. Rowland, and their colleagues, sampled in *Free At Last: A Documentary History of Slavery, Freedom, and the Civil War* (New York: The New Press, 1992).

15. See Davis, *Slavery and Human Progress,* for a sweeping perspective on this issue.

16. The classic history is Eric Foner, *Reconstruction: America's Unfinished Revolution, 1863–1877* (New York: Harper and Row, 1988), I have offered some thoughts on Reconstruction's legacy in "Exporting Reconstruction" in *What Caused the Civil War? Reflections on the South and Southern History* (New York: W. W. Norton, 2005).

17. On the legacy of Reconstruction, see David W. Blight, *Race and Reunion The Civil War in American Memory* (Cambridge, MA: Belknap Press of Harvard University Press, 2001).

18. For a fascinating essay on the South's loss of the cotton monopoly, see Sven Beckert, "Emancipation and Empire: Reconstructing the Worldwide Web of Cotton Production in the Age of the American Civil War," *American Historical Review* 109 (December 2004): 1405–38. On South Africa: John W. Cell, *The Highest Stage of White Supremacy: The Origins of Segregation in South Africa and the American South* (Cambridge: Cambridge University Press, 1982) and George M. Fredrickson, *White Supremacy: A Comparative Study in American and South African History* (New York: Oxford University Press, 1981).

19. See the discussion in the essays by Robert E. May and James M. McPherson in May, ed., *The Union, the Confederacy, and the Atlantic Rim.*

20. For the larger context, see Eric J. Hobsbawm, *The Age of Empire, 1875–1914* (New York: Pantheon, 1987) and Bayly, *Birth of the Modern World.*

21. I have described this literature and offered some thoughts on it in the essay "Worrying About the Civil War" in my *What Caused the Civil War?*

22. Reid, *American Civil War,* p. 213.

Bibliography

Surprisingly, no one book covers the themes of this essay. To understand this era of American history in global context, we need to piece together accounts from a variety of books and articles. For recent over-views of different components of these years, see Jay Sexton, "Towards a Synthesis of Foreign Relations in the Civil War Era, 1848–1877," *American Nineteenth-Century History* 5 (Fall 2004): 50–75, and Amy Kaplan, *The Anarchy of Empire in the Making of U.S. Culture* (Cambridge, MA; Harvard University Press, 2002).

Robert F. May, in the introduction to the book he edited, *The Union, the Confederacy, and the Atlantic Rim* (West Lafayette, IN: Purdue University Press, 1995), provides a useful summary of the larger context of the war. Though it is older, the perspective of D. P. Crook, *The North, the South, and the Powers, 1861–1865* (New York: Wiley, 1974) brings a welcome worldliness to the discussion. On the crucial debate in Britain, see Howard Jones, *Union in*

Peril: The Crisis Over British Intervention in the Civil War (Chapel Hill: University of North Carolina Press, 1992) and R. J. M. Blackett, *Divided Hearts: Britain and the American Civil War* (Baton Rouge: Louisiana State University Press, 2001).

James M. McPherson offers characteristically insightful, and hopeful, analysis in several places. Perhaps the single best focused portrayal of the interplay between events in the United States and in the Atlantic World is in his *Crossroads of Freedom: Antietam* (Oxford: Oxford University Press, 2002). McPherson's essay, " 'The Whole Family of Man': Lincoln and the Last Best Hope Abroad," in May, ed., *The Union, the Confederacy, and the Atlantic Rim,* makes the fullest case for the larger significance of the war in encouraging liberal movements and belief around the world.

Peter Kolchin's, *A Sphinx on the American Land: The Nineteenth-Century South in Comparative Perspective* (Baton Rouge: Louisiana State University Press, 2003), offers an elegant and up-to-date survey that puts the conflict in the larger context of emancipation movements. A useful overview appears in Steven Hahn, "Class and State in Postemancipation Societies: Southern Planters in Comparative Perspective," *American Historical Review* 95 (February 1990): 75–98.

Another pioneering work is Drew Gilpin Faust, *The Creation of Confederate Nationalism: Ideology and Identity in the Civil War South* (Baton Rouge: Louisiana State University Press, 1988). Faust changed historians' perspective on nationalism in the South, which had been considered largely fraudulent before her account. Building on Faust are two recent books that offer fresh interpretations: Anne S. Rubin, *A Shattered Nation: The Rise and Fall of the Confederacy, 1861–1868* (Chapel Hill: University of North Carolina Press, 2005) and Susan-Mary Crant, *North Over South: Northern Nationalism and American Identity in the Antebellum Era* (Lawrence: University of Kansas Press, 2000).

On the much-debated issue of the relative modernity and totality of the Civil War, see Stig Förster and Jörg Nagler, eds., *On the Road to Total War: The American Civil War and the German Wars of Unification,* 1861–1871 (Washington, DC: The German Historical Institute, 1997); the essays by Stanley L. Engerman and J. Matthew Gallman, Earl J. Hess, Michael Fellman, and Richard Current are especially helpful. Brian Holden Reid, in *The American Civil War and the Wars of the Industrial Revolution* (London: Cassell, 1999), offers a concise but insightful portrayal of the war in larger military context.

For a powerful representation of the role of slavery in this history, David Brion Davis's works are all helpful. His most recent account synthesizes a vast literature in an accessible way: *Inhuman Bondage: The Rise and Fall of Slavery in the New World* (Oxford University Press, 2006).

Excellent examples of what might be thought of as the new global history appear in Sven Beckert, "Emancipation and Empire: Reconstructing the Worldwide Web of Cotton Production in the Age of the American Civil War," *American Historical Review* 109 (December 2004): 1405–38; and Gordon H. Chang, "Whose 'Barbarism'? whose 'Treachery'? Race and Civilization in the Unknown United States-Korea War of 1871," *Journal of American History* 89 (March 2003): 1331–65.

EDWARD L. AYERS is Dean of the College of Art and Sciences at the University of Virginia, where he is also the Hugh P. Kelly Professor of History. He has published extensively on nineteenth-century Southern history, his most recent publication being *In the Presence of Mine Enemies: War in the Heart of America, 1859–1863 (2003),* which received the Bancroft Prize. An earlier book, *The Promise of the New South (1992),* was a finalist for both the Pulitzer Prize and the National Book Award. In addition, Ayers has created and directs a prize-winning Internet archive, "Valley of the Shadow: Two Communities in the American Civil War," containing original sources related to two towns at either end of the Shenandoah Valley, one in Virginia and the other in Pennsylvania.

1871 War on Terror

In the aftermath of the Civil War, America's federal authorities took unprecedented action to crack down on the Ku Klux Klan.

David Everitt

S ecret cells of violent zealots target civilians in their homes and workplaces. When not carrying out terrorist acts, they conceal themselves among the general population, aided by local officials. As waves of fear spread, an American president decides the time has come to strike back.

A description of recent world events? Not necessarily. The scenario also fits another time in America's history. The campaign against Al Qaeda and its allies is not the United States' first war on terror. In the American South during the aftermath of the Civil War, a terrorist organization emerged. Cloaked in ghostly disguise, it sought to murder and maim in the dead of night as it set out to impose its ideological agenda. For several years the governmental response was ineffectual. Finally, in 1871, the U.S. Congress and President Ulysses S. Grant took action and initiated a new policy in South Carolina, where the organization was especially brazen. The government took extraordinary—some said excessive—measures to crack down on the brutal crimes of this terrorist group, the Reconstruction-era Ku Klux Klan.

Some of the issues surrounding this 19th-century war on terror are reminiscent of those we face now. Like George W. Bush's today, Grant's administration was criticized for overstepping its authority and for not understanding the true nature of the problem. In the end, the offensive that Grant launched against the Klan produced some very tangible results, but the ultimate success of his effort is still open to debate.

Terrorism thrives on great turmoil, and in the conquered and humiliated South it found an ideal breeding ground. Reconstruction upended society as white Southerners knew it, not only freeing blacks from slavery but also providing opportunity for their advancement in both business and government. Enraged by those developments, many Southern white men looked for some way to lash out at emancipated slaves and their white supporters. More than that, they hoped to restore the old order. For them, the Ku Klux Klan was the answer.

In 1868, the Klan was imported to South Carolina from Tennessee, where it had originated earlier that same year. The organization immediately demonstrated it would not tolerate former slaves exercising their right to vote. During the 1868 South

Carolina election campaign, the Klan murdered eight blacks, two of them state congressmen.

The state government controlled by Republicans—the party of Abraham Lincoln—met the terrorist threat by raising a special militia and filling its ranks with black citizens. That proved to be dramatic enough to inflame the Klan, but not strong enough to defeat it.

During the 1870 election campaign, the new militia countered the Klan's intimidation tactics to some extent, and the ballot results enraged Klan members even further when the Republican governor, Robert Scott, was re-elected. The next day, South Carolina's wave of terror truly began.

South Carolina was by no means the only state plagued by Klan violence—the organization was active throughout the South—but in portions of South Carolina the acts of terror were especially alarming between the fall of 1870 and the summer of 1871. A public Klan proclamation announced that the organization's targets were "the scum of the earth, the scrapings of creation" and that they intended to do everything possible to oppose "negro rule, black bayonets, and a miserably degraded and thievish set of lawmakers." Over a nine-month period in South Carolina's York County alone, six murders were attributed to the Ku Klux Klan, while whippings and beatings might have numbered in the hundreds.

One of the most notoriously brutal cases was the murder of a black man named Tom Roundtree. The Klan shot him to death, then mutilated his body and sank it in a nearby stream. Other infamous crimes involved the black militia, an especially hated target of the Klan. In one instance, in Unionville, Klansmen lynched 10 black militiamen who had been jailed for the murder of a whiskey peddler. In another case, in the town of Yorkville, a black militia captain named Jim Williams allegedly issued a threat against whites in the area. The Klan dragged him from his house and hanged him. On his dangling body they left a card on which they had written "Jim Williams on his big muster."

The Klan cast a wide net and showed little mercy for those unlikely to be able to defend themselves. One of their whipping victims was a 69-year-old white man who had offended the Klan by acting as a Republican election officer, and another was a black preacher, incapacitated from birth by stunted arms and legs, who was charged with rabble-rousing from the pulpit. At times the Klansmen also took it upon themselves to punish what they considered domestic offenses. In an incident that would have pleased today's religiously fanatic terrorists, for example, Ku Kluxers in Spartanburg County once whipped a woman for the crime of leaving her husband.

As indefensible as the Klan's actions surely were, apologists for those acts were plentiful, and they did not necessarily come from the South.

As indefensible as the Klan's actions surely were, apologists for those acts were plentiful, and they did not necessarily come from the South. Sometimes their statements echo reactions to modern terrorism that we've heard in recent years. Certain pundits in the early 1870s, for instance, offered the terrorists-as-freedom-fighters rationalization. On the floor of the U.S. Congress, Representative S.S. Cox from New York argued that "South Carolina has been infested by the worst local government ever vouchsafed to a people." Comparing the Klan to the Carbonari, which fought for constitutional government in Italy during the early 1800s, Cox concluded, "All history shows that such societies grow by persecution and that they are the bitter fruits of tyranny." Even those in the South who criticized Klan excesses only did so because they considered them counterproductive as opposed to immoral, similar to the way some Middle Easterners today have criticized suicide bombers because they don't help the Palestinian cause, not because the acts themselves are unspeakable.

In the North, newspapers often minimized the Klan threat. A *New York Times* editorial stated that when there weren't enough real Klan atrocities to report, "the matter was put into the hands of literary gentlemen who thereupon started armed bands in all directions through the newspaper woods, dragged out newspaper negroes from newspaper homes, and, tying them up to trees of the mind, lashed their newspaper backs till blood ran down, awful to behold."

With little support for a forceful response, Governor Scott tried appeasing the South Carolina Klan. In February 1871, he disarmed York County's black militia, hoping that this would persuade the Klan to stop its raids. But the Ku Kluxers responded to that gesture as if it were a sign of weakness—they resorted to even more violence. At his wits' end, Scott requested help from Washington, and in March President Grant sent in federal troops.

The soldiers assigned to South Carolina belonged to the 7th Cavalry, Lt. Col. (Brevet Maj. Gen.) George Armstrong Custer's regiment, which had recently fought the Cheyennes on the Great Plains. The troops were headquartered in York County, the center for much of the Klan activity in the state, and they were commanded by 37-year-old Major Lewis M. Merrill. At first skeptical of the seemingly alarmist accounts of the KKK, Merrill soon became convinced of the basic truth of the allegations and would go on to play a crucial role in combating terrorism in the state.

Merrill quickly discovered that he faced great obstacles. Like terrorist organizations today, the Klan was highly compartmentalized. Klan chiefs had no direct contact with underlings, making it difficult for the Army to collect evidence against ringleaders. And even after Merrill and his men collected information on subordinates, local authorities sabotaged any effort to win a conviction in court. As Merrill later described it, "I never conceived of such a state of social disorganization being possible in any civilized community." Still, he continued to investigate in the hope that the federal government would find a way to bring the terrorists to justice.

In May 1870, Congress had passed the Enforcement Act, which had attempted to prevent the Klan from violating citizens' constitutional protections, but the law produced little result. Now, in 1871, Republicans in Congress considered passing a much stronger bill.

The Ku Klux Act, as it came to be called, targeted people who "conspire together, or go in disguise upon any public highway, or upon the premises of another" for the purpose of depriving any citizens of their legal rights. The bill authorized President Grant to dismantle those conspiracies in no uncertain terms: He could, in effect, place an area under martial law and suspend the writ of habeas corpus, which would allow authorities to imprison suspected Klansmen for extended periods of time without bringing them to court to face formal charges.

Democrats charged that the methods of enforcement amounted to tyrannical, unconstitutional powers. In rebuttal, Representative Robert B. Elliott, a black Republican from South Carolina, drew his fellow legislators' attention to more basic Constitutional protections. He pointed out that the Constitution states, "The United States shall guarantee to every State in the Union a republican form of government." States like South Carolina were denied this type of government, Elliott's argument went, as long as terrorists threatened citizens' right to vote. Strong as his case might have been, it could not overcome the congressional bickering that gridlocked the bill. What was needed was the moral authority of President Grant. The Ku Klux Act finally became law on April 20, only after Grant publicly urged Congress to ratify it.

Now, Major Merrill's efforts had a chance of making a difference. That summer, he testified before a congressional subcommittee that arrived in South Carolina to investigate the extent of Klan outrages in the state. The intelligence Merrill had gathered on whippings, beatings and murders painted a disturbing portrait for the congressmen.

'I never conceived of such a state of social disorganization being possible in any civilized community.'

—Major Lewis M. Merrill

During their four-week tour of the state, the congressmen could see for themselves how desperate the situation had become. Refugees from Klan violence congregated wherever the subcommittee convened. Many of them, both white and black, had been spending their nights in the woods for months to avoid Ku Klux attacks. According to a *New York Times* report, "It was found impossible for the Committee to examine more than a small part of the crowds of whipped, maimed, or terror-stricken wretches who flocked in upon hearing of their coming."

Pressing the case for forceful action was Grant's attorney general, Amos T. Akerman. A scalawag, according to conventional Southern wisdom of the day, Akerman was a transplanted Northerner who had spent his adult life as a citizen of Georgia and was now a staunch supporter of Reconstruction. He went to South Carolina to conduct his own investigation in late September and concluded that the Klan could be smashed quickly if the government took decisive steps that would rattle rank-and-file Ku Kluxers and convince them to confess. As Klan raids continued, Akerman met with Grant in early October and helped persuade him that the time had come to activate the Ku Klux Act's enforcement measures.

On October 12, Grant ordered the South Carolina Klan to disperse and disarm in five days. The warning was ignored. On October 17, Grant proclaimed that "in my judgment the public safety especially requires that the privileges of the writ of habeas corpus be suspended." The suspension applied to all arrests made by U.S. marshals and federal troops in nine of the state's western counties.

Akerman immediately met with Merrill to assemble a list of Klansmen to be arrested, based on information gathered by the major over the previous seven months. Their strategy was to hit several towns suddenly and simultaneously, with teams of federal marshals backed up by the 7th Cavalry, in order to instill panic throughout the organization. The plan could not have worked better.

Within 10 days of Grant's proclamation, marshals and troops made 100 arrests in York and Spartanburg counties. Many more Klansmen came in on their own, and by the end of November federal officials in South Carolina had made 600 arrests in all. A large number of those were very willing to "puke," the colorful slang term in those days for confess. There were 160 confessions in York County alone, and in the process investigators learned of five murders that had previously gone unreported. The federal crackdown had such a profound effect that York's county seat had "the look of a town in wartime recently captured by an invading army," according to a *New York Tribune* correspondent.

Louis F. Post, an aide to Merrill, contended that the mass confessions were the direct result of the suspension of habeas corpus. "For a time the prisoners were silent," he wrote. "But as hope of release died out and fears of hanging grew stronger, the weaker ones sought permission to tell Major Merrill what they knew."

Some editorialists saw grave dangers in the government's actions. Similar to some of today's critics of the war on terrorism, these people claimed that the government's aggressiveness was only making more enemies. "I shudder to think," wrote a *New York Herald* correspondent, "what the retaliation will be [from

the Klan] for the imprisoning of two hundred white men and the driving from their homes of three or four hundred others."

To be precise, hundreds of South Carolinians were not driven from their homes—they fled to avoid prosecution. This was both good news and bad. True, the flight of so many Ku Kluxers disrupted the organization, but the fugitives included some of the most prominent Klan chiefs. Federal prosecutors would only be able, for the most part, to press charges against the organization's underlings. Still, Akerman believed that convictions of these men would send a strong warning to anyone considering further Klan raids.

The Ku Klux court cases began November 27, 1871, in the U.S. Circuit Court in the South Carolina capital of Columbia. The first to go on trial was farmer Robert Hayes Mitchell, an ordinary, subordinate Klansmen whose case provided an extraordinary glimpse into the inner workings of the KKK and two of its most notorious crimes.

Like other defendants who followed, Mitchell was charged with conspiracy to prevent black citizens from voting. To illustrate the nature of the conspiracy, prosecutors called on one witness to outline the elaborate series of signs and passwords that Ku Kluxers used to identify one another and maintain security. The government also presented testimony on the Klan constitution. Acquired at Merrill's instigation, the document revealed the organization's deadly oath of secrecy: Anyone breaking this oath, the constitution stated, "shall meet the fearful penalty and traitor's doom, which is death, death, death."

Specific instances of conspiracy included the murder of Captain Jim Williams of the black militia. Klan supporters maintained that the organization's raids had been provoked by militia excesses, which typically amounted to arrogant, intimidating behavior. Federal prosecutors, though, established in court that the Klan had first resorted to violence two years before the black militia was formed in 1870.

Another count of conspiracy against Mitchell involved the assault against a black man named Amzi Rainey who had offended the Klan by voting for radical Republicans. The victim's testimony dramatized the savagery of the attack. Crashing into Rainey's house around midnight, the Klan beat not only Rainey but also his wife. At one point Rainey's little daughter ran at the Klansmen, yelling, "Don't kill my pappy; please don't kill my pappy!" One of the attackers responded by firing a shot that grazed the little girl's forehead.

> **'In my judgement the public safety especially requires that the privileges of the writ of habeas corpus be suspended.'**
>
> —U.S. Grant

In his summation for the defense, attorney Reverdy Johnson saw no point in trying to dispute the charges of Klan violence, conceding that the outrages "show that the parties engaged were brutes, insensible to the obligations of humanity and religion."

Instead, he argued that the Enforcement Act of 1870 and the Ku Klux Act were unconstitutional. The argument made little impression on the jury of 10 blacks and two whites who took only 38 minutes to bring in a guilty verdict.

Through the month of December, similar verdicts followed, along with a procession of guilty pleas. In pronouncing sentences, Judge Hugh L. Bond brought a finely tuned moral voice to the proceedings, showing both leniency for unsophisticated men pressured into the Klan ranks and severity for those who exercised some degree of authority. The most common of the 58 prison sentences ranged from three to six months, while others entailed both prison time and some sort of fine.

The most severe was a combination of five years and $1,000, reserved for the likes of Klan chief John W. Mitchell, a prominent member of his community and somebody, Judge Bond asserted, who should have known better. In his sentencing, the judge stressed Mitchell's abdication of responsibility: "Knowing all this [about the Klan's activities], hearing of the ravishing, murders and whipping going on in York County, you never took any pains to inform anybody; you never went to the civil authorities and you remained a chief till they elected somebody else."

The federal crackdown did not stop there. Through 1872, Major Merrill continued to make arrests, and in April the federal court in Charleston delivered 36 more convictions. At the same time, though—as critics branded Grant a dictator—the government began to back off.

Attorney General Akerman resigned in January 1872, and though his exit was amicable on the surface, some have speculated that he was frustrated by the lack of funding for ongoing Klan prosecutions. His replacement was less concerned with Klan violence, even though a federal marshal was killed in South Carolina while enforcing the Ku Klux Act, and a prosecution witness had his throat slit. Further impeding the anti-Klan campaign was Congress' decision in 1872 to restore habeas corpus rights. By August, the federal government began pardoning convicted Ku Kluxers. The government's war on Ku Klux Klan terror came to a definitive end in 1877, when President Rutherford B. Hayes ordered the end of Reconstruction.

Looking back upon this episode, we can see that the Grant administration faced two especially difficult questions that confront us today as once again we wage a war on terror. First, how much should the government limit constitutional rights when fighting an enemy that does not respect the rights of others? By imposing federal authority on local jurisdictions and suspending the writ of habeas corpus, the Grant administration was taking unprecedented measures in peacetime to deal with a dire crisis. In 1876, five years after the first Klan prosecutions, the U.S. Supreme Court ruled that the Enforcement Act of 1870 and the Ku Klux Act were indeed unconstitutional, that they had improperly superceded the rights of the states.

The second question is: How does one know when a war on terror is truly won? Although the Klan prosecutions did not last long, some historians maintain that they accomplished their immediate goal. According to Allen W. Trelease, author of *White Terror,* "The federal government had broken the back of the Ku Klux Klan throughout most of the South." And it is true that the Klan did not rise again until after World War I, some 50 years later. But the Grant administration left larger goals unrealized. Even though the outer trappings of the Klan might have disappeared, its attitudes and the willingness to impose those attitudes through violence remained. And once Reconstruction ended and the passage of repressive Jim Crow laws began, white supremacy reigned once again throughout the South. Jim Crow would continue to rule for another 80 years, until the dawn of the modern civil rights movement.

Union forces won the Civil War against the Confederacy. President Grant's marshals and troops won the battle against the Reconstruction-era Klan. Nevertheless, the federal government failed to see its war on terror as a long-term commitment, and it failed to come up with a practical plan for rebuilding the South and bringing the Old Confederacy into the modern, fully democratic age. As a consequence, some might say that the North ultimately failed to win the peace.

From *American History,* by David Everitt, June 2003, pp. 26–28, 30–33. Copyright © 2003 by Weider History Group. Reprinted by permission.

Little Bighorn Reborn

With a new Indian memorial, the site of Custer's last stand draws descendants of victors and vanquished alike.

TONY PERROTTET

"A beautiful place . . . ," I murmured to no one in particular, gazing down from a hilltop to cottonwood forests on both sides of a lazy river. A woman at my side finished the thought: ". . . to die."

A touch morbid for an exchange between strangers? Perhaps, but this was not just any hill top or any day. We were part of a small crowd gathered on Last Stand Hill on the 128th anniversary of the West's most famous battle. A few feet away, in the gently swaying grass, dozens of bone-white headstones mark the military's best guesstimates of where 42 of the Seventh Cavalry soldiers fell that June 25, 1876, some having held out behind a breastwork made of their dead horses. In the center of the markers, next to a small American flag, lay the headstone of their flamboyant, controversial leader, Lt. Col. George Armstrong Custer.

Still, on that clear, sunny summer morning, it seemed hard to believe that this quiet corner of Montana had been the scene of desperate hand-to-hand combat, when Custer and 209 men under his command were wiped out by the combined forces of the Sioux, Cheyenne and Arapaho Indians.

And then a voice rang out in the distance: "Here they come!"

Suddenly, the earth began to quiver, and the breeze carried shrill cries—*yip, yip, yip.* Bursting from behind Battle Ridge thundered 100 Lakota on horseback. Several were carrying wooden staffs adorned with colored tassels and eagle feathers, the sacred war standards of the Sioux (a name assigned to several Indian tribes, including the Lakota, who find the term offensive). For a moment, 128 years dissolved, and we were given a pale glimpse of the emotions those U.S. cavalrymen must have felt when they realized what Custer, hoping to attack an Indian camp before it could scatter, had led them into. On that fateful morning—a suffocatingly hot day—the entire valley basin had been covered with tepees, part of the largest Indian force on record. Custer and the five companies he was leading were surrounded and annihilated.

The news of Custer's defeat reached American cities just after jubilant Fourth of July centennial celebrations had concluded, stunning the nation. How could a group of "uncivilized" Indians have wiped out a modern military force, killing even a decorated Civil War hero?

Now, as I stood on Last Stand Hill, history seemed to have come full circle. Another 27 Lakota horsemen, these led by descendants of Crazy Horse, the most revered of the Sioux warriors at the 1876 battle, had ridden 360 miles in two weeks from their South Dakota reservation. They had followed the same route as their ancestors, and were now praying for their dead killed at the battle at an impressive new Indian memorial, just 50 yards northwest of Last Stand Hill. Dedicated in 2003, the memorial is a circular earth-and-stonework balustrade, with a weeping wall, interpretive panels and an elegant sculpture of Spirit Warriors—spirits of the Indian soldiers that were protecting the village that day

Until recently, the Great Sioux Nation Victory Ride—let alone the crowds of Native Americans participating in the anniversary festivities—would have been hard to imagine here. Indians "used to believe they weren't really welcome," said Tim McCleary, 42, a historian formerly at the battlefield who now teaches at Little Bighorn College. "And not surprisingly. All the interpretation was from the U.S. cavalry point of view." Kenneth Medicine Bull, a member of the Northern Cheyenne Nation visiting the battlefield, nodded in agreement. "Before, this place felt like it was a tribute to Custer," he said. "Nothing even mentioned the Cheyenne and Sioux."

Today, for Indians and whites alike, the June anniversary has become a three-day extravaganza of religious services, academic symposia and general whooping it up. (There is not one but two reenactments of the battle, held by rival groups.) After the Sioux had ridden off, John Doerner, the park's official historian, told me that there are still visitors who believe

Custer was an American martyr who died to tame the Indians as well as Custerphobes who consider him a war criminal. But the arguments over the site no longer carry the same venom they did in the 1970s, when the American Indian Movement disrupted memorial services here by carrying a flag upside down across the battlefield, singing "Custer Died for Your Sins."

"The shouts have died down to whispers now," Doerner said. "Time heals all."

Back in 1876, the first U.S. Army reports of the site sanitized the grisly fate of Custer's men. Lt. James H. Bradley arrived two days after the battle to help identify the slain officers and bury the dead. Not wishing to further upset the families of the fallen, he described for the *Helena Herald* an almost pastoral scene where few soldiers had been scalped and Custer's body was "that of a man who had fallen asleep and enjoyed peaceful dreams." But another eyewitness, Gen. Edward S. Godfrey, privately admitted that the reality was "a sickening, ghastly horror." Some soldiers had been stripped, scalped and mutilated. Many had had their genitals severed, some say in retaliation for the genital mutilation of Indian men and women by soldiers in previous battles. The burial party was not only sickened by the carnage but feared further attacks. With only a handful of shovels, the men hastily threw dirt over the dead, dug a shallow grave for Custer and beat a hasty retreat.

A year would pass before a second detail would come to remove the bodies of 11 officers and 2 civilians and send them to Eastern graveyards. (Indians had removed their dead shortly after the battle.) By now, as Lt. John G. Bourke noted, "pieces of clothing, soldiers' hats, cavalry coats, boots with the leather legs cut off, but with the human feet and bones still sticking in them, strewed the hill." Custer's shallow grave had been disturbed. After misidentifying one skeleton as Custer's—a blouse upon which the remains were lying identified it as belonging to a corporal—the party chose another. "I think we got the right body the second time," one member of the detail, Sgt. Michael Caddle, recalled in a letter to a historian; but another eyewitness remembered the commanding officer muttering: "Nail the box up; it is alright as long as the people think so."

The first actual sightseers at Little Bighorn were Indians. In the winter of 1876, Wooden Leg, a Cheyenne warrior and a veteran of the battle, led a nine-man hunting party to the desolate spot. Acting as tour guide, he and the group rode through hills still strewn with unexpended gun cartridges, spears, arrows and the bleached bones of cavalrymen.

Two years later, 25 recently surrendered Sioux and Cheyenne veterans provided a battlefield tour for Col. Nelson A. Miles, commander of Fort Keogh, in Montana, and a personal friend of the Custer family; who sought "the attainment of the Indian narrative of the engagement." As 400,000

visitors a year learn today, the battle involved more than just the cinematic debacle on Last Stand Hill. Early in the afternoon of June 25, Custer sent one of his three battalions, led by Maj. Marcus Reno, to attack the Indian encampment from the south. Repulsed, Reno retreated across Little Bighorn River to the bluffs beyond to be joined by a second battalion led by Capt. Frederick Benteen. The force dug in four miles southwest of Last Stand Hill, where they held out overnight against Indian attacks. After a harrowing siege, tormented by thirst and picked at by sniper fire, the soldiers saw the Indians withdraw the next afternoon; the battalions had suffered 53 killed and 52 wounded. Some 380 survived.

In 1879, the battle site fell under the jurisdiction of the War Department, and that year troops from the nearby Fort Custer erected a rough log memorial on the crest of Last Stand Hill. Native American visitation waned. The Indians who had won the battle had lost the war, and with it the right to interpret the past. Back East, Custer was turned into a hero.

It was not until 1881 that the bones of the remaining cavalrymen and their horses were finally gathered by hand into a mass grave, over which a 36,000-pound granite memorial was erected. Even then, the job was hardly thorough: in 1925, a decapitated skeleton of a trooper in Reno's command was found near the modern-day hamlet of Garryowen; another, wearing an Army tunic, was exposed in a shallow grave on Reno Hill in 1958.

The memorial, and the growing popularity of the automobile, brought more tourists to Little Bighorn. But it was not until the 1926 semicentennial of the battle that a major event was staged at the site: 50,000 people showed up, including western film star William S. Hart, to participate in services and watch a reenactment. There was an official burying of the hatchet ceremony in which General Godfrey, who had fought with Benteen and White Bull, Sitting Bull's nephew, came together to erase old hatreds. Bull gave Godfrey a blanket, and Godfrey gave White Bull an American flag. The tomahawk was buried in the grave of the soldier found the year before, as a symbolic gesture. But to some in the predominantly white audience, the ceremony suggested that the Indians had accepted domination by the white man.

About this time, Nellie Beaverheart, daughter of possibly the only Indian chief killed at the battle, Lame White Man, asked for a marker from the War Department at the place where he died. The request was ignored until the 1950s, when the National Park Service, now administering the site, erected a wooden marker. Still, it took until the 1970s—with the publication of works such as Dee Brown's poignant *Bury My Heart at Wounded Knee*—for the winds of cultural change to stir the battlefield. In 1991, Barbara Sutteer, the first Native American superintendent of the site, oversaw the name change, long requested by Indians, from Custer Battlefield to Little Bighorn Battlefield National Monument. An

11-member Indian memorial design committee, authorized by the same legislation, oversaw the design and content of a memorial. A sculpture, in an opening in the north wall of the memorial, was based on the pictograph drawings of White Bird, a Cheyenne warrior who had participated in the battle at age 15. It consists of three horsemen crafted from thick black wire, representing warriors riding out to defend the Indian village from Custer's attack; a fourth figure, a woman running alongside and passing up a shield to one of the soldiers, emphasizes the importance of women in Indian life. Within the circular earthworks of the memorial, designed by Philadelphians John R. Collins and Allison J. Towers, are interpretive panels about the Native American groups. A symbolic "spirit gate" welcomes the Indians' and soldiers' spirits.

I met Sutteer, who works today as a consultant on Native American issues, at the Hardin Dairy Queen. A soft-spoken woman in her 60s, she told me she had received death threats for wanting to introduce Native American viewpoints to the site. "Of course, the battlefield has been sacred to the Indians far longer than for white people," she told me. "The quality of the grass made it an excellent hunting place. That's one reason the groups had camped here in 1876."

The attention to Indian history at the monument has highlighted some complexities of Native American culture. "White people often take Native Americans as a single monolithic culture," says Tim McCleary. The Crow and Arikara were actually on Custer's side, working as scouts. They regarded the Sioux, Cheyenne and Arapaho as invaders of their homeland. "The opportunity to kill Sioux with the assistance of the U.S. military was really inviting," McCleary goes on, adding that the Arikara remain proud of their role as U.S. Army allies. To the Cheyenne and Sioux, on the other hand, the Battle of Little Bighorn climaxed long resistance to white incursions, and to this day they resent the favoritism they believe the government showed the Crow. (They also resent that the site of their greatest victory is on Crow land, adds McCleary, which allows Crow guides to give "Native American" tours. As for the Crow, they felt that the reservation they were given after the battle was too small and regard the creation of the Northern Cheyenne reservation right next door to their traditional home—with a slice of their original reservation carved off for their enemies—as a pointed insult.

These ancient rivalries still spill onto the battlefield today. Since 1999, five red-granite headstones have been placed to mark spots where Sioux and Cheyenne warriors fell, counterparts to white tablets erected for the men of the Seventh Cavalry in 1890. But their inscriptions, saying that each warrior "Died in Defense of His Homeland," enrage the Crow, who argue that the battle was actually on *their* homeland. "The Sioux and Cheyenne were migrating onto our land from the east and the Arapaho from the south," says Marvin Dawes, a Crow Indian historian. "Shall we say, they were passing through. They were visitors in the area."

When I got to Hardin, a lonely looking, hard-bitten prairie town with a string of boarded-up bars, the place was getting ready for the anniversary that keeps its economy alive. Every hotel room was booked, and reenactors wearing bluecoats and war paint thronged the streets.

The day of the anniversary, I got to the battlefield before dawn to see, along with about 50 others, seven Cheyenne elders in cowboy hats and dark glasses conduct a peace ceremony at the Indian memorial. Donlin Many Bad Horses lit a wooden pipe and said: "When things were bad for us, we could not do this. There were times when we could not come in here. But now a door has opened to us. We can come in and worship and pray. I hope this opening will continue to grow."

One morning a couple of days later, I met Ernie Lapointe, a great-grandson of Sitting Bull. "For many years," he said, "the Lakota, Cheyenne, Arapahos, everyone didn't like the Crow. We're natural enemies. But it's time now to settle those differences, to heal all those wounds." He told me that Sitting Bull had had a vision before the battle that "told him our warriors shouldn't take the spoils of war, or injure the dead—but they did. That's why we're oppressed to this day—by the losers in the battle!"

"Who wants to see Custer get killed?" a man with a loudspeaker asked the thousand-strong crowd at the longest-running reenactment of the battle, hosted by the mostly white businesses of Hardin on a dusty plain just outside town. "Y–e–s–s–s!" came the roar from the bleachers, as bluecoats on horseback rode out from a wooden fort. Next to me sat Joy Austin, the wife of Tony Austin, a 50-year-old postman now living in British Columbia who plays Custer. I asked how she felt about watching her husband die three times a day. "It's OK," she answered. "The only place I get choked up is when he leads the column of soldiers over the hill. You know that he and everyone else who rides with him won't be returning."

A Crow Indian, Joe Medicine Crow, wrote the script for this reenactment. It is based, he says, on interviews with a Cheyenne veteran of the battle, with echoes of the 1940 Errol Flynn film *They Died With Their Boots On,* and emphasizes reconciliation. "In this Battle of the Little Bighorn, there were no victors. . . . We red men and white men live in a united fortress of democracy, the United States of America."

Afterward, I went to the rival reenactment—hosted by the Real Bird family of Crow Indians by the Little Bighorn River—where I ran into Jason Heitland, who portrayed a federal soldier. "I'm going to fight here every year until I'm too old to do it," he told me breathlessly as we wandered among replica military tents by a shady creek. "You're fighting on the actual battlefield! You sleep where the actual Indian camp was, where the Cheyenne dog soldiers slept. And the battle itself is totally unscripted. You've got whooping Indians coming from all directions. It's quite a thrill."

"And the horses don't know it's fake," added Nicola Sgro, a coffee salesman from Michigan in his late-30s. "That's why it's so dangerous!"

By dusk on Sunday, after the last shot had been fired and the last memorial wreath had been laid, the battlefield had returned to its eerie silence. Visiting the site one last time, I was left with a sense of sadness for those on both sides—cavalrymen who were paid $13 a month to risk their scalps in an alien land, and Indian warriors desperately trying to preserve their nomadic way of life. "This was Custer's last stand," said John Doerner, "but it was also the last stand of the Indians. Within a year after the Little Bighorn, there wasn't a truly free Indian left on the plains."

TONY PERROTTET, a New York-based travel writer, is the author of *Pagan Holiday* and *The Naked Olympics*.

From *Smithsonian*, April 2005, pp. 90-95. Copyright © 2005 by Tony Perrottet. Reprinted by permission of the Tony Perrottet.

Gifts of the "Robber Barons"

JAMES NUECHTERLEIN

Even those who consider American history one long triumphal march tend to pass quickly over the decades of industrial expansion and consolidation between the Civil War and the early years of the 20th century. Industrialization was a necessary prelude to mass prosperity; but in America, as elsewhere, it often made for a dispiriting spectacle—pollution, urban blight, glaring material inequalities, ethnic and class conflict, moral dislocation.

To observers at the time, modern America's coining of age often seemed like an unraveling of the social fabric. Because so much had changed so quickly, precise explanations were hard to come by, but the responsibility for what had gone wrong settled quickly on those who had most obviously benefited. If, broadly speaking, industrialization was the problem, the men who ran the system—and who often got enormously rich doing so—had to be made to answer for its shortcomings.

Thus was born the notion of the "robber barons," and it has had a long historical shelf life. Until well into the second half of the 20th century, historians of post-Civil War industrial capitalism echoed contemporary observers both in their emphasis on the system's costs and in their indictment of those in charge.

In recent decades, a measure of economic sophistication has crept into accounts of the era, and the tendency to dwell on personal or institutional villainy has abated. For all its unlovely aspects, the period was one of dynamic economic growth, and those at the top must have been doing at least some things right. They may have gained disproportionately from economic progress, but most workers found their own real wages on the upswing. Industrial development was not the zero-stun game that progressive historians imagined it to be, nor is the concept of "robber barons" an adequate rubric to summarize either the men or the age to which it refers.

Evidence for this view abounds in two outstanding new biographies—David Nasaw's *Andrew Carnegie*[1] and David Cannadine's *Mellon: An American Life.*[2] Nasaw teaches at the Graduate Center of the City University of New York, Cannadine at the Institute of Historical Research, University of London. Neither author ignores or minimizes the flaws in his subject's behavior. But by offering portraits in the round, both resist historical reductionism. Readers may not come away admiring Andrew Carnegie or Andrew Mellon, but they will know better than simply to relegate them to historical pigeonholes.

That is particularly the case with Carnegie, a force of nature and, as Nasaw makes clear, a figure of fascinating complexity. In his business operations, he was sometimes a robber baron, sometimes an enlightened industrial statesman. More significantly, his life was about much more than business, and in his various non-business ventures he fit into no consistent analytical category. As a man, he was devious, deceptive, egomaniacal, and occasionally ruthless; he was also kindly, generous, dutiful, and possessed of an encompassing curiosity that suggested broad human sympathies. He defies convenient summing-up.

Carnegie's career was the American Dream personified. He was born in 1835 in Dunfermline, Scotland, to a poor, none-too-industrious weaver and his ambitious and resourceful wife. The family emigrated to America in 1848, settling near relatives and friends just outside Pittsburgh. Andrew, who had next to no formal education, went immediately to work as a bobbin boy in a cotton mill. Dissatisfied with the physical drudgery, he became a telegraph messenger, taught himself Morse code, and soon became the private telegraph operator and chief assistant to Thomas A. Scott, head of the Pennsylvania Railroad in the Pittsburgh region.

Bright, energetic, and personable—his inveterately optimistic and positive disposition attracted people to him all his life—Carnegie rose quickly in the railroad and considerably augmented his income with investments on the side, especially in oil.

After leaving the company at age thirty, he continued to work with Scott and the railroad's president, J. Edgar Thomson, in a number of joint ventures, contracting with the Pennsylvania and other railways to supply raw materials and grade crossings, and manufacture rails, bridges, and rolling stock of all varieties. He was already a rich man when he expanded from iron to steel in the early 1870's. By the time he retired in 1901, his share of the proceeds from the sale of Carnegie Steel to J.P. Morgan came to almost $120 billion in today's currency, making him the richest man in America, quite possibly the world.

Carnegie considered himself a businessman of probity and integrity and, by the standards of the day, he was. Attacks on his character genuinely baffled and appalled him. Nonetheless, as Nasaw notes, over the course of his career he engaged in activities that included sweetheart deals with corporate cronies, profiting from inside information, the floating of overvalued bonds, stock speculation, and involvement in pools to set minimum prices and allocate market shares. Carnegie operated in an intensely competitive and lightly regulated business environment. Although he acted decently enough by the lights of the day, those lights appear somewhat dim in retrospect.

The greatest blemish on Carnegie's reputation was the notorious lockout and strike at the Homestead steel works near Pittsburgh in July 1892. Carnegie considered himself a friend of the working man—he referred proudly to his family's involvement in the radical Chartist movement in Britain in the 1830's and 40's—but the theoretical rights of workers gave way when they came in conflict with his companies' profit margins. His operating partner Henry Clay Frick attempted to break the Homestead strike by bringing in Pinkerton men, but workers were there to block them. Violence broke out, and by the time order was restored there were dead and wounded on both sides. For the rest of his life, Carnegie, who was vacationing in Scotland at the time of the strike, disavowed responsibility for Homestead, but Nasaw shows that he had prior knowledge of Frick's intentions—they kept in contact by cable—and cites instances of earlier labor conflicts in which Carnegie employed similar tactics.

Still, Carnegie's image as an industrialist of generally enlightened opinions was not without substance. A member of the GOP's progressive wing—he had first been drawn to the party for its antislavery sentiments—he favored establishment of the Interstate Commerce Commission, backed Theodore Roosevelt on railroad regulation, and spoke in favor of a government commission to regulate prices. He defended the progressive income tax and proposed stiff levies on inherited fortunes. He was even known to speak favorably, if vaguely, of a possible socialist future. In foreign policy he was a fervent anti-imperialist, a strong internationalist, and a near fanatical advocate of world peace.

When he was just thirty-three, Carnegie determined that he would no longer preoccupy himself with material gain. "The amassing of wealth," he wrote in a personal memo, "is one of the worst species of idolatry." He began to work only three or four hours a day, spending the rest of his time at intellectual pursuits, philanthropy, and leisure. Much of his effort was devoted to self-education. More than anything else, Carnegie wanted recognition as a man of letters, and to a considerable degree he attained it. He moved in distinguished literary circles in America and Britain (Matthew Arnold and Samuel Clemens were among his close associates), published in fashionable journals of ideas, and wrote the best-selling *Triumphant Democracy* (1886), which, as its title suggests, was an extended celebration of the achievements wrought by America's political and economic institutions.

For Carnegie, America's moral and material progress showed it to be in conformity with the scientific imperatives of Herbert Spencer's Social Darwinism, under whose influence he himself had converted from "theology and the supernatural" to "the

truth of evolution." Evolutionary progress was not, to be sure, without its conundrums. "In particular," he wrote, "I don't at all understand the mysterious law of evolution, according to which the higher forms of life live upon the lower, rising through slaughter and extinction. That is profoundly, tragically obscure and perplexing." Still, the evolutionary consolation by which he overcame all doubts remained: "All is well, since all grows better."

Evolutionary theory provided, among other things, an argument for the social utility of millionaires like himself. Beginning in the 1880's, Carnegie elaborated that argument in a series of articles, later gathered into a book, that created the catchphrase with which his name is enduringly associated: the Gospel of Wealth. The simplest defense for great wealth was that it was a necessary byproduct of modern development. Earlier societies were restricted to the household or workshop method of manufacture and provided goods of uneven quality at high prices. Modern industrial society might generate greater inequalities of income, but it also produced dependable products at prices so low that now the poor could enjoy a style of material life available in the past only to the rich. Complex industrial society required as its leaders men with a special talent for organization and management; such men were relatively rare, and so could command a high level of compensation.

As Carnegie saw it, the emergence of the millionaire class resulted from the workings of immutable economic laws that societies ignored at their peril. Those in doubt about this "beneficent necessity," he explained, need only look about them: desperately poor nations like India, China, and Japan had few if any millionaires; as one went up the economic scale, from Russia to Germany to England, the incidence of millionaires proportionately increased. But none of these societies produced anything like America's abundant supply of the very rich, and in America—here, for Carnegie, was the clincher—the income of the many far surpassed that achieved anywhere else. The wealth gap was not a problem to be solved; it was an essential element in a system that worked to the good of all.

Another boon offered to society by millionaires was the proper use of the riches they accumulated that exceeded their personal needs. "The duty of the man of wealth," Carnegie said, is "to consider all surplus revenues which come to him simply as trust funds, which he is called upon to administer . . . in the manner which, in his judgment, is best calculated to produce the most beneficial results for the community."

That duty followed from the fact that, while the wealthy surely earned their riches, wealth itself came ultimately from the community. It was only the growth in the size and needs of the population that created the context in which business leaders could exercise their superior talents. In that sense, Carnegie noted, "the *community* created the millionaire's wealth."

Not all of his fellow millionaires, Carnegie conceded, did what duty required. Some left their fortunes not to the community but to their children, a practice Carnegie condemned as both self-regarding and, in the end, no favor to the children, for whom unearned wealth often turned out to be more blight than blessing. (Thus his support for steep inheritance taxes. Carnegie himself did not marry until he was past fifty, and he had only one child, a daughter.) Others earned Carnegie's rebuke by leaving their estates to be administered, often badly, by lesser men after their deaths. "It is well to remember," Carnegie warned, "that it requires the exercise of not less ability than that which acquired it to use wealth so as to be really beneficial to the community." Then there were those who gave their money away in their lifetimes but did so unwisely. Better to toss money into the sea, Carnegie thought, than to spend it "to encourage the slothful, the drunken, the unworthy." It was philanthropy that was needed, not heedless charity.

Whatever one thinks of his rationale, Carnegie was indeed serious about his philanthropic responsibilities. He did not quite succeed in his intention of giving away all of his money before his death in 1919, but he did disburse vast amounts and left the remainder (minus relatively modest bequests to his wife and various employees and friends) in a charitable trust.

His giving was diverse and sometimes idiosyncratic: it included, inter alia, thousands of community library buildings and endowments in America and Britain, thousands more organs for churches (to introduce parishioners to classical music), pensions for college professors, free tuition for students in Scottish universities, a scientific research institution in the nation's capital, a peace endowment, and a library, music hall, art gallery, and natural-history museum in Pittsburgh.

Carnegie's philanthropy was not motivated—as was the case with so many of his fellow millionaires—by guilt, religious convictions, or a desire to affect public opinion. He felt no pangs of conscience concerning his wealth, harbored no Calvinist or other theological beliefs, and settled on giving away his money long before he became a prominent target of public criticism. He surrendered his fortune because he thought it the right thing to do.

Carnegie had hoped that his retirement would be committed primarily to philanthropic activities. As it turned out, however, philanthropy became subordinate to the cause that consumed his final decades: world peace. He took a major role in opposing Britain's Boer War in South Africa and America's war with Spain and subsequent conflict with rebel forces in the Philippines. But his broader target was war itself, which he considered a moral anachronism among nations in the same way dueling had once been among individuals. The progress of civilization had eliminated the latter evil; that same progress, in combination with the increasing economic interdependence of nations, would do away with the former.

In this case, of course, what Nasaw terms his subject's "almost intolerable self-confidence" failed him. In his incessant, imperious, often condescending badgering of political leaders in Washington, London, and Berlin, he finally made himself "slightly ridiculous." Teddy Roosevelt bore more or less patiently with Carnegie's importunities in public, but referred to him privately as the leader of a "male shrieking sisterhood."

The outbreak of war in 1914 shattered, at least in the short run, Carnegie's naive faith that the ultimate result of the various policies he urged—bilateral arbitration treaties, international disarmament conferences, a permanent world court, a league of peace with enforceable powers—would be the cessation of armed conflict among nations. But if the Great War shook his pacifist dreams, it did not entirely destroy them. One of his last public acts was to write to Woodrow Wilson congratulating the President on his decision in 1917 to enlist America in what both of them believed would be the war to end war.

David Cannadine's biography of Andrew Mellon suffers in comparison with Nasaw's masterful work, but that has to do more with the book's subject than with its author. The historian Burton J. Hendrick, who wrote biographies of both Carnegie and Mellon (the latter was never published) and was thus uniquely positioned to offer a comparative judgment, concluded succinctly that "Mr. Mellon lacks the personal qualities that made Mr. Carnegie so attractive a subject, nor, in other ways, was he so great a man." Mellon's career was less interesting than Carnegie's, his mind less lively and original, his personality less compelling, his impact less memorable. Still, as Cannadine notes, his range of experience in business, politics, art collecting, and philanthropy has no equivalent among those commonly classed as robber barons, and it is well past time that he received full-scale treatment.

Cannadine concedes that he began his research prejudiced against his subject. At the outset, he says, he found Mellon "an unsympathetic person with unappealing politics." Mellon is best known to history as Secretary of the Treasury in the 1920's in the conservative administrations of Warren Harding, Calvin Coolidge, and Herbert Hoover. Cannadine, who is English (though he has studied and taught in the U.S.), admits that had he been an American during that period he would have voted against the Presidents whom Mellon served and thereafter in favor of Franklin D. Roosevelt. Nonetheless, he assures us that he has tried to remain evenhanded in his judgments, and he does scrupulously attempt to provide a comprehensive account of his subject that might satisfy both admirers and detractors. It does not, however, take a terribly perspicacious reader to conclude that the author's final estimation differs little from the one with which he began.

Mellon's career had none of the rags-to-riches romance of Carnegie's. He was born into comfortable circumstances in Pittsburgh in 1855; his father Thomas, whose Ulster Scots family had come to America in 1818 when he was five years old, had prospered as a lawyer, judge, businessman, and banker. Andrew inherited his father's aptitude for business, and already by 1882 had assumed control of T. Mellon and Sons Bank. Through the bank he gradually acquired interests in a broad range of enterprises: real estate, utilities, transportation, coal, steel, chemicals, oil, aluminum. By the turn of the century T. Mellon and Sons had become Mellon National Bank, and its head was now a very rich and powerful industrial financier.

Wealth and power did not translate into fame. Of the great industrialists of the age, Mellon was, until his entry into national politics in the 1920's, the least known. He was associated with no one major business, worked behind the scenes, and avoided publicity. He had none of Carnegie's flair and no desire for his notoriety. (The two men, twenty years apart in age, knew each other but were never close. In his dealings in steel, Mellon carefully avoided competition with Carnegie.) From childhood Mellon had been, even among his several siblings, a shy loner, remote and self-sufficient. He achieved his success through intellect and shrewd judgment, not force of personality.

Mellon's only experience in the public spotlight prior to the 1920's had been embarrassing and personally disastrous. He delayed marriage until 1901 when he was forty-six. He had met Nora McMullen on a cruise three years earlier, when she was nineteen, and had, for the first and only time in his life, fallen immediately and hopelessly in love. The two were utterly mismatched, their marriage a failure from the start. (Cannadine compares the union to that of Prince Charles and Diana Spencer.) Within a few years Nora had entered into a flagrant affair, and by 1912 the marriage was over, its dissolution marked by ugly, protracted, and widely publicized divorce proceedings that titillated the public and left the Mellons' two young children, Ailsa and Paul, with psychological scars that never entirely healed.

After the divorce, Mellon turned his attention not just to work but to the avocation of art collecting, which he had taken up in the late 1890's. Over the years, making his purchases through the prominent art dealers Roland Knoedler and Joseph Duveen, he built a magnificent personal collection. His greatest coup came in 1930-31, when he secretly purchased 21 of the finest paintings from the Hermitage collection in the Soviet Union for some $7 million, an acquisition—Cannadine calls it "the sale of the century"—made possible by Stalin's need for cash in his efforts to modernize the Soviet economy.

By 1920, Mellon was sixty-five and thinking about retirement. He was instead about to enter on a new career in national politics. Long active behind the scenes in the Republican party, he was particularly involved in the 1920 presidential campaign, pleased with the conservative turn in the party and nation that resulted in the nomination and landslide election of Warren Harding. His generous contributions and success at money-raising brought him to the attention of party leaders, and his name was put forward by conservatives to join Harding's cabinet as Secretary of the Treasury, in part to offset the presumed progressive influence of the incoming Secretary of Commerce, Herbert Hoover.

Mellon would serve under three Presidents, from 1921 to 1932. His major policies included reductions in interest rates and the national debt, cuts in taxes and government spending, and settlement of the huge debt that the European allies had incurred with the U.S. to finance their war efforts. On all these matters he achieved, over time, considerable success, and with the return of national prosperity he became a highly regarded figure. Mellon was hailed as "the greatest Secretary of the Treasury since Alexander Hamilton" and was even mentioned as a possible presidential candidate in 1928. This, of course, was before the stock-market crash of 1929 and the onset of the Great Depression, when praise turned to condemnation.

Examining Mellon's stewardship through the prism of the Depression, historians have more often than not been highly critical of his policies, even those prior to 1929. Cannadine, though a liberal in his politics and often disdainful of his subject's views, concludes that Mellon's tenure in the cabinet deserves "a more sympathetic appraisal than it has generally received." He defends in particular Mellon's tax policies, which have frequently been dismissed as special favors for the rich.

In cutting rates at the top, in fact, Mellon wanted to induce the wealthy to pay more in taxes, not less. The high wartime federal rates had prompted the wealthy to concentrate their investments in state and municipal bonds, which were tax-exempt. Mellon rightly supposed that lower income taxes would redirect investment from bonds, where returns were low, to taxable industrial stocks whose generally higher returns would offset the tax bite. Mellon, Cannadine notes, consistently held to the principle that payment of federal taxes should be proportionate to income. His reduction in top rates meant that the rich paid more than they had before, while his elimination of taxes for the first several thousand dollars of income meant that most Americans paid nothing.

Nor, Cannadine thinks, could Mellon have done much either to prevent the crash or to restore the economy in its aftermath. The government's monetary and fiscal tools were inadequate to both tasks. All in all, he concludes, "most of what happened in America between 1929 and 1932 would probably have happened regardless of who had been running the Treasury."

Where Cannadine *is* critical of Mellon concerns his practice, despite public denials, of continuing to look after his personal business interests while in office. There is no evidence of corrupt dealings, but there were times when Mellon urged policies that had favorable implications for companies he was involved in, like Gulf Oil and Alcoa. As Cannadine puts it, Mellon "simply never understood or accepted the notion of conflict of interest." Nor was this the first time that Mellon had cut ethical corners. Like Carnegie, Mellon thought of himself as a businessman of probity and honor, and by prevailing standards, he mostly was. On occasion, though, he indulged in practices that were similar to Carnegie's and that similarly would not pass muster today.

The triumph of Franklin Roosevelt and the New Deal turned Mellon's world upside down. As Cannadine writes, the new President considered Mellon "the embodiment of everything in the pro-business Republican world before 1932 that [he] loathed and was determined to destroy." Immediately upon assuming office in 1933, the administration ordered the Bureau of Internal Revenue to audit Mellon's income-tax returns during his last years in office. When the investigation found nothing amiss (the bureau's agents in fact recommended that Mellon be granted a refund for 1931) the administration, in an action Cannadine calls "wholly without precedent," turned the matter over to the Justice Department for criminal prosecution.

In May 1934, a grand jury unanimously refused to indict Mellon for knowingly filing a false return. But, instead of dropping the matter, the administration turned to a civil suit before the federal Board of Tax Appeals. Cannadine's careful analysis shows that Mellon had not, knowingly or unknowingly, violated the law. He died of bronchial pneumonia on August 26, 1937, some three months before the tax board announced its decision vindicating him.

What adds peculiar irony to this unsavory episode is that while the administration was proceeding in its political vendetta against Mellon, it was also negotiating with him about an extraordinary philanthropic gift he intended for the nation. For many years, Mellon had been planning to deed his art collection to "the people of the United States" and to build a gallery in the nation's capital in which that collection might be housed. In December 1936, after the tax board had concluded its hearings in his case, he made a formal offer to the President. Whatever his personal feelings toward Mellon, Roosevelt accepted the offer in a cordial meeting that proceeded as if the tax case did not exist.

Thus was born the National Gallery of Art, a philanthropic contribution that, in Cannadine's estimation, is without "precedent or parallel in the nation's history." The final worth of the gift, including the art, the building, and a substantial endowment, came to some $60 million in 1936 dollars. Mellon's gesture was self-effacing as well as generous: in an effort to encourage other patrons to make their own gifts of art to expand the collection, he stipulated that his name not appear on the building. Mellon's philanthropy, Cannadine makes clear, was as straightforward in motivation as Carnegie's had been: he felt no guilt for his fortune, was only nominally religious, and had always been disdainful of public opinion.

Cannadine devotes the final pages of his book to weighing Mellon's life in the balance. Though he attempts to do his subject justice, his own expressed support for the New Deal makes it difficult for him fully to comprehend Mellon's conservative political and social views, about which he offers frequent denigrating comments. Mellon should have been more critical of the social order in which he grew up, Cannadine suggests, and more sympathetic toward a Roosevelt who, he says again and again, was only striving to preserve capitalism. Thus he characterizes Mellon's antipathy to the New Deal as "imprudent, unimaginative, chilling." That anachronistic criticism, one feels sure, would utterly have baffled Andrew Mellon.

Cannadine is even harder on Mellon's personality than on his politics. He consistently places the overwhelming burden of blame on Mellon for his troubled relations with his wife and children, a judgment that appears to discount evidence of ambiguities and mutual misunderstandings that Cannadine himself presents. His sweeping condemnations of Mellon—"one of the most famously cold, taciturn, and repressed men of his generation"; "a hollow man, with no interior life"—seem imposed and gratuitous, unwarranted extrapolations from a life that, in the author's own account, sounds more complicated than the conclusions he puts forward about it.

None of this is to belittle Cannadine's achievement in writing an absorbing, intelligent, well-researched biography. But David Nasaw's approach seems preferable to me. While describing and analyzing Andrew Carnegie in brilliant detail, and offering occasional critical comments along the way, Nasaw does not attempt to characterize him. He says to his readers, in effect: here is a fascinating and multifaceted man, make of him what you will. Nasaw's own political views are decidedly liberal—as I discovered by stumbling across an op-ed piece he recently wrote—but they do not intrude on his narrative.

Carnegie and Mellon were very different creatures, but both of their lives bring into question the stereotype of the robber baron. Two men do not an era make, of course, but other recent biographical studies of industrial titans—Ron Chernow on John D. Rockefeller and Jean Strouse on J.P. Morgan, for example—point in the same direction.

In one key respect, however, the accounts of Nasaw and Cannadine do not support the efforts of an earlier generation of revisionists. In the 1950's, for instance, Allan Nevins defended John D. Rockefeller in part by arguing that he brought necessary order out of the chaos of the oil industry in the immediate post-Civil War period. Similar cases have been made for leaders in other industries. In this view, early industrial competition—cut-throat and frequently corrupt—had led to an untrustworthy boom-and-bust economy that undermined national prosperity. Against the backdrop of a reigning laissez-faire philosophy that precluded effective government intervention, the great industrial oligopolists supplied a measure of rough-and-ready economic stability that preceded the more formal controls on industry provided by Progressive and New Deal reforms.

Neither Cannadine nor Nasaw tries to make this case. Cannadine does not raise the issue, and Nasaw says quite explicitly that "the source materials I have uncovered do not support the telling of a heroic narrative of an industrialist who brought sanity and rationality to an immature capitalism plagued by runaway competition, ruthless speculation, and insider corruption." ("Nor," he immediately adds, "do they support the recitation of another muckraking exposé of Gilded Age criminality.")

Ultimately, the most persuasive way to rebut the robber-baron school of thought is to step back from its emphasis on the actions and intentions of particular individuals. Critics have presupposed that during this era the rich became rich at the expense of the general population. But (as I noted at the outset) this supposition flies in the face of the evidence of rising real wages. Indeed, as Milton Friedman once observed: "There is probably no other period in history, in this or any other country, in which the ordinary man had as large an increase in his standard of living as in the period between the Civil War and the First World War, when unrestrained individualism was most rugged." If Friedman is correct—or even anywhere near correct—the robber barons stand rehabilitated.

More precisely, they may be somewhat beside the point. Friedman did not mean to suggest that, but for specific men, the greatest economic boom in human history would not have occurred. Carnegie and Mellon were players—not interchangeable, of course, but also not indispensable—in an epic economic story whose outcome they only incidentally determined. Just as they were neither creators nor despoilers of general economic abundance, so too were they neither heroes nor villains in the roles they played. Like the rest of us, Carnegie and Mellon were made of mixed stuff, and were morally accountable as individuals, not as members of a class.

In that perspective we can appreciate the biographies of David Nasaw and David Cannadine without worrying whether they help to make or unmake a thesis. The stories they tell are not without larger significance; but the best stories, and the people who inhabit them, have never been reducible to neat moral and ideological categories.

Notes

1. Penguin, 878 pp., $35.00.
2. Knopf, 779 pp., $35.00.

JAMES NUECHTERLEIN, a former professor of American studies and political thought at Valparaiso University, is a senior fellow of the Institute on Religion and Public Life.

The Spark of Genius

Thomas Edison created the first light bulb 125 years ago. But he was not only America's greatest inventor. He was also a master entrepreneur.

HAROLD EVANS

It sits in isolation on a slope in the middle of a cow pasture, a two-story white clapboard house surrounded by a picket fence. Approached from the front, it looks like an ordinary home, with high sash windows, a gracefully arched porch ascended by sagging wooden steps, and a little balustraded balcony above. The first surprise is how far back the house extends. From the modest 30-foot facade, it runs at least 100 feet to the fringe of a virgin forest.

It is late on a winter's night in 1876. There is snow on the ground, and wood smoke curls from two brick chimneys. Inside, up the dark, uncarpeted stairs, a big bare-boarded room lit by gas jets and kerosene lamps stretches the building's full 100 feet. Its ceiling is laced with wire and piping, its walls lined floor to roof with jars of liquids and bottles of powder of every color. A rack in the center of the room is stacked with galvanic batteries, and every other nook and surface is covered with bits of copper, brass, lead, and tinfoil; crucibles, phials, and small darkened panes of glass; microscopes, spectrometers, telegraph keys, and galvanometers; rubber tubing and wax and small disks of some obscure material. At scattered workbenches and heaped-up tables there are a dozen young men engrossed in what they are doing: A bearded pair observe a spark jumping from an electromagnet to a metal lever; another boils a smelly chemical; another has his ear to some kind of telephone receiver; another, chewing tobacco, bends his head to frown at the needle on an instrument. In the far corner, stretched out on the floor amid a score of open books, is a pale young man with a mop of brown hair and stains on his hands, entirely lost to this world because he is concentrating on making a new one.

This is Thomas Alva Edison at 30. If we stay long enough, we will see him uncoil his shabby 5 feet, 8 inches and, stooping slightly, move slowly among the workbenches, cupping an ear to listen to observations on the night's work, reaching over to tweak an instrument, breaking out in laughter as one of the fellows makes a joke at his expense. His black frock coat and waistcoat are dusty, and a white silk handkerchief around his neck is tied in a careless knot over the stiff bosom of a white shirt rather the worse for wear, but what stands out is the extreme brightness of his eyes.

Around midnight he and his comrades in discovery will settle in front of a blazing fire for pie, ham, crackers, smoked herring, and beer. There is as likely to be a competition in mocking doggerel or crude cartoons as a debate on the proper expression of Newton's law of gravitation. Someone, maybe Edison himself if he has had a good day, will blast out a melody on a huge pipe organ at the end of the big room and they will raise the rafters singing sentimental (and censorable) ditties. Then they will all go back to their benches and books until the early hours while down the hill in Edison's farmhouse home, Mary Edison, his wife and the mother of two of his children, will have given up and gone to sleep with a revolver under her pillow. One late night soon a disheveled Edison will forget his keys, climb onto the roof, and let himself in through an open bedroom window. Mary, ever fearful of intruders, will nearly shoot him with her .38 Smith & Wesson. In the words of his journal, he will again "resolve to work daytimes and stay home nights," but he cannot keep a promise to himself when his head is filled working out the complexities standing between a panoramic vision and the steps to its realization.

Thomas Edison was America's most productive inventor in the 19th century and remains so into the 21st. His 1,093 patents are by no means the proper measure of the man. To Edison, the patents were the easy part, before "the long, laborious trouble of working them out and producing apparatus which is commercial"—and then fighting off the pirates. Edison's greatness lies not in any single invention, not even in the whole panoply, but in what he did with his own and other men's cleverness.

The invention for which he is most remembered, the incandescent bulb, is emblematic. The technology was a marked advance over the work of other inventors, but the piercing vision—and it was Edison's alone—was how he would bring light and power to millions of homes and offices. The historian Ruth Cowan writes that Edison from the beginning wanted to build a technological system *and* a series of businesses to manage that system. By the time he applied for any patent, Edison had already envisaged how he could translate the invention into a tangible, commercial product; indeed, he would not begin the research otherwise. Still, he was a classic innovator. "Only Leonardo da Vinci evokes the inventive spirit as impressively," writes the historian Thomas Hughes, "but, unlike Edison, Leonardo actually constructed only a few of his brilliant conceptions." Purists might respond that Leonardo was on his own whereas Edison had clever men at his beck and call—but what a sensible notion that was! One man could hardly hope to keep up with the efflorescence of knowledge in the sciences and the profusion of new techniques and new materials. In the decades after 1870, when industrialization in manufacturing superseded the machine-shop culture, it was quite brilliant to finance and focus multidisciplinary research in an organized manner with the deliberate intention of manufacturing the results. The momentum by which the United States surpassed Britain as the greatest industrial power near the turn of the century was in significant part due to the culture of research and development. In the year Edison was born, 1847, only 495 inventors won patents; in the year of his 40th birthday, he had more than 20,000 lesser mortals for company.

Little Al, as he was called then, did not do well at school. At the age of 8, in 1855, Edison was described by a teacher as "a little addled." Edison himself recalled, "I was always at the foot of the class. I used to feel that the teachers did not sympathize with me." Part of the trouble was that he missed years of lessons because of a series of infections, one of which seriously damaged his hearing. He was also ill-suited to rote learning; he could reach understanding only by doing and making.

His father, Sam, was a handsome jack-of-all-trades of Dutch extraction who became a lighthouse keeper on moving his family to Port Huron, Mich., in 1854. He had endless schemes for getting rich that never quite came off, but the little family was comfortable by the standards of the day, if erratically in debt. But it was Al's very protective mother, Nancy, a devout Presbyterian (who always dressed in black in memory of three children dead in infancy), who would be the boy's salvation. She divined that Al had a visual imagination and unusual powers of reasoning, and made it her business to take him out of the school that found him defective. She read him classics like Gibbon's *Decline and Fall of the Roman Empire* and Sear's *History of the World,* and when he kept asking questions she could not answer (*What is electricity? What is pitch made of?*) she put into his hands, at the age of 9, R. G. Parker's *A School Compendium of Natural and Experimental Philosophy.* It illustrated simple home experiments in chemistry and electricity, and Al attempted every one of them. When he left school for good at 13, a boy with a large head and jutting jaw, Alva was "dead set on being an engineer of a locomotive."

His first job was to climb aboard a train at Port Huron at 7 A.M. with copies of the Detroit *Free Press* to sell to passengers on the three-hour journey to Detroit and back. The budding entrepreneur persuaded the conductor to let him store berries, fruit, and vegetables, as well as sandwiches and peanuts, and deputized two other boys to sell the food for him. He also made a cheeky habit of walking into the composing room of the *Free Press* to find out what the next day's headlines would be, and

a year into the Civil War, on April 6, 1862, he scored a coup. A proof of next day's sensational front page reported that as many as 60,000 might be dead in a battle at Shiloh (actual deaths were 24,000). He had enough money to buy only 300 papers but talked his way into the sanctum of the fierce managing editor, Wilbur F. Storey, and got 1,000 copies on credit. Edison had already bribed officials at the railroad office to telegraph the fact that there had been a battle to every train station on the way back to Port Huron. He was mobbed at the first stop, raised prices at every station thereafter, and ended with a sell-out auction—and the princely sum of around $150. "I determined at once to be a telegrapher," he recalled later.

His luck was in. Late that summer, he plucked a 3-year-old boy from the path of a boxcar, and the grateful father—the railroad's stationmaster—offered telegraph lessons as a reward. Five months later, Al—now to be called Tom—began wandering Middle America as one of the hundreds of young "tramp" telegraph operators. In demand because so many telegraphers had been called into the armies on both sides, the tramps were fond of gambling, cursing, drinking, smoking, playing jokes, and carousing with women. Edison chewed tobacco ceaselessly, gambled a little, and played practical jokes, but he spent most of his spare time reading in lonely boardinghouse rooms and fiddling with telegraph equipment in railway stations on his preferred night shifts.

By the time he arrived in Boston in 1868, after jobs with Western Union and the military, Edison was a haunted man. The little sleep he had was populated by polarized magnets, springs, cylinders, rotating gears, armatures, batteries, and rheostats, all dancing intricate patterns with labyrinthine strands of wire to make the most marvelous advances in telegraphy, and all vanishing as soon as he awoke. He rented a corner of Charles Williams Jr.'s instrument workshop (the same workshop where Alexander Graham Bell encountered his collaborator Thomas A. Watson). Here Edison improved on the standard stock telegraph tape printer and went into business with other telegraphers to sell his machine and a stock-and-gold quotation service.

But there was not enough money for all his ideas in Boston, so Edison decamped for New York. Soon after his arrival in Manhattan in June 1869, at the age of 22, he was in the office of Dr. Sam Laws's Gold Indicator's wire service as a piecework assistant when its machine broke down. Hundreds of brokers' messengers fought at the door for the information while Wall Street came to a stop and the experts responsible for transmission worked themselves into impotent rage.

Edison fixed the machine.

He was now the golden boy in the dizzily evolving telegraph world. When he went before the directors of a Western Union subsidiary to present a device that aligned stock tickers in outside offices with the central station, they offered an astounding $30,000. His confidence, already sublime, came to border on the reckless.

He boldly contracted to deliver private telegraph machines and electrical equipment as well as 1,200 sped-up stock tickers for Western Union, manufacturing them with a machinist in Newark. By working 16 hours at a stretch, living on coffee, apple pie, and cigars, he delivered all the machines, though his bookkeeping mixed up the accounts of rival companies. Then he bought out his machinist partner. He was now his own man. He acted as foreman of 50 or more pieceworkers in the Newark factory, but this was a secondary preoccupation. He set up a laboratory equipped with the latest scientific equipment. One of his associates described seeing him go through a 5-foot-high pile of journals from Europe, eating and sleeping in his chair over six weeks, and conducting hundreds of experiments.

Most important, in the early 1870s, he recruited three men who would be crucial: Charles Batchelor, an English textile machinist; John Kruesi, a Swiss clockmaker; and Edward Johnson, a voluble railroad and telegraph engineer. Batchelor would render a rough Edison sketch into a precise drawing, Kruesi would make a model that could be entered into an application for a patent, and Johnson would organize patent applications, contracts, and payroll. Edison had an instinct for the kind of people he needed to stimulate and service his fertile imagination, and the right people were drawn like moths to his creative flame. His journal of February 1872 had more than 100 sketches; with the help of Batchelor and Krusei, he won 34 patents in that single year.

In 1875 Edison gave his 71-year-old father an assignment. Sam had an eye for property, and it was he who found the pasture in New Jersey and oversaw the building of the curiously shaped house where Edison set up his laboratory in March 1876. Thomas Hughes describes Menlo Park as a cross between Camelot and a monastic cloister. Every downstairs room in the lab had a needling quotation from the English painter Joshua Reynolds: "There is no expedient to which a man will not resort to avoid the real labor of thinking." Every clock had its spring removed to show that the place would not be a slave to time as measured by a machine; the length of the days would be fixed by Edison, who would often work for 24 hours, with tiny naps stretched out on floor or bench, and then sleep for 18.

His happy band of brothers knew something big was brewing at the end of August 1878 when a well-tanned Edison bounced into the lab wearing a big black sombrero. His exuberance was so different from July when, sick and exhausted, he had gone off by himself to the Rockies for a vacation, watching the total eclipse of the sun with a group of scientists. One of the scientists, George Barker of the University of Pennsylvania, had enthused about a system of lights the inventor Moses Farmer had installed at an Ansonia, Conn., foundry. They were arc lights, so called because the light was an arch of elongated sparks reaching between two carbon electrodes. Bright as searchlights, they had been familiar since the '60s in British and American lighthouses and a few places of public assembly but were too blinding (and hazardous) for domestic use.

Epiphanies. When he took the train to Ansonia with Barker and Batchelor on Sunday, September 8, it was not so much the eight big arc lamps at the foundry that excited Edison as the system he examined that morning: electric light generated not by batteries but by a primitive little dynamo, the current wired a quarter mile to the foundry. It was a double epiphany. Edison

was seeing for the first time practical proof that electric power could be sent a distance—and subdivided between lamps. His next question: Could it be done at a profit? A reporter for Charles Dana's New York *Sun,* who had come along, captured the moment of realization: "Edison was enraptured. . . . He ran from the instrument to the lights and from the lights back to the instrument. He sprawled over a table with the *simplicity of a child,* and made all kinds of calculations. He estimated the power of the instrument and of the lights, the probable loss of power in transmission, the amount of coal the instrument would save in a day, a week, a month, a year, and the result of such saving on manufacturing."

Edison's intuition was to think small. Instead of sending current to create a leap of light between the electrodes of big arc lamps, useless for domestic lighting, why not send it along the wire and into a filament in a small incandescent lamp? Back at Menlo Park he worked euphorically through two nights. "I discovered the necessary secret, so simple that a bootblack might understand it," he wrote. Edison went public only a week after his visit to Ansonia. His spicy quotes got full play in the newspapers: He had not only found the way to create an incandescent bulb but would be able to light the "entire lower part of New York" with one engine and 15 or 20 dynamos: "I have it now! With a process I have just discovered, I can produce a thousand—aye, ten thousand (lamps) from one machine. Indeed, the number may be said to be infinite. . . . with the same power you can run an elevator, a sewing machine, or any other mechanical contrivance, and by means of the heat you may cook your food."

It was hot air. The "secret" was something he had visualized but not realized, a thermal regulator to cut off current to the filament before it melted or burned out. The Edison scholars Robert Friedel and Paul Israel underline his audacity: "For Edison, the search for a practical incandescent light was a bold, even foolhardy, plunge into the unknown guided at first more by overconfidence and a few half-baked ideas than by science. To suggest otherwise is to rob the inventive act of its human dimension and thus to miss an understanding of the act itself."

Other experimenters in both arc and incandescent lighting had pushed a great deal of current along a thick wire to a low-resistance filament. The real secret, Edison found, arguing it out with Charles Batchelor, was to raise the voltage to push a small amount of current through a thin wire to a high-resistance filament. It was an application of the law propounded in 1827 by the German physicist George Ohm, but it was still imperfectly understood. Edison himself said later, "At the time I experimented I did not understand Ohm's law. Moreover, I do not want to understand Ohm's law. It would stop me experimenting." This is Edison in his folksy genius mode. Understanding the relationship linking voltage, current, and resistance was crucial to the development of the incandescent lamp, and he understood it intuitively even if he did not express it in a mathematical formula.

Scientists in America and England who were still thinking of low resistance and thicker and thicker wires (at great cost) dismissed Edison's project to light New York as both scientifically stupid and economically hopeless. But he had to find a filament of high resistance—and heat it up to incandescence in a bulb as close to airless as he could get to hinder oxidization. Edison was not even close to resolving these dilemmas in the early fall of 1878 when his friend and lawyer Grosvenor Lowrey (who had encouraged Edison to fly his colorful kite in the press) moved on his behalf in New York's banking parlors. Lowrey swiftly raised $300,000 to form the Edison Electric Light Co. The filament proved more elusive than Edison had hoped. He had discarded carbon because it burned up so readily. Platinum wire offered only low resistance but did not oxidize and therefore seemed to offer the best prospect. They worked on making long spirals of thin platinum, to increase the resistance, but it was delicate and dangerous work. In mid-April, Lowrey led a group of investors into the darkened lab where Edison had installed 12 lamps with a platinum filament linked in series. Edison told John Kruesi to turn on the current slowly. Francis Jehl, an assistant, recalls: "I can see those lamps rising to a cherry red and hear Mr. Edison saying, 'A little more juice,' and the lamps began to glow. A little more . . . and then one emits a light like a star after which there is an eruption and a puff, and the machine shop is in total darkness." Batchelor replaced the dud lamp; the same thing happened a few minutes later. Only Lowrey's eloquence and the steadfastness of 42-year-old John Pierpont Morgan held the group together.

The other challenge was the vacuum; nobody had been able to get enough air out of the bulb. Edison did a simple thing. He had put a classified advertisement in the New York *Herald* for a glass blower, which netted an 18-year-old in a little red German student cap. The mechanics were amused by the dainty Ludwig Boehm and his pince-nez, but he blew a better bulb to Edison's design and he helped work out a new way of evacuating a bulb by infusions of mercury. It was laborious, frustrating work, but in September, after weeks of effort, Edison and his team achieved a vacuum of one hundredth of an atmosphere. Edison discovered that at this level they had so reduced the oxygen in the bulb that a carbon stick did not burn up quickly and it gave a better light than platinum ever had. That was the good news; the less good was that resistance to this particular piece of carbon was only around 2 ohms (which would mean more current, more copper). Resistance could be raised by shaping a tiny filament in a small spiral, but the filament would have to be no thicker than 15 thousandths of an inch. Edison set everyone in a frenzy trying to roll carbon into reeds no thicker than thread. Day after day, night after night, the spiral reeds kept breaking.

Success. After two sleepless weeks, Edison relieved the carbon rollers. His new idea was to bake the carbon into a length of plain cotton thread. On the eighth attempt, on October 21, the dexterous Batchelor held his breath carrying a tiny thread bent into the shape of a horseshoe to Boehm's house for insertion in a bulb. "Just as we reached the glass blower's house, the wretched carbon broke," Edison recalled. "We turned back to the main laboratory and set to work again. It was late in the afternoon before we produced another carbon, which was broken by a jeweler's screwdriver falling against it. But we turned back again and before nightfall the carbon was completed and inserted in the lamp. The bulb was exhausted of air and sealed,

the current turned on, and the sight we had so long desired to see met our eyes."

Thread No. 9, lit at 1:30 A.M., lasted until 3 P.M.—13½ hours, whereupon Edison added a stronger battery to boost the light to 30 candles, or three times gaslight. They watched the tiny filament struggle with the intense heat. The light continued for 60 minutes. It was a crack in the glass that turned the room back into darkness—amid the cheers of exhausted men. They had proved that a carbon filament in a vacuum would work.

After examining the charred filament under a microscope, Edison launched another search for an organic fibrous material, some form of cellulose that might yield even more resistance than cotton. By November 16, they settled on a piece of common cardboard. Edison records: "None of us could go to bed, and there was no sleep for any of us for 40 hours. We sat and watched it with anxiety growing into elation. The lamp lasted about 45 hours, and I realized that the practical incandescent lamp had been born."

Already, Edison was preparing to establish electric beachheads in New York, Paris, and London. The lab staff worked frantically making bulbs by hand, one by one, so that on New Year's Eve, when Edison opened Menlo Park to a public exhibition, he had around 300 bulbs. Some 3,000 people came to gaze and put questions to the great man. Still, the experts in America and England refused to be dazzled. Henry Morton of the Stevens Institute, who had been on the Rockies expedition, charged that Edison was perpetrating "a fraud upon the public," provoking Edison to make another promise: He would erect a statue of Morton at Menlo Park and shine an eternal electric light on his gloomy countenance.

What Edison attempted next can be characterized only as awesome, as if having climbed Everest he sprouted wings and flew from the top. "There is a wide difference," he said, "between completing an invention and putting the manufactured article on the market," but marketing an electric light bulb was the least of it. He had to invent the electrical industry. He had to conceive a system down to its very last detail—and then manufacture everything in it. He had to build a central power station; design and manufacture his own dynamos to convert steam power into electrical energy; ensure an even flow of current; connect a 14-mile network of underground wiring; insulate the wiring against moisture and the accidental discharge of electrical charges; install safety devices against fire; design commercially efficient motors to use electricity in daylight hours for elevators, printing presses, lathes, fans, and the like; design and install meters to measure individual consumption of power; and invent and manufacture a plethora of switches, sockets, fuses, distributing boxes, and lamp holders.

Luckily, Edison was worth around half a million dollars by then; Western Union had made big payments for his telegraph and telephone patents. Shuttling between Menlo Park and his grand new headquarters in a double brownstone mansion at 65 Fifth Avenue, Edison the industrialist organized a group of companies from 1880 to 1881, the progenitors of the modern Con Edison and General Electric. For his power station,

Edison bought a couple of dilapidated warehouses at 25–257 Pearl Street within sight of the high towers of the unfinished Brooklyn Bridge. In December 1881, he began to dig up cobblestones for conduits radiating symmetrically outward from Pearl Street. He was often down in the trenches in the raw early hours checking the connections made by the wiring runners. It took six months to do the work.

Lights on. Sunday was normally the one day of the week reserved for his neglected wife, Mary, and their two children, but Sunday, Sept. 3, 1882, was different. All day and into the night Edison was on Pearl Street rehearsing every part of the operation for the system's debut due on Monday afternoon. So much might go wrong when he gave the orders for the steam to flow. "The gas companies were our bitter enemies, ready to pounce upon us at the slightest failure," he recalled later. When the chief electrician pulled the switch at 3 P.M., only one of the six dynamo sets worked and the steam engine was wobbly.

But Edison, over at the offices of Drexel, Morgan & Co., ready for the big moment when he would ceremonially connect the 106 lamps there, was not disappointed. They all came on! They came on, too, at the offices of the *New York Times,* "in fairy tale style," said the paper, 52 filaments appearing to glow stronger as the night drew in.

Edison's success was at once a vindication and an incitement. His patent was swiftly challenged, his ideas stolen. But Edison would not sue; he would out-invent and undersell them all. When Pearl Street went on line in 1882, no fewer than 200 companies across America had already signed up with the Edison Company for Isolated Lighting, using 45,000 lamps a day: companies like Marshall Field's dry goods store in Chicago, George Eastman's Photographic Company in Rochester, N.Y., the Stetson Hat Co. in Philadelphia, and Dillard's Oregon Railway and Navigation Co. The electrical evangelists Edison had sent overseas had done their work well. A London newspaper summed up the acclaim: "There is but one Edison."

Global Cooling

In the 19th century, winter ice, cut from the frozen ponds, lakes and rivers of the American North, was transported around the world, initiating a new age of cool.

MARK BERNSTEIN

On September 10, 1833, the brig *Tuscany* docked in Calcutta and began unloading cargo—100 tons of crystal-clear ice, cut from the winter ponds of Massachusetts and transported from Boston across 15,000 miles of mostly tropical waters.

The British colony in Calcutta was, likewise, transported. Servants were sent scurrying to acquire the commodity, which had gone promptly on sale. One resident Briton wrote: "How many Calcutta tables glittered that morning with lumps of ice! The butter dishes were filled; the goblets of water were converted into miniature Arctic seas with icebergs. . . . Everybody invited everybody to dinner, to taste of claret and beer cooled by the American importation."

Ice to Calcutta was the grandest coup of a 19th-century entrepreneur, Frederic Tudor, who by the time of this passage to India had been shipping ice to ports throughout the Caribbean for a quarter century. Tudor—whom one biographer cheerfully termed "a diminutive, pig-headed Bostonian"—had overcome the scorn of many, and a serious bout with bankruptcy, to pursue a business plan as dazzling as his ice in its simplicity. "In a country," Tudor once wrote, "where at some seasons of the year the heat is almost unsupportable, where at times the common necessary of life, water, cannot be had but in a tepid state—ice must be considered as out doing most other luxuries."

In warmer climes, ice had long ranked as a luxury. By one account, ice was stored in deep pits almost 4,000 years ago near the Euphrates River in Mesopotamia; the Roman emperor Nero used snow brought from the Apennines to cool his wine; England's James I had brick-lined pits built at Greenwich to capture the cold of snow; and, later, ships from England gathered the floating ice of the North Atlantic to be brought to London.

In the 19th century, ice, like many things, made its way from luxury to necessity. Tudor's most important contribution, perhaps, was to demonstrate to commercially minded America that a good return could thereby be had, and many followed in his footsteps. The world wanted cold. New England in winter had plenty of surplus cold to export, cold that conveniently stored

itself in clear slabs of ice up to 2 feet thick. The region also had mounds of sawdust, the waste product of lumbering—and a cheap, effective insulator for the frozen commodity.

> **'In a country where at some seasons of the year the heat is almost unsupportable . . . ice must be considered as out doing most other luxuries.'**

Ice made its way from the ponds and rivers of New England, where it was cut, packed in sawdust and stored until the following summer. It was then sold to the city dwellers of the East Coast, to whom it was delivered by, of course, the iceman. Ice also made its way from the Great Lakes and freshwater ponds of the Midwest to Chicago, where Swift, Armour and others used it to introduce fresh meat to the American table, and to Milwaukee, where German brewers used it to produce the cold-fermented lager beers that went with that meat. The whole process was like a miniglacier, which by the late 19th century saw 8 million tons of ice moving south each year.

Ice is peculiar stuff. It forms in the open—lakes, ponds and elsewhere—whenever water of less than 40 degrees Fahrenheit is exposed to air that is below freezing. The ice industry was dependent on one simple fact of nature: Unlike most things, water expands when it freezes. A cubic foot of ice weighs about 58 pounds—10 percent less than an equal volume of water. Were this not the case, ice would not float, and there would be no surface ice available to harvest.

Ice is hard, often slippery and unyielding to the touch. It is also startling to the uninitiated. In his *Second Jungle Book,* Rudyard Kipling writes of a bird that, present when a cargo of ice is being unloaded in India, catches and straightaway swallows a chunk of ice casually tossed its way. The adjutant bird reported: "Never have I felt such cold. I danced in my grief and amazement until I recovered my breath, and then I danced and cried out against the falseness of the world; and the boatmen derided me until they fell down."

Ice is sometimes a commodity of contemplation. Henry David Thoreau wrote: "Why is it that a bucket of water soon becomes putrid, but frozen remains sweet forever? It is commonly said that this is the difference between the affections and the intellect." Thoreau, America's best-known naturalist, reported on a commercial ice harvest when in 1847 workmen came to, in Thoreau's phrase, "unroof the house of fishes"—stripping the ice from Walden, America's best-known pond.

As Thoreau described the scene: "A hundred Irishmen, with Yankee overseers, came from Cambridge every day to get out the ice. They divided it into cakes ... and these, being sledded to the shore, were rapidly hauled off on to an ice platform, and raised by grappling irons and block and tackle, worked by horses, on to a stack, as surely as so many barrels of flour. They told me that in a good day they could get out a thousand tons, which was the yield of about one acre." The resulting pile, Thoreau reported, stood 35 feet high and 100 feet square. With its gaps stuffed with meadow hay, it looked like "a venerable moss-grown and hoary ruin, built of azure-tinted marble, the abode of Winter, that old man we see in the almanac." Told that some of the ice was destined for India, Thoreau struck a globalizing note: "Thus it appears that the sweltering inhabitants ... of Madras and Bombay and Calcutta, drink at my well."

Although Thoreau called the methods of ice harvesting "too well known to require description," as with many 19th-century chores, those methods are now all but entirely forgotten. Thoreau's description was of a small commercial operation; more commonly, ice harvesting was a rural task, one that, like butchering hogs and raising a barn, was part of the communal side of farm life. Farmers worked in teams to cut and store the ice that they would need the following summer to chill and preserve milk and butter.

The ice harvest had no fixed date, falling anytime from the week before New Year's to late February. Climate influenced its timing. On winter's southern tier—that is, the Ohio River valley and Pennsylvania—the fear that an unseasonable thaw might spoil the crop prompted farmers to harvest when ice had reached 6 inches thick. Farther north, in Maine, where winter's cold could be better relied upon, the harvest waited until 15 inches or more of ice had formed.

The work of commercial harvesting was done by coordinated teams, well described in such contemporary sources as *Scribner's Magazine* and Henry Hall's *The Ice Industry in the United States,* both published in 1875. Crew members had specialized tasks. First, horse-drawn wooden snowplows would clear the surface snow that overlay the ice. A snow-ice plane followed, to shave off any crusted or pocketed ice that remained. Then, a horse-drawn marker would scratch a 2- or 3-inch-deep groove into the ice. The marker was then fixed with a sliding guide; with the guide set into the previously made cut, the marker would create a second cut, generally 22 inches from the first. By this rather tedious means, the surface would be scratched first in one direction, then at 90 degrees, creating something resembling a large, frozen checkerboard.

Cutting then began. Commonly, ice would be cut through most of its thickness by teams of horses pulling ice plows. Workers would free the ice using long-handled pry bars, breaking it into rafts of perhaps 30 cakes long by 12 wide, then cutting smaller units to be floated toward shore. In her account of late-19th-century ice harvesting in Maine, Jennie G. Everson wrote: "Moving ice was called 'live ice,' while blocks that had come to a stop were known as 'dead ice,' and hard labor was required to start it moving again. In warm or rainy weather, when the ice was sticky and slushy and went slowly, shouts of 'Come on, boys, don't let her die,' 'Catch her while she's hot,' or perhaps taunts by older and more experienced men, rang through the house." On shore, the often 300-pound blocks were pulled by horses up a chute that extended into the water, and then dispatched for storage.

The trade had its own specialized tools, many designed by Nathaniel Jarvis Wyeth of Boston, an associate of Tudor's and the inventor of the first practical ice cutter and other tools that improved the work's efficiency. Tools included ice saws of varying sizes, a grapple used in towing sheets of ice by horse, breaking-off bars to separate pieces from flows, splitting chisels to separate sheets into blocks, bar chisels to loosen and trim cakes, ice hooks to pull or push the floating ice, and scoop nets to remove ice from the channel through which the cakes were floated. There were dozens of other tools as well.

Once harvested, the ice had to be stored. Here, again, the debt was to Tudor, who realized that melted ice would turn no profit and who did much to master methods of insulation. In 1816 he built an icehouse in Havana that used wood shavings 3 feet thick as insulation. The resulting loss from melting was just seven gallons an hour; at that rate, its stockpile of 150 tons would take six months to disappear.

Less elegant constructions often sufficed. A visiting Midwestern farmer noted that his neighbor's icehouse was of a plain rough-board construction, 16 feet square, with a simple roof and openings back and front. According to the farmer, the neighbor reported that "his ice kept perfectly until the next winter. He put a layer of sawdust about a foot thick on the ground, and then stacked the ice snugly in the center, 18 or 20 inches from the walls; and then filled it in with sawdust, and up over the top a foot or more thick." With the understanding gained from this visit, the farmer built his own icehouse, later affirming: "At the present time I have an abundance of ice, and the cakes seem to come out as square and perfect as when they went in, seemingly nothing lacking except what is used out. I am satisfied how to build an ice house."

While harvesting ice in teams meant the work got done, the camaraderie that developed was apparently not enough to make the work a pleasure. Ice harvesting made for long, cold days—days made longer and colder if one failed to remain dry. Horses, their shoes fitted with special steel cleats for traction, provided much of the power—and much of the uncertainty if their 1,500-pound bulks found a weak spot or air pocket in the ice and suddenly broke through. In *America's Icemen,* author Joseph Jones described one scene: "If a horse broke through the ice the driver immediately grabbed the rope and pulled it tight around the [horse's] neck. By shutting off the wind the horse would not struggle in the water." Planks were placed under the horse and then a second team would haul it from the water. Chilled to the core, "the frightened horse was wiped down, blanketed, thoroughly exercised." In addition to the shock and cold, horses sometimes drowned.

The work may seem picturesque today, but those who performed it did not necessarily recall it fondly. One upstate New York resident said: "Looking back I cannot see any romantic side to the ice harvest. It was just cold, hard work that was necessary to protect milk and food during the hot summer months. . . . The ice harvest, like hog raising, has gone from upstate New York, but it is one industry that is not missed."

Early on, commercial ice remained a product for the affluent, and, in the case of Tudor, an item for export. In 1847 Tudor sent 23,000 tons of ice to 31 foreign destinations. Tudor had his rivals. To promote its sale in England, Wenham Lake Ice Company, an American concern, sent a block of ice to Queen Victoria. To promote it further, the company's office on The Strand in London kept a 2-foot block of ice on display in its window—so clear, it was claimed, that one could read a newspaper through it. A second entrepreneur, Gage, Hittinger and Company, tried to build a market for ice by introducing the British to mint juleps and other drinks best served chilled. This effort, in a country that allegedly still drinks its beer warm, was not entirely successful.

As a product for affluent consumers, ice had its hierarchy, and Wenham's was considered the best. Food writer Elizabeth David wrote that, at mid-19th century, "No British dinner party was considered complete without Wenham's ice"—a small block decorating each table, larger blocks for cooling. (When Norway displaced America as the source of England's ice, a lake there was renamed Wenham so that its product could be marketed under that name.)

Ice was an exotic export, but its real impact was in the United States, where about 97 percent of domestically harvested ice was used. The most notable impact was on the American diet. And it was a good thing, too.

Most mid-19th-century Americans lived on salted pork, bread or corn mush, a diet low in many vitamins, high in fat, exceedingly long on monotony and not all that safe—intestinal illnesses traceable to spoiled food were widespread, often fatal. Monotony and danger stemmed from the same cause. Unless chilled, meats and most types of produce would spoil; they could not, therefore, be delivered to markets far from their point of origin. Thus, diets were largely restricted to what nearby agriculture could produce. The danger had mostly to do with bacteria associated with spoilage. And to prevent or, at least, retard that spoilage, people had for centuries been storing produce in cellars and salting, pickling, smoking, drying or spicing meats—indeed, the preservative properties of spices had done much to drive early trade with the Orient.

In 1867 a revolution in food preservation came when J.B. Sutherland of Michigan patented a refrigerated railway car that channeled air through bunkers of ice located at either end of the car, thus cooling the contents. That same year, the Illinois Central Railroad put a refrigerated car into service, with 100 pounds of ice used to cool 200 quart batches of strawberries. Brewers, wishing to produce cold-fermented German lagers, became major users of ice, permitting year-round production of brews previously available only in cooler months.

The most important step came in 1878, when Chicago cattle dealer Gustavus Swift sought an alternative to shipping live cattle east for slaughter; if already butchered beef could be shipped cooled, the costs would greatly decrease. Swift commissioned the design of a railway car that was chilled by bins of ice positioned near its top. The cooler air produced by the melting ice would sink to the bottom of the car, preserving its contents. The consequence: Chicago became the cattle and hog butcher to the world, and fresh meat found its place in the American diet nationwide. Soon, other perishable goods—apples from Washington, peaches from Georgia—were being carried across the country in rapidly moving refrigerated cars, and produce could be shipped from wherever it could be grown most economically, all year long.

The railways had created cool. Families maintained cold storage in their homes by purchasing ice chests, which became a standard item in a middle-class home by the 1880s. Sturdily made of oak, the containers could store up to 100 pounds of ice—generally, a day's worth of cooling. That ice was delivered from the slow-moving cart of the iceman, who—rather like the Good Humor men of later years—was a creature of interest to neighborhood children. By one account: "Children loved the iceman! Little kids would string along behind and beg for ice chips. If that didn't work they would climb on the back of the delivery wagon or truck, while the iceman was making a delivery, and steal a piece of ice to suck." By the late 19th century, such home use accounted for half the national consumption of ice.

As ice went from luxury to acknowledged necessity, massive quantities were required to meet the demand. In the Chicago area, 3,000 men worked at harvesting ice from the rivers that flowed into Lake Michigan. By 1883, Chicago ice companies had an aggregate capacity of 1.3 million tons. Meat packers maintained huge railroad-side warehouses filled with ice where refrigerated cars could be replenished. In Pewaukee, Wis., Armour built a 6-acre icehouse that stored 175,000 tons in a single location.

The ice business prospered. With demand rising, the industry sought out new sources. Weather played a role. The winter of 1879–80 was unseasonably warm in New York's Hudson River Valley, and by February 1880 its local crop of ice was largely ruined. Wholesale prices in New York City rose above $4 a ton, which spelled opportunity for ice harvesting in Maine. There, the Kennebec, Sheepscot and Penobscot rivers lay coated in 15 or more inches of glistening ice. That ice could be cut, loaded and freighted to New York, Jones wrote, for barely $1.50 a ton. Four thousand men were soon bringing in the crop. So much sawdust was required for insulation that the former nuisance suddenly gained commercial value, selling for $3 a cord. About 1.3 million tons of ice was harvested in Maine, three-quarters of it from the Kennebec, a yield that represented about one-fourth of the nation's consumption. From 1880 onward, Maine ranked ahead of Massachusetts as the leading provider of ice.

Maine achieved preeminence, however, just as the foundations of the ice industry began to melt from under its feet. One cause was technological innovation. The basic elements of mechanical ice making—compressor, condenser, expansion valve and evaporator—had been established as long ago as 1834, when a device incorporating such components was patented in Britain by Jacob Perkins, an American living in London. In 1848, a Frenchman, Ferdinand Carre, devised an ammonia-based refrigerating system. In 1851, a Florida physician, Dr. John Gorrie—who had been treating malaria patients by placing them in a room cooled by air circulating over blocks of ice—completed an automatic ice-making machine, for which he received a U.S. patent that year. In 1856, an Australian, James Harrison, produced a working refrigerator on the principle of vapor compression.

None of these inventors thrived—indeed, Dr. Gorrie went broke trying to promote his invention. The central problem was that none of the inventions were, at least as yet, particularly efficient. The ice they produced was far more costly than the going rate for natural ice. That rate varied, depending on where the ice was headed. Ice being bulky, much of its retail price in any city reflected the costs of getting it there. Ice that in New York City might sell for $8 a ton, delivered, brought 10 or more times that amount in inland Southern cities. Those faced with such prices welcomed alternatives.

The country's first artificial ice-making company opened in New Orleans in 1868; it placed its ice on sale at $35 a ton, exorbitant by New York City rates, but a bargain locally. The *New Orleans Crescent* reported, "So great has been the demand of late for this ice that the immense quantity of 60 tons per day is inadequate to meet it." The efficiency of mechanical refrigeration increased with the years; larger volumes brought lower prices, and the affordability of the mechanical alternative worked its way northward.

Holding the bulk of the market, natural ice makers sloughed off their upstart mechanical rivals. In January 1889, the Bath, Maine, *Daily Times* reported that a Chicago ice-making machine had blown up, setting several buildings ablaze and inflicting $200,000 in damage. It editorialized: "Kennebec ice men can now chuckle under their collars and mark up several points for their natural river product. A few accidents like this will discourage the general introduction of such concerns, and Maine's winter industry will continue to flourish as of old."

He who chuckles last, however, chuckles best. A key selling point of pond and river ice was that it was "natural"—formed by nature's cold on nature's lakes and ponds and, as such, "superior." This point was about to be lost. Then, as now, the word "natural" had no very certain meaning; it covered a multitude of sins. Those sins were quite small—the billions of bacteria contained in the raw sewage and general sludge of industrial life that were being dumped untreated into the nation's water system. That water, when frozen, was sawed up, sold and used to cool drinks. Thoreau had observed that ice remained pure over time, but only, as events were to demonstrate, if that water was pure to begin with. Doubts about the purity of ice harvested from rivers and ponds began to surface in the 1880s, a few years before the Maine newspaper's confident prediction. Doubt grew. In the summer of 1901, a typhoid epidemic in Chicago was blamed on polluted ice.

And finally, the "natural industry" was the victim of Mother Nature. In the early 19th century, Tudor realized that the simple cold of New England's winters was a valuable commercial asset. Cold was indeed the natural ice industry's key raw material, but it was a material the industry itself could not produce. In 1905–06, a warm winter devastated the crop. And on February 2, 1906, *The New York Times* headlined: "ICE FAMINE THREATENS UNLESS COLD SETS IN—Twenty Days' Hard Frost Needed to Make a Crop—NONE HARVESTED ON HUDSON. New York needs 4,000,000 Tons a year and Artificial Plants can supply only 700,000."

The availability of cheap natural ice had turned it into a necessity, and as such, it was a precious commodity people were unwilling to leave to the vicissitudes of Old Man Winter. Mechanically produced ice was not only safer, it was also more reliable. The number of commercial ice-making houses in America, 787 in 1899, rose to more than 2,000 by 1909. And it was perhaps a good thing for New Yorkers that the ice harvest failed on the Hudson River in 1906. The following year, Dr. Daniel D. Jackson of the state's Department of Water Supply, Gas and Electricity declared Hudson River ice unfit for cooling drinks. The natural ice industry died swiftly. Just before the turn of the century, the Kennebec River in Maine had produced 1.3 million tons of ice a year; in 1907–08, no ice was commercially harvested on the Kennebec.

As ice went from luxury to acknowledged necessity, massive quantities were required to meet the demand.

The death of the natural ice industry came less than a century after Frederic Tudor's entrepreneurial insight that cold—the bane of New England's winters—was itself a commercial commodity. With that principle established, inventors followed: first, to create the cooled railcars that brought fresh meat and produce to America's table; and second, to devise mechanical methods of producing cold more cheaply, more reliably, more safely and in greater abundance than the lakes and rivers of Massachusetts and Maine could manage.

What Tudor introduced to the world of trade was a new concept, that of a self-contained zone of cold that would protect goods in transit. Known in today's world of trade as "cold chain," it is how all manner of temperature-sensitive goods—including 80 million shipments of pharmaceuticals a year—reach their destinations, following in the wake of *Tuscany's* 15,000-mile passage to India in 1833.

From *American History,* by Mark Bernstein, August 2006, pp. 49–55. Copyright © 2006 by Weider History Group. Reprinted by permission.

Lockwood in '84

In 1884, a woman couldn't vote for the president of the United States, but that didn't stop activist lawyer Belva Lockwood from conducting a full-scale campaign for the office. She was the first woman ever to do so, and she tried again for the presidency in 1888. It's time we recognized her name.

JILL NORGREN

In 1884, Washington, D.C., attorney Belva Lockwood, candidate of the Equal Rights Party, became the first woman to run a full campaign for the presidency of the United States. She had no illusion that a woman could be elected, but there were policy issues on which she wished to speak, and, truth be told, she welcomed the notoriety. When challenged as to whether a woman was eligible to become president, she said that there was "not a thing in the Constitution" to prohibit it. She did not hesitate to confront the male establishment that barred women from voting and from professional advancement. With the spunk born of a lifelong refusal to be a passive victim of discrimination, Lockwood told a campaign reporter, "I cannot vote, but I can be voted for." Her bid for the presidency startled the country and infuriated other suffrage leaders, many of whom mistakenly clung to the idea that the Republican Party would soon sponsor a constitutional amendment in support of woman suffrage.

In the last quarter of the 19th century, Lockwood commanded attention, and not just from the columnists and satirists whom she led a merry chase. Today she is virtually unknown, lost in the shadows of the iconic suffrage leaders Elizabeth Cady Stanton and Susan B. Anthony. That's an injustice, for Belva Lockwood was a model of courageous activism and an admirable symbol of a woman's movement that increasingly invested its energies in party politics.

Lockwood was born Belva Ann Bennett in the Niagara County town of Royalton, New York, on October 24, 1830, the second daughter, and second of five children, of Lewis J. Bennett, a farmer, and Hannah Green Bennett. Belva was educated in rural schoolhouses, where she herself began to teach at the age of 14. In her first profession she found her first cause. As a female instructor, she received less than half the salary paid to the young men. The Bennetts' teenage daughter thought this treatment "odious, an indignity not to be tamely borne." She complained to the wife of a local minister, who counseled her that such was the way of the world. But bright, opinionated, ambitious Belva Bennett would not accept that world.

From her avid reading of history, Belva imagined for herself a life different from that of her mother and her aunts—the life, in fact, of a great man. She asked her father's permission to continue her education, but he said no. She then did what she was expected to do: On November 8, 1848, she married Uriah McNall, a promising young farmer. She threw herself into running their small farm and sawmill, wrote poetry and essays, and determined not to let marriage be the end of her individuality. She wanted to chart her own course, and tragedy gave her an opportunity to do so. In April 1853, when she was 22 and her daughter, Lura, three, Uriah McNall died.

The young widow had a second chance to go out into the world. She resumed her teaching and her education. In September 1854, she left Lura with her mother and traveled 60 miles east to study at the Genesee Wesleyan Seminary in Lima. The seminary shared a building with the newly coeducational Genesee College, which offered a more rigorous program. Belva transferred to the college (becoming its third woman student), where she took courses in science and politics. She graduated with a bachelor's degree (with honors) on June 27, 1857, and soon found a position teaching high school in the prosperous Erie Canal town of Lockport. Four years later, she took over a small school in the south-central New York town of Owego. In 1866, Belva McNall traveled to Washington and began to reinvent herself as an urban professional. She was neither flamboyant nor eccentric. Indeed, had she been a man, it would have been apparent that her life was following a conventional 19th-century course: Talented chap walks off the farm, educates himself, seeks opportunities, and makes a name. But because Belva strove to be that ambitious son of ordinary people who rises in the world on the basis of his wits and his work, she was thought a radical.

In Washington, Belva taught school and worked as a leasing agent, renting halls to lodges and organizations. She tutored herself in the workings of government and the art of lobbying by making frequent visits to Congress. In 1868 she married Ezekiel Lockwood, an elderly dentist and lay preacher who shared her reformist views. We do not know precisely when she fell in love with the law. In antebellum America the profession belonged to men, who passed on their skill by training their sons and nephews and neighbors' boys. After the Civil War a handful of women, Lockwood among them, set out to change all that. She believed from her reading of the lives of great men that "in almost every instance law has been the stepping-stone to greatness." She attended the law program of Washington's National University, graduated in 1872 (but only after she lobbied for the diploma male administrators had been pressured to withhold), and was admitted to the bar of the District of Columbia in 1873 (again, only after a struggle against sex discrimination). When the Supreme Court of the United States refused to admit her to its bar in 1876, she single-handedly lobbied Congress until, in 1879, it passed, reluctantly, "An act to relieve the legal disabilities of women." On March 3, 1879, Lockwood became the first woman admitted to the high Court bar, and, in 1880, the first woman lawyer to argue a case before the Court.

From her earliest years in Washington, Lockwood coveted a government position. She applied to be a consul officer in Ghent during the administration of Andrew Johnson, but her application was never acknowledged. In later years, she sought government posts—for women in general and for herself in particular—from other presidents. Without success. When Grover Cleveland passed over Lockwood and appointed as minister to Turkey a man thought to be a woman izer, she wrote to compliment the president on his choice: "The only danger is, that he will attempt to suppress polygamy in that country by marrying all of the women himself." A year later, in 1886, in another communication to Cleveland, she laid claim to the position of district recorder of deeds and let the president know in no uncertain terms that she had a "lien" on the job. She did not give up: In 1911 she had her name included on a list sent to President William Howard Taft of women attorneys who could fill the Supreme Court vacancy caused by the death of Justice John Marshall Harlan.

W hat persuaded Lockwood that she should run for the highest office in the land? Certainly, she seized the opportunity to shake a fist at conservatives who would hold women back. And she was displeased with the enthusiasm for the Republican Party shown by suffrage leaders Susan B. Anthony and Elizabeth Cady Stanton. More than that, however, campaigning would provide an opportunity for her to speak her mind, to travel, and to establish herself on the paid lecture circuit. She was not the first woman to run for president. In 1872, New York City newspaper publisher Victoria Woodhull had declared herself a presidential candidate, against Ulysses Grant and Horace Greeley. But Woodhull, cast as Mrs. Satan by the influential cartoonist Thomas Nast, had to abandon her campaign barely a month after its start: Her radical "free love" views were too much baggage for the nascent women's movement to bear, and financial misfortune forced her to suspend publication of Woodhull & Claflin's Weekly at the very moment she most needed a public platform.

Years later, Lockwood—and the California women who drafted her—spoke of the circumstances surrounding her August 1884 nomination, their accounts colored by ego and age. Lockwood received the nod from Marietta Stow, a San Francisco reformer who spoke for the newly formed, California-based Equal Rights Party, and from Stow's colleague, attorney Clara Foltz. Foltz later insisted that Lockwood's nomination amounted to nothing more than a lighthearted joke on her and Stow's part. But Stow's biographer, Sherilyn Bennion, has made a strong case that the nomination was, in fact, part of a serious political strategy devised by Stow to deflect attention from the rebuff given suffrage leaders that year at the Republican and Democratic conventions, and to demonstrate that "the fair sex" could create its own terms of engagement in American party politics. Women were becoming stump speakers, participants in political clubs, candidates for local office, and, in a handful of places, voters. (By 1884 the Wyoming, Utah and Washington Territories had fully enfranchised women, who in 14 states were permitted to vote in elections dealing with schools.) Marietta Stow began the Equal Rights Party because she had long been interested in matters of public policy and because readers of her newspaper, *The Women's Herald of Industry,* had expressed an interest in a "new, clean, uncorruptible party."

In July 1884 Stow urged Abigail Scott Duniway, an Oregon rights activist and newspaper editor, to accept the Equal Rights Party's nomination. But Duniway declined, believing, as Bennion writes, that "flaunting the names of women for official positions" would weaken the case for equal rights and provide "unscrupulous opponents with new pretexts and excuses for lying about them." Undiscouraged, Stow continued her search for a candidate. In August, she hit her mark.

Belva Lockwood, *Women's Herald* reader, had already begun to think of herself as a standard-bearer. On August 10 she wrote to Stow in San Francisco and asked rhetorically, and perhaps disingenuously, "Why not nominate women for important places? Is not Victoria Empress of India? Have we not among our country-women persons of as much talent and ability? Is not history full of precedents of women rulers?" The Republicans, she commented, claimed to be the party of progress yet had "little else but insult for women when [we] appear before its conventions." (She had been among those rebuffed that summer by the Republicans.) She was exasperated with the party of Lincoln and maddened by Stanton and Anthony's continuing faith in major-party politics: "It is quite time that we had our own party, our own platform, and our own nominees. We shall never have equal rights until we take them, nor respect until we command it."

Stow had her candidate! She called a party convention on August 23, read Lockwood's letter to the small group, and proposed her as the party's nominee for president of the United States, along with Clemence S. Lozier, a New York City physician, as the vice presidential nominee. Acclamation followed, and letters were sent to the two women. The dispatch to Lockwood read as follows: "Madam: We have the honor to inform you that you were nominated, at the Woman's National Equal-Rights Convention, for President of the United States. We await your letter of acceptance with breathless interest."

Lockwood later said that the letter took her "utterly by surprise," and she kept it secret for several days. On September 3, she wrote to accept the nomination for "Chief Magistrate of the United States" from the only party that "really and truly represent the interests of our whole people North, South, East, and West. . . . With your unanimous and cordial support . . . we shall not only be able to carry the election, but to guide the Ship of State safely into port." Lockwood went on to outline a dozen platform points, and her promptness in formulating policy signaled that she (and the party) intended to be taken seriously about matters of political substance.

Forecasters in '84 were predicting another close presidential race. Four years earlier, James Garfield had defeated Winfield Hancock by just 40,000 votes (out of nine million cast), and people were again watching the critical states of New York and Indiana. The nearly even division of registered voters between the two major parties caused Democratic candidate Grover Cleveland and Republican candidate James G. Blaine to shy away from innovative platforms. Instead, the two men spent much of their time trading taunts and insults. That left the business of serious reform to the minor parties and their candidates: Benjamin Butler (National Greenback/Anti-Monopoly), John St. John (Prohibition), and Samuel Clarke Pomeroy (American Prohibition). Butler, St. John, and Pomeroy variously supported workers' rights, the abolition of child and prison labor, a graduated income tax, senatorial term limits, direct election of the president, and, of course, prohibition of the manufacture, sale, and consumption of alcohol. Lockwood joined this group of nothing-to-lose candidates, who intended to promote the public discussion of issues about which Blaine and Cleveland dared not speak.

The design of Lockwood's platform reflected her practical savvy. The platform, she said, should "take up every one of the issues of the day" but be "so brief that the newspapers would publish it and the people read it." (She understood the art of the sound bite.) Her "grand platform of principles" expressed bold positions and comfortable compromise. She promised to promote and maintain equal political privileges for "every class of our citizens irrespective of sex, color or nationality" in order to make America "in truth what it has so long been in name, 'the land of the free and home of the brave." She pledged herself to the fair distribution of public offices to women as well as men, "with a scrupulous regard to civil service reform after the women are duly installed in office." She opposed the "wholesale monopoly of the judiciary" by men and said that, if elected, she would appoint a reasonable number of women as district attorneys, marshals, and federal judges, including a "competent woman to any vacancy that might occur on the United States Supreme Bench."

Lockwood's views extended well beyond women's issues. She adopted a moderate position on the contentious question of tariffs. In her statement of September 3, she placed the Equal Rights Party in the political camp that wanted to "protect and foster American industries," in sympathy with the working men and women of the country who were organized against free trade. But in the official platform statement reprinted on campaign literature, her position was modified so that the party

might be identified as middle-of-the-road, supporting neither high tariffs nor free trade. Lockwood urged the extension of commercial relations with foreign countries and advocated the establishment of a "high Court of Arbitration" to which commercial and political differences could be referred. She supported citizenship for Native Americans and the allotment of tribal land. As was to be expected from an attorney who earned a substantial part of her livelihood doing pension claims work, she adopted a safe position on Civil War veterans' pensions: She argued that tariff revenues should be applied to benefits for former soldiers and their dependents; at the same time, she urged the abolition of the Pension Office, "with its complicated and technical machinery," and recommended that it be replaced with a board of three commissioners. She vowed full sympathy with temperance advocates and, in a position unique to the platform of the Equal Rights Party, called for the reform of family law: "If elected, I shall recommend in my Inaugural speech, a uniform system of laws as far as practicable for all of the States, and especially for marriage, divorce, and the limitation of contracts, and such a regulation of the laws of descent and distribution of estates as will make the wife equal with the husband in authority and right, and an equal partner in the common business."

Lockwood's position paper of September 3 was revised into the platform statement that appeared below her portrait on campaign flyers. The new version expanded on certain points, adopted some sharper rhetoric, and added several planks, including a commitment that the remaining public lands of the nation would go to the "honest yeomanry," not the railroads. Lockwood stuck to her radical positions of support for women's suffrage and the reform of domestic law, but, in a stunning retreat, her earlier promises of an equitable allotment of public positions by sex and any mention of the need for women in the judiciary were absent from the platform.

Armed with candidate and platform, the leaders and supporters of the Equal Rights Party waited to see what would happen. A great deal depended on the posture adopted by the press. Fortunately for Lockwood and the party, many of the daily newspapers controlled by men, and a number of weeklies owned by women, took an interest in the newest contender in the election of '84. A day after she accepted the nomination, *The Washington Evening Star* made her candidacy front-page news and reprinted the entire text of her acceptance letter and platform of September 3. The candidate told a *Star* reporter that she would not necessarily receive the endorsement of activist women. Indeed, leaders of the nation's two top woman suffrage associations had endorsed Blaine, and Frances Willard had united temperance women with the Prohibition Party. "You must remember," Lockwood said, "that the women are divided up into as many factions and parties as the men."

On September 5, an editorial in the *Star* praised Lockwood's letter of acceptance: "In all soberness, it can be said [it] is the best of the lot. It is short, sharp, and decisive. . . . It is evident that Mrs. Lockwood, if elected, will have a policy [that] commends itself to all people of common sense." Editor Crosby Noyes rued the letter's late appearance: Had it existed sooner, "the other candidates might have had the benefit of perusing it and framing their several epistles in accord with its pith and candor." Newspaper reporting elsewhere was similarly respectful.

Abigail Duniway's warning that women candidates would meet with "unpleasant prominence" and be held up "to ridicule and scorn" proved correct, but Lockwood actually encountered no greater mockery than the men in the election. She had to endure silly lies about hairpieces and sham allegations that she was divorced, but Cleveland was taunted with cries of "Ma, Ma Where's My Pa" (a reference to his out-of-wedlock child). Cartoonists for *Frank Leslie's Illustrated and Puck,* mass-circulation papers, made fun of all the candidates, including Lockwood. This was a rite of passage and badge of acceptance. *Leslie's* also ran an article on Lockwood's campaign and contemplated the entrance of women into party politics with earnest good wishes: "Woman in politics. Why not?. . . . Twenty years ago woman's suffrage was a mere opinion. Today, it is another matter."

After establishing campaign headquarters at her Washington home on F Street, Lockwood wrote to friends and acquaintances in a dozen states asking that they arrange ratification meetings and get up ballots containing the names of electors (as required by the Constitution) pledged to her candidacy. This letter to a male friend in Philadelphia was a typical appeal: "That an opportunity may not be lost for the dissemination of Equal Rights principles, cannot, and will not the Equal Rights Party of Philadelphia hold a ratification meeting for the nominee, put in nomination a Presidential Elector, and get up an Equal Rights ticket? Not that we shall succeed in the election, but we can demonstrate that a woman may under the Constitution, not only be nominated but elected. Think of it."

Closer to home, party supporters organized a ratification meeting in mid-September at Wilson's Station, Maryland. (They bypassed the District to make the point that, under federal law, neither men nor women could vote in the nation's capital.) Lockwood delivered her first speech as a candidate at this gathering of about 75 supporters and journalists, and two Lockwood-for-president electors were chosen. She did not disclose at the rally that Clemence Lozier had declined the nomination for vice president—and not until September 29 did Marietta Stow decide to run in the second spot and complete the ticket.

Throughout September the national press spread the story of the Equal Rights Party and its candidate, and letters poured in to the house on F Street. They contained "earnest inquiries" about the platform, nasty bits of character assassination, and, from one male admirer, the following poem, which so amused Lockwood that she gave it to a reporter for publication:

O, Belva Ann!

Fair Belva Ann!

I know that thou art not a man;

But I shall vote,

Pull off my coat,

And work for thee, fair Belva Ann.

For I have read

What thou hast said,

And long I've thought upon thy plan.

Oh no, there's none

Beneath the sun

Who'd rule like thee, my Belva Ann!

The letters also brought invitations to speak in cities across the East and the Midwest. In late September, Lockwood prepared to go on the stump, her expenses covered by sponsors. Many of the lectures she gave were paid appearances; indeed, she claimed to be the only candidate whose speeches the public paid to hear. She was a widowed middle-class woman (her second husband, who was more than 30 years her senior, had died in 1877), and her livelihood depended on the earnings of her legal practice. So the time she devoted to politics had to pay. When the election was over, she told reporters that she had a satisfaction denied the other candidates: She had come out of the campaign with her expenses paid and "$125 ahead."

Lockwood took to the field in October. She made at least one full circuit in October, beginning in Baltimore, Philadelphia, and New York. Mid-month she delivered speeches in Louisville and in Cleveland, where she appeared at the Opera House before 500 people. In a loud and nasal voice, she attacked the high-tariff position of the Republicans on the grounds that it would injure American commerce, But she also assailed the free-trade policy of the Democrats, arguing that they were "willing to risk our manufacturing interests in the face of the starving hordes of pauper labor in other countries." She applauded the good that capital had done and said that "capital and labor did not, by nature, antagonize, and should not by custom."

If the people who came to hear Lockwood expected nothing but women's rights talk, they were disappointed. She and her party colleagues believed that the Equal Rights Party should not run a single-issue campaign. Of course, the platform introduced "feminist" ideas. But it also allowed Lockwood to address many other issues that preoccupied Americans. So she directed only a small part of her talk to describing how women had helped to make the country "blossom as a rose." She intended her candidacy to make history in the largest sense—by demonstrating that the Constitution did not bar women from running in elections or serving in federal elective office.

People who saw her for the first time said that her campaign photographs did not do her justice: The lady candidate had fine blue eyes, an aquiline nose, and a firm mouth, and she favored fashionable clothes. The cartoonists naturally focused on her sex, and the public had its own fun by creating dozens of Belva Lockwood Clubs, in which men meaning to disparage Lockwood paraded on city streets wearing Mother Hubbard dresses, a new cut of female clothing with an unconstructed design that freed movement and was considered improper to wear out of doors.

On November 3, the day before the election, Lockwood returned from a campaign tour of the Northwest. She had stayed "at the best hotels; had the best sleeping berths." Her last stop was Flint, Michigan, and she told a Washington reporter that 1,000 people had attended her (paid) talk there, a larger number than Ohio congressman Frank Hurd drew the following night. When asked on November 4 where she would await the election news, she replied that her house would be open throughout the evening, "the gas will be lighted," and reporters were welcome to visit. The historic first campaign by a woman for the presidency of the United States had ended, though in politics, of course, nothing is ever over.

When the ballots were tallied, Cleveland was declared the winner, with an Electoral College vote of 219 to 182. In the popular vote, he squeaked by with a margin of 23,000.

In 1884 the United States had yet to adopt the "Australian" ballot, which has the names of all candidates for office printed on a single form. The system then in effect, dating from the beginning of the Republic, required that each political party in a state issue ballots that contained the names of that party's slate and the electors pledged to them. A supporter cast his vote by depositing the ballot of his chosen party in a box. Some states required that voters sign the back of their ballot, but the overall allocation of ballots was not controlled by polling place officials, and stuffing the box was not impossible. It was also possible for officials in charge of the ballot boxes to discount or destroy ballots. And that, Lockwood claimed, is precisely what happened.

In a petition sent to Congress in January 1885, she wrote that she had run a campaign, gotten up electoral tickets in several states, and received votes in at least nine of the states, only to determine that "a large vote in Pennsylvania [was] not counted, simply dumped into the waste basket as false votes." In addition, she charged that many of the votes cast for her—totalling at least 4,711—in eight other states ("New Hampshire, 379 popular votes; New York, 1,336; Michigan, 374; Illinois, 1008; Iowa, 562; Maryland, 318; California, 734 and the entire Electoral vote of the State of Indiana") had been "fraudulently and illegally counted for the alleged majority candidate."

She asked that the members of Congress "refuse to receive the Electoral returns of the State of New York, or count them for the alleged majority candidate, for had the 1,336 votes which were polled in said state for your petitioner been counted for her, and not for the one Grover Cleveland, he would not have been awarded a majority of all the votes cast at said election in said state." (Cleveland's margin of votes in New York was 1,149). Lockwood also petitioned Congress for the electoral vote of Indiana, saying that at the last moment the electors there had switched their votes from Cleveland to her. In fact, they had not; it was all a prank by the good ol' boys of Indiana, but either she did not know this or, in the spirit of political theater, she played along with the mischief and used it to her advantage.

The electoral votes of New York (36) and Indiana (15) had been pivotal in the 1880 presidential race. With her petition and credible evidence, Lockwood—perhaps working behind the scenes with congressional Republicans—hoped to derail Cleveland's victory and keep him from becoming the first Democratic president since James Buchanan in 1856. She failed when the legislators ignored her petition, which had been referred to their Committee on Woman Suffrage. On February 11, Congress certified the election of New York governor Grover Cleveland as the 22nd president of the United States.

Subsequent interviews suggest that Lockwood was satisfied with the campaign, if not with the vote counting. The U.S. Constitution had betrayed women in the matter of suffrage, but it did not, as she said, prohibit women's speech and women's candidacies. As a celebration of the First Amendment, Lockwood's campaign was a great success. It served the interests of women (though it angered Susan B. Anthony), the candidate, and the country. Lockwood ran as an acknowledged contender and was allowed to speak her mind. American democracy was tested, and its performance did not disappoint her.

After the election, while maintaining her law practice, Lockwood embarked on the life of travel that she had long sought—and that she continued until her early eighties. Not unlike 21st-century politicians, she capitalized on the campaign by increasing her presence on the national lecture circuit; she even made at least one product endorsement (for a health tonic). She had long worked as a pension claims attorney, and, while traveling as a lecturer, she used the publicity surrounding her appearances to attract clients who needed help with applications and appeals. In 1888, the Equal Rights Party again nominated her as its presidential candidate. She ran a more modest campaign the second time around, but she still offered a broad domestic and foreign policy platform and argued that "equality of rights and privileges is but simple justice."

Lockwood always spoke proudly of her campaigns, which were important but not singular events in a life that would last 87 years. She was a woman of many talents and interests. Blocked from political office or a high-level government position because of her sex, she sought new realms after the campaigns of 1884 and 1888 where she might raise questions of public policy and advance the rights of women. Representing the Philadelphia-based Universal Peace Union, she increased her work on behalf of international peace and arbitration at meetings in the United States and Europe. She participated in an often-interlocking network of women's clubs and professional organizations. And she maintained a high profile in the women's suffrage movement, which struggled throughout the 1890s and the first two decades of the 20th century to create a winning strategy. In the spring of 1919, the House of Representatives and the Senate acted favorably on legislation to amend the Constitution to give women the right to vote; the proposed Nineteenth Amendment went out to the states in a ratification process that would not be completed until August 1920. But Belva Lockwood never got the right to vote. She died in May 1917.

Lockwood remains the only woman to have campaigned for the presidency right up to Election Day. (In 1964, Senator Margaret Chase Smith of Maine entered several Republican primaries and received 27 delegate votes; in 1972, Representative Shirley Chisholm of New York ran in a number of Democratic primaries and won 151 delegates.) In 1914 Lockwood, then 84 years old, was asked whether a woman would one day be president. The former candidate answered with levelheaded prescience and the merest echo of her former thunder: "I look to see women in the United States senate and the house of representatives. If [a woman] demonstrates that she is fitted to be president she will some day occupy the White House. It will be entirely on her own merits, however. No movement can place her there simply because she is a woman. It will come if she proves herself mentally fit for the position."

JILL NORGREN, a former Wilson Center fellow, is professor of government and legal studies at John Jay College and the University Graduate Center, City University of New York. She is writing the first full biography of Belva Lockwood, to be published in 2003. Copyright © 2002 by Jill Norgren.

From *Wilson Quarterly,* August 2002, pp. 12–20. Copyright © 2002 by Jill Norgren. Reprinted by permission of the author.

A Day to Remember: December 29, 1890

CHARLES PHILLIPS

The intermittent war between the United States and the Plains Indians that stretched across some three decades after the Civil War came to an end on December 29, 1890, at the Pine Ridge Reservation in South Dakota. The events leading up to its final act—the Wounded Knee Massacre—had been building since the late 1880s, when the son of a Paiute shaman named Wovoka had first introduced a series of new beliefs and practices to the Indian reservations of the West.

Fundamentally peaceful, Wovoka's movement envisioned the coming of a new world populated solely by Indians living on the Great Plains where buffalo were again plentiful. Generation upon generation of Indians slain in combat would be reborn into this new world, and all—the living and the formerly dead—would live in bliss, peace and plenty. U.S. Indian authorities claimed that in the hands of the defeated and embittered leaders of the Teton Sioux—men like Short Bull, Kicking Bear and eventually Sitting Bull himself—Wovoka's peaceful religion had taken on the militant overtones of a millennial uprising. Wovoka had created a ceremony called the Ghost Dance to invoke the spirits of the dead and facilitate their resurrection. The Sioux apostles of the Ghost Dance purportedly preached that it would bring about a day of deliverance—a day when they were strong enough again to wage all-out war against the whites. They had fashioned "ghost shirts," which they claimed white bullets could not penetrate. In any case, Ghost Dancing had quickly become the rage of the Western reservations such as Pine Ridge and Rosebud.

"Indians are dancing in the snow and are wild and crazy," an anxious Pine Ridge Reservation agent, Daniel F. Royer, telegraphed Washington in November 1890. "We need protection and we need it now. The leaders should be arrested and confined at some military post until the matter is quieted, and this should be done at once."

The Indian Bureau in Washington quickly branded the Ghost Dancers "fomenters of disturbances" and ordered the Army to arrest them. On November 20, cavalry and infantry reinforcements arrived at the Pine Ridge and Rosebud reservations, but their arrival did not intimidate the Sioux followers of Short Bull and Kicking Bear. Quite the contrary, it seemed to galvanize their resolve. A former Indian agent, Dr. Valentine McGillycuddy, advised Washington to call off the troops: "I should let the dance continue. The coming of the troops has frightened the Indians. If the Seventh-Day Adventists prepare their ascension robes for the second coming of the savior, the United States Army is not put in motion to prevent them. Why should the Indians not have the same privilege? If the troops remain, trouble is sure to come."

About 3,000 Indians had assembled on a plateau at the northwest corner of Pine Ridge in a nearly impregnable area that came to be called the Stronghold. Brigadier General John R. Brooke, commander of the Pine Ridge area, quickly dispatched emissaries to talk with the "hostiles." Brooke's commanding officer, hard-nosed Civil War veteran and Indian fighter Maj. Gen. Nelson A. Miles, did not approve of such parleys. He saw in them evidence of indecision, and, furthermore, believed the Indians would interpret talk as a sign of weakness. Miles decided to prosecute the campaign against the Ghost Dancers personally and transferred his headquarters to Rapid City, S.D.

While Miles was preparing this move, Sitting Bull—the most influential of all Sioux leaders—began actively celebrating the Ghost Dance and its doctrine at the Standing Rock Reservation that straddled the North and South Dakota border. The agent in charge there, James McLaughlin, weighed his options. He did not want to repeat the hysterical mistake of his colleague at Pine Ridge by telegraphing for soldiers. He decided instead to use reservation policemen—Indians—to effect the quiet arrest and removal of the old chief.

Unfortunately, General Miles would not accept it. For Miles, the arrest of Sitting Bull would be a momentous act in a great drama. It should not be left to Indians, and it should not be done secretively; if anything, it called for showmanship. Miles contacted the greatest showman the West had ever known: William "Buffalo Bill" Cody. As everybody in the country probably knew—Buffalo Bill had seen to that himself—he and Sitting Bull were friends, or, at least, Sitting Bull held Cody in high regard. Sitting Bull, after all, had been a star attraction in Buffalo Bill's Wild West Show. If any white man could convince Sitting Bull to step down, it would be Buffalo Bill.

Agent McLaughlin was aghast at the notion of carting in the likes of Buffalo Bill Cody to carry out what should be done quietly and without publicity. He was convinced that Buffalo Bill's presence would only inflame tempers and transform the proceedings into a circus or something worse. Accordingly, when Cody arrived at Standing Rock on November 27, McLaughlin saw to it that the celebrity was glad-handed and subtly shanghaied by the commanding officer of nearby Fort

Yates, Lt. Col. William F. Drum. Drum entertained Cody all night at the officers' club while McLaughlin worked feverishly behind Miles' back to have the showman's authority rescinded. It was a desperate plan, and McLaughlin had missed one crucial fact: The man capable of drinking Buffalo Bill Cody under the table had yet to be born. Come morning, Cody was bright eyed and ready to set out for Sitting Bull's camp. McLaughlin hastily arranged for additional delays—just long enough for the arrival of orders canceling Cody's mission. The old entertainer seethed but boarded the next train back to Chicago. He had not set eyes on Sitting Bull.

But the situation at Pine Ridge Reservation was heating up. Word reached McLaughlin that Short Bull and Kicking Bear had formally invited Sitting Bull to leave Standing Rock and join them and their people at the Stronghold on the reservation. The time had come to act. McLaughlin dispatched 43 reservation policemen on December 15 to arrest Sitting Bull before he set out for Pine Ridge. Officers surrounded the old chief's cabin as Lieutenant Bull Head, Sergeant Red Tomahawk and Sergeant Shave Head entered it.

The chief awoke from slumber, and, seeing the men, asked, "What do you want here?"

"You are my prisoner," said Bull Head. "You must go to the agency."

Sitting Bull asked for a moment to put his clothes, on. By the time the reservation police officers emerged with their prisoner, a crowd had gathered. A warrior named Catch-the-Bear called out, "Let us protect our chief!" and he leveled his rifle at Bull Head. He fired, hitting him in the side. The wounded police-man spun around with the force of the impact. His own weapon discharged, perhaps accidentally, perhaps intentionally. A round hit Sitting Bull, point blank, in the chest. Then policeman Red Tomahawk stepped into the fray and shot Sitting Bull in the back of the head.

McLaughlin had hoped to avoid a circus. As the reserva-tion police officers scuffled with Sitting Bull's followers, the slain chief's horse—which Buffalo Bill had presented to him back when he was part of the Wild West Show—was apparently stimulated by the familiar noise of a crowd, and performed his repertoire of circus tricks.

Miles had not intended that Sitting Bull be killed, but it had happened, and the general accepted it as he would any casualty in the fog of war. Just now he had yet another Ghost Dancer to arrest, and that's where he focused his attention. Chief Big Foot was leader of the Miniconjou Sioux, who lived on the Cheyenne River. Unknown to Miles, Big Foot had recently renounced the Ghost Dance religion, convinced that it offered nothing more than desperation and futility. Miles was also unaware that Chief Red Cloud, a Pine Ridge leader friendly to white authorities, had asked Big Foot to visit the reservation and use his influ-ence to persuade the Stronghold party to surrender. All Miles knew—or thought he knew—was that Big Foot was on his way to the Stronghold, and it was up to the Army to prevent him from joining Short Bull, Kicking Bear and the others. Miles dispatched troops across the prairies and badlands to intercept any and all Miniconjous, especially Big Foot.

On December 28, 1890, a squadron of the 7th Cavalry located the chief and about 350 Miniconjous camped near a stream called Wounded Knee Creek. Big Foot was in his wagon, hud-dled against the bitter winter. He was feverish, sick with pneu-monia. During the night of the 28th, additional soldiers moved into the area, so that by daybreak on the 29th, 500 soldiers, all under the command of Colonel James W. Forsyth, surrounded Big Foot's camp. Four Hotchkiss guns, small cannons capable of rapid fire, were aimed at the camp from the hills around it. The mission was to disarm the Indians and march them to the railroad, where a waiting train would remove them from the "zone of military operations."

As the Indians set up their tepees on the night of the 28th, they saw the Hotchkiss guns on the ridge above them. "That evening I noticed that they were erecting cannons up [there]," one of the Indians recalled, "also hauling up quite a lot of ammunition." The guns were ominously trained on the Indian camp. A bugle call woke up the Indians the next morning. The sky was clear and very blue as the soldiers entered the camp. Surrounded by bluecoats on horses, the Indians were ordered to assemble front and center. The soldiers demanded their weapons. Outraged, medicine man Yellow Bird began dancing, urging his people to don their sacred shirts. "The bullets will not hurt you," he told them. Next, Black Coyote, whom another Miniconjou called "a crazy man, a young man of very bad influence and in fact a nobody," raised his Winchester above his head as the troopers approached him to collect it. He began shouting that he had paid much money for the rifle, that it belonged to him and that nobody was going to take it. The soldiers, annoyed, crowded in on him and then began spinning him around and generally roughing him up.

A shot rang out. Instantly, troopers began firing indiscrimi-nately at the Indians. "There were only about a hundred war-riors," Black Elk reported. "And there were nearly five hundred soldiers." The warriors rushed to where they had piled their guns and knives. Hand-to-hand fights broke out, and some of the Indians started to run. Then the Indians heard the "awful roar" of the Hotchkiss guns. Shells rained down, almost a round a second, mowing down men, women and children—each shell carrying a two-pound charge, each exploding into thousands of fragments. The smoke was thick as fog; the Indians were running blind. Louise Weasel Bear said, "We tried to run, but they shot us like we were buffalo." Yellow Bird's son, just 4 years old at the time, saw his father shot through the head: "My father ran and fell down and the blood came out of his mouth." Those who fled the camp were chased down by soldiers. Rough Feathers' wife remembered: "I saw some of the other Indians running up the coulee so I ran with them, but the soldiers kept shooting at us and the bullets flew all around us. My father, my grandfather, my older brother and my younger brother were all killed. My son who was two years old was shot in the mouth that later caused his death." Black Elk added: "Dead and wounded women and children and little babies were scattered all along there where they had been trying to run away. The soldiers had followed them along the gulch, as they ran, and murdered them in there." In one of the gulches, "two little boys" who had found guns were lying in ambush, and "they had been killing soldiers all by themselves."

An hour later the guns stopped. The place was silent. Trails of blood trickled along the ground heading out of camp toward the gulches. Hundreds of Indians lay dead or dying on the frosted earth alongside a score of soldiers, hit mostly by the fire of their own Hotchkisses. Clouds filled the sky, and soon a heavy snow began to fall. Three days later, New Year's Day 1891, after the blizzard had passed, a burial party was sent to pull the frozen Indians from beneath the blanket of snow and dump them in a long ditch, "piled one upon another like so much cordwood, until the pit was full." Many of the corpses were naked because soldiers had stripped the ghost shirts from the dead to take home as souvenirs.

General Miles scrambled to distance himself from what public outrage there was over the massacre at Wounded Knee. He relieved Forsyth of command and convened a court of inquiry, which exonerated the colonel. Miles protested, but his immediate superior, General John M. Schofield, together with Secretary of War Redfield Proctor, eventually reinstated Forsyth's command.

In the meantime, the massacre at Wounded Knee caused "hostile" and "friendly" Sioux factions to unite. Even though Chief Red Cloud protested and repudiated his people's participation, on December 30, Sioux under Kicking Bear attacked the 7th Cavalry near the Pine Ridge Agency along White Clay Creek. At first it looked like it might be another Custer debacle, but black troopers of the 9th Cavalry rode to the rescue and drove off the Indians.

General Miles acted quickly to assemble a force of 8,000 troops, deploying them to surround the Sioux, who had returned to the Stronghold. This time Miles was careful, acting slowly and deliberately to contract the ring—almost gently—around the Indians. As he did this, he urged them to surrender, and he pledged good treatment. Whether anyone believed Miles or not, it had become clear that what the Ghost Dance foretold was a hope forlorn. The Sioux laid down their arms on January 15, 1891, bringing decades of war to an end. While lives were lost on both sides at White Clay Creek and in other skirmishes here and there, the massacre at Wounded Knee is generally considered to be the last major engagement of the Indian wars.

UNIT 2

The Emergence of Modern America

Unit Selections

Key Points to Consider

- Discuss the kinds of conditions Jacob Riis found in the slums. What combination of factors made it difficult for individuals to escape this environment?

- What does the article "The Murder of Lucy Pollard" tell us about race relations in the South during the 1890s? What were "Jim Crow" laws?

- Who was Joe Hill? Why did he become a legend to large number of American workers?

- Discuss the Triangle Waist fire? Why did it cause such outrage? Did anything positive come out of the disaster?

Student Web Site

www.mhcls.com/online

Internet References

Further information regarding these Web sites may be found in this book's preface or online.

The Age of Imperialism
http://www.smplanet.com/imperialism/toc.html

William McKinley 1843–1901
http://lcweb.loc.gov/rr/hispanic/1898/mckinley.html

American Diplomacy: Editor's Corner—If Two By Sea
http://www.unc.edu/depts/diplomat/AD_Issues/amdipl_15/edit_15.html

Great Chicago Fire and the Web of Memory
http://www.chicagohs.org/fire/

The United States underwent enormous changes during the 1880s and 1890s. Millions of people continued to live on family farms or in small towns. Millions of others flocked to the cities in search of a better life. It was a period of huge immigration, most of which landed in the poorer parts of cities. Most of these people came from Southern and Eastern Europe, and became known as the "new" immigration (previous waves had come from Ireland and Germany). Because their dress, their languages, and their customs differed so markedly from native-born Americans, they were seen by many as inferior peoples. One of the essays in this section, "Where the Other Half Lived," shows the incredible poverty and crowded conditions some of these people had to endure.

Small and medium sized businesses continued to exist, but corporations on a scale previously unheard of came to dominate the marketplace. Though the gross national product increased dramatically, the gap between rich and poor steadily widened. Corporate leaders, on the one hand, amassed unprecedented fortunes on which they paid no income taxes. Urban working families, on the other hand, often lived in unhealthy squalor even though all their members—including young children—worked in some shop or factory. Depressions, one beginning in 1873 and another in 1893, threw more people out of work than ever before. Farmers had to sell what they produced in markets that fluctuated widely, but had to purchase equipment and other necessities at prices often fixed by the large companies. They also had to contend with the monopolistic practices of railroads, which charged "all the traffic would bear" for shipping and storing farm products. Minority groups, such as Indians and blacks, continued to suffer socially and economically through good times as well as bad.

"The Murder of Lucy Pollard" tells the story of three Southern black women and a black man who were arrested on charges of a murder they almost certainly did not commit, and of a crusading black journalist who was determined to expose this travesty of justice. The essay uses the incident to depict conditions in the South during the 1890s, when blacks were increasingly denied the right to vote and lynchings were at an all time high.

Working conditions during this period often were abominable, and laborers usually had no choice but take whatever wages were offered. Indeed, for most companies labor was just another cost of doing business. It should be purchased as cheaply as possible and exploited to the utmost without regard for human consequences. Workers' efforts to create unions to give them some protection were vigorously fought, often with violence. "Joe Hill: I Never Died" describes the life and times of Joe Hillstrom, better known as "Joe Hill," a legendary labor organizer and agitator. He became a martyr in the eyes of many workingmen after his execution for a murder he may not have committed.

Library of Congress

"A Day to Remember: March 25, 1911," provides another glimpse of the miserable conditions under which people had to work. In 1909 employees of the Triangle Waist Company had joined in a strike led by the Women's Trade Union League, calling for better pay, shorter hours, and improvement of miserable working conditions. They gained little from the strike, and the company management continued to impose the most degrading working conditions. A fire at Triangle in 1911 cost the lives of 146 women and brought to public attention the squalid and dangerous circumstances that existed there and in other sweatshops. Blocked exits and leaky fire hoses caused many unnecessary deaths.

"Alice Roosevelt Longworth" tells the story of an individual who would have been remarkable in any era. As a young woman during the early years of the 20th Century, however, she was considered scandalous. She was independent, outspoken, and possessed a devastating wit. She delighted in embarrassing her father, Theodore Roosevelt, and he in turn regarded her as virtually unmanageable. She lived to a ripe old age, and remained controversial almost to the end.

Where the Other Half Lived

The photographs of Jacob Riis confronted New Yorkers with the misery of Mulberry Bend—and helped to tear it down.

VERLYN KLINKENBORG

A block below canal street in lower Manhattan, just a few hundred yards from City Hall, there is a small urban oasis called Columbus Park. Early on a spring morning, the sun rises over an irregular threshold of rooftops to the east of the park—a southern spur of Chinatown—and picks out details on the courthouses and state office buildings looming over the west side of the park. Carved eagles stare impassively into the sunlight. Incised over a doorway on the Criminal Courts Building is a strangely senseless quotation from Justinian. "Justice is the firm and continuous desire to render to every man his due," it says, as though justice were mainly a matter of desire.

Beneath the sun's level rays high overhead, Columbus Park seems almost hollow somehow, and since it is open ground—open playground, to be accurate—it exposes the local topography. The land slopes downward from Bayard Street to Park Street, and downward from Mulberry to Baxter. At the north end of the park, temporary fencing surrounds an ornate shelter, the sole remnant of the park's original construction in 1897, now given over to pigeons. Plane trees lean inward around the perimeter of the asphalt ball field, where a tidy squadron of middle-aged and elderly Asian women stretches in unison, some clinging to the chain-link fence for balance. One man wields a tai chi sword to the sound of Chinese flutes from a boom box. A gull spirals down out of the sky, screeching the whole way. All around I can hear what this city calls early morning silence, an equidistant rumble that seems to begin a few blocks away.

I watch all of this, the tai chi, the stretching, the old men who have come to sit in the cool spring sunshine, the reinforced police vans delivering suspects to the court buildings just beyond it all, and as I watch I try to remember that Columbus Park was once Mulberry Bend. Mulberry Street still crooks to the southeast here, but the Bend proper is long gone. It was the most infamous slum in 19th-century New York, an immeasurable quantity of suffering compacted into 2.76 acres. On a bright April morning, it's hard to believe the Bend ever existed. But then such misery always inspires disbelief.

The Bend was ultimately torn down and a park built on its site in 1897 after unrelenting pressure from Jacob Riis, the Danish-born journalist and social reformer. In *How the Other Half Lives,* an early landmark in reforming literature whose title became a catchphrase, Riis provides some numbers for Mulberry Bend, which he obtained from the city's Registrar of Vital Statistics. In 1888, he wrote, 5,650 people lived on Baxter and Mulberry streets between Park and Bayard. If Riis means strictly the buildings within the Bend, as he almost certainly does, then the population density there was 2,047 persons per acre, nearly all of them recent immigrants.

By itself, that's an almost meaningless figure. But think of it this way: In Manhattan today, 1,537,195 persons live on 14,720 acres, a density of slightly more than 104 per acre. (In 1890, the average density within the built-up areas of Manhattan was about 115 per acre.) If Manhattan were peopled as thickly today as the Bend was in 1888, it would have more than 30 million inhabitants, an incomprehensible figure, the equivalent of nearly the whole of California jammed onto a single island. To put it another way, if the people who live in Manhattan today were packed as tightly as the immigrants in Mulberry Bend were, they could all live in Central Park with room to spare. But these are suppositions, imaginary numbers. The truly astonishing figure, of course, is 5,650 persons—actual human beings, every one of them—living in Mulberry Bend, among the highest population density ever recorded anywhere.

Now consider a final set of numbers: According to Riis and the city statistician, the death rate of children under five in Mulberry Bend was 140 per 1,000, roughly 1 out of 7. This is likely to be an underestimate. (Citywide, the number was just under 100 per 1,000 and falling fast.) Today, Mulberry Bend would rank between Lesotho and Tanzania in under-five mortality and worse than Haiti, Eritrea, Congo, and Bangladesh. Last year, the under-five mortality rate for the United States was 8 per 1,000, or 1 out of 125.

Numbers, even numbers as striking as these, do not do a good job of conveying horror. But when the horror is literally fleshed out, it begins to make an impression, as it did on Riis himself. After coming to America in 1870, at age 21, and enduring a vagrant existence for a few years, he found work at the *New York Tribune* as a police reporter and was sent to the office at 303 Mulberry Street, a few blocks north of the Bend and across from police headquarters. Night after night, Riis visited the Bend, sometimes in police company, often not, and he reported what he saw—especially the extreme overcrowding—to the Board of Health. "It did not make much of an impression," Riis wrote in *The Making of an American*. "These things rarely do, put in mere words."

So Riis put them in pictures. With a flashgun and a hand-held camera, invented just a few years earlier, Riis began to take photographs of what he found in the Bend. "From them," he wrote, "there was no appeal." They made misery demonstrable in a way that nothing else had. No political or economic or cultural theory could justify the crowding his photographs document. There was no explaining away the sense of oppression and confinement they reveal. In picture after picture you see not only the poverty and the congestion of the Bend—the stale sweatshops and beer dives and five-cent lodging houses—but the emotional and psychological consequences of people living on top of each other.

Since the mid-20th century, Riis has been considered one of the founders of documentary photography. Over the years, his photographs of Mulberry Bend and other New York slums have become a part of the city's conscience. But his approach to photography was flatly utilitarian. "I had use for it," Riis wrote of the camera, "and beyond that I never went." Printing technology at the time meant that in books and articles his pictures had to be redrawn as wood engravings, considerably reducing their impact. The actual photographs were seen only in lantern slides accompanying his lectures. What mattered was not aesthetics but what the pictures showed. Riis had a similar use for words and statistics. They were merely tools to persuade New Yorkers to witness what was right in front of their eyes.

In one of his many articles on tenement housing, Riis printed a map of the Bend drawn from overhead, a silhouette showing the proportion of open space to buildings. Looking at that map is like looking at an old-fashioned diagram of a cell, a hieroglyphic of dark and light. It's hard to know what to call the spaces depicted by the white areas on Riis's map. *Yard* is too pastoral and *air shaft* too hygienic. Riis calls them "courts" and "alleys," but even those words are too generous. What the white spaces really portray are outdoor places where only a single layer of humans could live, many of them homeless children who clustered in external stairwells and on basement steps. In the tenements of the Bend—three, four, and five stories each—families and solitary lodgers, who paid five cents apiece for floor space, crowded together in airless cubicles. "In a room not thirteen feet either way," Riis wrote of one midnight encounter, "slept twelve men and women, two or three in bunks set in a sort of alcove, the rest on the floor."

For reformers, Riis included, the trouble with the Bend wasn't merely the profits it returned to slumlords and city politicians, nor was it just the high rents that forced tenants to sublet floor space to strangers. The problem was also how to portray the Bend in a way that conveyed its contagious force, the absence of basic sanitation, of clean water and fresh air, the presence of disease, corruption, and crime, the enervation and despair. It was, for Riis, the problem of representing an unrepresentable level of defilement. The power of his silhouette map, for instance, is flawed by its white margins, which falsely imply that conditions improved across the street, when, in fact, the entire Sixth Ward was cramped and impoverished. Even the grimmest of Riis's photographs show only a few people, at most, in the back alleys and basement dives. Powerful as they are, these pictures fail to convey the simple tonnage of human flesh in those dead-end blocks.

But the problem of Mulberry Bend was also how to interpret it. On a bright spring morning in the 1880s or early 1890s, a New Yorker—curiosity aroused, perhaps, by one of Riis's articles—might have strolled over to Mulberry or Baxter Street to see for himself. What he found there would depend on his frame of mind. It might have been, as photographs suggest, a bustling streetfront crowded with people going rather shabbily about the ordinary sorts of business, much as they might in other neighborhoods. Such a New Yorker—disinclined to push through to the dark inner rooms a few flights up or to the dismal courts and alleys behind or to the dank beer dives below—might conclude that perhaps Riis had exaggerated and that perhaps all there was to see here was a people, immigrants nearly all of them, who were insufficiently virtuous or cleanly or hardworking or American. It would be possible for such a person to blame Mulberry Bend on the very people who were its victims. But when the tenements were condemned and their inhabitants moved into decent housing, particularly in Harlem, they blended imperceptibly into the fabric of the city.

Riis has been faulted for his glib descriptive use of racial and ethnic stereotypes, a convention of his time that sounds raw and coarse to us now. In his defense, he came to understand that the power of a place like Mulberry Bend was enough to corrupt its residents, no matter who they were, as it had the Irish, and then the Italians who were their successors in the Bend. No iniquity within the Bend was as great, to Riis, as the political and financial iniquity that sustained the tenements there.

But the tragedy of Mulberry Bend isn't only that it came to exist and, once in existence, to be tolerated. It was also that when the city finally tore down the Bend and at last built the park that Calvert Vaux had designed for the site, a kind of forgetfulness descended. A New Yorker coming to the newly built Mulberry Bend Park in 1897, or to its renaming in 1911, or merely to watch the sun rise on a bright spring morning in 2001, might never know that there had been such a place as the Bend. The park that stands in its place is some kind of redemption, but without memory no redemption is ever complete. And without action of the kind that Riis undertook, justice remains only a matter of desire.

From *Mother Jones*, July/August 2001, pp. 54–57. Copyright © 2001 by Foundation for National Progress. Reprinted by permission.

The Murder of Lucy Pollard

CALEB CRAIN

O n July 12, 1895, in Lunenburg County, Virginia, a retired farmer complained to his diary that the state was spending $300 a day to keep four blacks accused of murder safe in jail. "They should and ought to have been promptly lynched at once," wrote Robert Allen, who had recently been elected to his twentieth consecutive term as a justice of the peace, "for there is not the least shadow of doubt about the guilt of all four of them."

In *A Murder in Virginia: Southern Justice on Trial,* Suzanne Lebsock, a historian, has chronicled the efforts that frustrated Allen and other would-be lynchers in Lunenburg County. The prisoners, three women and one man, were being held for the murder and robbery of a white woman named Lucy Pollard. The story is full of suspense and complex characters, with a plot so rich in incident and irony that Lebsock is puzzled that the case vanished from history for nearly ninety years. After all, Lebsock writes, "it had bedeviled some of Virginia's most prominent politicians, engaged its best legal minds, and inspired some of the state's most creative investigative reporting."

In a footnote, she names the historian who broke the silence. Ann Field Alexander, who wrote her 1973 Ph.D. dissertation on John Mitchell Jr., the editor of the black newspaper *The Richmond Planet,* who covered the trials and their aftermath. With *Race Man: The Rise and Fall of the 'Fighting Editor' John Mitchell Jr.,* a book based on Alexander's dissertation, readers may supplement Lebsock's account of the case with a biography of the journalist who was largely responsible for its surprising outcome.

T he body of Lucy Pollard, a white planter's daughter, was discovered by her husband at dusk on Friday, June 14, 1895, lying between her house and her chicken coop. A nearby meat ax accounted for the wounds to her face and head, while a struggle with her killer was the likely cause of the bruises on her neck and wrists. A lens had been knocked out of her glasses, and a dozen eggs had fallen from her basket and were lying broken beside her on the ground.

Lucy had married down. Her husband, Edward Pollard, a former peddler, had, thanks in part to the land brought to him by a series of wives, become a farmer and moneylender. When he came upon the body he rang the alarm bell twice, then stopped to check the liquor cabinet, where he kept his cash, and found that he had been robbed as well as widowed. His bell-ringing and shouting brought neighbors to the scene, including two black women, Mary Abernathy and Pokey Barnes, who kept vigil over the body through the night while Edward slept beside it. The next day, the women were arrested as suspects by the local constable. Soon Mary Barnes, a black woman who worked in Pollard's garden and was the mother of Pokey Barnes, was also arrested. Mary Abernathy and Mary Barnes were the last people known to have seen Lucy Pollard alive. They had shared a drink of water with her and Edward at four o'clock, and after Edward had left, they had stayed behind for a few minutes to chat. Pokey Barnes, meanwhile, admitted to having been in the vicinity at the time.

Edward Pollard thought that some of his wife's clothes were missing and, as Lebsock explains, stealing clothes was considered to be a crime characteristic of black women. All of this evidence was circumstantial, and it failed to convince a coroner's jury. On Monday, three days after the murder, the women were released. But shortly afterward they were fingered as accomplices in the murder by a fourth suspect, a mulatto laborer named William Henry "Solomon" Marable, who had been seen the day after the murder spending twenty-dollar bills, then a large denomination, in nearby Chase City. The women were rearrested.

Despite angry crowds carrying ropes, the suspects were not lynched. Local officials smuggled them from one jail to another until they reached the relative safety of the city of Richmond, where they fell under the protection of the new governor, Charles O'Ferrall. During the last weeks of O'Ferrall's 1893 election campaign, an unemployed black laborer had been hanged, shot, and burned in Roanoke before an audience of four thousand onlookers, and in response, O'Ferrall had committed himself politically to the suppression of lynching. At the request of Lunenburg County's sheriff, O'Ferrall ordered two infantry units to escort the suspects back to Lunenburg for their trials. There a captain in the militia named Frank Cunningham pacified the crowds outside the courthouse by organizing baseball games and concerts and offering free medical care. Marable and the three women were safely tried. They were convicted and sentenced, and it looked as if Marable and two of the women would unjustly but legally hang, until a young black newspaper editor, John Mitchell Jr., involved himself in the case.

Mitchell was born in 1863 at Laburnum, an estate outside Richmond, the property of James Lyons, a genteel and well-connected attorney. Lyons was a close friend of Jefferson Davis, owned more than two dozen slaves, and decried Lincoln's Emancipation Proclamation as "inhuman and atrocious." Among his possessions were Mitchell's mother, a seamstress, and his father, a coachman. Alexander suggests that young Mitchell studied his master's grand manner, which he later used to social advantage. As an adolescent, Mitchell took advantage of the schools that opened for blacks during the early years of Reconstruction and was educated to become a teacher. While teaching in Richmond's schools, he began in 1883 to write for the black press. His first column, for *The New York Globe,* the most prominent black newspaper in the country, narrated the hanging of a black murderess in Henrico County, Virginia, in a suspenseful and sentimental style.

When a new black weekly, *The Richmond Planet,* was founded in December 1883, Mitchell and several other teachers began to write for it. No clippings from the paper's first two years have survived. A few months after the Planet's inception, white Democrats ousted blacks and their allies from the Richmond school board, and many of the city's black teachers were purged, among them Mitchell and ten others who had been moonlighting for the *Planet.* Unable to find any other work that satisfied him, at the end of 1884, Mitchell, at age twenty-one, took over the paper.

Under Mitchell's leadership, the *Planet* had an exuberant, even militant tone. In every issue, beneath an image of a hanged black man, Mitchell published a list of lynching victims. He urged blacks to arm themselves against lynch mobs, writing that "the best remedy for a lyncher or a cursed mid-night rider is a 16-shot Winchester rifle in the hands of a dead-shot Negro who has nerve enough to pull the trigger." He presented himself in his articles as a swashbuckling character, and at times he was. In 1886, when his articles about a recent lynching provoked an anonymous death threat, Mitchell printed the letter and then toured the scene of the lynching, sporting a pair of Smith & Wesson revolvers. In 1889 he saved a fifteen-year-old from hanging by riding all night to hand-deliver the governor's stay of execution. In 1893 he helped obtain the acquittal and release from jail of a black farmhand who had miraculously survived a beating, shooting, and hanging by a white mob. He became well known for his bravado, and in 1888 he was elected to the lower house of Richmond's city council. In 1890 he was elected alderman.

Mitchell made his newspaper a financial success. He found odd outside jobs to keep his printing press running. Alexander suggests that the *Planet* may have been subsidized by the local Republican Party in return for its support. Most important, black readers responded to its appeal. Alexander quotes an ad for subscribers that ran in the *Planet* in 1891:

Do you want to see what the Colored People are doing? Read the *Planet.* Do you want to know what Colored People think? Read the *Planet.* Do you want to know how many Colored People are hung to trees without due process of law? Read the *Planet. . . .*

Anti-lynching was the principal cause of the *Planet,* but by the time of the Lunenburg cases, Mitchell realized that he had to press the *Planet's* campaign further. Even when blacks received due process in the courts, they could be the victims of racism in the community. The threat of lynching could function as blackmail, intimidating judges and juries into disregarding evidence, or the lack of it.

For righting this subtler injustice, Mitchell realized, the murder of Lucy Pollard was an opportune case. As he must have suspected when he read accounts in the white press of the four Lunenburg trials, and as he recognized as soon as he interviewed the four prisoners in Richmond in late July 1895, the case against the women was extremely thin. The principal witness against them was Solomon Marable, who had confessed to the murder and, under a surprisingly vigorous cross-examination by Pokey Barnes herself, had also confessed to perjury. Moreover, only one of the women, Mary Abernathy, had been represented by a lawyer. He had represented her only for as long as it took to request a change of venue; as soon as the request was denied, he quit.

During his first jailhouse interview, Mitchell learned from Mary Abernathy that a local white man whose last name was Thompson had threatened to kill Edward Pollard the day of the murder, calling him "a thief in every degree"—a fact that had gone unmentioned in all four trials. In the Lunenburg courtroom there had been such flagrant disregard of the facts—lack of interest in them, really—that it was clear to Mitchell that the trials' outcome was the result of pressure on the part of lynch-hungry people like the justice of the peace and diarist Robert Allen, the lack of mob violence notwithstanding. Mitchell at once hired three conservative white lawyers to appeal the verdicts against the women. To pay their fees, he appealed to the generosity of readers of the *Planet.*

Thompson's threat to "squash [Edward Pollard] in hell" turned out to be only the first in a series of revelations that undermined the case against Mary Abernathy, Pokey Barnes, and Mary Barnes. The case further unraveled when Solomon Marable began to tell a new story: not three black women but a white man had enlisted him to help with the killing, and that man's name was also Thompson. But the Thompson who had threatened to "squash" Edward Pollard turned out to be William G. Thompson, Edward Pollard's stepson, whereas the Thompson accused by Solomon Marable was David James Thompson, the son of one of Lucy Pollard's cousins. Neither Thompson was charged with murder, although Solomon continued to repeat the name of David James Thompson to the press, until Thompson took the precaution of suing one of Richmond's white newspapers for libel.

Was David James Thompson the murderer? Lebsock leads the reader through a thicket of conflicting theories and irreconcilable testimony. Since David James Thompson was never tried, there isn't enough evidence to judge him in retrospect. But Marable's story about Thompson was more credible than his story about the three women had been. He made his accusation against Thompson in court only once, and retracted it almost immediately, but it must have helped to sow doubt, especially in the minds of the judges, who later granted retrials in the women's cases.

Doubt over the identity of the killer persists. No one ever found the eight hundred dollars stolen from Edward Pollard, or at least no one ever admitted to finding it. And in his last statement before hanging, Solomon Marable insisted that authorities were executing the wrong man.

At the end of her narrative, Lebsock speculates on who the murderer or murderers might have been. She suggests that the crime may have been the work of David James Thompson's brother, Herbert Thompson, and that Cass Gregory, an amateur detective, may have encouraged Solomon to name the right family but the wrong man, so that Gregory could blackmail Herbert Thompson. This strikes me as somewhat too complex to be likely. But unresolved murders are tempting, and it is one of the merits of Lebsock's book that readers acquire so detailed a knowledge of the case that they can invent theories of their own.

I myself was struck by an odd bit of dialogue that Marable repeated almost every time he blamed the murder on David James Thompson. According to Marable, just before Thompson murdered Lucy Pollard, he asked her, "Do you know me?" and she replied, "You are a white man." While Lebsock observes that "the statement is just strange enough to ring true," her explanation doesn't quite account for its strangeness. Was Marable struggling to make up a story about a killer unlike himself, while also struggling riot to pin the crime on a real and identifiable person, as his story about the three black women had done? As an invented line of dialogue, "You are a white man" would have been such a story, though not a very convincing one. On the other hand, what if Marable was telling the truth? Perhaps he reported Lucy Pollard's statement accurately but misunderstood what she had said. Perhaps when the killer had asked, "Do you know me?" Mrs. Pollard had answered, "You are a Whiteman." She would have been replying that she did know him, by giving his family name. Therefore, having robbed her, Mr. Whiteman would have had to kill her.

The 1890 census records for Virginia were destroyed in a fire long ago, but the names "Whiteman" and "Whitman" appear in Richmond city directories for 1889 and 1890. But unless there are descendants of people named Whiteman with pertinent information, my theory isn't any more susceptible of proof than Lebsock's.

Alexander points out that the close of the nineteenth century has been called "the nadir" of African-American history. In the 1890s, lynching in the United States was at its peak, with 161 cases reported in 1892. Virginia had a better record than most Southern states. Racial violence there tapered off steeply around the time of the Lunenburg cases. Yet even in Virginia, the situation of African-Americans continued to be bleak for years to come. In 1896, flush with his success in exonerating the three black women, Mitchell failed to win reelection as an alderman when white election officials obstructed the voting in the polls in black districts and discarded many black ballots on the grounds that they were incorrectly marked.

The disfranchisement of blacks soon became systematic; after Mitchell's defeat, there would be no blacks on Richmond's city council for the next fifty years. In 1901, Virginia's trains were segregated for the first time. In 1904, Richmond's streetcars were segregated. Indeed, the transit company responsible for the segregation order was represented by one of the lawyers Mitchell had hired to defend the Lunenburg women a decade earlier.

Lebsack believes that the Lunenburg cases were forgotten because few people had both the power and the motive to recall them publicly once white supremacy took hold in Virginia. When blacks lost their political voice, they also lost the ability to keep alive the memory of past victories, and whites found the Lunenburg cases inconvenient to remember, perhaps because, as Lebsock suggests, their story was exceptional, involving "a united and highly mobilized African American citizenry, formidable African American leadership, and a critical mass of whites and blacks who worked in concert to the same end."

Yet the Lunenburg cases coincide with the decline of lynching in Virginia, and so to some degree they reflect the historical moment. Without Mitchell's intervention, Mary Abernathy and Pokey Barnes would no doubt have been hanged, but once Mitchell took up their cause, a number of powerful whites were willing to bend the rules to assist him. When Lunenburg's sheriff would not accept a military escort to prevent the lynching, the governor refused to hand the prisoners over to him, even though he had no legal authority to hold them. In the original trials no one had filed a bill of exceptions on behalf of the defendants, but Virginia's Supreme Court of Appeals nonetheless granted writs that allowed lawyers to request retrials. A commonwealth attorney spontaneously halted his county's prosecution of Pokey Barnes in what seems to have been an act of conscience. In 1896, the year of *Plessy* v. *Ferguson,* the white elite of Virginia seems to have been ready to set aside both lynching and the railroading of juries by the threat of lynching. Why?

Perhaps the state's leaders were able to feel ashamed of these clumsy and brutal tools of oppression because they had taken up a new, bloodless, and more efficient one: disfranchisement. It may be no coincidence that Mitchell was turned out of office just as he was winning the Lunenburg cases. White supremacy had shifted its strategy. The shift was never a complete one. Lynching survived, side by side with denying blacks the vote, until the 1960s, and it would turn out that in order to end lynching, one had to allow black people to vote.

The shift does not make Mitchell's part in the Lunenburg cases any the less heroic, but it does complicate the story's ending. In the difficult decades that followed, he seems to have become demoralized. "We find as we grow older that nothing speaks so loud as money," he wrote in 1905. Although he kept his newspaper, he turned most of his attention to banking, insurance, and real estate speculation, and in the pursuit of financial success, he ceased to challenge the people he began to call "quality white folks." After his bank failed in 1922, he was found guilty of fraud and theft. The conviction was overturned on technicalities, but his career was over. A. Philip Randolph's journal, *The Messenger,* did not regret Mitchell's fall from grace: "When one loses his courage and devotes most of his time [to] urging the victims of oppression to be polite to the persecutors, it is time for him to go." Perhaps we remember the Lunenburg cases now because we can appreciate a victory in a cause that did not achieve everything that had been hoped for.

Joe Hill: 'I Never Died,' Said He

During the first years of the 20th century, Joe Hill moved like a phantom 'Johnny Laborseed' through the far-flung corners of the United States, everywhere planting working class solidarity through his songs, speeches— and even his death—to foster the growth of a burgeoning labor movement.

BEN LEFEBVRE

At one point in the early 20th century, 49 of the 50 United States had in their possession some of the ashes of one man. Inside envelopes sent to union halls around the country were the remains of Joe Hillstrom, popularly known as Joe Hill, a drifter, songwriter and, for some members of the organized labor movement, a martyr. His story is not as well known as it once was, but his ghost still walked the land vividly enough in 1925 that Alfred Hayes was able to compose a poem commemorating it:

From San Diego up to Maine

In every mine and mill,

Where workers strike and organize,

Says he, "You'll find Joe Hill."

Hill's life had all the elements of classic American myth: back roads wandering, music, ideals and confrontations with the law. It also proves the point that for individuals to become legends, the way they die is just as important as the way they live.

Joe Hill stepped onto Ellis Island in October 1902. Born Joel Emmanuel Hägglund in Gävle, Sweden, in 1879, he sailed with his brother to America after the deaths of their parents—their father, a railway conductor, died from injuries suffered in a workplace accident, and their mother died 15 years later from illness. Far from finding the sidewalks paved with gold, Hill had to take whatever odd job he could find just to survive, at one point even cleaning bar spittoons in the roughest parts of New York City for a few pennies a day. Tired of city life, he abandoned the slums and hit the road, armed only with the English he had learned at the Gävle YMCA and on the streets of New York.

The labor pool he entered—before organized unions had any influence—was a turbulent one. Just finding a job was in itself an enormous task. "Employment sharks" would sell supposed job opportunities to unemployed men, who would then travel great distances only to find that the job did not exist; other "sharks," working in cahoots with the employer, would sell jobs that were only good for a few days before they were resold to someone else. In addition, the working conditions in those jobs were more often than not abominable. Management during the early 20th century exploited child labor and immigrant workers to the hilt. This was the era in which 146 workers died in New York's Triangle Shirtwaist Company fire; 362 West Virginia coal miners perished in the Monongah mine disaster; and Pittsburgh steel workers endured 12-hour shifts, six days a week. Workers who asked for higher wages or safer conditions were fired, beaten or, in some cases, killed. Faced with these horrific conditions, Hill gradually became a labor activist.

Gathering information to chronicle Hill's life between 1902 and his arrest in Utah in 1914 is difficult, because so much of it is scattered all over the map. The tall man with blue eyes and dark hair was reportedly sighted in Philadelphia, the Dakotas and Hawaii. In 1905 he sent a Christmas card from Cleveland to his sisters in Sweden, and in 1906 he sent a letter to the Gävle newspaper describing his experience in the Great San Francisco Earthquake. Reports and personal letters, many contradictory, depict a sort of "Johnny Laborseed" traveling through the country doing odd jobs, assisting strikes and furthering the union cause. In 1910 he joined the Industrial Workers of the World's San Pedro chapter while working on the California waterfront.

The IWW, still in existence, is a radical offshoot of the American Federation of Labor. The split represented the difference between reform and revolution. Whereas the AFL fought for "A fair day's wage for a fair day's work," the IWW, or Wobblies, as they are known, have flown a banner reading "Abolition of the wage system" since the group's inception in 1905. The Marxist group strives to organize the workers of the world into "one big union," arguing that separate unions are too easily manipulated by the managerial establishment. Though the group eschews violence, it does advocate "direct action," including industrial sabotage, as a means to persuade management to see things from labor's point of view. The IWW claimed about 100,000 members during its golden age before World War I, but wielded influence disproportionate to its size. During the opening decades of the 20th century, it directed or took part in at least 150 strikes.

Hill was dedicated to the cause and participated in his fair share of organizing before and after becoming formally affiliated with the IWW. Louis Morean, a Wobbly in British Columbia striking against the Canadian Northern Railroad in 1912, wrote of a typical Joe Hill sighting in a letter: "Joe Hill made his appearance at our strike camp at Yale a week or 10 days after the strike. I didn't know Joe before but quite a few fellow workers knew him and [he] was very popular. Joe wrote [his song] 'Where the Fraser River Flows' the first few days he was in our strike camp. It became very popular with everybody."

Morean also brought up what was another of Hill's trademarks: his ability to move in and out of camps almost without a trace. After a raid by strikebreakers broke up the union's activities, Morean wrote: "One thing puzzled us. We had not seen Joe Hill either during or after the raid."

Hill was also reported to be participating in some of the union's more extreme activities. He is believed to have joined a group of several hundred Wobblies and Mexican rebels who temporarily seized control of Tijuana, Mexico, in January 1911. The group attempted to overthrow dictator Porfirio Díaz and establish "industrial freedom" in that country, but was forced to retreat when government troops beat them back. Wobbly participants in the event recalled Hill being there, but Hill himself later denied it. That was part of the mystery of Hill's life—he had an uncanny ability to be simultaneously everywhere and nowhere within the labor movement.

Hill's songwriting was part of the reason behind that mystery. Regardless of which strikes Hill did or did not attend, his songs put him there in spirit. He was musically inclined since childhood, and during his time in the IWW he composed tunes and lyrics while on the road and while in prison. He wrote songs in Malgren's Hall, the San Pedro local's meeting place, composing the tunes on the piano, violin, banjo or guitar. His fellow Wobblies bought the sheet music for such songs as "Mr. Block," "It's a Long Way Down to the Breadline" and "Rebel Girl" for a few cents apiece. When the IWW collected his work and published it as part of their Little Red Songbook, a collection of labor songs subtitled Songs to Fan the Flames of Discontent, Hill's fame grew among the Wobblies and helped energize the movement.

"Songs became a distinguishing element of IWW—supported strikes," wrote Gibbs M. Smith, author of the biography Joe Hill. "Strike songs infused heterogeneous groups of workers with a sense of unity and solidarity," Smith continued. "They were great morale builders and, as such, important tools." A number of Hill's songs rank among the group's best. His understanding of the common laborer's plight and the satiric criticism of management in his lyrics endeared him to the rank and file. Wobblies sang his songs in picket fines and during mass meetings and demonstrations; the songs echoed in the "hobo jungles"—makeshift encampments where drifters could find respite from their search for work.

Though his songs were popular with the rank and file, he still had to justify them to some of his union brethren. Some officials considered music a frivolous waste of time that distracted workers from a more serious education. "Now I am well aware of the fact that there are lots of prominent rebels who argued that satire and songs are out of place in a labor organization," Hill wrote in a letter to the editor of Solidarity, an IWW newspaper. "A pamphlet, no matter how good, is never read more than once, but a song is learned by heart and repeated over and over; and I maintain that if a person can put a few cold, common sense facts into a song, and dress them in a cloak of humor to take the dryness off them, he will succeed in reaching a great number of workers who are too unintelligent or too indifferent to read a pamphlet or an editorial on economic science."

Hill wrote one of his most famous songs in support of the 35,000 workers striking against the Illinois Central Railroad. Protesting the introduction of nonunion workers to break the strike, Hill composed "Casey Jones—The Union Scab." Workers took up the song's refrain after it was published in a bulletin issued to the strikers. Sung to the tune of "Casey Jones," it dealt with the fate of a hapless strikebreaker after his untimely demise:

> The angels got together, and they said it wasn't fair,
>
> For Casey Jones to go around a-scabbing everywhere.
>
> The Angel Union No. 23, they sure were there,
>
> And they promptly fired Casey down the Golden Stair.

Another of Hill's songs, "The Preacher and the Slave," is considered one of the best protest songs ever written in America. Folk musicians still perform it today, singing it to the tune of "In the Sweet Bye and Bye." Hill's lyrics satirize religious leaders who asked hard-up laborers to endure destitution today for promised riches in the afterlife. Its opening verse and chorus set the tone:

> Long-haired preachers come out ev'ry night
>
> Try to tell you what's wrong and what's right;
>
> But when asked, how about something to eat?
>
> They will answer with voices so sweet:
>
> You will eat bye and bye
>
> In the glorious land above the sky;
>
> Work and pray, live on hay,
>
> You'll get pie in the sky when you die.

Hill's final chorus, however, extols the virtues of concentrating on the here and now, instead of depending on the powers that be:

> You will eat bye and bye
>
> When you've learned how to cook and to fry.
>
> Chop some wood, it'll do you good,
>
> And you'll eat in the sweet bye and bye.

Little did Hill know that his life would be dependent on those powers that be in the very near future.

Shortly before 10 P.M. on January 10, 1914, John G. Morrison and his son Arling were closing their grocery store in Salt Lake City when they were violently interrupted. According to Morrison's youngest son, Merlin, the only eyewitness, two masked men entered the store brandishing guns, shouting, "We have got you now!" Arling pulled out a gun his father kept in the store and shot one of the assailants. The two masked men returned fire, killing Arling and John. They then escaped into the night, one of them clutching his chest as he ran.

The police deigned the murders a revenge case. John Morrison had been a police officer in the city at one time, and lived in fear of retribution from the men he had arrested during his five-year stint. That, along with the fact that no money had been taken from the till, made robbery an unlikely motive. The police started searching for suspects right away, and eventually found three or four likely perpetrators.

Unfortunately for Hill, he was one of a number of people who had suffered gunshot wounds that night. Hill had stopped in Utah while en route to Chicago, and had taken odd jobs to earn money for the remainder of the trip. Unemployed due to illness, he eventually found lodging with the Eseliuses, a Swedish family he knew in Salt Lake City. On the night of January 10, 1914, Hill left the family's home between 6 P.M. and 9 P.M. He did not return until around 1 the next morning. Neither Hill nor his accusers were ever able to satisfactorily account for his actions before midnight.

What is known is that Hill, his shirt and undershirt soaked with blood, visited the office of Dr. Frank McHugh at about 11:30 P.M. He had been shot, he said, in a quarrel with a friend, something to do with the friend's wife. The bullet had gone cleanly through Hill's chest and only grazed his left lung—no permanent damage had been done. The doctor patched him up, took him to the Eselius house and eventually took his story to the police. On January 13, the police arrested Hill for the murders of John and Arling Morrison. He was formally arraigned 15 days later.

The trial, which began on June 17, 1914, and lasted more than a year, was by all accounts a shambles. Neither side could, or would, give concrete descriptions of what had happened on the night of the 10th. Moreover, it became quickly evident that conservative Utah did not like Hill or the IWW. This was fine by the union—they did not like Utah either. Mormon church leaders had voiced strong anti-union sentiments throughout the IWW's attempts to organize Utah's workers.

Once Hill's membership in the IWW became apparent, the bad blood spilled into the courtroom. The court not only allowed the prosecution's dependency on circumstantial evidence to make its case, but also defended the ploy. Merlin Morrison could not positively identify Hill as the masked gunman until he was goaded to do so by state attorneys. The prosecution never established a past connection between Hill and Morrison, nor supplied any substantial motive for the killing.

Hill did not help his own case, either. Though stubbornly insisting that Utah was determined to "fix" the case against him, Hill refused to give a concrete alibi for the night of the 10th. Worse, he declined to clarify the circumstances under which he had received his gunshot wound, only saying that any explanation would sully a certain lady's honor. He disastrously acted as his own attorney during the preliminary trial, conducting amateurish questioning when he bothered to question the witnesses at all. His erratic behavior eventually turned the jury against him. When he stood up in the courtroom and attempted to fire his state-appointed attorneys, instructing them to "get out of that door," his case was as good as lost in the eyes of most Utahans. The evidence may not have been enough to find him guilty in a court of law, but it did not need to be. He was found guilty in the court of public opinion long before the judge's gavel fell.

On June 27, 1915, after brief deliberations, the jury decided against Hill. The judge sentenced him to death. His lawyers filed an appeal on July 3, 1915, which the Utah State Supreme Court denied.

When Wobblies heard that the man who wrote "The Preacher and the Slave" and "Mr. Block" was facing execution, thousands of letters poured into Utah from around America. The IWW mobilized, sending representatives to Salt Lake City to protest his conviction. They did this peaceably, if loudly, but fights still broke out between them and residents who did not like unions. Outside interests got into the act, too. Concerned about the court's obvious bias against Hill, the Episcopal bishop of the Salt Lake City diocese requested that Hill's sentence be commuted, as did a member of the Utah State House of Representatives. W.A.F. Ekengren, the Swedish minister to the United States, became personally involved in the case. Workers in Boulder City, Australia, threatened to boycott American-made goods if Hill was executed.

Then, on September 30, Utah Governor William Spry received a telegram:

> Respectfully ask if it would not be possible to postpone execution of Joseph Hillstrom, who I understand is a Swedish subject, until the Swedish minister has an opportunity to present his view of the case fully to your Excellency.
>
> —Woodrow Wilson

This kind of heavy political pressure could not be ignored. It did win Hill a reprieve, but it was short-lived. Utahans found it absurd that the president of the United States would lend a hand to a person they believed to be the embodiment of anarchism, and the court once again refused to reconsider the case. On October 18, Hill was brought into the courtroom and again sentenced to die. The press reported that when Hill tried to make a statement in the courtroom after the sentencing, officials silenced him. "The judge didn't want to hear what I had to say," Hill was quoted as saying while being escorted out, "and I don't blame him."

Hill's next month was taken up with waiting in the death house, giving interviews and writing letters. "One thing this jail has made out of me is a good correspondent," he wrote in one of his epistles. His surviving letters from that time show not only a man dealing with the issues of appearing a court case, but also one adept at turning his case into a rallying cry for "the cause." At times he seems to consciously contribute to the making of his own myth, describing himself as a "rebel true blue" and ready to die as such. At other times, Hill seems genuinely weary: ". . . all this notoriety stuff is making me dizzy in the head," he wrote to a friend. "I am afraid I am getting more glory than I really am entitled to." His last letter to "Big" Bill Haywood, leader of the IWW in Chicago, asks that his body be hauled out of the state: "I don't want to be caught dead in Utah," he wrote. That letter contained a phrase that still reverberates throughout labor unions today: "Don't waste any time mourning—organize!" He also wrote his last will and testament, published in the *Salt Lake Herald-Republican:*

> My Will is easy to decide
>
> For there is nothing to divide
>
> My kin don't need to fuss and mourn
>
> "Moss does not cling to a rolling stone."
>
> My body? Oh! If I could choose
>
> I would to ashes it reduce
>
> And let the merry breezes blow
>
> My dust to where some flowers grow.
>
> Perhaps some fading flower then
>
> Would come to life and bloom again.

On November 19, 1915, Hill was taken to the execution grounds. Wearing a dark blue suit of coarse material, he was sat down on a chair and blindfolded. A doctor used a stethoscope to search for his heart's exact position and placed a heart-shaped paper target over the spot. Five soldiers lined up, one of whom had a blank cartridge in his rifle. Deputy Shettler began the sequence of commands, calling out, "Ready . . . aim . . . "

"Fire," Hill called from his chair. "Go on and fire."

Shettler went on to command, "Fire," and the five rifles cracked. With that, Joe Hill—man, émigré, idealist, union activist, poet and, perhaps, even murderer—was dead. Four blackened circles on the target began to turn crimson, and the white paper heart turned red.

By the time of Hill's two funerals, the myth-making process had already begun. The Salt Lake Herald-Republican reported that the several thousand people who came to see Hill's body at a Salt Lake City funeral home included "newspaper boys, workingmen with their lunch boxes beneath their arms, business and professional men and women, people who were well dressed and poorly clad. The expressions of opinion were as varied as the appearance of the visitors."

More than 90 years later, they still are. Joe Hill was considered a militant labor agitator by some and a hero of enlightenment by others, but his life in many ways is overshadowed by his death. Clouding the issue are the scores of "eyewitness" testaments to his character that surfaced after his death, all of uncertain credibility. Some claimed he had the soul of a poet and would never take another's life; others said he was the Robin Hood sort, one who would not mind kilting another human being if it furthered the cause of the workingman. The unions idolized Hill; the newspapers mostly vilified him. His family in Sweden collected and destroyed most records of him after he was executed, not wanting to be associated with the incident. Whether Hill was guilty of murder or not, he clearly did not receive a fair trial, one that might have credibly determined the truth.

When the IWW brought Hill's body back to the union's home base in Chicago, an estimated 30,000 people jammed the streets to catch a glimpse of his funeral procession. By midmorning, 5,000 people failed the West Side Auditorium to capacity to attend his funeral. The audience sang Hill's songs and listened to speeches; they celebrated the man they considered a martyr, and badmouthed Utah. His body was later cremated, his ashes placed in envelopes and sent to IWW locals in every state but Utah. Years later, his last wishes would be honored, when the IWW collected his ashes and scattered them to the wind. Hill's story, embedded with elements of classic American mythology, still stirs the imagination of some. The sentiment is probably best captured in Alfred Hayes' 1925 poem:

> I dreamed I saw Joe Hill last night,
>
> Alive as you or me.
>
> Says I, "But Joe, you're ten years dead."
>
> "I never died," said he.

From *American History,* by Ben Lefebvre, December 2005, pp. 57–62. Copyright © 2005 by Weider History Group. Reprinted by permission.

Alice Roosevelt Longworth

STEVEN LEE CARSON

America was horror-stricken in September 1901. Mourning bells tolled throughout the stunned land, and cannons thundered farewell salutes to assassinated President William McKinley. Extended, elaborate Victorian bereavement rituals were still in vogue as news reporters, wearing heavy black crepe on their hats and sleeves, trudged to the home of Vice President Theodore Roosevelt. On the front lawn his teenage daughter Alice was playing with her younger brother as the representatives of the press sadly asked, "And how does young Miss Roosevelt feel about this terrible tragedy to afflict the nation?" Looking up, Alice replied: "Utter rapture! Daddy always wanted to be president and now he is!"

Alice Roosevelt Longworth, as she would become known, had just stepped onto the stage of American history, and, unlike any other presidential daughter, she stayed in the spotlight for the rest of her long life, well past her White House years. Today she is still mentioned or portrayed in books, plays and motion pictures for the sake of a laugh, a quip, a quote or an anecdote about America, Washington society or White House families.

Her father, America's youngest president, was a colossus of his time, striding both the nation and the world—from battling big interests for the common man to building the Panama Canal to negotiating the end of the Russo-Japanese War. Teddy Roosevelt was the first of only three presidents to win the Nobel Peace Prize. By the time he entered the White House in 1901, he was already a hero of the Spanish-American War, a governor, assistant naval secretary, vice president and prolific author and expert on history, political science and nature, specifically ornithology. No one had ever seen such a dramatic president, and he and his family captured the American spirit in a way that was unrivaled until the Kennedys in the 1960s. Yet in many ways his personal rival was his firstborn

In an era when women were expected to be dainty dolls dressed in stays, corsets, bustles, high-neck collars and long, sweeping gowns, Alice was the exception. One year, when she entered the White House East Room for the annual grand diplomatic reception, the soothing sound of violins suddenly was drowned out by the shrieks of fleeing, fainting ladies. The president's daughter had arrived with her hissing pet snake wrapped around her neck. Alice was constantly finding other inventive ways to challenge her father's authority. Seen smoking when doing so branded a woman a prostitute, she was ordered by her enraged father to never smoke under his roof again. So Alice went up on top of the White House roof to smoke. She also joined her siblings in driving barnyard animals through the State Dining Room or the East Room. Alice organized a club whose express purpose was to oppose her father's views that a woman should concentrate on cooking, church and children; it met in the White House. When TR's friend Owen Wister, author of *The Virginian,* complained about the president's eldest daughter in the White House, Theodore Roosevelt made a rare admission of defeat: "Look Owen. I can control Alice or run the country. I can't do both."

Yet few know that her outrageousness and fun-loving antics were meant to keep people from getting too close to her and discovering a series of catastrophic tragedies. She captured the headlines before they could capture her. One interpretation of Alice's outrageous behavior, comments and attempts to throw herself into the headlines was that she simply wanted her father to notice her—and love her. Yet she also resented feeling the need to do that.

In fact, almost from the day she was born, February 12, 1884, Alice Lee Roosevelt felt abandoned. Within two days of her birth both her mother, for whom she was named, and her grandmother died—and in the same house. So devastating were the losses of his wife and his mother to Theodore Roosevelt that he gave his infant daughter to his sister to raise for the next two years while he went out West to ranch and hunt. He killed so many animals that it seemed like a slaughter to vent his rage. Shortly after his return home to New York in 1886, he married a childhood friend, Edith Carow, who was dutiful and loving enough toward Alice, but Alice's very name served as a constant reminder to Edith that she was not her husband's first love.

Because of the family's painful loss and the arrival of a new woman on the scene, Alice's mother's identity was wiped out. Albums and drawers were searched, and all photos, letters and mementoes of her were destroyed. In his autobiography, Theodore Roosevelt never mentions his first wife. And while Alice was discouraged from ever asking about her, at night she was forced by her family to say prayers for her dear departed mother in heaven. In a sense, then, young Alice's identity was destroyed too. Even her name became anathema to the new family; she was never called by her first name—ever. From being "Baby Lee," she was soon called "Sister" and to the end of her days even "Auntie Sister" by her siblings' children. All of this and her father's disappearance in her early childhood were the only two personal things Alice would comment upon throughout her adult life. Years later someone, without mentioning Alice's name or the time in which she lived, described the circumstances of her early life and asked a psychiatrist for an evaluation of such a person. The doctor said: "These symptoms are very unusual and are common to an older era. This person could be a hysteric."

To her friend Michael Teague, Alice admitted she disliked her father. He was impossible to be around, she claimed. Others agreed, describing TR as "radioactive," "TNT" and "a steam engine in pants." He was overwhelming, impossible and imperious. (His son Ted Jr. had a nervous breakdown at the age of 12. The doctor blamed Teddy Roosevelt, who ruefully accepted the charge.) When TR was in his vice presidential years, Harvard psychologist and philosopher, and his former professor, William James, described Roosevelt as "still in the *Sturm und Drang* period of early adolescence."

Claiming, "My father wants to be the corpse at every funeral, the bride at every wedding and the baby at every christening," Alice tried to upstage him at every opportunity. At her marriage to Congressman and future Speaker of the U.S. House of Representatives Nicholas Longworth in 1906, Alice delighted the White House crowd by suddenly seizing a Marine's dress sword and slashing her wedding cake. Since just before the wedding ceremony Alice had been told by her stepmother Edith that they were glad to be rid of her, Alice's slashing of the cake with that sword takes on another meaning.

Her marriage was a disaster, and Longworth, who was 15 years older than Alice, soon abandoned her, too. A voracious womanizer, he even kept a humidor of condoms on his office desk. Once a freshman congressman came up behind him and rubbed his head saying, "This feels like my wife's ass." Longworth rubbed his own head and said, "You know, I think you are right."

Longworth and Alice soon led separate lives. When daughter Paulina was born, it was widely believed that the father was Senator William E. Borah of Idaho, whom Paulina resembled—certainly no one in the know thought the father was Longworth. Yet Longworth and Paulina adored each other, while Alice was often brutal to her daughter. Paulina was seemingly catatonic at dinner parties and very shy. Alice had no patience for someone so different from herself. She veered between abandoning her daughter, as she herself had been abandoned, and savagely squelching whatever personality or individuality Paulina could muster. Paulina rushed into marriage to escape her mother and found catastrophe. Beforehand, paralleling another nasty wedding scene decades before, Alice began her daughter's wedding day by telling Paulina some upsetting news—that the late Nick Longworth was not her real father.

Paulina's husband, Alexander Sturm, turned out to be a raging alcoholic and ne'er-do-well whose only interests appeared to be heraldry and framing fancy menus. Moreover, his family had ties to prominent Nazi collaborators at the highest levels. Sturm died at the age of 29, leaving Paulina with a daughter, Joanna. When Joanna was 10 years old, she came home one day to find her mother dying with an empty pill bottle at her side. Paulina had swallowed 60 barbiturates with hard liquor.

Alice had lost her brother Kermit to suicide in World War II, and her youngest brother, Quentin, had been shot down in aerial combat in World War I. Then Ted Jr. died of a heart attack a few weeks after leading a charge on D-Day. He would posthumously be awarded the Congressional Medal of Honor. With Paulina's death, however, Alice's veneer finally cracked. To her cousin Eleanor Roosevelt she admitted that she had "crumpled" upon hearing the news. But she was the daughter of Theodore Roosevelt. Devastated, racked with guilt and largely incommunicado for six months, she nonetheless emerged to be as good a grandmother as she had not been a mother.

In her post-White House years, despite all the personal tragedies, Alice reigned as the queen of Washington society. Popular with the public and the press, she appeared on the cover of *Time* magazine, and a popular song, "Alice Blue Gown," penned in 1919, was dedicated to her. While she was well-read, Alice seemed interested only in social intrigues and being entertained and entertaining. Once, when compared to her famous cousin, she snapped, "I leave the good deeds to Eleanor!" They were "too boring" for her, she claimed.

Movers and shakers from all walks of life came together in her salon and became friends, or enemies. Richard Nixon first met J. Edgar Hoover there, and a banker friend once found himself with the chairman of the Federal Reserve Board for a dinner companion. Bob Hope was no stranger to her home, and neither were some presidents. She was a great morale booster, and her vitality and wit were incandescent. But no one got much sympathy from her either. Her attitude was perhaps best summed up by a pillow on her sofa with the embroidered saying, "If you haven't got anything good to say about anyone, come and sit by me."

When her poker-playing crony, President Warren G. Harding, unexpectedly died in office and the press asked for an appropriate tribute, she said: "Harding was not a bad man. He was just a slob." President Calvin Coolidge, she reportedly claimed, "looked like he was weaned on a sour pickle." Even family members did not escape her quips. Her cousin Franklin Roosevelt was "one part Eleanor and nine parts mush." The White House was "supposed" to be for brother Teddy Jr., she said, and she never really forgave her "upstart" cousin who also grew more famous than her Republican father. When FDR was elected president, Ted Jr. was the Republican governor general of the Philippines. Asked what his blood relationship was to the new chief executive, Alice's brother said, "Fifth cousin about to be removed." When FDR took the country off the gold standard, Alice paid him a visit wearing every bit of gold jewelry she could find. To her, Eisenhower was "a nice boob." In contrast, she and the Kennedys became a mutual admiration society. "There's been nothing like the Kennedys since the Bonapartes," she said. Even that, however, was something of a barb, for many of the world's old society considered the Bonapartes nouveau riche upstarts.

Other presidential children were not usually included in her circle, perhaps because she felt they might be possible rivals. While willing to comment on almost anyone, she refused to talk about her parents. When the chairman of the White House Conference on Presidential Children invited her to join others in commenting upon their fathers and life in the White House, Alice was harsh and abrupt: "What utter nonsense! I am glad I am too old for such things!"

Her offbeat reactions to events were also legendary. When the erection of a hotel next to her home caused the wall of her bedroom to collapse and the construction superintendent came by to apologize, Alice said, "But you forgot to knock." Swirling tear gas from demonstrations at the nearby South Vietnam Embassy during the Vietnam War elicited the comment, "Great for the lungs," as she opened the window. When late in life Alice suffered through a second mastectomy, she handled it in her typical fashion. "Well," she said, when asked to comment on modern sexual attitudes at the time, "you are asking the hospital's oldest topless octogenarian, but when it itches, scratch it."

While being interviewed for a front-page *New York Times* article to mark her 90th birthday, Alice casually looked over at a photo and suddenly blurted out: "No one must ever touch me. I don't want to be touched. That's probably some psycho thing that I don't understand." Her trademark, unfashionable large-brimmed hats, may have been worn to help avoid such contact. Lyndon B. Johnson had once complained, "Alice, I can't kiss you with that big hat of yours." She replied, "That's why I wear it, Mr. President." Although Senator Joseph McCarthy's picture was displayed in her home and she believed much of what the anti-Communist crusader said, she once lashed out at him for coming up behind her, slipping his arm around her and trying to kiss her. "The policeman on the block, the trash man and the gardener may call me Alice," she firmly stated. "You call me Mrs. Longworth!"

Incredibly, it wasn't until 1974 that Alice learned for the first time that her father had loved her mother. The word came from, of all people, Alice's old friend, Richard Nixon. In his televised rambling and weepy farewell to his White House staff on the day of his resignation, Nixon said that the previous night he had found a small book while he was reading in the White House library. The book was about a young man in his 20s, TR, who thought that his life was over. "This was in his diary," Nixon said, and he quoted, " 'And when my heart's dearest died, the light went out of my life forever.' " Until that moment, Alice claimed, she thought her mother had done something wrong.

Alice had come to know every president from Benjamin Harrison to Gerald Ford by the time she died in 1980 at the age of 96. When her doctor wondered what he should fill in on her death certificate where it said "Business or Profession," her grand-daughter's boyfriend remarked, "Gadfly."

From *American History,* by Steven Lee Carson, August 2005, pp. 38–40, 77. Copyright © 2005 by Weider History Group. Reprinted by permission.

A Day to Remember: March 25, 1911
Triangle Fire

CHARLES PHILLIPS

At the end of the work day on March 25, 1911, Isidore Abramowitz, a cutter at the Triangle Waist Company located on the corner of Greene Street and Washington Place in the heart of Manhattan's Garment District, had already pulled his coat and hat down from their peg when he noticed flames billowing from the scrap bin near his cutting table. It was about 4:40 P.M., and within minutes the fire swept through the factory and killed more than 140 of the 500 people who worked there. The conflagration, for some 90 years considered the deadliest disaster in New York City history, would usher in an era of reform with implications far beyond those of mere workplace safety.

The Jewish and Italian immigrants working at Triangle, most of them young women, produced the fashionable shirtwaists—women's blouses loosely based on a man's fitted shirt—popularized by commercial artist Charles Dana Gibson, whose famous "Gibson Girl" had become the sophisticated icon of the times. Beginning in late 1909, these workers participated in a major strike led by the Women's Trade Union League demanding a shorter working day and a livable wage. The garment workers had also protested the deplorable working conditions and dangerous practices of the industry's sweatshops. A large proportion of these firetraps, like Triangle, were located in Manhattan's crowded Lower East Side.

The factory workers had support not only from the left wing of the American labor movement but also among the city's wealthy progressives. Such socially prominent women as Anne Morgan (banker J.P Morgan's daughter) and Alva Belmont (tycoon William H. Vanderbilt's ex-wife, who married banker Oliver Hazard Perry Belmont) ensured tremendous publicity for the strikers, and they helped stage a huge rally at Carnegie Hall on January 2, 1910. But they met with adamantine resistance from factory owners, led by Triangle partners Max Blanck and Isaac Harris, who hired thugs from Max Schlansky's private detective agency to break up the strike. The owners in general enjoyed the backing of Tammany Hall boss Charles E Murphy, which meant not only that the New York police were hostile to the workers but that strikebreakers were also available from the street gangs employed as muscle by Murphy's political machine.

When the strike ended, although the owners had agreed to some minor concessions and the radical newspaper *The Call*

declared the strike a victory, little had truly changed, and everyone on the Lower East Side knew it. Certainly the workers at Triangle still put in long hours for penurious wages, without breaks, in an airless factory located on the top three floors of a hazardous 10 story firetrap. Scraps from the pattern cutters piled up in open bins and spilled over at the workers' feet, where the higher paid cutters, often men, dropped the ashes or even tossed the smoldering butts of the cheap cigars they smoked.

Because Blanck and Harris feared pilfering by their employees, access to the exits was limited, despite the city's fire regulations. At closing, workers were herded to the side of the building facing Greene Street, where partitions had been set up to funnel one worker at a time toward the stairway or the two freight elevators before they could leave the building for the day. This allowed company officials to inspect each exiting employee and his or her belongings for stolen tools, fabric or shirtwaists. The stairway and passenger elevators on the opposite side of the building, facing Washington Place, were reserved for management and the public. The only other egress was a narrow and flimsy fire escape on the back side of the building, opposite Washington Place, that corrupt city officials in 1900 had allowed Blanck and Harris to substitute for the third stair way legally required by the city. Access to it was partially blocked by large worktables.

These arrangements all led the disaster when the fire broke out as the result—the fire marshal later ruled—of a match or a smoldering cigarette or cigar tossed into Abramowitz's scrap bin. The loosely heaped scraps of sheer cotton fabric and crumpled tissue paper flared quickly, and the fire was blazing within seconds. Accounts of the chaos that erupted vary greatly, but apparently Abramowitz reached up, grabbed one of the three red fire pails on the ledge above his coat rack, and dumped it on the flames. Other cutters snatched pails and tried in vain to douse the exponentially spreading blaze. Despite their efforts, the fabric-laden old structure, ironically called the Asch Building, began to burn quickly and fiercely.

Factory manager Samuel Bernstein directed his employees to break out the fire hoses, only to find them completely useless. Some claimed the uninspected hoses had rotted through, while others asserted that either the water tanks on the roof were empty or the flow of water from them was somehow blocked.

Having lost precious minutes in fruitless attempts to control the blaze, the workers looked for the means of escape.

A few rushed to the solitary, poorly constructed and inadequately maintained fire escape, which descended from the 10th floor to the 2nd, stopping above a small courtyard. Some of the young women who used it fell from one landing to the next; one of the male employees fell from the 8th floor to the ground. Others madly rushed toward the inward-opening doors on the Washington Place side, preventing them from being opened. (Some later claimed these doors were locked.) As more and more workers piled up at the doors, those at the front were nearly crushed. Only with great effort did Louis Brown, a young shipping clerk, bully his way through the pressed bodies and muscle them away from the exit so that he could open the doors. On the opposite side of the building, panicked workers who tried to exit the 8th floor on the Greene Street side were slowed by the funneling partitions, and found the stairway and elevators already jammed with workers fleeing from the 9th and 10th floors.

Afterward, there was much confusion and a lot of debate about which floor the Washington Place passenger elevators visited and when. The elevator operators—Joseph Zito and Gaspar Mortillo—certainly risked their lives by returning to burning floors to carry their co-workers to safety. They probably visited the 8th floor first, saving a lot of lives even as the panic there set in. Then they headed up to the 10th floor, the executive floor. Zito later guessed that they went to 10 twice, dropping off the first group only to find the floor empty on the next trip up.

All 70 workers on the 10th floor managed to escape, as did Blanck (and the two daughters he'd brought to work with him) and Harris, who showed a good deal of bravery in his efforts to save many of his 10th-floor employees. They all got out either by the early elevator trips, by way of the staircases or by ascending to the roof. New York University law students in a taller, adjacent building lowered ladders to the roof of the Asch Building, and the workers inched their way up them to safety.

Of all the Triangle employees, the 260 who worked on the 9th floor suffered the worst fate. According to some accounts, the alert and the fire reached them at the same time. The Greene Street exit was quickly jammed, and the doors to the Washington Place stairwell were found to be locked. Since the elevator car itself was packed with 10th-floor employees, some clambered down the greasy cables of the freight elevator.

Elevator operator Zito peered up the elevator shaft as those left behind faced grim choices. "The screams from above were getting worse," he later reported. "I looked up and saw the whole shaft getting red with fire. . . . They kept coming down from the flaming floors above. Some of their clothing was burning as they fell. I could see streaks of fire coming down like flaming rockets."

Others on the 9th floor wedged their way into the Greene Street staircase and climbed up to the roof. Still others ran to the fire escape, which proved incapable of supporting the weight of so many. With an ear-rending rip, it separated from the wall, disintegrating in a mass of twisted iron and falling bodies. In complete desperation, some 9th-floor workers fled to the window ledges. The firemen's ladders would not reach beyond the 6th floor, so the firefighters deployed a safety net about 100 feet below, and they exhorted the victims to jump. Some of the young women, in terror, held hands and jumped in pairs. But the weight of so many jumpers split the net, and young men and women tore through it to their deaths.

An ambulance driver bumped his vehicle over the curb onto the sidewalk, hoping against hope that jumpers might break their fall by landing on his roof. Deliverymen pulled a tarpaulin from a wagon and stretched it out. The first body to hit it ripped it from their hands. "The first ten [to hit] shocked me," wrote reporter William Gunn Shepherd before he looked up and saw all the others raining down.

Fifteen minutes after the fire started, the firemen—even then New York's finest, the pride of the city—were within moments of bringing the fire on the 8th floor under control. But the 9th was hopeless. On the 9th, the fire took over the entire floor. Later, burned bodies were found piled up in a heap in the loft. A second scorched cluster was discovered pressed up against the Greene Street exit, where they had been caught by the blaze before they could get out. At the time, the crowds watching could see groups of girls trapped in burning window frames, refusing to jump. When they could hold out no longer, they came tumbling through the windows in burning clumps.

Then it was over. The last person fell at about 4:57 P.M., and there was nothing left to do but deal with the dead—146 broken bodies. During the next few days, streams of survivors and relatives filed through the temporary morgue on 26th Street to identify the dead. Eventually, all but six were given names.

Even before the bodies stopped falling, veteran newsman Herbert Bayard Swope had interrupted District Attorney Charles Seymour Whitman's regular Saturday news briefing at his apartment in the Iroquois Hotel to announce the disaster. Whitman immediately rushed to the scene and began looking for somebody to blame. Since he couldn't go after the city itself, he got a grand jury to charge Blanck and Harris with negligent homicide for locking the doors to the back stairway. Defended in a celebrated trial by famed Tammany mouthpiece Max D. Steuer, himself a former garment worker, the "Shirtwaist Kings" were acquitted, much to the outrage of progressives everywhere.

But watching the fire that day was a young woman named Frances Perkins. Perkins happened to be enjoying tea with a friend who lived on the north side of Washington Square. She heard the fire engines and arrived just in time to see the bodies begin to fall. Already a rising star in the progressive firmament, she never forgot what she saw, and she never let it go. Through her efforts, and the efforts of others like her, the horrible images of the Triangle fire brought an anguished outcry for laws to compel heedless, greedy, cost-cutting manufacturers to provide for the safety of employees.

The pre-fire strikes, coupled with the Triangle disaster and its aftermath, unified union organizers, college students, socialist writers, progressive millionaires and immigrant shop workers. Tammany Hall boss Murphy quickly sensed that a transformation of the Democratic Party could take advantage of this new progressive coalition at the ballot box. As a result, he fully supported the New York Factory Investigating Commission, formed three months after the fire, to inspect factories throughout the state. The "Tammany Twins," Alfred E. Smith and Robert F. Wagner, who were the driving force behind the investigation, backed Perkins as she sat on the commission and took the lead in shaping its findings. The commission's report, compiled during $2\frac{1}{2}$ years of research, brought dramatic changes to existing laws and introduced many new ones.

Smith, of course, went on to become governor of New York and the Democratic nominee for the presidency in 1924 and 1928. When Franklin Delano Roosevelt followed in his footsteps and actually won election to the office in 1932, he brought Perkins with him into his New Deal, as the first female Cabinet member (secretary of labor), and Wagner as an adviser who drafted some of the most important progressive legislation in the country's history. In many ways, it is fair to say that the modern American welfare state of the 20th century's middle decades rose from the ashes of the Triangle fire.

From *American History,* by Charles Phillips, April 2006, pp. 16, 18, 70. Copyright © 2006 by Weider History Group. Reprinted by permission.

UNIT 3

From Progressivism to the 1920s

Unit Selections

Key Points to Consider

- What factors were at work in the trial and ultimate lynching of Leo Frank? That he was Jewish was obvious, but what else did he represent that seemed so threatening?

- What did women progressives hope to achieve and how did they go about it? What is meant by their "ambiguous legacy"?

- Why did the question of evolution seem so important to people at the time?

- Why does the issue continue to stir up controversy?

- What is meant by a "consumer society?" How did the move from production to consumption affect politics?

Student Web Site

www.mhcls.com/online

Internet References

Further information regarding these Web sites may be found in this book's preface or online.

International Channel
  http://www.i-channel.com/
World War I—Trenches on the Web
  http://www.worldwar1.com/
World Wide Web Virtual Library
  http://www.iisg.nl/~w3vl/
The Roaring 20's and the Great Depression
  http://www.snowcrest.net/jmike/20sdep.html

Reform movements in the United States have most often developed in the face of economic dislocation. The Populist crusade in the 1890s and the New Deal in the 1930s are typical. Progressivism was an exception. It developed during a period of relative prosperity. Yet more and more people became dissatisfied with existing conditions. Individuals who became known as "muckrakers" published books and articles that revealed the seamier side of American life. One focused on the terrible working conditions in the meat packing industry, another on corruption and cronyism in the Senate, still another on the "bossism" and "machine politics" he found in a number of cities. The popularity of muckraking in newspapers, journals, and books showed that many segments of the public were receptive to such exposures.

The Progressive movement generally was led by white, educated, middle or upper-middle class men and women. They were not radicals, though their opponents often called them that, and they had no wish to destroy the capitalist system. Instead they wanted to reform it to eliminate corruption, to make it function more efficiently, and to provide what we would call a "safety net" for the less fortunate. The reforms they proposed were modest ones such as replacing political appointees with trained experts, having senators elected directly by the people, and conducting referenda on important issues. The movement arose on local levels, then percolated upward to state governments, then into the national arena.

Teddy Roosevelt as president had responded to progressive sentiment through actions such as his "trust busting." He did not seek a third term in 1908, and anointed William Howard Taft as the Republican candidate for the presidency. Taft won the election but managed to alienate both progressives and conservatives during his tenure of office. By 1912, progressivism ran strongly enough that the Democrat party nominated Woodrow Wilson, who had compiled an impressive record as a reform governor in the state of New Jersey. Roosevelt, now counting himself a full-blown progressive, bolted the Republican Party when Taft was re-nominated and formed the Progressive or "Bull Moose" party. Roosevelt was still popular, but he managed only to split Republican support with the result that Woodrow Wilson won the election with just 42 percent of the popular vote.

Those progressives who held or competed for political offices were almost exclusively white males. Women had not yet been granted the right to vote, let alone be elected to positions in government, and the prevailing racism ensured that blacks would be excluded from the power structure. "Jim Crow" laws in the South had virtually pushed blacks out of the political arena altogether. Yet members of both groups were attracted to progressivism. Blacks, at least as much as whites, wanted to change the power structures that kept them down. Female progressives shared these goals as well. "The Ambiguous Legacies of Women's

Library of Congress

Progressivism" points out that, contrary to what one might think the movement did not always serve to liberate women.

Anti-Semitism was a fact of life during this era and beyond. "The Fate of Leo Frank" describes how a Northern Jew was convicted for the murder of a little girl, and later removed from jail and lynched. He was almost certainly innocent, yet the things he represented enraged those who persecuted him.

What we call "World War I" (contemporaries called it "The Great War") broke out in the summer of 1914. President Woodrow Wilson called upon the American people to remain neutral "in thought and deed" toward the warring powers. By April 1917, however, after Germany resorted to "unrestricted submarine warfare" against neutral shipping, he asked Congress for a declaration of war. American entry into the conflict proved decisive, but this nation suffered nothing like the enormous casualties incurred by those who had fought the entire war. Between

September 1918 and June 1919 more Americans died from a worldwide pandemic of influenza or, as it was called at the time, the "Spanish flu," than they did on the battlefield. Some officials tried to downplay the seriousness of this catastrophe by subordinating it to the war effort.

There had been a number of movements in the United States to prohibit the sale and consumption of alcoholic beverages. "A Day to Remember: January 16, 1920" describes these movements and the conditions that resulted in what some called the "noble experiment." Prohibition, its supporters claimed, would end the curse of alcoholism, lead to a healthier citizenry, and assure that money previously wasted on booze would be spent in beneficial ways. It did none of these things, and some have claimed that Prohibition actually led to increased alcohol consumption during what became known as the "Roaring Twenties." Too many people were willing to flout the law, and enforcement proved impossible because it was so easy to manufacture alcoholic beverages or smuggle them in from other countries.

"Evolution on Trial" discusses the highly publicized Scopes trial of 1925 in Dayton, Tennessee. The teaching of evolution in public schools was a hot-button issue in many areas because it appeared to undermine the teachings of fundamentalist Christianity. Interest in the case was stimulated by the clash of opposing lawyers William Jennings Bryan and Clarence Darrow. Former presidential candidate Bryan argued for a literal interpretation of the bible, including the proposition that the earth was created in seven days. Darrow's cross-examination of Bryan proved devastating to the latter's claims. The author of this essay points out that 80 years later many residents of Dayton still refuse to accept Charles Darwin's theory about the common ancestry of humans and primates.

The progressive spirit of the early years of the 20th Century had waned by the 1920s, partly as a result of the Great War and its aftermath. "Rethinking Politics: Consumers and the Public Good during the 'Jazz Age'" argues that " . . . rather than attacking political and corporate corruption, Americans bought Model T's; rather than cleaning up slums they purchased a vast array of new brand-name consumables." This consumer society was marked by a number of innovations that are familiar to us today. These include: an increasingly sophisticated advertising industry, the growth of installment buying, a shift to mass production as exemplified by Henry Ford's assembly lines, and the emergence of chain stores such as Woolworth's that could sell goods at lower prices than local merchants could match. Consumption rather than production came to be acknowledged as the prime mover of economic life.

That virulent racism continued in this nation can be seen in the essay, "Unearthing a Riot." Author Brent Staples reveals the facts of a bloody race riot that took place in Tulsa, Oklahoma in 1921. Hundreds of black people were shot, burned alive, or dragged to death behind automobiles. Staples not only describes what happened but how this catastrophe was covered up for decades before being brought to light.

America's entry into World War I or "The Great War," as people at the time called it, to a great degree stifled the progressive impulse. Furthering the war effort seemed more important than experimenting with this or that reform, and the perceived threat of espionage or sabotage by German agents brought about drastic curtailments of civil liberties. The suspicions and fears engendered by the war carried over when the fighting ended. Now, instead of being directed only at Germans, they were extended to foreigners in general and to radicals in particular. "The Fire Last Times" describes what happened in the wake of an explosion on Wall Street in September, 1920. Without a shred of evidence to go on, Attorney General A. Mitchell Palmer arrested the head of a radical labor union as "a precaution." Others, equally lacking any evidence, attributed the bombing to an Italian anarchist gang.

After numerous crusades against inequities at home and the consequences of waging war abroad, the American people in 1920 yearned to return to what Republican presidential candidate Warren G. Harding referred to as "normalcy." Harding was elected in a landslide. Following a recession brought about by postwar reconversion, prosperity returned again although not equally shared by all. The genial Harding presided over this economic boom and was an extremely popular president at the time of his death in 1923. "The Dark Side of Normalcy" reveals the facts that emerged after Harding's death, showing that his was one of the most corrupt administrations in American history.

The final selection, "Marcus Garvey and the Rise of Black Nationalism," shows how this remarkable figure tapped into the yearning of black people to take pride in their heritage. The Garvey movement ultimately collapsed amidst charge of corruption but, author Elwood D. Watson believes the movement was significant in appealing to the ambitions and emotions of black people.

Marcus Garvey was a charismatic leader to some, a charlatan to others. Regardless of what he was, analyze the great appeal his movement had for black people in a racist society.

The Fate of Leo Frank

He was a Northerner. He was an industrialist. He was a Jew. And a young girl was murdered in his factory.

LEONARD DINNERSTEIN

On December 23, 1983, the lead editorial in the Atlanta *Constitution* began, "Leo Frank has been lynched a second time." The first lynching had occurred almost seventy years earlier, when Leo Frank, convicted murderer of a thirteen-year-old girl, had been taken from prison by a band of vigilantes and hanged from a tree in the girl's hometown of Marietta, Georgia. The lynching was perhaps unique, for Frank was not black but a Jew. Frank also is widely considered to have been innocent of his crime. Thus the second "lynching" was the refusal of Georgia's Board of Pardons and Paroles to exonerate him posthumously.

Frank's trial, in July and August 1913, has been called "one of the most shocking frame-ups ever perpetrated by American law-and-order officials." The case became, at the time, a cause célèbre in which the injustices created by industrialism, urban growth in Atlanta, and fervent anti-Semitism all seemed to conspire to wreck one man.

Until the discovery of Mary Phagan's body in the basement of Atlanta's National Pencil Company factory, Leo Frank led a relatively serene life. Born in Cuero, Texas, in 1884, he was soon taken by his parents to Brooklyn, New York. He attended the local public schools, the Pratt Institute, and Cornell University. After graduation he accepted the offer of an uncle, Moses Frank, to help establish a pencil factory in Atlanta and become both co-owner and manager of the plant. He married Lucille Selig, a native Atlantan, in 1910, and in 1912 he was elected president of the local chapter of the national Jewish fraternity B'nai B'rith. Then, on the afternoon of April 26, 1913, Mary Phagan, an employee, stopped by Frank's factory to collect her week's wages on her way to see the Confederate Memorial day parade and was murdered.

Hugh Dorsey built a case around Frank's alleged perversions. Four weeks after the murder the grand jury granted the indictment he sought.

Courtesy of the Atlanta History Center

Leo M. Frank, manager and co-owner of National Pencil Company (above), was accused of the murder of Mary Phagan.

Courtesy of the Atlanta History Center

Mary Phagan, found dead in the factory's basement.

A night watchman discovered the girls' body in the factory basement early the next morning. Sawdust and grime so covered her that when the police came they could not tell whether she was white or black. Her eyes were bruised, her cheeks cut. An autopsy would reveal that her murderer had choked her with a piece of her own underdrawers and broken her skull. The watchman, Newt Lee, summoned the police; they suspected that he might have committed the murder, and they arrested him. After inspecting the scene, the officers went to Frank's home and took him to the morgue to see the body. The sight of the corpse unsettled him, and he appeared nervous. He remembered having paid the girl her wages the previous day but could not confirm that she had then left the factory. The police would find no one who would admit to having seen her alive any later.

A number of unsolved murders had taken place in Atlanta during the previous eighteen months, and the police were under pressure to find the culprit. Early newspaper reports erroneously suggested that Mary Phagan had been raped, and crowds of people were soon milling about the police station, anxious to get their hands on whoever had committed the crime. Frank's uneasy behavior and the public's hunger for justice made him a prime suspect. He was arrested two days later.

Shortly thereafter some factory employees told a coroner's jury, convened to determine the cause of death and suggest possible suspects for investigation, that Frank had "indulged in familiarities with the women in his employ." And the proprietress of a "rooming house" signed an affidavit swearing that on the day of the murder Frank had telephoned her repeatedly, seeking a room for himself and a young girl. Both these charges were later proved false (many witnesses recanted their accusations later), but newspapers headlined them, fueling talk of Jewish men seeking Gentile girls for their pleasure. The solicitor general, Hugh Dorsey, built a case for the prosecution around

Frank's alleged perversions. Four weeks after the murder the grand jury granted the indictment Dorsey sought.

Unknown to the members of the grand jury, however, another suspect had also been arrested. He was Jim Conley, a black janitor at the factory who had been seen washing blood off a shirt there. He admitted having written two notes found near her body. They read: "Mam that negro hire down here did this i went to make water and he push me down that hole a long tall negro black that hoo it was long sleam tall negro i wright while play with me" and "he said he wood love me land dab n play like the night witch did it but that long tall black negro did buy his slef."

At first almost all investigators assumed that the author of these items had committed the crime. But Conley claimed to have written them as Frank dictated the words, first the day before the murder occurred, then, according to Conley's second affidavit, on the day of the crime.

Conley ultimately signed four affidavits, changing and elaborating his tale each time. Originally he said he had been called to Frank's office the day before the murder and asked to write phrases like "dear mother" and "a long, tall, black negro did this by himself;" and he claimed to have heard Frank mumble something like "Why should I hang?" But the newspapers found the idea of Frank's having prepared for an apparent crime of passion by asking a black janitor to write notes about it utterly ridiculous. So Harry Scott, the chief detective, said he then "pointed out things in [Conley's] story that were improbable and told him he must do better than that." Another lengthy interrogation led to the second affidavit. It stated that Frank had dictated the notes just after the murder and that Conley had removed the dead body from a room opposite Frank's office, on the second floor, and taken it by elevator to the basement. (Later evidence showed that the elevator had not been in operation from before the time of the girl's death until after her body was discovered.) A third affidavit spelled out in greater detail the steps Conley had allegedly taken in assisting Frank with the disposal of the dead girl. The Atlanta *Georgian* had already protested after the janitor's second statement that with Conley's "first affidavit repudiated and worthless it will be practically impossible to get any court to accept a second one." But Atlantans had been so conditioned to believe Frank guilty that few protested the inconsistencies in the janitor's tale.

Among those who questioned the prosecution's case against Frank were the members of the grand jury that had originally indicted him. They wanted Dorsey to reconvene them so that they could charge Conley instead. Dorsey refused, so the jury foreman did it on his own. It was the first time an Atlanta grand jury had ever considered a criminal case against the wishes of the solicitor general. Then Dorsey came back before the group and pleaded with them not to indict the black man. Exactly what he told them was not made public, but the next day the Atlanta *Constitution* reported that "the solicitor did not win his point without a difficult fight. He went in with a mass of evidence showing why the indictment of the negro would injure the state's case against Frank and stayed with the grand jurors for nearly an hour and a half."

It is difficult to say why the grand jury ultimately supported Dorsey. Perhaps they accepted the Atlanta *Georgian*'s explanation: "That the authorities have very important evidence that has not yet been disclosed to the public is certain." Or, given Southern values, they may have assumed that no attorney would base his case on the word of a black man "unless the evidence was overwhelming." In any case, the solicitor prevailed and prepared to go to trial.

The trial began on July 28, 1913, and brought forth large and ugly-tempered crowds. The heinous nature of the crime, rumors of sexual misdeeds, newspaper reports of "very important evidence that has not yet been disclosed," the solicitor general's supreme confidence, and anti-Semitism (a Georgia woman had written that "this is the first time a Jew has ever been in any serious trouble in Atlanta, and see how ready every one is to believe the worst of him") combined to create an electric tension in the city. Gossip about Frank had been widespread, and many Georgians wondered if an unbiased jury would be possible. But jury selection was swift, and in an atmosphere punctuated by spontaneous applause for the prosecuting attorney and shouts of "Hang the Jew" from throngs outside the courthouse, the proceedings unfolded.

Solicitor Dorsey opened his presentation by trying to establish where and when the crime had occurred. He elicited testimony from several witnesses about blood spots on the floor and strands of hair on a lathe that Mary Phagan had allegedly fallen against in the room opposite Frank's office. (The state biologist had specifically informed the prosecution that the hair was not Mary Phagan's, and many witnesses testified that the bloodstains could have been merely paint spots; Dorsey ignored them.)

The heart of the state's case, however, revolved around Jim Conley's narrative. Although his story had gone through several revisions during the previous weeks—all of them published in

Courtesy of the Atlanta History Center

Frank's wife, Lucille Selig Frank, sits close by him during the murder trial.

the newspapers—his courtroom account mesmerized the spectators. Conley told how he had served as a lookout in the past when Frank "entertained" women in the factory (no such women ever appeared at the trial), how after an agreed-upon signal he would lock or unlock the front door or go up to the superintendent's office for further instruction. He claimed that on the fatal day Frank had summoned him to his office, and when he arrived there, he had found his boss "standing up there at the top of the steps and shivering and trembling and rubbing his hands. . . . He had a little rope in his hands. . . . His eyes were large and they looked right funny. . . . His face was red. Yes, he had a cord in his hands. . . . After I got up to the top of the steps, he asked me 'Did you see that little girl who passed here just a while ago?' and I told him I saw one. . . . 'Well . . . I wanted to be with the little girl and she refused me, and I struck her and . . . she fell and hit her head against something, and I don't know how bad she got hurt. Of course you know I ain't built like other men.' The reason he said that was, I had seen him in a position I haven't seen any other man that has got children." Conley did not explain that last sentence; instead he went on to detail how Frank had offered, but never given him, money to dispose of the body. He said Frank had then asked him if he could write and, when he said yes, had dictated the murder notes.

When Dorsey concluded his presentation, *Frost's Magazine* of Atlanta, which had previously made no editorial comment about the case, condemned both the solicitor and Atlanta's chief detective for misleading the public into thinking that the state had sufficient evidence to warrant an accusation against Frank. "We cannot conceive," the commentary read, "that at the close of the prosecution, before the defense has presented one single witness, that it could be possible for any juryman to vote for the conviction of Leo M. Frank."

Frank had retained two of the South's best-known attorneys to defend him: Luther Z. Rosser, an expert at cross-examination, and Reuben R. Arnold, a prominent criminal lawyer. Despite their brilliant reputations, they failed to display their forensic talents when they were most needed. Rosser and Arnold cross-examined Conley for a total of sixteen hours on three consecutive days and could not shake his basic tale. He continually claimed to have forgotten anything that tended to weaken the case against Frank, and some observers thought Conley had been carefully coached by the solicitor general and his subordinates. The murder and disposal of the body would have taken at least fifty minutes to accomplish as the janitor described them, yet witnesses corroborated "Frank's recollection of his whereabouts for all but eighteen minutes of that time. Furthermore, much of Conley's narrative depended on his having removed the body to the basement via the elevator, but floor markings, the absence of blood in the elevator, and other incontrovertible evidence proved that he hadn't. Why Frank's attorneys failed to exploit these facts, and why they also failed to request a change of venue before the trial began, has never been explained. But their inability to break Conley undermined their client's case. A reporter who attended every session of the hearings later observed, "I heard Conley's evidence entire, and was impressed powerfully with the idea that the negro was repeating something he had seen. . . . Conley's story was told with a wealth of infinitesimal detail that I firmly believe to be beyond the capacity of his mind, or a far more intelligent one, to construct from his imagination."

One juror had allegedly been overheard to say, "I am glad they indicted the God damn Jew. They ought to take him out and lynch him."

Rosser and Arnold's biggest error was probably their attempt to delete from the record Conley's discussion of times he had "watched for" Frank. For a day the two men got the janitor to talk about Frank's alleged relationships with other women, hoping to poke holes in the testimony; then they tried to get the whole discussion stricken. Even one of Dorsey's assistants agreed this information should not have been allowed into the record but added that once Conley had been examined and cross-examined on the subject, it was wrong to try to expunge. "By asking that the testimony be eliminated," the Atlanta *Constitution* noted, the defense "virtually admit their failure to break down Conley."

It did not matter thereafter that witnesses came in to attest to Frank's good character and his whereabouts before, during, and after the murder. It also made little difference that Frank's explanation of his activities on the day of the murder carried, according to the *Constitution,* "the ring of truth in every sentence." Conley's narrative absolutely dominated the four-week trial.

In their summations Arnold and Rosser accused the police and solicitor general of having fabricated the evidence. Arnold stated that "if Frank hadn't been a Jew, there would never have been any prosecution against him," and he likened the entire case to the Dreyfus affair in France: "the savagry [*sic*] and venom is . . . the same."

But once again Dorsey emerged the winner. The *Constitution* described his closing argument as "one of the most wonderful efforts ever made at the Georgia bar." The solicitor reviewed the evidence, praised his opponents as "two of the ablest lawyers in the country," and then reemphasized how these men could not break Conley's basic narrative. He went on to state that although he had never mentioned the word *Jew,* once it was introduced he would use it. The Jews "rise to heights sublime," he asserted, "but they also sink to the lowest depths of degradation." He noted that Judas Iscariot, too, had been considered an honorable man before he disgraced himself. The bells of a nearby Catholic church rang, just as the solicitor was finishing. Each time Dorsey proclaimed the word *guilty* the bells chimed, and they "cut like a chill to the hearts of many who shivered involuntarily" in the courtroom.

The jury took less than four hours to find Frank guilty, and the judge, fearing mob violence, asked the defense to keep their client out of court during sentencing. Rosser and Arnold agreed. Solicitor Dorsey requested that they promise not to use Frank's absence as a basis for future appeals—even though barring a defendant from his own sentencing might constitute a denial of his right to due process of law—and the two defense attorneys assented.

Frank's attorneys kept their word and ignored the issue in their appeals for a new trial. According to state law, appeals in a capital case could be based only on errors in law and had to be heard first by the original trial judge. Rosser and Arnold based their appeal on more than 115 points, including the alleged influence of the public on the jury, the admissibility of Conley's testimony about Frank's alleged sexual activities, and affidavits from people who swore that two of the jurors were anti-Semitic. (One had allegedly been overheard to say, "I am glad they indicted the God damn Jew. They ought to take him out and lynch him. And if I get on that jury I'd hang that Jew sure.") Dorsey and his associates countered with affidavits from the jurors swearing that public demonstrations had not affected their deliberations. In his ruling, Leonard Roan, the trial judge, upheld the verdict and commented that although he was "not thoroughly convinced that Frank is guilty or innocent. The jury was convinced."

The next appeal, to the Georgia Supreme Court, centered on Roan's doubt of Frank's guilt, but the justices went along with the earlier decision. This court concluded that only the trial judge could decide whether the behavior of the spectators had prevented a fair trial and whether the jurors had been partial. The judges also ruled Conley's testimony relevant and admissible and dismissed Roan's personal expression of doubt.

At this point Frank replaced his counsel. The new attorneys did not feel bound by their predecessors' promise to Dorsey, and they pressed the argument that Frank had been denied due process by being absented from his sentencing. But the state supreme court responded that "it would be trifling with the court to . . . now come in and . . . include matters which were or ought to have been included in the motion for a new trial."

The new attorneys went on to try to get the United States Supreme Court to issue a writ of habeas corpus, on the ground that the mob had forced Frank to absent himself from the court at the time of his sentencing, and thus he was being held illegally. The Court agreed to hear arguments on that question and, after two months, rejected the plea by a vote of 7–2.

Justice Mahlon Pitney explained that errors in law, no matter how serious, could not legally be reviewed in a request for a writ of habeas corpus but only in a petition for a writ of error. And Frank's contention of having been denied due process "was waived by his failure to raise the objection in due season. . . ." In a celebrated dissent, Justices Oliver Wendell Holmes and Charles Evans Hughes concluded, "Mob law does not become due process of law by securing the assent of a terrorized jury."

It is difficult for those not well versed in the law to follow the legal reasoning behind such procedural and constitutional questions, especially when judges are not even considering disputes in testimony or blatantly expressed prejudices. Thus many people assumed that the Court was reconfirming the certainty of Frank's guilt. Afterward his attorneys sought commutation to life imprisonment rather than a complete pardon because they concluded that after all the judicial setbacks they would have a better chance with the governor that way.

Once the case came before him, Gov. John M. Slaton moved with dispatch. He listened to oral presentations from both sides, read the records, and then visited the pencil factory to familiarize himself with the scene of the crime. Since the two sides differed in their arguments on where the murder had actually taken place—the metal-lathe room on the second floor versus the factory basement—and whether the elevator had been used, the governor paid particular attention to those parts of the building. Besides the voluminous public records, Slaton received a personal letter written by the trial judge recommending commutation, a secret communication from one of Hugh Dorsey's law partners stating that Jim Conley's attorney believed his own client was guilty, and a note from a federal prisoner indicating that he had seen Conley struggling with Mary on the day of the murder.

For twelve days Slaton wrestled with the materials. On the last day he worked well into the night, and at 2:00 A.M., on June 21, 1915, he went up to his bedroom to inform his wife. "Have you reached a decision?" she asked.

"Yes," he replied, ". . . it may mean my death or worse, but I have ordered the sentence commuted."

Mrs. Slaton then kissed her husband and confessed, "I would rather be the widow of a brave and honorable man than the wife of a coward."

A ten-thousand-word statement accompanied the governor's announcement. Slaton appeared thoroughly conversant with even the minutiae of the case. He saw inconsistencies in Conley's narrative and zeroed in on them. The first significant discrepancy dealt with the factory elevator. Conley had admitted defecating at the bottom of the shaft on the morning before the murder. When police and others arrived the next day, the feces remained. Not until someone moved the elevator from the second floor was the excrement mashed, causing a foul odor. Therefore, Slaton concluded, the elevator could not have been used to carry Mary Phagan's body to the basement. Furthermore, according to scientific tests, no bloodstains appeared on the lathe or on the second floor—where the prosecution had contended that the murder had taken place—or in the elevator. But Mary's mouth, nostrils, and fingernails had been full of sawdust and grime similar to that in the basement, not on the second floor.

Other details also incriminated Conley. The murder notes found near the body had been written on order pads whose numerical sequence corresponded with those stored in the basement and not at all with those in Frank's office. Another major discrepancy that Slaton noticed concerned the strand of hair found on the metal lathe. Since the state biologist had determined that it could not have come from Mary's head, testimony from Dorsey's witness that "it looked like her hair" had to be dismissed.

Although most of Marietta knew who the killers were, a coroner's jury concluded that Frank had been lynched by persons unknown.

Privately Slaton told friends that he believed Frank was innocent, and he claimed that he would have pardoned him except that he had been asked only for a commutation and he assumed the truth would come out shortly anyway, after which the very people clamoring for Frank's death would be demanding his release. Slaton's announcement of the commutation sent thousands of Atlantans to the streets, where they burned Frank and the governor in effigy; hundreds of others marched toward Slaton's mansion, where state troopers prevented them from lynching him.

A wave of anti-Semitic demonstrations followed. Many Georgians assumed that the governor's "dastardly" actions resulted from Jewish pressures upon him. Atlanta Jews feared for their lives, and many fled the city. Responding to these actions a few days later, Slaton declared: "Two thousand years ago another Governor washed his hands of a case and turned over a Jew to a mob. For two thousand years that Governor's name has been accursed. If today another Jew were lying in his grave because I had failed to do my duty I would all through life find his blood on my hands and would consider myself an assassin through cowardice."

But the mob would not be thwarted. A fellow inmate at the state prison farm cut Frank's throat. While he was recovering in the hospital infirmary, a band of twenty-five men, characterized by their peers as "sober, intelligent, of established good name and character—good American citizens," stormed the prison farm, kidnapped Frank, and drove him 175 miles through the night to Marietta, Mary Phagan's hometown, where, on the morning of August 17, 1915, they hanged him from an oak tree. Although most of the people in Marietta knew who the killers were, a coroner's jury concluded that Frank had been lynched by persons unknown. The Pittsburgh *Gazette* restated that finding: "What the coroner's jury really meant was that Frank 'came to his death by hanging at the hands of persons whom the jury wishes to remain unknown.'

Many of Frank's friends and later defenders attributed the hanging to unbridled mob passions, but the explanation cannot suffice. "The very best people," a local judge opined at the time, had allowed the Frank case to go through all the courts, letting the judicial process take its course. Then, after every request for a new trial had been turned down, the governor had outrageously stepped in. "I believe in law and order," the judge said. "I would not help lynch anybody. But I believe Frank has had his just deserts."

Obviously, much more than just a wish to carry out the court's decision motivated Frank's killers. The man symbolized all that Georgians resented. He was the Northerner in the South, the urban industrialist who had come to transform an agrarian society, a Jew whose ancestors had killed the Savior and whose co-religionists rejected the truth of Christianity. Thus, despite the fact that the state used a black man as its key witness, something that would have been unthinkable had the accused been a Southern white Christian, Atlantans could easily believe the worst about this particular defendant.

Over the years scores of people have wondered why many Georgians were loath to suspect that a black man might have committed the murder. The answer may have come from the pastor of the Baptist church that Mary Phagan's family attended. In 1942 the Reverend L. O. Bricker wrote: "My own feelings, upon the arrest of the old negro night-watchman, were to the effect that this one old negro would be poor atonement for the life of this little girl. But, when on the next day, the police arrested a Jew, and a Yankee Jew at that, all of the inborn prejudice against the Jews rose up in a feeling of satisfaction, that here would be a victim worthy to pay for the crime."

As time passed, people no longer remembered the specific facts of the case, but they told the story of Mary Phagan and Leo Frank to their children and grandchildren. As with all folktales, some details were embellished, others were dropped; however, as the first three verses of "The Ballad of Mary Phagan" unfold, no listener can have any difficulty knowing what happened:

> *Little Mary Phagan*
> *She left her home one day;*
> *She went to the pencil-factory*
> *To see the big parade.*
>
> *She left her home at eleven,*
> *She kissed her mother good-by;*
> *Not one time did the poor child think*
> *That she was a-going to die.*
>
> *Leo Frank he met her*
> *With a brutish heart, we know;*
> *He smiled and said, "Little Mary,*
> *You won't go home no more."*

People have argued the Frank case again and again, but usually without specific knowledge, falling back on hearsay to support their positions. However, in 1982 a dramatic incident put the case back in the public spotlight. Alonzo Mann, who had been a fourteen-year-old office boy in the Atlanta pencil factory in 1913, swore that he had come into the building on the day of the murder and witnessed Jim Conley carrying Mary Phagan's body toward the steps leading to the basement. The janitor had warned him, "If you ever mention this, I'll kill you." Lonnie Mann ran home and told his mother what he had seen and she advised him to "not get involved." He obeyed her but eventually began telling his tale to friends. Finally, in 1982, two enterprising reporters filed the story in the Nashville *Tennessean.*

Mann's revelations stimulated a renewed effort to achieve a posthumous pardon for Leo Frank. Newspapers editorialized on the need to clear his name, public-opinion polls showed a majority in Georgia willing to support a pardon, and the governor of the state announced in December 1983 that he believed in Frank's innocence. But three days before Christmas the Board of Pardons and Paroles denied the request. It asserted that Mann's affidavit had provided "no new evidence to the case," that it did not matter whether Conley had carried the body to the basement or taken it via the elevator, and that "there are [so] many inconsistencies" in the various accounts of what had happened that "it is impossible to decide conclusively the guilt or innocence of Leo M. Frank."

Once again a storm broke as editorials and individuals excoriated the Board of Pardons and Paroles. The *Tennessean* said that "the board turned its back on the chance to right an egregious wrong."

The *Tennessean,* and others that were so certain about what the board should have done, had the advantage of hindsight. While this historian believes there is no question that Frank was an innocent man, the fact is that his case was much more complex than those who have read about it afterward recognize. One should not dismiss the impact of Jim Conley's performance on the witness stand or the electrifying effects of the innuendoes and charges in the courtroom that Frank might have engaged in improper sexual activities with the young people who worked in the pencil factory. Aside from the defendant's partisans, most people who heard the evidence or read about it in the newspapers during the summer of 1913 accepted its truthfulness. No reporter who attended the proceedings daily ever wrote of Frank's innocence. Long after the trial ended, O. B. Keeler and Herbert Asbury, newspapermen who covered the case, still regarded him as guilty; Harold Ross, another writer and later the founding editor of *The New Yorker,* stated merely that the "evidence did not prove [Frank] guilty beyond that 'reasonable doubt' required by law."

Another factor is the ineptitude of Frank's counsel. They failed to expose the inaccuracies in Conley's testimony, and they blundered by asking him to discuss occasions when Frank had allegedly entertained young women. This opened the door for a great deal of titillating but irrelevant material and allowed Dorsey to bring in witnesses to corroborate Conley's accusation. The defense attorneys demonstrated their limitations once more by ignoring relevant constitutional questions in their original appeal to the Georgia Supreme Court. Thus a reinvestigation of the case in the 1950s led one observer to write that "the defense of Leo Frank was one of the most ill-conducted in the history of Georgia jurisprudence."

Still another consideration is the environment in which the trial took place. Today judicial standards have been tightened, and it is unlikely that any court proceedings would be conducted in so hostile an atmosphere as that in which Frank met his doom. But that does not necessarily outweigh the effect of the witnesses' testimony and the subsequent cross-examinations. To be sure, many of the jurors feared going against popular opinion, but perhaps they might have reached an identical judgment in a hermetically sealed chamber.

There is no reason to doubt that Alonzo Mann's affidavit is accurate. Had he ignored his mother's advice and gone to the police with his information right away, Conley would surely have been arrested, the police and district attorney would not have concentrated their efforts on finding Frank guilty, and the crime would most likely have been quickly solved. But by the time the trial began, in July 1913, Mann's testimony might hardly have even seemed important.

When reviewing the case, one need not be so one-sided as to ignore the very real gut reactions that Atlantans had to Mary Phagan's murder, the trial, and Leo Frank. Prejudice did exist in Atlanta, some people did lie at the trial, and anti-Semitism did contribute to the verdict. There were also contradictions in the case that people could not understand. Rational persons believed Conley's tale, and there is no denying that the janitor made a tremendously good impression on the stand. A reporter listening to him wrote that "if so much as 5 per cent" of his story was true, it would suffice to convict Frank.

The struggle to exonerate Leo Frank continued, and in March 1986 the state Board of Pardons and Paroles reversed itself and granted a pardon. It had been granted, said the accompanying document, "in recognition of the state's failure to protect the person of Leo Frank and thereby preserve his opportunity of continued legal appeal of his conviction, and in recognition of the state's failure to bring his killers to justice, and as an effort to heal old wounds."

Not, that is, because Frank was innocent.

In the late 1980s a Georgia citizen, firmly convinced of Frank's guilt, vehemently underscored the point in a letter to the Marietta *Daily Journal:* "The pardon expressly does not relieve Mr. Frank of his conviction or of his guilt. Rather, it simply restored to him his civil rights, permitting him to vote and serve on juries, activities which, presumably, at this date are meaningless."

Meaningless they may be. Still, Leo Frank's unquiet spirit continues to vex the conscience of many Georgians eighty-one years after he died on an oak tree in Marietta.

LEONARD DINNERSTEIN is a professor of history and the director of Judaic Studies at the University of Arizona. His books include *The Leonard Frank Case* (available in paperback from the University of Georgia Press), *America and the Survivors of the Holocaust,* and *Antisemitism in America.*

From *American Heritage,* October 1996, pp. 98–102, 105–109. Copyright © 1996 by American Heritage, Inc. Reprinted by permission.

The Ambiguous Legacies of Women's Progressivism

ROBYN MUNCY

Most undergraduates come into my classroom convinced that men have so dominated American political life that they are responsible for all the good and evil in America's public past. The history of progressive reform usually persuades them otherwise. Students discover that black and white women, by the hundreds of thousands—even millions—threw themselves into progressive reform, helping to chart the direction of public policy and American values for the century to come. When they learn this, students want to believe that such activism and power must have tended unambiguously to liberate women. My job is to explain that this is not altogether the case.

The truth is that female progressive activism left a complicated legacy to twentieth-century American women. First, women reformers generally failed to overcome (and white activists often worked to sustain) racial divisions in American life. Second, black and white female progressives changed "the place" of American women in many important senses, especially in winning admittance to the polls and the policymaking table. Third, despite carving out significant public space for women, female progressives—mostly white in this case—embedded in public policy the notion that motherhood and economic independence were incompatible. Women reformers thus empowered successive generations of women in some ways while continuing to deny them the multiplicity of roles open to men.

Most women's activism took place through the many local, regional, and national organizations that women formed around 1900. The sheer number of women participating in these associations boggles the late-twentieth-century mind and suggests an engaged, cohesive female citizenry well before the achievement of women's suffrage. For instance, two hundred local white women's clubs joined together in 1890 to form the General Federation of Women's Clubs (GFWC), which by 1920 claimed over a million members. Along with the National Mothers' Congress (NMC), formed in 1897, the GFWC became a vehicle for moderate white women's political activism. In similar fashion, one hundred middle-class black women's clubs created the National Association of Colored Women (NACW) in 1896, and by 1914 this group claimed fifty thousand members in one thousand local clubs. Jewish women organized the National Council of Jewish

Women in 1893, and black Baptist women founded the Woman's Convention of the National Baptist Convention in 1900. That organization alone embraced over one million members.[1]

Although gender and race segregation were the rule among civic organizations early in this century, there were exceptions. Some women participated in gender-integrated groups like the National Child Labor Committee, which targeted child labor as an urgent public problem, and some women helped to found such gender- and race-integrated groups as the National Association for the Advancement of Colored People and the National Urban League. One of the most important progressive organizations, the National Consumers League (NCL), was ostensibly a gender-integrated group, though white women dominated it throughout the period, and thousands of women—overwhelmingly white—invigorated the Progressive party of 1912.[2]

In these organizations, women pursued an agenda that set them squarely in the social justice wing of progressivism. They aimed to ameliorate the worst suffering caused by rapid industrialization, immigration, and urbanization without forsaking

The mansion of the late Chicago businessman Charles Hull served as the original home of Jane Addams's famous social settlement. This photo of Hull House was taken around 1893. (Courtesy of the Jane Addams Memorial Collection, Special Collections, The University Library, The University of Illinois at Chicago, Negative 146.)

capitalism altogether. To do so, they strove to make government at all levels more responsible for the social and economic welfare of citizens, and though many hoped ultimately to improve the lives of America's entire working class or the whole community of color, most women reformers found that they were especially effective when they spoke specifically to the needs of women and children. Their agendas ran the gamut from anti-lynching campaigns to the prohibition of alcohol, from maximum hours laws to women's suffrage, from improved educational opportunities for African-American children to the abolition of prostitution. A brief article can glimpse only a tiny portion of their work.

One example, the campaign for protective labor legislation, reveals some of the complex meanings of women's progressivism. Although many working-class women believed the solution to workplace problems lay in unionization, some accepted the middle-class preference for legislation as the surest route to job-related improvements. Thus, both groups—organized, for instance, in the National Women's Trade Union League—lobbied their states for guarantees of factory safety, maximum hours laws, and less often, minimum wage provisions as well. Many states passed such laws and even hired women as factory inspectors to enforce them.

These legislative successes were threatened in 1905, when the U.S. Supreme Court handed down its famous *Lochner* decision. In it, the Court struck down a New York law that regulated the hours of bakers, an overwhelmingly male group. The Court ruled that states could interfere in the freedom of contract only if long hours constituted a clear health risk either to the workers themselves or to the general public.

Women reformers would not see their protective laws undone. Indeed, their determination to sustain protective labor legislation led to their participation in a second case, *Muller v. Oregon*. In 1903, Oregon passed a law that limited the hours of women in industrial work to ten per day. Two years later, the state prepared a case against laundry owner Curt Muller for violation of the law. Muller took the case to the U.S. Supreme Court, where he expected the reasoning in *Lochner* to strike down Oregon's law. The NCL, with the fiery Florence Kelley at its head, took up Oregon's fight, leading the charge for protective legislation for women workers.

Kelley, who had fought for and implemented a similar law in Illinois, hired Louis Brandeis to argue against Muller. Kelley's colleague, Josephine Goldmark, aided Brandeis in preparing a precedent-setting brief. Providing over one hundred pages of evidence that showed that women workers were hurt by long hours in ways that men were not, the brief argued that women workers warranted the state's interference in freedom of contract even when men did not. In 1908, the Supreme Court accepted their arguments, concluding that "woman's physical structure and the performance of maternal functions place her at a disadvantage in the struggle for subsistence".[3]

Women reformers thus won a progressive end—government intervention in the economy on behalf of workers—by perpetuating an older belief in male/female difference and moreover inscribing that difference into law. In this crusade, activist women, mostly middle-class and white, gained public power for themselves while at the same time cementing in public policy a view of working women as peculiarly vulnerable workers. This image of working women, while justifying legislation that genuinely helped many, made it impossible for women to compete effectively with men in many sectors of the labor market. This law created a complicated bequest to later generations of American women. Moreover, these maximum hours laws, antecedents of the Fair Labor Standards Act of 1938, also supported racial difference, not explicitly as in the case of gender, but implicitly, by omitting from coverage the occupations in which African-American women were heavily represented: agricultural labor and domestic service.

Another campaign rooted in a belief in the difference between women and men was the movement for mothers' pensions. Mothers' pensions were public stipends paid to mothers—usually widows—who found themselves without male support. The purpose of these payments was to allow impoverished mothers to remain at home with their children rather than having to put them in an orphanage or neglect them while working for wages. Led especially by the NMC and the GFWC, white activists lobbied their state governments for such programs and won them in virtually every state by the mid 1920s. These programs, unfortunately poorly funded and often unjustly administered, set the precedent for Aid to Dependent Children, a federal program enacted as part of the Social Security Act in 1935 during Franklin Roosevelt's New Deal.[4]

African-American women reformers, seeing that social workers often reserved mothers' pensions for white women, lobbied for their extension to qualified African-American women. Simultaneously however, they promoted day care services as an alternative response to mothers' need to work for pay. These services revealed not only black women's suspicion of government programs—based in part on the disenfranchisement of African-American men and spread of Jim Crow laws in the early twentieth century—but also their greater acceptance of working mothers. Poor wages for men were so endemic to African-American communities that black reformers could not so easily envision a world in which mothers were spared paid labor, and so they were more ready than white women to create institutions that allowed women to be both good mothers and good workers.[5]

In both black and white neighborhoods, day care services were often provided by other, multifaceted progressive women's institutions. Indeed, the quintessential progressive women's institutions were social settlements and neighborhood unions. Social settlements first appeared in the United States in the 1880s. They were places where middle-class women and men lived in the midst of working-class, largely immigrant neighborhoods. Their purpose was to bridge the gap between the classes. By the turn of the century, settlements existed in most sizable cities. Educated women took the lead in the establishment of settlement communities. Once acquainted with their working-class neighbors, these middle-class women created social services that they believed their neighbors needed. Much of the time, settlement residents piloted local health services, educational series, or recreational programs and then lobbied their municipal, county, or state government to provide permanent

To counter the claim that suffragists deserted their families or disrespected motherhood, suffragists often took their children on parade with them, as some did in this 1912 demonstration in New York City. (Library of Congress, Division of Prints and Photographs.)

funding and oversight. In this way, settlement residents became leaders in progressive reform.

The most famous social settlement was Hull House in Chicago. Founded in 1889 by Jane Addams and Ellen Gates Starr, Hull House set the standard for the hundreds of settlements that subsequently opened in cities all over the country. Beginning with a day nursery (considered a regrettable, stop-gap measure by the white reformers) and evening classes and clubs for its immigrant neighbors, Hull House eventually housed seventy middle-class residents, a library for the neighborhood, a community theater, a gym, playground, labor museum, many classrooms and clubhouses for adults and children, and a coffee house. It offered a visiting nurse and employment counseling to the neighborhood, as well as a meeting ground for unions and political groups. It was a vital hub of neighborhood life and provided the initiative and/or support for much progressive legislation, including protective legislation for women workers and children, women's suffrage, workers' compensation programs, increased funding for public education, and the creation of the U.S. Children's Bureau.

Besides women's suffrage, the Children's Bureau may have been progressive women's most significant national achievement. The idea for a federal agency devoted to child welfare is usually credited to Lillian Wald, founder and head resident of the Henry Street Settlement in New York City. Herself a visiting nurse, Wald joined Jane Addams in creating a female reform network that stretched across the country by 1903. That year Wald first proposed that the U.S. government create a bureau to collect information and propose legislation of benefit to the country's children. In 1912, Congress finally rewarded the women's lobbying efforts by establishing the Children's Bureau in the U.S. Department of Labor.

Addams immediately argued that a woman should head the new agency and proposed in particular Julia Lathrop, a long-time resident of Hull House. To everyone's surprise, President William Howard Taft accepted the recommendation, and

Lathrop became the first woman ever to head a federal agency. She quickly hired other women to staff the bureau, which became a female beachhead in the federal government for decades to come. In 1921, Lathrop and her staff drafted and won from Congress the first piece of federal social/welfare legislation: the Sheppard-Towner Maternity and Infancy Act, which sent public health nurses into nearly every corner of America to teach pregnant women how best to care for themselves and their newborns. This set another precedent for New Deal programs.[6]

Although African-American women also founded social settlements, as did some interracial groups, more typical of black women's institution building was the neighborhood union. Such entities differed from social settlements mainly in that few reformers actually lived in them, reflecting in part the tendency of black women reformers to be married while their white counterparts often remained unmarried. Many of these progressive institutions called themselves missions, community centers, institutional churches, or even schools, but like settlements, they provided meeting places and services for those living nearby, and they joined the middle and working classes in local political crusades.[7]

The most famous such center was the Neighborhood Union in Atlanta. Founded in 1908 by Lugenia Burns Hope, the union provided day care services, health care and health education, and playgrounds. It sponsored clubs and classes for children and adults alike, and organized lobbying campaigns to obtain greater funding for the education of African-American children, as well as improved street lights and sanitation in black neighborhoods. Members urged public relief for the unemployed. The Neighborhood Union's appeals for governmental support remind us that even though black women had less hope for a positive response from government officials than white women, they did not—even in this hour of miserable race relations—give up entirely on obtaining government resources.[8]

Just as social settlements and neighborhood unions were usually race-segregated, so were organizations that fought for women's suffrage. Ratification of the Nineteenth Amendment in 1920 stood as a monumental victory for women progressives; it is one of the signal achievements of progressive reform. But even that fight to expand democracy was marked by racial division and hierarchy. Hoping to win support from white southerners, leaders in the North refused to admit black women's clubs to the National American Woman Suffrage Association, which, with two million members in 1917, was the largest suffrage organization in U.S. history. In response, black women formed their own suffrage associations—like the Equal Suffrage League founded by Ida Wells-Barnett in Chicago—or fought for enfranchisement through multi-issue groups like the NACW or the black Baptist Women's Convention.[9] Complicating black women's struggle for suffrage was their simultaneous fight for the re-enfranchisement of African-American men in the South, whose right to vote was eroding in the face of brutal violence, literacy tests, and poll taxes. When the women's suffrage amendment passed, no state could deny suffrage on

Lugenia Burns Hope founded the Neighborhood Union in Atlanta. While white progressives in the South usually pursued policies that assured white dominance, Hope's activism reminds us that southern African Americans were also progressives. (Courtesy of the National Park Service, Mary McLeod Bethune Council House National Historic Site, Washington, DC.)

the basis of sex, but the same measures that disenfranchised black men in the South also prevented most black women from approaching the polls. Thus, not until the Voting Rights Act of 1965 did women's suffrage achieve a complete victory.

Black and white women were integral to progressivism. No history of progressive reform could possibly be complete without discussing the campaign for women's suffrage, the work of neighborhood unions, or the struggle for protective legislation.

These efforts by millions of American women suggest several conclusions. This history illuminates the source of sometimes contradictory views of women embedded in public policy and personal identities since the Progressive Era: while most American women received the vote by 1920, imparting a new parity with men in public life, the same period produced legislation that construed women primarily as mothers rather than as workers and as more vulnerable, weaker workers than men. This ambiguous legacy has reverberated through the twentieth century.

The history of these women reformers moreover reveals some of the ways that race has shaped women's experience and political agendas in the past, and it embodies the ways that racism has crippled democracy and betrayed democratic movements in the United States. It reminds us that the renewed political life we might create in the twenty-first century, if it is to fulfill

the promise of democracy, must strive to overcome the racial hierarchy that progressives—and all of their successors—failed to defeat.

Notes

1. Karen J. Blair, *Clubwoman as Feminist. True Womanhood Redefined, 1868–1914* (New York: Holmes and Meier, 1980); Evelyn Brooks Higginbotham, *Righteous Discontent. The Women's Movement in the Black Baptist Church* (Cambridge: Harvard University Press, 1993), 8; and Stephanie Shaw, "Black Club Women and the Creation of the National Association of Colored Women," *Journal of Women's History 3* (Fall 1991): 10–25.

2. Dorothy Salem, *To Better Our World: Black Women in Organized Reform, 1890–1920* (Brooklyn: Carlson, 1990), 45–46, 100–14, 146–96, 274; Kathryn Kish Sklar, "The Historical Foundations of Women's Power in the Creation of the American Welfare State, 1830–1930," in *Mothers of a New World: Maternalist Politics and the Origins of Welfare States,* ed. Seth Koven and Sonya Michel (New York: Routledge, 1993), 43–93; and Robyn Muncy, "'Women Demand Recognition': Women Candidates in Colorado's Election of 1912," in *We Have Come to Stay: American Women and Political Parties, 1880–1960,* ed. Melanie Gustafson, Kristie Miller, and Elisabeth Israels Perry (Albuquerque: University of New Mexico Press, 1999), 45–54.

3. Muller v. Oregon, 208 U.S. 412; Nancy Woloch, *Muller v. Oregon: A Brief History with Documents* (Boston: Bedford Books, 1996); Sybil Lipschultz, "Social Feminism and Legal Discourse," *Yale Journal of Law and Feminism 2* (Fall 1989): 131–60; and Kathryn Kish Sklar, "Hull House in the 1890s: A Community of Women Reformers," *Signs* 10 (Summer 1985): 658–77.

4. Molly Ladd-Taylor, *Mother-Work: Women, Child Welfare, and the State, 1890–1930* (Urbana: University of Illinois Press, 1994), 135–66; and Theda Skócpol, *Protecting Soldiers and Mothers: The Political Origins of Social Policy in the United States* (Cambridge: Belknap Press of Harvard University, 1992), 424–79.

5. Linda Gordon, "Black and White Visions of Welfare: Women's Welfare Activism: 1890–1945," *Journal of American History 78* (September 1991): 559–90; Eileen Boris, "The Power of Motherhood: Black and White Activist Women Redefine the 'Political,'" *Yale Journal of Law and Feminism 2* (Fall 1989): 25–49.

6. Robyn Muncy, *Creating a Female Dominion in American Reform, 1890–1935* (New York: Oxford University Press, 1991).

7. Salem, *To Better Our World;* and Elisabeth Lasch-Quinn, *Black Neighbors: Race and the Limits of Reform in the American Settlement House Movement, 1890–1945* (Chapel Hill: University of North Carolina Press, 1993).

8. Jacqueline Anne Rouse, *Lugenia Burns Hope: Black Southern Reformer* (Athens: University of Georgia Press, 1989).

9. Rosalyn Terborg-Penn, "Discrimination Against Afro-American Women in the Woman's Movement, 1830–1920," in *The Afro-American Woman: Struggles and Images,* ed. Sharon Harley and Rosalyn Terborg-Penn (Port Washington, NY: National University Publications, 1978); and Higginbotham, *Righteous Discontent, 226.*

Bibliography

In addition to the works cited in the endnotes, the following sources are helpful for studying women's activism in the Progressive Era.

Boris, Eileen. *Home to Work: Motherhood and the Politics of Industrial Homework in the United States.* New York: Cambridge University Press, 1994.

Cott, Nancy F. *The Grounding of Modern Feminism.* New Haven: Yale University Press, 1987.

Crocker, Ruth Hutchinson. *Social Work and Social Order: The Settlement Movement in Two Industrial Cities, 1889–1930.* Urbana: University of Illinois, 1992.

Goodwin, Joanne L. *Gender and the Politics of Welfare Reform: Mothers' Pensions in Chicago, 1911–4929.* Chicago: University of Chicago Press, 1997.

Gordon, Linda. *Pitied But Not Entitled: Single Mothers and the History of Welfare, 1890–1935.* New York: Maxwell MacMillan International, 1994.

Hewitt, Nancy A. and Suzanne Lebsock, eds. *Visible Women: New Essays on American Activism.* Urbana: University of Illinois Press, 1993.

Knupfer, Anne Meis. *Toward a Tenderer Humanity and a Nobler Womanhood: African American Women's Clubs in Turn-of-the-Century Chicago.* New York: New York University Press, 1996.

Neverdon-Morton, Cynthia. *Afro-American Women of the South and the Advancement of the Race, 1895–1925.* Knoxville: University of Tennessee Press, 1989.

Scott, Anne Firor. *Natural Allies: Women's Associations in American History.* Urbana: University of Illinois Press, 1991.

Robyn Muncy is an associate professor of history at the University of Maryland. She is the author of *Creating a Female Dominion in American Reform, 1880–1935* (1991) and coauthor with Sonya Michel of *Engendering America: A Documentary History, 1865–The Present* (1999).

From *OAH Magazine of History,* Spring 1999, pp. 15–19. Copyright © 1999 by Organization of American Historians. Reprinted by permission of Organization of American Historians.

Influenza 1918

The Enemy Within

In the midst of an unprecedented public health crisis, can a government protect the welfare of its citizens at home while rushing millions of troops to battlefields half a world away? In 1918 America faced just such a challenge.

CHRISTINE M. KREISER

Horse-drawn carts plied the streets with a call to bring out the dead in the city where bodies lay unburied for days. The afflicted died by the thousands, and survivors lived in fear. But this wasn't medieval Europe being stalked by the Black Death. This was Philadelphia, October 1918, and the city was under siege from a new variant of one of mankind's oldest specters: influenza.

Between September 1918 and June 1919, 675,000 Americans died as a result of the "Spanish flu" epidemic—more than the combined combat deaths of U.S. forces in World War I, World War II, Korea and Vietnam. Conservative estimates place the worldwide death toll at 30 million to 40 million. It was, however, a largely forgotten episode until the recent avian flu scare raised concerns that, today, a quickly mutating influenza virus could paralyze entire nations and claim a billion or more lives.

Before the autumn of 1918, Americans were more likely to be stricken with war fever than the flu. The United States had entered World War I late, but it did so with gusto. Millions mobilized for deployment overseas, and those on the home front braved gasless days, meatless days and wheatless meals. Making the world safe for democracy wouldn't come cheap, and the government funded more than 50 percent of its war effort with money borrowed from the public. Liberty Loan drives were held all across the country, and not chipping in was tantamount to treason. In the words of Secretary of the Treasury William McAdoo, "A man who can't lend his govt $1.25 a week at the rate of 4% interest is not entitled to be an American citizen."

The flu lurking in the midst of this patriotic fervor, however, would prove far more lethal than trench warfare and poison gas. Most alarming was the fact that the disease ravaged previously healthy young adults in their 20s and 30s: the men and women who worked the factories, cleaned the streets, tended the sick—and fought the wars.

Many assumed, wrongly, that the flu had originated in Spain, where 8 million fell ill during a wave of relatively mild flu that had swept the globe in the spring of 1918. Because Spain was neutral and its press uncensored during the war, it was one of the few places in Europe where news about the epidemic was being reported. Whatever its origins, the flu was taking a toll on front-line troops. Commander Erich von Ludendorff blamed the disease for the failure of Germany's major spring offensive. "It was a grievous business," he said, "having to listen every morning to the chiefs of staff's recital of the number of influenza cases, and their complaints about the weakness of their troops."

Influenza wasn't Ludendorff's only obstacle. General John "Black Jack" Pershing, commander in chief of the American Expeditionary Forces in Europe, pushed relentlessly to build up troop strength. The U.S. Army had fewer than 100,000 soldiers when it entered the war—the general's plans called for approximately 4 million. The Americans would not simply plug holes in the British and French lines. The AEF would stand alone, and march to victory under the American flag. To do that, Pershing needed more men, more materiel. Always, endlessly, more.

Back home, the ramp-up hit a snag. On March 4, 1918, the Army installation at Camp Funston, Kan., reported a single case of flu. Before the end of the month, 1,100 men had been hospitalized, and 20 percent of those men developed pneumonia. Flu spread rapidly among Army camps as troops were rushed through on their way to the front. But the outbreak had subsided by summer, and it looked like the worst was over.

It wasn't.

Only a Matter of Hours

Camp Devens, 35 miles northwest of Boston, was seriously overcrowded. Built to house 36,000 troops, it contained more than 45,000 in early September 1918. The flu struck there with a suddenness and virulence that had never been seen before. "These men start with what appears to be an ordinary attack

Flu Facts

- The average age of flu victims was 33.
- The Actuarial Society of America determined in 1918 that the average loss of active life for every flu victim was 25 years, and that the total number of years lost in the U.S. was 10 million.
- The flu virus had an incubation period of 24 to 72 hours, meaning that a person who showed no symptoms could pass on the virus.
- The flu virus could survive in the air for up to 24 hours. The lower the humidity, the longer the virus lived.
- In most cities, the epidemic lasted 6 to 8 weeks.
- Home remedies for the flu included a teaspoon of sugar with turpentine or kerosene, or poultices made from goose grease and onions tied in a piece of red flannel and placed on the chest.
- 3 Navy nurses were posthumously awarded the Navy Cross for "distinguished service and devotion to duty" during the epidemic. They all died of the flu.

of LaGrippe or Influenza, and when brought to the Hosp. they very rapidly develop the most vicious type of Pneumonia that has ever been seen," wrote Roy Grist, a doctor at the Camp Devens hospital. "Two hours after admission they have the Mahogany spots over the cheek bones, and a few hours later you can begin to see the Cyanosis extending from their ears and spreading all over the face, until it is hard to distinguish the coloured man from the white. . . . It is only a matter of hours then until death comes. . . . We have been averaging about 100 deaths per day. . . . We have lost an outrageous number of Nurses and Drs."

Flu victims were wracked by fevers often spiking higher than 104 degrees and body aches so severe that the slightest touch was torture. Cyanosis was perhaps the most terrifying hallmark of the pneumonia that often accompanied this flu. A lack of oxygen in the blood turned one's skin a bluish-black—leading to speculation that the Black Death had again come calling.

While Devens tried unsuccessfully to contain the outbreak, a similar situation was developing at Commonwealth Pier, a naval facility in Boston. Flu was reported there in late August, but the war would not wait. Sailors were shipped out to New Orleans, Puget Sound and the Great Lakes Naval Training Station near Chicago. Josie Mabel Brown was a young Navy nurse living in St. Louis, Mo., when she was called to duty at Great Lakes. "There was a man lying on the bed dying and one was lying on the floor," she said of her first visit to a sick ward. "Another man was on a stretcher waiting for the fellow on the bed to die. . . . We wrapped him in a winding sheet and left nothing but the big toe on the left foot out with a shipping tag on it to tell the man's rank, his nearest of kin, and hometown. . . . Our Navy bought the whole city of Chicago out of sheets. There wasn't a sheet left in Chicago. All a boy got when he died was a winding sheet and a wooden box; we just couldn't get enough caskets."

Three hundred sailors from Boston landed at the Philadelphia Navy Yard on September 7; on the 19th the *Philadelphia Inquirer* reported that 600 sailors and marines had been hospitalized with the flu. It should have been apparent to city officials that a potential crisis loomed. In Massachusetts the flu had spread rapidly from military encampments to the public at large. Medical practitioners in Philadelphia called for a quarantine, but Wilmer Krusen, director of the city's Department of Public Health and Charities, declined. There was recent precedent for such action: Quarantines were regularly enacted during a terrifying polio epidemic in 1916. But that was in peacetime. No civilian deaths from flu had been reported locally, and a Liberty Loan parade—perhaps the largest parade Philadelphia had ever seen—was scheduled for the end of the month. A quarantine would only cause panic, and the city would most certainly not meet its quota of war-bond sales.

'I was very sick. . . . The doctor told my mother it wasn't necessary to feed me anymore.'

Every American seemingly had a personal stake in winning the war. Even children were eager to do their bit. Anna Milani, who was a child in Philadelphia during the epidemic, remembered the rhyme she and her friends would sing in the street:

Tramp, tramp, tramp the boys are marching
I spied Kaiser at the door
We'll get a lemon pie
And we'll squash it in his eye
And there won't be any Kaiser anymore

The parade stepped off as planned on September 28 with marching bands, military units, women's auxiliaries and Boy Scout troops. Some 200,000 spectators thronged the two-mile-long parade route in a show of civic pride. Three days later, 635 new civilian cases of flu, and 117 civilian deaths from the disease and its complications, were reported in Philadelphia.

Worry Is Useless

October 1918 was brutal in the City of Brotherly Love. Schools, churches, theaters and saloons were closed. So many Bell Telephone operators were home sick that the company placed notices in city newspapers pleading with the public to "cut out every call that is not absolutely necessary that the essential needs of the government, doctors and nurses may be met." Krusen authorized Bell to discontinue service to those making unnecessary calls, and 1,000 customers were eventually cut off.

Even if emergency calls did get through, there weren't enough people to answer them. A quarter of Philadelphia's doctors and nurses were away serving in the military. Volunteers were called, but many were too sick themselves—or too frightened of contracting the disease—to be of much help. Entire families were stricken, and the prognosis was often grim. "My mother called the doctor because the whole family was sick with this flu," said Harriet Hasty Ferrell. "And I, being an infant baby, was very sick, to the point that the doctor thought that I would not make it. He told my mother it wasn't necessary to feed me anymore."

Still, there were those who tried to quell panic. An October 6 editorial in the *Inquirer* advised: "Live a Clean life. Do not even discuss influenza. . . . Worry is useless. Talk of cheerful things instead of the disease."

No amount of happy talk could make the nightmare go away. Between October 12 and October 19, 4,597 Philadelphians died of the flu and related respiratory diseases, and survivors struggled to carry out familiar mourning rituals. "We couldn't go inside the church," one city native remembered. "The priest would say Mass on the step, and we would all be congregated outside. . . . They figured maybe outside you wouldn't catch the germ." Another recalled that her 13-year-old cousin, who was sick with the flu, had to be carried to the cemetery wrapped in a blanket in order to say the traditional Jewish prayers at his mother's funeral service. Hundreds of unburied corpses posed another serious health risk. Caskets were in such short supply that the J.G. Brill Co., which manufactured trolley cars, donated packing crates to fill the need. The Bureau of Highways used a steam shovel to dig mass graves in a potter's field. By the end of the month, the Spanish flu had claimed 11,000 victims in Philadelphia and 195,000 nationwide.

The tragedy played out with varying degrees of severity across the country. The city of San Francisco, where the flu hit hardest in late October, mandated that gauze masks be worn in public at all times. The mandate was widely followed, though in reality, masks did little to prevent the spread of flu. They were also uncomfortable and inconvenient, and the public would not tolerate them for long. Even officials showed a less than vigilant attitude when the mayor, a city supervisor, a Superior Court judge, a congressman and a rear admiral were photographed at a prizefight sans their protective masks. And there were those who claimed the act was an unconstitutional attack on personal freedom: "If the Board of Health can force people to wear masks," said the *San Francisco Chronicle,* "then it can force them to submit to inoculations, or any experiment or indignity."

Doctors searched desperately for a cure, or at least a stop-gap measure. But they were on the wrong track. Conventional wisdom held that the flu was caused by bacteria; vaccines to fight bacterial infections, however, had no effect on the disease. (Flu was not identified as a virus until 1933.) The epidemic was a crushing blow to medical science, which had only recently come to be seen as a professional discipline.

Government agencies fared no better. Surgeon General Rupert Blue, head of the U.S. Public Health Service, was aware that an outbreak of flu was possible. But in July 1918, he denied a request for $10,000 to be dedicated to pneumonia research, and he made no other preparations. Blue's first public warning came in mid-September and included such tips as "Avoid tight clothes, tight shoes, tight gloves—seek to make nature your ally not your prisoner" and "Help by choosing and chewing your food well." Congress appropriated $1 million in emergency

funding for USPHS; Blue eventually returned $115,000 to the government.

Worse still, the government contributed to the national paranoia surrounding all things German. The USPHS officer for northeastern Mississippi planted stories in the local papers that "the Hun resorts to unwanted murder of innocent noncombatants. . . . He has [at]tempted to spread sickness and death thru germs, and has done so in authenticated cases." Lieutenant Colonel Philip Doane, head of the Health and Sanitation Section of the Emergency Fleet Corporation, which oversaw U.S. shipyards, theorized that U-boats had delivered German spies to America "to turn loose Spanish influenza germs in a theatre or some other place where large numbers of persons are assembled." So persistent was the belief that Germany had somehow launched a biological attack that USPHS laboratories devoted precious time to investigating claims that Bayer aspirin, which was manufactured in the States under a German-held patent, had been laced with deadly flu germs.

"Let the curse be called the German plague," declared *The New York Times* in October. "Let every child learn to associate what is accursed with the word German not in the spirit of hate but in the spirit of contempt born of the hateful truth which Germany has proved herself to be."

Over There

The death toll mounted at home through September and October even as President Woodrow Wilson was faced with General Pershing's demands for more soldiers. Through the summer, Americans were being sent to Europe at the rate of 250,000 a month. But flu was running rampant on troopships, and those who survived the interminable voyage simply spread the disease to frontline staging areas. Wilson was urged by several advisers not to dispatch additional troops until the epidemic had been contained. The president consulted with his chief of staff General Peyton March, who conceded that conditions on the overseas transports were hardly ideal. He would not, however, concede anything that might stand in the way of winning the war. "Every such soldier who has died [on a troopship]," said March, "just as surely played his part as his comrade who died in France." Wilson relented. The transports continued.

Wilson had won a second term in 1916 because he had kept the United States out of the war. Once war was declared in 1917, however, he could not afford to waver in his commitment to seeing the conflict through to Allied victory. To shore up public support, Wilson created the Committee on Public Information a week after declaring war on Germany. (One of its lasting contributions was the Uncle Sam "I want you" recruiting poster.) The CPI'S news division issued thousands of press releases and syndicated features about the war that made their way, often unedited, into newspapers across the country. The CPI also had a pictorial publicity division, an advertising division and a film division. In short, it used every possible media source to influence public opinion.

Wilson's zeal for advancing democratic ideals abroad was secured by his willingness to suppress them at home. Dissent

1918 Flu Deaths Compared to 20th-Century U.S. Battle Fatalities

Influenza	675,000
World War I	53,000
World War II	292,000
Korea	34,000
Vietnam	58,000

1918 Flu Deaths Compared to Other 20th-Century Epidemics in the U.S.

Influenza	675,000
HIV/AIDS*	540,000
Polio**	13,000

* cumulative for 1981–2004
** cumulative for three worst outbreaks: 1916, 1949, 1952

was not tolerated. Under the 1917 Espionage Act, roundly criticized as being unconstitutional, Socialist leaders Eugene Debs and Victor Berger were sentenced to a combined 30 years in prison for their antiwar protests. The act also gave the postmaster general the right to determine what constituted unpatriotic or subversive reading material and ban it from the U.S. mail. The Justice Department authorized the 200,000 members of a volunteer group called the American Protective League to report on suspected spies, "slackers" who didn't buy war bonds and anyone who voiced opposition to the government.

In this hyper-patriotic atmosphere, fighting the flu came Second to winning the war. Public officials, and the public itself, downplayed the seriousness of the silent enemy within and focused on the more tangible enemies of a nation at war. The Germans could be defeated on the battlefield overseas and by surveillance at home. Nothing could stop a disease that immobilized great cities for weeks and carried off hundreds of thousands in the prime of life.

And then, it was over. By the end of 1918, deaths from flu and pneumonia nationwide had subsided greatly, and a third wave in the spring of 1919 left far fewer casualties in its wake. "In fight of our knowledge of influenza and the way it works," explained Dr. Shirley Fannin, an epidemiologist and current director of disease control for Los Angeles County, Calif., "we do understand that it probably ran out of fuel. It ran out of people who were susceptible."

Those who survived their exposure to the flu developed immunity to the disease, but not to its lasting consequences. William Maxwell, writer and longtime editor at *The New Yorker,* was a 10-year-old in Lincoln, Ill., when the flu struck his family, killing his mother. "I realized for the first time, and forever, that we were not safe. We were not beyond harm," he remembered eight decades later. "From that time on there was a sadness, which had not existed before, a deep down sadness that never quite went away. . . . Terrible things could happen—to anybody."

For all the advances in medical science, it is still not clear where the 1918 virus originated, or why it took such a toll on healthy young adults. Flu viruses are avian in origin and extremely adaptable. According to the National Institutes of Health, one new strain of flu appeared in humans between the Hong Kong flu outbreak in 1969 (the last flu pandemic) and 1977. Between 1997 and 2004, five new strains appeared.

Modern researchers agree that it is probably impossible to prevent an outbreak of flu, but it is possible to prepare for one—if the public, health officials and government agencies can agree on a plan of action. Today, as in 1918, a global conflict demands an ever-increasing amount of resources. The government has enacted extraordinary measures in the name of national security. And a public health crisis of the magnitude of the 1918 epidemic is almost incomprehensible. After all, it's only the flu.

A Day to Remember: January 16, 1920

CHARLES PHILLIPS

The night before the manufacture, transport and sale of alcoholic beverages became illegal in the United States of America, saloons and liquor stores held cut-rate sales. Nightclubs across the country staged mock funerals, some of them featuring coffins for the dying god John Barleycorn, whose effigy they would soon lay to rest. A rich habitué of the Park Avenue Club in New York City hosted a fancy formal at which the black-clad attendees tasted black caviar and toasted the coming of a society that banned drinking with champagne served in specially crafted black glasses. Newspaper reporters scoured the streets of New York and New Orleans and San Francisco looking for sensational accounts of last minute revelers before the Volstead Act, which was passed to provide for the enforcement of the 18th Amendment, went into effect on January 16, 1920.

The amendment itself had been ratified by a sufficient number of state legislatures to become the law of the land in 1919, plunging the country into what future U.S. President Herbert Hoover would call a "noble experiment" but what American citizens described more soberly as "Prohibition." The morning the Volstead Act went into effect, activists and supporters of Prohibition celebrated the victory of the "drys" over the "wets." The parades and extravagant rallies held in some cities, but especially in small towns throughout the land, boasted local politicians and celebrities who gave endless speeches extolling the virtues of abstinence and condemning the evils of demon rum, just as they had been doing for most of a century. In Washington, D.C., hundreds of congressmen attended the parade along with members of the Anti-Saloon League. Among the speakers was Secretary of State William Jennings Bryan, who in his many failed campaigns for president had become the spokesman for rural America.

"They are dead," came his famous clarion-call voice, "that sought the child's life. They are dead! They are dead! King Alcohol has slain more children than that Herod ever did." But now, he predicted, "The revolution that rocked the foundation of the Republic will be felt all over the earth."

It was a change that had been a long time coming. Since the late 18th century, Americans occasionally banded together to try to persuade, cajole or force other Americans to quit drinking. Such temperance movements were cyclical, much like American religious revivals, and they usually appealed to evangelical, middle-class, native-born Protestants. In the two decades before the Civil War, temperance movements had some effect in reducing the amount of liquor Americans drank, which from Colonial times had been prodigious. By the 1840s, middle-class Americans no longer automatically entertained guests with a drink as they had in the previous century, and a country intent on developing its industry had begun to demand discipline among its workforce by banning the once frequent practice of drinking during special breaks on the job.

Alcohol consumption, however, began to increase again after the mid-19th century with the coming of German, Irish and other immigrants, whose drinking habits were European and who tended to congregate in saloons after work to socialize and discuss politics. In fact, by the late 19th century, saloons had become immigrant political institutions, the home of city bosses and political mechanics who found work for their ethnic kin in return for political loyalty and votes on Election Day. Prohibition, the heir to the temperance movement, took on a nativist cast and was often associated with progressive campaigns against corruption and bossism. It had become an attempt by middle-class Protestants, who felt their social and political dominance threatened by Catholic immigrants, urbanization and industrialization, to preserve the status quo.

By the 1870s, the temperance movement had also become associated with women's reform, because of the real threat that male drunkards posed to their wives and children. By common law, men controlled not only their own property but also that of their wives, and they could literally drink the family into destitution. Tales of wayward drunkards who physically abused their mates became standard fare in temperance tracts and at temperance meetings, where attendees might pledge total abstinence, place a capital T by their names and become Tee-Totalers. But the prominence of mostly middle-class women in the temperance movement of the late 19th century had also to do with a century's worth of social, economic and ideological developments.

As American society grew more industrial it developed what historians call the doctrine of separate spheres—the notion that a man's world was in the workplace and a woman's at home, but that both were of equal importance to family life. Male and female patterns of drinking began to diverge, as men did their social drinking outside the home and women, especially middle-class women, aspired to "true womanhood," which meant that while they were more delicate than men, they were also more morally refined. Once considered weak and immoral as a sex, they were now viewed as passionless and proper. It was their duty to see to the moral education and refinement of future generations, to use their roles as mothers to set good examples for their children and as ladies for their employees and less fortunate neighbors. With such a charge, most middle-class women quit drinking altogether.

When cheap immigrant labor provided middle-class families with domestics to handle the household drudgery, those morally upright women expanded their duties from managing the household to participating in charitable work in the community and, eventually, to taking up social issues such as abolition, suffrage and temperance.

On December 23, 1873, a Harvard-educated temperance advocate trained in homeopathic medicine, Dr. Diocletian Lewis, gave a temperance lecture in Hillsboro, Ohio, called "The Duty of Christian Women in the Cause of Temperance" that inspired local women to do as he said his mother had done when she was at wit's end over his father's drinking: invade saloons and shops that sold alcoholic beverages and persuade the owners to quit trafficking in drink. Throughout the winter, women in other towns followed their example, and after *The New York Times* picked up the story, thousands of women in hundreds of communities also organized into groups that invaded saloons and demanded pledges from bartenders, prayed, sang hymns, marched on the streets outside bars and drugstores, formed picket lines to prevent beverage deliveries, took down the names of patrons who ignored them and held mass temperance meetings. The short-lived Women's Temperance Crusade gave birth to the Women's Christian Temperance Union (WCTU), which under the leadership of Frances Willard became the major vehicle for prohibition over the next two decades. Willard and others spread the organization into the South and West, where they became associated with the whole gamut of agrarian and radical Western reforms, from suffrage to the free-coinage of silver.

By 1890 more than half the counties in America contained WCTU organizations and a Prohibition Party had been formed to take the fight to the ballot box. Republicans uneasily adopted prohibition as a cause, while Democrats—outside the South—opposed it. Catholics, Germans (both Lutheran and Catholic), the Irish, eastern Europeans, the working class, urbanites, and those in counties where a disproportionate number of residents were male tended to vote against such amendments. Evangelical Protestant farmers tended to support them. Prohibition was a domestic issue and a small town and rural issue, all arenas in which the effects of excessive drinking tended to be most obvious.

The turn of the century witnessed the birth of the Anti-Saloon League. Prohibition Party gatherings could have been mistaken for revivals, but not so Anti-Saloon League meetings: They were all business. Like the Women's Temperance Crusade, the Anti-Saloon League began in Ohio, but unlike the women's temperance organizations, the Anti-Saloon League limited itself to one issue, prohibition, and would back any candidate, accept any proposal and support any group that advanced the cause in any fashion. The prototype of modern political pressure groups, the first league was formed in 1893 and became national in 1895 when the Ohio group merged with an organization in Washington, D.C.

The league depended not on volunteers but paid staff, mostly recruited from Protestant churches, and its general counsel and legislative superintendent, Wayne B. Wheeler, would actually write the Volstead Act. Though league members would use any argument to advance their cause, they concentrated not on individual drinkers or domestic issues, but on propaganda about the massive influence of the liquor "interests" in American—especially big-city—politics, and on economic arguments that claimed intemperance hurt worker productivity and that saloon districts discouraged growth. Knowing that prohibition seemed a way to instill discipline for emerging manufacturers confronting workers with traditional drinking habits, the league pitched its message to businessmen; John D. Rockefeller and Henry Ford, for example, were early and substantial patrons.

The Anti-Saloon League and other prohibitionists pointed to the growing incidence of radical protest from such organizations as the Industrial Workers of the World (IWW) and argued that it spread in step with liquor consumption. Blaming working-class drinking for industrial conflict was disingenuous at best, since almost all unions—including the IWW—insisted that their members remain sober, and many required a pledge to that effect in order to become a member.

But middle-class voters accepted the link between drinking and labor militancy because they did not wish to face the true source of the disorder: industrial growth. Meanwhile, unions and workers were hostile to the Anti-Saloon League not for its anti-alcohol message but for diverting attention from pressing issues of wealth and power. Industrialists, on the other hand, supported the league for just that reason, and most league leaders were members of the Republican Party. The result was that farmers and their wives voted rural areas dry under local option laws in order to protect their families from—and impose their sober Protestant-American values and work habits on—a "foreign" working class. Their native-born allies in the urban middle class voted their states dry to restore the order they believed was being disrupted by slum-dwelling alien anarchists. Once again, small towns proved the seedbed for the struggles over liquor, with nativism its engine of growth.

By 1916, 21 state legislatures had outlawed saloons. That year, too, voters sent a "dry" majority to Congress. Those congressmen secured the passage of the 18th Amendment. Intended to create a nation of hardworking, sober, responsible citizens, Prohibition instead quickly transformed a nation of basically law-abiding citizens into a nation of lawbreakers. In the big cities, Prohibition had consistently been voted down, and it was in urban America that the new law was consistently violated. Neighborhood folk set up stills in their basements, brewing bathtub gin and other alcoholic concoctions. Within the neighborhoods, informal networks quickly developed, as grocers stocked the raw materials necessary to brew moonshine and former saloon-keepers, restaurant owners and ice cream and soft drink parlor operators helped local bootleggers distribute their wares. And that wasn't all. The friendly (and often corrupt) cop on the beat usually didn't pay the law any more heed than the citizens he was supposed to police. Routinely, he looked the other way. When higher authorities moved in, as they periodically did, to conduct surprise raids, typically the neighborhood was informed well in advance.

But the liquor business was not by nature a mom and pop affair. Even before the 18th Amendment went into effect on January 16, 1920, the urban underworld geared up to supply what it knew would be a very lucrative demand for an illegal indulgence. And certain elements among the underworld realized that meeting the demand effectively would require a degree of organization hitherto unheard of in criminal circles. Thus the amendment's most enduring legacy to 20th-century America was what soon came to be called organized crime.

The mobsters moved in on the neighborhood operations. The gangsters, like those they preyed on, were immigrants, but they were ruthless and brutal, convinced that crime was the quickest route to riches in America. Such men tended to be at home with violence, and neighborhood bootlegging looked like a good, easy mark. They began by extorting protection money from the illegal traffickers and brutalizing the uncooperative. The terrorized bootleggers could hardly turn to the police for help, so they paid or gave up the business altogether. Within a short time, the gangs scrapped their protection schemes in favor of outright control of all liquor production and smuggling as well as distribution, including illicit bars, saloons and nightclubs, establishing a network of "speakeasies." Rival gangs, their members often no more than teenagers, battled each other for control of territory, making liberal use of sawed-off shotguns and the Thompson submachine guns ("tommy guns"), which in post-World War I America were available cheaply and in quantity as U.S. government surplus. Gangland slayings became commonplace, and terms like "hit" and "rub out" entered the language.

The mainstream press, pandering to its nativist, middle-class audience, tried to make a racial issue out of the crime wave that Prohibition created in the major American cities, and their headlines announced almost weekly still another Sicilian gang war or the discovery of yet one more illegal warehouse in this or that town's Little Italy. But the first well-known mobster in New York was an Englishman, Owney Madden, and the second a Jew, Arnold Rothstein. The Irish and Germans, too, had their own highly formidable gangs in almost every major city. The mobsters worked hand in glove with local political machines, securing votes and furnishing graft in return for protection from police interference. They poured their profits into clubs where jazz was played over the machine gun rat-tat-tat in the background. The deals struck in the mean streets of the 1920s steadily percolated up the power structure, until much of the country's political administration and law enforcement had been corrupted and co-opted.

The year Prohibition went into effect was the year the U.S. Census documented that for the first time the number of people living in American cities had surpassed those living in rural areas. And in those cities industrialization was ushering in yet another change. In an economy that was producing more goods than it could sell, one that relied increasingly on advertising to foster new needs and create fresh markets for its surplus, pleasure-seeking became an approved pastime. The Broadway club life that developed from the cabarets of the 1890s began attracting young middle- and upper-class urbanites, who mixed with mobsters in a modern culture that exalted consumption and display rather than industry and thrift. Those thoroughly modern guys and dolls valued self-expression and individuality rather than sacrifice and family, and found fulfillment in leisure rather than work.

The Jazz Age was born in the speakeasies of Prohibition. Even before the Great Depression brought to office the Democrats who repealed the 18th Amendment in April 1933, prohibitionists were losing all the ground it had taken them more than a century to gain, except in areas of the rural South and Midwest: Dry laws would linger on there in spots well into the second half of the 20th century.

From *American History,* by Charles Phillips, February 2005, pp. 38, 72–73. Copyright © 2005 by Weider History Group. Reprinted by permission.

Evolution on Trial

Eighty years after a Dayton, Tennessee, jury found John Scopes guilty of teaching evolution, the citizens of "Monkeytown" still say Darwin's for the birds.

STEVE KEMPER

In the summer of 1925, when William Jennings Bryan and Clarence Darrow clashed over the teaching of evolution in Dayton, Tennessee, the Scopes trial was depicted in newspapers across the country as a titanic struggle. Bryan, a three-time presidential candidate and the silver-tongued champion of creationism, described the clash of views as "a duel to the death." Darrow, the deceptively folksy lawyer who defended labor unions and fought racial injustice, warned that nothing less than civilization itself was on trial. The site of their showdown was so obscure the *St. Louis Post-Dispatch* had to inquire, "Why Dayton, of all places?"

It's still a good question. Influenced in no small part by the popular play and movie *Inherit the Wind,* most people think Dayton ended up in the spotlight because a 24-year-old science teacher named John Scopes was hauled into court there by Bible-thumping fanatics for telling his high-school students that humans and primates shared a common ancestry. In fact, the trial took place in Dayton because of a stunt. Tennessee had recently passed a law that made teaching evolution illegal. After the American Civil Liberties Union (ACLU) announced it would defend anyone who challenged the statute, it occurred to several Dayton businessmen that finding a volunteer to take up the offer might be a good way to put their moribund little town on the map.

One morning in early May, the enterprising boosters interrupted a tennis game Scopes was playing behind the high school and invited him to join them at Robinson's Drug Store on Main Street. After treating him to a soft drink at the soda fountain, they asked the young teacher if he had ever use the state's standard biology textbook, which contained a section on evolution. Scopes said yes. The men then told him what they were up to and wanted to know if he was willing to be arrested for teaching evolution. Although Scopes, a recent graduate of the University of Kentucky, certainly believed Darwin's theory, it's unclear whether he ever actually taught it in his classroom. Nevertheless, he amiably agreed to go along with the scheme and then returned to the tennis court. Neither he nor his fellow conspirators had any idea, of course, what an uproar their gambit would create, let alone how badly it would backfire, or with what long-lasting repercussions.

Today, 80 years later, the Scopes trial is still reverberating in the nation's consciousness. After President Bush was reelected last fall, commentators invoked it to help explain the cultural divide between blue and red, urban and exurban, secular and religious, scientific and evangelical. Many pointed to the seemingly decisive boost given to Bush by those who voted for him because of their conviction that he stood for moral values. Historian Garry Wills called the vote "Bryan's revenge for the Scopes trial." Implicit in more than a few election postmortems was the notion that Bryan's creationists had somehow contrived to come back from the dead. In truth, they have been here all along, living in places like Dayton.

A century or so ago, Dayton was a prosperous farming and mining center with 2,000 people and a blast furnace. After the furnace closed in 1913, the community fell on hard times and since then has undergone many changes. The population is currently 6,180 and counting. The big employer these days is a La-Z-Boy plant; up-to-date emporiums like Blockbuster and Wal-Mart have arrived on the scene, and the long-dormant downtown area, dominated by the old courthouse square, shows signs of revitalization. But one thing about Dayton has not changed and probably never will: its bedrock fundamentalism. Even now, it's hard to find a teacher who goes along with Darwin. "We all basically believe in the God of creation," says the head of the high-school science department.

Many residents, however, do wince at the ridicule that comes with Dayton's place in history. H. L. Mencken, who coined the term "Bible Belt," covered the Scopes trial along with 200 other newspapermen. He called the locals "primates," not to mention yaps, yokels, morons and anthropoids. The mockery lingers still. "If something bad happens here to people from Memphis or Chattanooga," says lifelong resident Bobbie McKenzie, "they'll say, 'It's just a monkey-town anyway.' They associate Dayton with ignorance." Then she brightens up a bit. "Well, for us it's a blissful state. I'm so glad I was born here and raised my kids here."

Bobbie is sitting with her husband, James "Jimmy" McKenzie, Rhea County's family-court judge, in his office at the three-story brick courthouse where, right upstairs, his grandfather Ben, and uncle, Gordon, helped prosecute Scopes. "It gave Dayton a black eye," Judge McKenzie acknowledges, referring to the trial. But in spite of all the hoopla and history associated with it, he notes wryly, "the case didn't solve anything."

Bryan and the creationists claimed victory because the jury in Dayton upheld the state's ban against teaching evolution and, by implication, the right of parents to control what their children learned. Darrow and the evolutionists, on the other hand, believed that in exposing the ignorance behind creationism they had stymied its threat to academic freedom. Time has proved both sides wrong. "As a result of the Scopes trial, evolution largely disappeared in public school science classrooms," says historian Edward J. Larson, a professor at the University of Georgia and author of *Summer for the Gods,* a Pulitzer Prize-winning account of the trial and its aftermath. Larson acknowledges that there is "more mandated teaching of evolution now than ever before." But that doesn't translate into actual teaching. According to a recent report in the *New York Times,* many teachers simply ignore evolution or play it down to duck controversy.

The level of support among Americans for creationism—and for what is now called "intelligent design"—remains high. "Polls say it's stayed pretty stationary over time," says Larson. "About half answer with a creationist viewpoint." These true believers are continuing to press for curricular changes in schools across the country. As in the Scopes case, the new creationists tend to focus on textbooks. They've persuaded Alabama to place evolution disclaimers on its biology texts. Kansas removed evolution from its science standards in 1999; it was subsequently reinstated. Early last year, Georgia purged the word "evolution" from a proposed biology curriculum because, explained the state's superintendent of schools, Kathy Cox, it causes "a lot of negative reaction" by bringing up "that monkeys-to-man sort of thing." The resulting furor forced Cox to back down. Since 2002, however, schools in Georgia's Cobb County have been putting stickers in its biology textbooks stating that "evolution is a theory, not a fact." The ACLU, riding to the defense of evolution once again, sued to have the stickers removed, and in January a judge agreed. The school board is appealing the ruling.

"If something happens here to people from Memphis or Chattanooga," says a resident, they'll say, 'it's just a monkeytown anyway.'"

With help from their main think tank, the Discovery Institute in Seattle, advocates of intelligent design have also tried to persuade school boards to add "alternative theories" and criticisms of evolution to their science curricula. Three years ago, Ohio required its biology teachers to "critically analyze" evolution. Last year, a Wisconsin school board followed suit, and a school board in Pennsylvania voted to mandate the teaching of intelligent design. "These local revolts are started by people who are upset by what they consider to be the dogmatism of Darwin," says Phillip E. Johnson, an emeritus professor at the University of California at Berkeley's school of law.

An adviser to the Discovery Institute, Johnson ignited the intelligent-design movement with his influential 1991 book, *Darwin on Trial.* He's published a number of anti-evolution books and has been instrumental in reframing creationism as a "fairness" issue—as in, it's only fair to listen to both sides of an argument. "The Darwinists insist that only fully naturalistic explanations can be considered, regardless of the evidence," he says. "I would describe this as a faith in naturalism as a philosophy, rather than in science as an investigative process that considers all possibilities toward which the evidence may point."

"The idea that evolution is shaky or just a theory—this is absolutely amazing to scientists," says Eugenie C. Scott, executive director of the National Center for Science Education in Oakland, California. Scott has made a career out of playing Clarence Darrow to Johnson's William Jennings Bryan. She spearheads the defense of basic science education, including evolution, and has won many public service awards from scientific organizations. "On the street, a theory is just an opinion, but in science, a theory is an explanation," she says. "The theory of gravity is not an opinion or an observation, it explains why things fall. Creationists point to scientific arguments about how evolution takes place and the mechanisms of it, and then say evolution is controversial, so 'teach the controversy,' as if scientists are arguing about whether evolution is true. And that's just plain bad education."

In the aftermath of the November election, Scott anticipates many more challenges to the teaching of evolution. Religious conservatives "feel empowered now," she says. "For another four years, federal district court judges will be appointed, and conceivably one or more Supreme Court judges. Basically, it's court decisions that have kept creationism out of the classroom. But the law evolves too, and we can't stay confident the courts will continue to interpret the First Amendment as courts have in the past."

At Dayton's Rhea County High School, students do learn that species can change over time, a process modern creationists call "micro-evolution." Joe Wilkey, a genial bear of a man who heads the science department, can't think of anyone on his staff of nine teachers who believes in "macro-evolution"—the evolutionary origins of all life—and no one teaches it. If a student asks why a textbook states that dinosaurs lived 65 million years ago when his parents and his minister have told him that God created the world 6,000 years ago, Wilkey answers that people disagree about the earth's origins, and that some scientists trace the fossil record to the biblical flood. He doesn't teach creationism; it's not part of the state curriculum. "But I do not believe it would hurt a thing to teach intelligent design."

"Darrow and others would go to my grandfather's office at the end of the day and tell war stories. My daddy said it was a show."

The scopes trial ran for eight days in the middle of a July heat wave. Dayton worked hard to get ready for it. The big courtroom got a new coat of paint and was outfitted with 500 additional seats and a platform for a newsreel camera. New microphones installed in the courtroom were connected to speakers out on the lawn, so the expected overflow crowds could follow the proceedings, and a Chicago radio station arranged to use those same microphones to broadcast the trial live. Western Union strung wire for 22 telegraph operators to transmit breaking news to newspapers and radio stations across the country. To meet increased demand, the Southern Railway expanded its passenger service to Dayton.

Although folks in town couldn't abide the notion of monkeys as kinfolk, they had no reservations about exploiting them for fun and profit. While vendors sold popcorn, ice cream and cold drinks, hucksters hawked monkey souvenirs, including a coin minted by the Progressive Dayton Club that featured a monkey wearing a boater. A circus sent a gorilla in a freight car and charged a dime to see it. At his drugstore, Frank Robinson entertained customers with a besuited chimp that sipped "simian soda" and played a toy piano. Other stores advertised their wares with monkey displays, and the constable decorated his motorcycle with a "Monkeyville Police" sign. Meanwhile, Mencken observed, the courthouse lawn was "peppered" with evangelists, "and their yells and bawlings fill the air with orthodoxy."

More than 3,000 visitors showed up for the trial and the monkeyshines, and they all needed a place to eat and sleep. Some Daytonians rented their houses and left town. Many others let out rooms or sold home-cooked meals. Ann Gabbert Bates, druggist Robinson's 61-year-old granddaughter, remembers her mother telling how her own mother fed lots of journalists, "except Mr. Mencken. He wasn't welcome."

The visiting members of the press did not ingratiate themselves with their hosts. When an elderly woman asked one of the two reporters staying with her why he wrote that people in Dayton said "hain't" and "sech" and wore ragged clothes, he told her his paper wanted him to add "color." The other reporter never even bothered going to the courthouse because, he said, "I know what my paper wants me to write."

Longtime resident Richard Cornelius, a retired English professor, used to get his hair cut at Wilkey's Barbershop, where older habitués still laughed about a trick that was cooked up there for the newspapermen. After George Rappleyea, one of the chief drugstore plotters, sauntered in one day and began praising evolution, his partner, Thurlow Reed, yelled, "You can't call my ancestors monkeys!" and pretended to attack him. The Northern reporters ate it up because it matched their preconceptions about volatile Southerners. When another Dayton jokester shot off his pistol in front of the barbershop one day, he generated still more colorful copy—and more local glee at the reporters' expense.

Eloise Reed, an elegant 92-year-old widow whose attractive home sits a few blocks from the courthouse, was 12 that summer. Her brother Crawford had been playing tennis with John Scopes when the schoolteacher was summoned to the drugstore. After Scopes returned to the tennis court, he told Crawford about the scheme, which the youngster relayed to the family that night at supper. "We laughed," Reed recalls. "It didn't seem like any big deal." But then Bryan announced he was coming, followed by Darrow, and the excitement started to build.

When Bryan gave a sermon against evolution at the Southern Methodist church one Sunday, Eloise Reed was sitting near the front. Later, she shook his hand. She saw him and Darrow many times. Bryan was taller, she says. "And he stood tall. Darrow draped a little." Darrow was indeed stooped, and he wore baggy clothes and colorful wide suspenders. In contrast to Bryan's orotund grandiloquence, Darrow's speaking style was conversational, down-home and cuttingly quick. Working pro bono for the ACLU, he led a team of big-city lawyers. Tom Stewart, the astute district attorney, directed the prosecution with help from, among others, Bryan, his son, William Jr., old Ben McKenzie and his son Gordon. Judge John Raulston, a conservative lay Methodist minister, presided. All but one of the jurors belonged to local evangelical churches. On the trial's opening day, Judge Raulston read aloud the first chapter of Genesis.

Bryan, 65, and Darrow, 68, shook hands like boxers before the bell. They had once been political allies, back in the days when Bryan, who served as Woodrow Wilson's secretary of state, was known as "the Great Commoner," a passionate advocate of corporate reform, female suffrage and a progressive income tax. Teddy Roosevelt, no admirer, called him "a professional yodeler, a human trombone." Bryan left politics to become a crusader against Darwinism, which he blamed for atheism and a host of social and corporate ills. By the time of the trial, Darrow, a fierce rationalist, had long since concluded that Bryan was hazardous to the country's intellectual health. He intended to demolish him. "Nothing will satisfy us but broad victory, a knockout which will . . . prove that America is founded on liberty and not on narrow, mean, intolerable and brainless prejudice of soulless religio-maniacs," Darrow said.

Darrow's strategy was aimed less at exonerating Scopes than in discrediting the anti-evolution law. He assembled a distinguished group of scientists and religious leaders to testify that there was no conflict between evolution and belief in God; that many devout people also believed in evolution, and that the state should not allow a particular religious viewpoint to dictate or censor public-school curricula. His opening speech lasted two hours and awed even the opposition. Ben McKenzie told Darrow it was "the greatest speech that I have ever heard on any subject in my life."

Though McKenzie wryly referred to all of the Northern attorneys as "foreigners," he and Darrow struck up a lasting friendship. Ben's grandson, Jimmy, recently came across the family copy of Darrow's 1932 autobiography, inscribed: "To my esteemed and valued friend . . . with the kindest remembrances." A black-and-white photograph in Jimmy's office at the Dayton courthouse shows Ben with his arm around Darrow. It was no secret both men liked to drink, Jimmy says. "Darrow and others would go to my grandfather's office at the end of the day and tell war stories. My daddy said it was a show."

Since the town was dry, the booze consumed during those raucous get-togethers had to be bootlegged. Mary Welch, a 72-year-old widow, heard all about that from her father-in-law,

Luther Welch. He was a road commissioner and a good Christian, she says, but he didn't mind having a drink once in a while. At the time of the trial, he was a teenager, she recalls, and "he would go to Chattanooga in an old farm truck to get liquor for the lawyers on both sides."

Prosecutor Tom Stewart didn't want Darrow's shrewd eloquence and all-star experts to derail the trial. As it wore on, he constantly reminded Judge Raulston the case wasn't about creationism or academic freedom but solely about whether Scopes had broken the law. After Raulston agreed to prevent Darrow's experts from testifying before the jury, Mencken and many of the other reporters decided that was it for Scopes, so they left town and missed out on the biggest fireworks of all.

On the seventh day, the trial was moved from the stifling courtroom to a platform beneath the big oak trees on the lawn. There, after challenging Bryan to take the stand, Darrow asked him a series of questions designed to show that belief in the literal truth of the Bible was preposterous in light of current knowledge, and also that the Bible was subject to interpretation. Did Joshua really make the sun stand still? If so, did Bryan think the sun revolved around the earth? Did Jonah really live inside a whale for three days?

In the 1960 film version of *Inherit the Wind,* the Bryan-based character (played by Fredric March) melts down on the stand—becomes pathetic and incoherent. Actually, Bryan acquitted himself quite well, answering Darrow (Spencer Tracy in the movie) with wit and clever evasion. But eventually he did reveal that he knew little or nothing about fossils, geology, ancient civilizations or world religions. Such things did not interest him, he explained, because the Bible sufficed: "I have all the information I want to live by and to die by."

When Tom Stewart realized Bryan was not helping himself or the prosecution's case, he asked Judge Raulston, "What is the purpose of this examination?"

"The purpose," answered Bryan, "is to cast ridicule on everybody who believes in the Bible."

"We have the purpose," retorted Darrow, "of preventing bigots and ignoramuses from controlling the education of the United States."

The next day, Raulston expunged Bryan's testimony as immaterial to the case. Darrow responded by asking the court to instruct the jury to go ahead and find Scopes guilty so he could proceed with an appeal. The jury returned its unanimous verdict nine minutes later.

Scopes never spent time in jail, but the judge did fine him $100. Darrow's appeal lost (although Scopes' conviction was eventually reversed on a technicality), and Tennessee's anti-evolution law stayed in force until 1967. The Dayton school board asked Scopes to stay on, and he also had offers from Hollywood and vaudeville, but instead he accepted a scholarship to study geology at the University of Chicago. He worked as a geologist in South America and later for an oil and gas company in Texas and Louisiana. He married, had two boys, John Jr. and William, and stayed out of the spotlight.

In 1960, Scopes returned to Dayton for the world première of *Inherit the Wind* at a local drive-in (the town's only movie theater was too small), and in 1967 he published a memoir, *Center of the Storm.* He died three years later at 70. Son John Jr., 72, spent his entire career in the insurance business and now lives on Long Island. Son Bill, semi-retired at 69, also worked mainly in the insurance field. Speaking by phone from his home in Guntersville, Alabama, recently, he said: "If anybody ever got to Heaven, it was Dad. He was just a real nice person—easygoing, modest, well liked, tolerant." John senior did not talk about the trial when the boys were growing up, Bill says, and he never discussed evolution.

The Scopes case was one of Darrow's last major trials. He visited Dayton with his family a few years later to be feted by the business club of Dayton, which gave him a dinner at the Aqua Hotel. When Darrow noticed a new church across from the hotel, he quipped, "Well, I didn't do so much good here after all." He died of heart disease at age 80 in 1938.

Bryan died of apoplexy five days after the trial ended while taking a nap in a bedroom of the house on S. Market Street in Dayton where he had been staying. (The house burned down in the late 1920s and has long since been replaced by another.) Some wondered whether the trial had broken his spirit and contributed to his death, but in fact Bryan felt vindicated and energized, and was enthusiastically planning another lecture tour.

In 1930, funded by donations from creationists throughout the country, William Jennings Bryan Memorial University opened in Dayton to carry on his work. Now known as Bryan College, the 110-acre campus consists of a dozen or so brick buildings scattered across a hill overlooking the town. Last year, the undergraduate enrollment was 600. According to the college's catalog, the curriculum is "based upon unequivocal acceptance of the inerrancy and authority of the Scriptures."

Kurt Wise teaches science at Bryan. His credentials are impressive—an undergraduate degree in geology from the University of Chicago and a PhD from Harvard, where he studied with the late Stephen J. Gould, the eminent paleontologist and anti-creationist. Wise believes that God created the world and everything in it 6,000 years ago.

On this July day, he is leading a group on a field trip through Grassy Cove Saltpeter Cave. Wearing headlights, the students crawl through muddy tunnels, run their hands over rough limestone columns and peer at fossil shells embedded in rock. Wise tells his students that water may have carved this extensive cave in a matter of hours about 4,000 years ago, a few centuries after Noah's Flood. He thinks the same phenomenon sculpted the Grand Canyon, though that, he says, took about three weeks.

This "catastrophic" explanation radically compresses geologic history to make it fit a literal interpretation of the Bible. For instance, Wise puts the Cambrian rock layers, usually dated from 540 million to 505 million years ago, at 2500 B.C. He tells students that geological events don't require long timelines—limestone can be simulated in a lab in two days, wood will petrify rapidly under certain conditions. Basically, what Wise and other "young earth" creationists are attempting to do is empirically explain the world in light of Genesis. "God's truth should be used to interpret—to properly interpret—all the data of the universe," Wise writes in his 2002 book, *Faith, Form, and Time.* "All the stars of the universe, all the rocks of the earth, all the organisms on its surface must be reinterpreted, as well as all the world's literature, philosophies, and religions. They can and should be reinterpreted from a Christian perspective so all these things can be taken captive under the mind of Christ."

What do most other paleontologists and geologists think of this? "Absolute bunk!" says Wise with a laugh. Does he believe evolution is flawed in and of itself, or flawed because it contradicts Genesis? His answer could have come straight from the college's namesake himself: "Scripture trumps interpretations of physical data."

Though the Scopes trial made Dayton a laughingstock in some quarters, it also made it a tourist destination. A steady stream of people visits the old courthouse these days and a few stop at the plaque where Robinson's Drug Store used to stand. Every July, Dayton puts on a three-day Scopes Festival, a modest affair that faintly echoes the original event—a few musicians on the courthouse lawn; a few vendors selling food, crafts and monkey souvenirs. In the main event put on daily, local actors restage the trial in the courtroom, speaking dialogue culled from the transcript by the wife of a Dayton minister. This time around, Bryan fares much better.

H. L. Mencken said he expected "a squalid southern village," but found instead "a country town full of charm and even beauty."

Richard Cornelius, 70, helped start the festival as a sort of damage-control project. He attended Bryan College and has lived in Dayton since 1961, when he joined the faculty, and over the years he has interviewed eyewitnesses and written articles "to show that perhaps we don't need to be quite so embarrassed."

Actually, not all of the publicity Dayton received at the time of the trial or since has been embarrassing. Mencken said he expected "a squalid Southern village," but instead found "a country town full of charm and even beauty," where the "Evolutionists and the Anti-Evolutionists seem to be on the best of terms." The next day he reported that "there is an almost complete absence, in these pious hills, of the ordinary and familiar malignancy of Christian men. . . . There is absolutely no bitterness on tap. But neither," he added, "is there any doubt."

That description still applies. Dayton has more than 30 churches; Rhea Country, with 28,400 people, has more than 140. The semiweekly *Herald-News* runs a biblical quote on every front page, the Dayton Coffee Shop sells religious CDs near the Jesus posters, and evangelical preachers compete with each other on the radio day and night. Even so, many Daytonians cringe anytime the extremists among them reinforce old stereotypes, as happened last year when the county commissioners voted not only to oppose gay marriage, but to recommend that the state prosecute homosexuals for crimes against nature. Sure enough, most outside news stories mentioned the monkey trial, implying that history was repeating itself.

Mary Brooks says she is "a pretty strong Christian person," but she doesn't like "the way people get lumped into backwoods ignorant stereotypes. I know there's some of that here, but it's not the majority." As one of Dayton's new boosters, Brooks focuses on economic rather than religious revival. Seven years ago, she bought the empty hardware store near the courthouse and turned it into an upscale shop that sells antiques and home accessories, with a coffee bar on one side. The store did well enough that Brooks bought six more run-down buildings. One became a deli, another houses her daughter's bakery. Brooks' example has inspired other merchants to open their own specialty gift stores. "It's a work in progress," she says of the budding revival, "but I do think we're on our way. The other morning we must have had 40 kids in here from Bryan College getting cappuccinos and espressos."

After Scopes returned to the tennis court, he told about the scheme. "We laughed," Reed recalls. "It didn't seem like any big deal."

Those old soda fountain plotters would be every bit as proud of Dayton's progress as Bill Hollin, 68, who was the town's director of development and tourism until he retired last year. "Rhea County is going to change," he predicts. But Hollin knows as well as anyone that still more change in his fundamentalist neck of the woods will require some earnest soul-searching. Hollin is convinced, for example, that Dayton, which remains almost as dry as it was in John Scopes' time, needs "some medium-to-better" restaurants, like Appleby's or O'Charlies. "But it's hard to bring them in, because they can't make it without a bar," he acknowledges. Two years ago a neighboring town approved liquor-by-the-drink. "And now they've got all those major restaurants!" says Hollin, sounding envious. "Not that I can recommend liquor-by-the-drink," he quickly adds. "I'm a deacon."

STEVE KEMPER'S book about the *Segway, Code Name Ginger,* has been reissued as a paperback entitled *Reinventing the Wheel*.

From *Smithsonian,* April 2005, pp. 52, 54–59, 61. Copyright © 2005 by Steve Kemper. Reprinted by permission of the author.

Rethinking Politics: Consumers and the Public Good During the "Jazz Age"

Lawrence B. Glickman

The 1920s are often understood as a time of economic abundance and political quiescence. Frequently the decade's supposed political lethargy and conservatism is seen as a consequence of its supposed affluence. With progressive energies exhausted—weakened by World War I and the domestic repression that accompanied and followed it—and with the economy booming. Americans, in this stereotypical vision, turned inward. Enjoying the private pleasures afforded by the new affluence of the "jazz age," they displayed either indifference or cynicism to the well-being of the public sphere.

Commentators often speak of the rise of "consumer society" in the 1920s as a way to encapsulate these political and economic transformations. They frequently use the term to explain the economic vibrancy and political passivity that they take to characterize the decade, and to link the two. In this view, privatized consumption undermined the public-spirited citizenship that had characterized the producerist nineteenth century and Progressive era. Rather than attacking political and corporate corruption, Americans bought Model-T's; rather than cleaning up slums, they purchased a vast array of new, brand-name consumables; rather than throwing themselves into political struggles—such as the campaigns for suffrage, socialism, and prohibition which had absorbed so much energy in the previous decade—they visited chain stores and ordered goods from catalogs. Whatever critical spirit remained from the previous decade transmogrified itself from progressive activism to the cynicism characteristic of the "lost generation." Thus Paul Carter entitles the introductory chapter of his survey text on the decade, "Of Bohemians and Consumers." This title characterizes the two sides of declining political engagement: the cynical artiste and the solipsistic shopper.[1]

Indeed, the 1920s did represent a takeoff period for consumer society. During the decade, pundits, scholars, and many ordinary Americans claimed to be observing an epochal and multifaceted transformation whose key feature was a shift from production to consumption. While a robust consumer economy had been developing since at least the market revolution of the early nineteenth-century, several elements converged in the 1920s to create a fully mature consumer society. Those elements included a much-expanded advertising industry, the advent of installment buying and consumer credit industries, the mass production on Henry Ford's assembly lines, and the mass consumption at Woolworth's chain stores. Increasingly, American life, not just economically but culturally, centered on mass consumption. The decade witnessed an increase in leisure time, as well as the rise of a full-fledged culture of celebrity (notably Babe Ruth) and a self-conscious youth culture.[2]

In this industrializing and urbanizing society (the census of 1920 showed that, for the first time, more Americans lived in towns and cities than in the country), consumption was acknowledged as the prime mover of economic life, dislodging the traditional American faith in "producerism," the belief that the makers and growers of goods lay at the heart of the nation. Similarly, Americans knocked thrift, another guiding concept of the nineteenth century, off its pedestal. Recognizing that consumption is what drove the economy, many Americans—including an influential group of businessmen and politicians that the historian Meg Jacobs labels the "purchasing power progressives"—redefined thrift not as saving (which was redefined by some as 'hoarding') but as what a business group called "wise spending." In this sense, thrift meant purchasing quality merchandise, since as the *New York Times* editorialized, "Poor Stuff Never is Cheap." In this new understanding of thrift, not spending or underspending was an unaffordable "extravagance." Henry Ford gave his imprimatur to this view when he noted that "No successful boy every saved any money." On the contrary, the wizard of Detroit claimed, they "spent it as fast they could for things to improve themselves." When, in the early 1920s, his advertising department came up with the slogan, "Buy a Ford and Save the Difference," Ford replaced the word "save" with "spend." Spending, he insisted, "is the wiser thing to do." If spending was the lever of the economy, and prosperity was a social good, then it followed that, if Americans were to practice thrift at all, they should do so in this redefined manner. Thrift in effect became redefined as mass consumption.[3]

The advent of consumer society, however, was not only an economic and cultural process. Historians are beginning to show that the decade of the 1920s was also a crucial decade in the development of consumer politics.[4] For, rather than a diminution of political energy, the decade witnessed new kinds of political engagements, many of them centered on the politicization of consumers and consumption. In the milieu of the consumer economy of the 1920s, many Americans, far from losing interest in politics, developed new political engagements based in large measure on their identities as consumers. For many Americans—aware that they were living in a distended, urbanizing society with national markets—consumer politics provided a way for the private to reconnect to the public, an avenue for individuals to overcome urban anomie and anonymity to assert their will and to unite in common cause.

Older forms of consumer politics were re-energized too. A keyword search of the *New York Times* for the word "boycott," during the decade of the 1920s, produces more than 2,000 hits. Alongside such traditional forms of consumer politics, new ones were invented, such as the "Spend Your Money Where You Can Work" campaigns, in which, starting in 1929, members of Chicago's African American community demanded that businesses, which depended on their patronage, hire black workers. During the Great Depression, these would change into the well-known "Don't Buy Where You Can't Work" demands in Harlem, Baltimore and elsewhere.[5] In addition, for the first time, consumers began to organize as consumers—forming what became known as the "consumer movement"—and both business and government began to conceive of the "consumer interest" as an important, perhaps the defining, political and social force in modern America. One indication of this reorientation was the coinage in 1921 of the term "consumerism" by the economist Sidney A. Reeve. Just as nineteenth-century advocates of producerism held that those who provided useful goods and services to the nation deserved to be the political leaders, advocates of this new concept of consumerism—who ranged from labor leaders, to economists, to eminences in the world of business—held that the economic centrality of consumers necessitated that they be accorded a central political role.

To say that consumption and politics were linked in intriguing new ways in the 1920s is not to claim that consumer politics had a single meaning. Indeed, at least five understandings of the relationship between consumption and politics emerged in this decade. A variety of pundits, politicians, and purchasing-power proponents described consumers (and sometimes simultaneously) as: economically central, potentially powerful, befuddled and victimized, in need of organization, and universal citizens. While some of these understandings overlapped, they also diverged in crucial respects. Taken as a whole, they reveal that in the 1920s, as in other periods, it is difficult—as well as inaccurate—to pigeonhole consumer politics as either liberal or conservative. While a growing number of Americans agreed that consumers and consumption had reached a new level of importance, they disagreed about the implications and the plan of action to follow from this insight. Business leaders understood consumer politics, as the implementation of policies that would yield maximum mass consumption (hence profits); self-appointed experts understood consumer politics as the creation of a lobby on behalf of ordinary consumers; finally many ordinary consumers understood that the wallet and the cash register provided a site for the expression of collective interests.

Perhaps the most commonly expressed—and widely accepted—view of the 1920s was that consumers were essential to the American economy. From the 1930s through the end of the twentieth century, this insight—labeled Keynsianism in the postwar years—drove federal monetary policy. But in the 1920s, this was a relatively new idea, put forward by businessmen as diverse as the conservative Henry Ford and the progressive Edward Filene, as well as a wide variety of economists and politicians, who came to accept that consumers were the prime movers of economic activity; as the U.S. Chamber of Commerce put it in 1924, "Production cannot be possible unless it produces, first of all, consumers." Rather than understanding people as primarily producers, they came to be seen as most important in their consuming capacities. For different reasons, labor groups and many politicians supported the increase of working-class purchasing power as both good economic policy, and smart as well as ethical politics. Roy Dickinson, an economist for the American Federation of Labor, writing in the advertising trade journal *Printer's Ink* in 1921, warned that "lower wages reduce purchasing power; men on starvation wages do not buy phonographs, clothes, shoes, etc." In a 1927 article summarizing what he called, "The New Economic Gospel of Consumption," journalist Edward S. Cowdrick, noted that "the worker has come to be more important as a consumer than he is as a producer." This was also a trend that Robert and Helen Lynd discovered in their famous study of Muncie, Indiana.[6]

Recognizing their dependence on mass consumption meant that businessmen were acutely concerned with promoting purchasing power. For the most part, however, they did not see the need for independent political action on the part of consumers. Indeed, they sometimes disclaimed a link between consumption and citizenship. The Muncie Chamber of Commerce, for example, declared that since consumption was a "new necessity," the "American citizen's first importance to his country is no longer that of citizen but that of consumer." The consumer's job, in this vision, was to buy and it was their job, as businessmen, to entice consumers to do so. This was the essence of what became known as "Fordism," the model of mass consumption, not as empowerment for ordinary individuals—although that may have been a by-product—but as necessary fuel for the engines of corporate capitalism.[7]

Because the mass production economy of the 1920s depended on mass consumption, many commentators came to see consumers as a potentially powerful group, perhaps even a new political and social force.

Others, however, pushed to make consumers an independent political force. Because the mass production economy of the 1920s depended on mass consumption, many commentators came to see consumers as a potentially powerful group, perhaps even a new political and social force. Many businessmen took the so-called "buyers' strikes" of the early 1920s, in which shoppers refused to buy what they deemed to be overpriced goods, as a warning about the need to cultivate consumers through low prices and high quality goods and about the potential power of consumers to either help or weaken their businesses. The buyers' strike, the economic theorist Ralph Borsodi warned businessmen in 1927, "was a dramatic demonstration of the supreme importance" of mass consumption. In what he called "The Distribution Age," consumers, not producers, held the cards. Similarly, in an editorial on "embattled consumers," the *New York Times,* also made reference to the buyers' strikes and observed that "the docile and long-suffering consumer" was finally beginning to recognize her "latent power." The home economist Christine Frederick made this claim as well in her 1929 book, *Selling Mrs. Consumer.* The renewed popularity of boycotts over a range of issues, from the high cost of meat, to racist practices at stores, to unhappiness with foreign governments' policies, and even to dissatisfaction with theatrical performances and prices, demonstrated that Americans used their pocketbooks to achieve their social and political goals. Ultimately, some Americans began to push for a political party to promote the interests of consumers.[8]

Yet even as they recognized the fundamental importance of consumers to the economy, many commentators described the average consumer as an embattled figure. In this view, the powerful forces arrayed against consumers made the consumer a weak, easily duped, even pathetic, presence in American life. As early as 1917, the pundit Walter Lippmann compared American consumers to "a bewildered child in a toy shop." He concluded, "the simple act of buying has become a vast, impersonal thing which the ordinary man is quite incapable of performing without all sorts of organized aid." Similarly, the pioneering consumer activists, Stuart Chase and F. J. Schlink, famously compared consumers to Lewis Carroll's fairy-tale character Alice, helplessly facing "conflicting claims, bright promises, fancy packages, soaring words," with an "almost impenetrable ignorance."[9] The economist Hazel Kyrk described the consumer as "the helpless victim of powerful interests."[10] The Lynds determined that the citizens of Muncie were not knowledgeable enough to pursue their interests as consumers. Lynd called this problem of ignorance in the ways of consumption, "the new illiteracy".[11]

Furthermore, in this view, consumers were not only duped but inefficient and, as a result, wasteful. Through a combination of commercial complexity, which made face-to-face observations an insufficient mode of policing economic transactions and through what the experts believed was the ordinary consumers' appalling ignorance, consumers were not exercising the potential power that so many commentators claimed that they had. Asserting that few "consumers feel any of that sense of power which economists say is theirs," Lippmann argued that this made sense because shoppers could not be expected to understand the complexity of the modern economy.[12] If any group was in need of scientific assistance and an organized lobby, it was consumers. In the absence of comparative information about goods, efficient and intelligent consumption would be impossible to achieve. Similarly, many consumer advocates argued, in a pluralist society, in which pretty much every group in society from workers, to businessmen, to doctors, to lawyers was represented by an organized lobby, consumers could not be expected to gain ground without such representation. These advocates of consumer politics did not call on consumers to take action in their own hands, but to delegate these responsibilities to experts who were capable of rising to the challenge. If anything the tone toward consumers taken by Chase and Schlink, and others was one of scolding. "Why do you buy the toothpaste you are using," reads a typical passage, on the first page of *Your Money's Worth,* "do you know if it has, beyond a pleasant taste, any merit at all? . . . Have you any evidence, except blind hope, that the package of insecticide under your arm will actually rid a house of flies?" Despite this hectoring tone, the book became a manifesto of a new kind of expert-led consumer politics.

The first organization on behalf of consumers that arose, came in the wake of the publication of Chase and Schlink's 1927 bestseller, *Your Money's Worth*—a book Robert Lynd called the "Uncle Tom's Cabin" of the consumer movement. With accounting and engineering backgrounds, the authors claimed that they had the numeracy and technological skills that most consumers lacked. They carried forward the progressive concern with efficiency into the consumer programs they developed. The organization, Chase argued, would substitute "science for magic and persuasion" on the part of advertisers and "eliminate the waste of brands" resulting from the proliferation of inferior products hyped through "mysticism." Based on the demands of enthusiastic readers, who, apparently were not put off by the harsh diagnosis of their condition put forward in the book, Chase and Schlink organized a club in New York City to help consumers get accurate information about goods. The two men also offered advice on a local radio station. As interest in this group blossomed, the informal buyers' club transformed itself in 1929 into the world's first consumer products testing service, Consumers Research (CR). By the end of the decade, CR had 5,000 members and by the mid-1930s, it had about 50,000 members.[13]

CR was in many ways very different from earlier consumer groups. Previously, consumer organizations called on citizens to organize their collective consumption on behalf of a group needing assistance or a cause. For example, the National Consumers League, founded in 1899, called on middle-class consumers to use their purchasing power on behalf of poor working-class women. The raison d'être of CR was that consumers needed to organize on behalf of another maltreated group—themselves. Moreover, the organization needed to be run, not democratically, but from the top down by experts who could combat the problems that drove consumers to join the group in the first place.

If the main draw for CR members was the advice they received about the relative merits of foods and other consumables, the group also maintained a strong political element. In its newsletter, CR leaders regularly lobbied for increased government intervention on behalf of the consumer. CR pushed the government to develop standards that would aid the consumer. And it was one of the first organizations to call for a cabinet level, federal Department of the Consumer. Although CR later disavowed its broad-based conception of consumer politics, in the 1920s it was—in spite of its elitism—widely seen as the vanguard of a broad-based consumer politics, which would include the full array of political strategies developed or re-energized during this decade: from boycotts, to lobbying, to political party formation.[14]

In the 1920s, then, some Americans began to reverse the nature of consumer politics; rather than consumers acting on behalf of the oppressed, as the NCL urged, they began to argue that it was consumers themselves who were oppressed and needed assistance. The consumer movement, which blossomed into a powerful social force in the 1930s grew from this insight of the 1920s. Since that time, it has periodically re-emerged as an important social force, notably in the 1960s and 1970s in the figure of Ralph Nader. The 1920s was thus a pivotal decade in shaping, for better or worse, not just a consumerist economy but a consumerist polity.

Notes

1. Paul Carter, *The Twenties in America, 2nd ed.* (Arlington Heights, IL: AHM Publishing, 1975), 1–34.

2. See Paula S. Fass, *The Beautiful and the Damned: American Youth in the 1920s* (New York: Oxford University Press, 1979). Historians have demonstrated that affluence was not as widespread as many of these stereotypes suggest. As the historian Lizabeth Cohen points out, "Not all Americans participated equally in mass consumer markets; many more lacked a car; a washing machine; vacuum cleaner and radio than had one." [Lizabeth Cohen, *Consumers' Republic: The Politics of Mass Consumption in Postwar America* (New York: Knopf, 2003), 22].

3. "A Business Message: The Buyers Strike: Thrift vs. Spending," *New York Times*, Jan. 18, 1921; "Poor Stuff Never is Cheap," *New York Times*, Jan. 19, 1921. Ford is quoted in Steven Watts, *The People's Tycoon: Henry Ford and the American Century* (New York: Alfred A. Knopf, 2005), 118, 134.

4. See, for example, Lizabeth Cohen, *Making a New Deal: Industrial Workers in Chicago, 1919–1939* (New York: Cambridge University Press, 1990); Kathleen Donahue, *Freedom From Want: American Liberalism and the Idea of the Consumer* (Baltimore: Johns Hopkins University Press, 2004); Dana Frank, *Purchasing Power: Gender in Seattle, 1919–1929* (New York: Cambridge University Press, 1994); Meg Jacobs, *Pocketbook Politics: Economic Citizenship in Twentieth-Century America* (Princeton: Princeton University Press, 2005).

5. St. Clair Drake and Horace Cayton, *Black Metropolis: A Study of Negro Life in a Northern City* (New York: Harcourt, Brace and Company, 1945), 84, 733, 743. For notice of the aggregate consuming power of African Americans, see Paul K. Edwards,

6. *The Southern Urban Negro as a Consumer* (College Park, MD: McGrath Publishing, 1932).

6. Chamber of Commerce quotation is from Jacobs, *Pocketbook Politics*, 80. Dickinson quoted in John B. Judis, *The Paradox of American Democracy: Elites, Special Interests, and the Betrayal of the Public Trust* (New York: Pantheon, 2000), 88; Edward S. Cowdrick, "The New Economic Gospel of Consumption: Revolutionary Changes Brought About by Our Highly Geared Production Machine," *Industrial Management* (Oct. 1927), 209-II; Robert S. Lynd and Helen Merrell Lynd, *Middletown: A Study in Modern American Culture* (New York: Harcourt Brace Jovanovich, 1929), 88.

7. Muncie Chamber of Commerce is quoted in Lynd and Lynd, *Middletown*, 88.

8. Ralph Borsodi, *The Distribution Age: A Study of the Economy of Modern Distribution* (New York: D. Appleton and Company, 1927), 276. For contemporary analyses of the "buyers' strikes," see: J. H. Collins, "Coming, another buyers' strike?" *Saturday Evening Post*, June 23, 1923, 29; P. D. Vroom, "Is there a buyers' strike?" *Colliers*, July 16, 1921, 5–6; "How to break the buyers' strike," *Literary Digest*, March 26, 1921, 7–9; "Should the buyer cease from striking?," *Literary Digest*, January 22, 1921, 72; "Embattled Consumers," *New York Times*, December 27, 1927. On the call for a "consumers party," see, for example, the letter to the editor from C. E. Nixdorff, *New York Times*, February 15, 1927.

9. Walter Lippmann, *Drift and Mastery: An Attempt to Diagnose the Current Unrest* (New York: Henry Holt and Company, 1917), 65, 67; Stuart Chase and F. J. Schlink, *Your Money's Worth: A Study in the Waste of the Consumer's Dollar* (New York: Macmillan, 1927), 2.

10. Kyrk is quoted in Jacobs, *Purchasing Power*, 81.

11. Lynd and Lynd are quoted in Stuart Chase, *The Economy of Abundance* (New York: Macmillan, 1934), 272.

12. Lipmann, *Drift and Mastery*, 64.

13. Lynd quoted in "The Consumer Movement," *Business Week*, April 22, 1939, 40. Chase's first book, *The Tragedy of Waste* (New York: Macmillan, 1925) condemned the fact that consumers produced what he called (following the English critic John Ruskin) "illth" rather than "wealth" through their inaccurate understandings of modern economic processes. Schlink too was extremely critical of the ability of consumers to shop efficiently. "Memorandum for the Establishment of The Consumers Foundation," Container 2, Subject File: Consumers' Research Folder: Correspondence, memoranda, clippings, and documents, 1928–1931, Stuart Chase Papers, Library of Congress. On the growth of Consumers Research see, "Consumers' Group Grows; To Incorporate Club That Advises Members Through Tests," *New York Times*, Dec. 8, 1929; "Consumers' Group Grows; Membership in Testing Bureau Has Reached 5,700 Since Jan. 1," *New York Times*, Oct. 19, 1930.

14. Stuart Chase and F. J. Schlink, "Few billions for consumers [government testing and standards]," *New Republic*, December 30, 1925, 153–55; F. J. Schlink, "Improving purchasing methods through specifications," *American City* 42 (April 1930): 157–58; "Wanted, a consumers' advocate," *Nation*,

February 6 1929, 151. This idea became more popular during the New Deal: "Cabinet Department Urged For Consumer; Emergency Conference Declares in Letter to Roosevelt NRA Board Has No Power," *New York Times,* Dec. 12, 1933. On the transformation of CR in the 1930s, see Lawrence B. Glickman, "The Strike in the Temple of Consumption: Consumer Activism and Twentieth-Century American Political Culture," *Journal of American History* 88 (June 2001): 99–128.

LAWRENCE B. GLICKMAN is professor of history at the University of South Carolina. He is the author of *A Living Wage: American Workers and the Making of Consumer Society* and the editor of *Consumer Society in American History: A Reader* (both Cornell University Press). He is currently working on *Buying Power: Consumer Activism in America from the Boston Tea Party to the Twenty-First Century* (University of Chicago Press, forthcoming).

UNIT 4

From the Great Depression to World War II

Unit Selections

Key Points to Consider

- Describe the personality and character of Franklin D. Roosevelt. What made him such an effective president?

- Discuss the "repatriation" of people of Mexican ancestry during the Great Depression? What justifications were used for these blatant violations of human rights and what methods were employed?

- What is a "sit down" strike? How effective were sit-down strikes both in the short and long run? What other means of bettering their pay and working conditions did laboring people have at the time?

- Analyze the situation President Truman faced at the time the atomic bombs were dropped on Japan. What alternatives did he have, and how were they likely to have turned out?

Student Web Site

www.mhcls.com/online

Internet References

Further information regarding these Web sites may be found in this book's preface or online.

Works Progress Administration/Folklore Project
http:///lcweb2.loc.gov/ammem/wpaintro/wpalife.html
Hiroshima Archive
http://www.lclark.edu/~history/HIROSHIMA/
The Enola Gay
http://www.theenolagay.com/index.html

After a brief postwar depression, the economy took off during the 1920s. Sales of relatively new products such as automobiles, radios and telephones mushroomed. Farmers, who sold their goods on a fluctuating market, tended not to fare as well as others but even many of them were purchasing the sundry goods pouring off assembly lines. Successive Republican administrations understandably took credit for this prosperity—attributing it to their wise economic and financial policies. They proclaimed the 1920s as a "New Era." When people ran out of things to buy and still had many left over they dabbled in the stock market in ever-increasing numbers. As stock prices rose dramatically, a kind of speculative mania developed in the latter half of the decade. In the past most people had bought stocks as long-term investments. That is, they wanted to receive income from the dividends reliable companies would pay over the years. Speculators had no interest in the long run; they bought stocks on the assumption that they would make money when they were sold on the market in a matter of months or even weeks. Rumors abounded, some of them true, about individuals who had earned fortunes "playing" the market.

By the end of the 1920s stock market prices had soared to unprecedented heights. So long as people were confident that they would continue to rise, they did. There were a few voices warning that stocks were overpriced, but they were denounced as doomsayers. Besides, had not the highly regarded President Herbert Hoover predicted that "we are on the verge of a wave of never ending prosperity?" No one can say why this confidence

began to falter when it did and not months earlier or later, but on October 24, 1929 the market crashed. "Black Thursday" set off an avalanche of selling as holders dumped their shares at whatever price they could get, thereby driving prices even lower. Some large banks tried to shore up confidence by having representatives appear at the stock exchange where they ostentatiously made large purchase orders. Despite such efforts, prices continued to tumble in the months following.

President Herbert Hoover tried to restore confidence by assuring the public that what had happened was merely a glitch, a necessary readjustment of a market that had gotten out of hand. The economy of America was sound, he claimed, and there was no reason business should not go on as usual. His reassurances met with increasing disbelief as time went on. Businessmen as well as stockholders were worried about the future. In order to protect themselves they laid off workers, cut back on inventory, and put off previous plans to expand or to introduce new products. But their actions, however much sense they made for an individual company, had the collective result of making the situation worse.

Hoover endorsed more federal programs than had any of his predecessors to combat the depression, but they failed to stop the downward slide. Just as people tend to credit an incumbent when times are good, they also blame him when things go sour. He became the most widely detested man in America: trousers with patches on them were scoffingly referred to as "Hoover" pants and in every city the collection of shacks and shanties in which homeless people lived were called "Hoovervilles." As discussed in "A Promise Denied," his reputation sank further when he used the United States Army to roust veterans of the Great War who had come to Washington seeking early payment of bonuses promised them by Congress. In the presidential election of 1932, the discredited Hoover lost by a landslide to Democrat candidate Franklin D. Roosevelt. Although Roosevelt had compiled an impressive record as governor of New York State, his greatest asset in the election was that he was not Hoover.

Roosevelt assumed the presidency without any grand design for ending the depression. Unlike Hoover, however, he was willing to act boldly and on a large scale. His "first 100 days" in office resulted in passage of an unprecedented number of measures designed to promote recovery and to restore confidence. "A Monumental Man" provides a portrait of Roosevelt as president: his appearance, his confidence, and his ability to persuade people that he cared about them.

Unfortunately, FDR's "New Deal" mitigated the effects of the depression but did not end it. Several articles discuss aspects of the 1930s. "When America Sent Her Own Packing" tells how the depression fueled an anti-immigration frenzy that resulted in up to 1 million people of Mexican descent being driven across the border. "Labor Strikes Back" discusses "sit down" strikes such as the one launched by the United Mine Workers against General Motors in 1936. On a lighter note, "Wings Over America" describes the "golden age" of American aviation as exemplified by the 1936 Bendix air race. What was unusual about this event was the number of women pilots who participated in it.

The depression ended with the advent of war in Europe. Massive purchases from abroad and the American preparedness program stimulated the economy as no New Deal legislation had been able to do. Unlike Woodrow Wilson, Roosevelt made no effort to remain neutral when conflict engulfed Europe and Asia. He believed the United States ought to cooperate with other nations to stop aggression, but had to contend with a congress and public that was deeply influenced by those who thought the United States should remain aloof. After war broke out, Roosevelt took decidedly unneutral steps when he transferred 50 overage destroyers to Great Britain and later pushed through congress a "Lend Lease" program providing aid for those nations fighting the Axis Powers. Alarmed at Japan's attempt to conquer China, Roosevelt tried to use economic pressure to get Japan to back off. His efforts only stiffened the will of Japanese hard liners who planned and carried out the raid on Pearl Harbor on December 7, 1941. An aroused Congress almost unanimously approved the declaration of war Roosevelt asked for. "World War II: 1941 to 1945" analyzes a number of outstanding books about the conflict.

Pearl Harbor and Germany's declaration of war against the United States a few days later united Americans in their determination to win the war. For the next six months the Japanese ran rampant as they inflicted a string of defeats against British and American forces in the Pacific. The British suffered a humiliating setback at Singapore, and though American forces fought with greater determination in the Philippines they too had to surrender. The tide of Japanese expansion was halted during the summer of 1942 by the naval battles at the Coral Sea and at Midway. The United States launched its first offensive operations on Guadalcanal in the Solomon Islands. Though much bitter fighting remained, American military and industrial might rendered Japan's ultimate defeat inevitable.

Roosevelt and his military advisers agreed at the beginning of the war that the European theater should receive top priority. Offensive operations against the Germans and Italians began when U.S. forces invaded North Africa in November 1942, Sicily and Italy during the next year. Still, the main effort against Germany was put off until June 6, 1944, when Allied forces invaded the French beaches at Normandy. After tough going against determined German opposition, the invaders broke out across France and began approaching the German border. Hitler launched the last great German offensive in December. In what became known to Americans as "The Battle of the Bulge," the Germans initially made rapid advances but finally were stopped and then pushed back. After more months of fighting, with Germany caught between the western Allies and Soviet armies advancing from the east, Adolf Hitler committed suicide and Germany finally surrendered on May 8, 1945.

Meanwhile, American forces in the Pacific were steadily advancing toward the Japanese homeland. Capture of the Mariana Islands enabled the United States to mount massive air attacks against Japanese cities, and naval actions progressively strangled their war machine. Some historians have argued that President Harry S. Truman could have attained a Japanese surrender by the summer of 1945 if only he had assured them that they could retain their sacred emperor. That is incorrect. The Japanese will to resist still ran strong, as the bloody battles of Iwo Jima and Okinawa during the first half of 1945 had shown. Indeed, Japanese generals claimed that they welcomed an invasion of the home islands, where they would inflict such staggering casualties that the United States would settle for a negotiated peace instead of unconditional surrender. "The Biggest Decision: Why We had to Drop the Bomb" shows that Truman used atomic weapons to end a bloody war that would have been far bloodier if an invasion had been necessary.

A Promise Denied

The Bonus Expeditionary Force

In 1932 World War I veterans seeking a bonus promised by Congress were attacked and driven out of Washington, D.C., by troops of the U.S. Army under the command of Douglas MacArthur, Dwight D. Eisenhower and George Patton.

Wyatt Kingseed

Army chief of staff and Major General Douglas MacArthur watched a brigade of steel-helmeted soldiers precisely align themselves in a straight four-column phalanx, bayonets affixed to rifles. He nodded his head in satisfaction. Discipline was wonderful. Up ahead, Major George Patton kicked his heels against his mount, and the big horse reared forward to signal a line of cavalry. The riders drew their sabers, and the animals stepped out in unison, hoofs smacking loudly on the street. Five Renault tanks lurched behind. Seven-ton relics from World War I and presumably just for show, the old machines nonetheless left little doubt as to the seriousness of the moment. On cue, at about 4:30 P.M. on July 28, 1932, the infantry began a slow, steady march forward. Completing the surreal atmosphere, a machine gun unit unlimbered, and its crew busily set up.

This was no parade, although hundreds of curious office workers had interrupted their daily routines to crowd the sidewalk or hang out of windows along Pennsylvania Avenue between the White House and the Capitol to see what would happen. Up ahead, a group of weary civilians, many dressed in rags and ill-fitting, faded uniforms, waited in anticipation amid their sorry camp of tents and structures made from clapboard and sheets of tin covered in tar paper. Some loitered in the street. They had heard something was afoot—expected it after what happened earlier. Now, a murmur rose from the camp crowd. Upon seeing the Army's menacing approach, they were momentarily stunned, disbelieving.

Recovering their senses, a few of the men cursed and sent bottles and bricks flying toward the troops—ineffective weapons against so formidable a force. The missiles shattered on impact on the hard pavement or bounced off the flanks of horses and soldiers. Undaunted, the roughly 600 troops maintained their discipline with tight-lipped determination. The extra training MacArthur had recently ordered was paying off.

Some of the camp inhabitants had already begun running from the oncoming soldiery, but angry packs held their ground, defiantly wielding clubs and iron bars, yelling profanities. An officer signaled, and the infantry halted to don masks and toss gas grenades. Forming into two assault waves, they continued their push. Clouds of stinging, gray fumes wafted through the air, forcing most of the remaining unarmed veterans to flee in panic. One particularly pesky truckload continued to throw debris, prompting a quick response from Patton: "Two of us charged at a gallop and [striking with the flat of our swords] had some nice work at close range with the occupants of the truck, most of whom could not sit down for some days."

As cavalry dispersed a group of outnumbered veterans waving a U.S. flag, a shocked bystander, his face streaked with tears from the gas, accosted MacArthur as he rode along in a staff car. "The American flag means nothing to me after this," the man yelled. The general quieted him with a stern rebuke, "Put that man under arrest if he opens his mouth again." The energetic officer was in his element. One reporter observed, "General MacArthur, his chest glittering with medals, strode up and down Pennsylvania Avenue, flipping a riding crop against his neatly pressed breeches."

MacArthur could not help being euphoric. If the tactics were not textbook, the results were everything he hoped for—a complete rout. The troops had exercised perfect restraint in completely clearing the downtown area without firing a shot. Within hours it was all over. Troopers set the abandoned camp ablaze as the former inhabitants retreated, demoralized and beaten, across the Third Street bridge. MacArthur called a halt to allow his troops to rest and eat while he considered his next move.

As many as 20,000 former soldiers and their families had converged on Washington in the summer of 1932, the height of the Great Depression, to support Texas Congressman Wright Patman's bill to advance the bonus payment promised to World War I veterans. Congress had authorized the plan in 1924, intending to compensate the veterans for wages lost while serving in the military during the war. But payment was to be deferred until 1945. Just one year earlier, in 1931, Congress overrode a presidential veto on a bill to provide, as loans, half the amount due to the men. When the nation's economy worsened, the half-bonus loans were not enough, and the unemployed veterans now sought the balance in cash. Known as Bonus Marchers, they came in desperation from all across the nation, hopping freight trains, driving dilapidated jalopies or hitchhiking, intent on pressuring Congress to pass the legislation. The administration vehemently opposed the measure, believing it inflationary and impractical given the $2 billion annual budget deficit.

At first the march was a trickle, led by Walter Waters, a 34-year-old former sergeant from Portland, Ore. It soon became a tidal wave, drawing national press attention. The first contingent reached the nation's capital in May 1932. They occupied parks and a row of condemned buildings along Pennsylvania Avenue, between the White House and the Capitol. When new arrivals overflowed that site, they erected a shanty-town on the flood plain of the Anacostia River, southeast of Capitol Hill. Theirs was a miserable lot, alleviated somewhat by the beneficence of the city's superintendent of police, Pelham Glassford, himself a war veteran.

Glassford pitied the beleaguered itinerants and solicited private aid to secure medical assistance, clothing, food and supplies. During a May 26 veterans meeting, Glassford suggested they officially call themselves the Bonus Expeditionary Force. Adopting the name—which was commonly shortened to Bonus Army—they asked him, and he agreed, to serve as secretary-treasurer of the group. Working together, Waters and Glassford managed to maintain enough discipline and order in the ranks to ward off eviction. Glassford likely hoped that the horde would eventually lose interest and return home, but Waters had other ideas. "We'll stay here until the bonus bill is passed," Waters told anyone who would listen, "till 1945, if necessary." He staged daily demonstrations before the Capitol and led peaceful marches past the White House. President Herbert Hoover refused to give him an audience.

In June the House of Representatives narrowly passed the Patman bill, but the Senate defeated the measure with a lop-sided vote of 62 to 18. Congress was scheduled to adjourn in mid-July, and about one-quarter of the veterans accepted the government's offer of free transportation home. Hoover had apparently won. Perhaps now he could concentrate on an economic recovery plan and the upcoming reelection campaign. But many of the marchers felt betrayed and disillusioned. With nowhere else to go, they decided to stay. Ominously, their disappointment festered in Washington's muggy summer heat. To complicate matters, at this point the American Communist Party saw an opportunity to cause trouble, and sent forth John Pace as the catalyst with instructions to incite riot. The degree of his success is uncertain and will be forever a matter of debate, but his presence alarmed the Washington power structure.

'General MacArthur, his chest glittering with medals, strode up and down Pennsylvania Avenue, flipping a riding crop against his neatly pressed breeches.'

Historian Kenneth S. Davis theorizes that Pace may have had a hand in escalating the tensions, goading the angry veterans to become more aggressive. A more plausible explanation for rising tension may simply be that frustrations finally reached a boiling point. In any case, Secretary of War Patrick Hurley had had enough. On July 28 he ordered Glassford to immediately evacuate the occupied buildings, which were scheduled for demolition to make way for new government offices. The veterans stubbornly refused to budge. For whatever reason, Glassford and his police officers became the target of bricks and stones, and one officer suffered a fractured skull. As the melee got out of hand, an angry veteran, apparently feeling that Glassford had betrayed the Bonus Marchers, tore off the chief's gold police badge. Fearing for their safety, police opened fire, killing one veteran and mortally wounding another.

The officers retreated while Glassford sought the advice of his Board of Commissioners. Quick to pass on the responsibility, and perhaps overreacting, the commissioners called the president to deploy the Army from nearby Fort Myer to restore order. Describing the attack on police as a "serious riot," the commissioners asserted, "It will be impossible for the Police Department to maintain law and order except by the free use of firearms." They went on to argue that only the presence of federal troops could resolve the crisis.

Hoover, upset by the continued presence of the Bonus Marchers, now had the excuse he was looking for to expel them from the capital. He directed Secretary Hurley to unleash MacArthur, who received the following instruction: "You will have United States troops proceed immediately to the scene of the disorder. Surround the affected area and clear it without delay. Any women and children should be accorded every consideration and kindness. Use all humanity consistent with the execution of this order."

Not surprisingly, MacArthur now executed his orders in a manner seemingly designed to maximize media attention. In a highly unusual but characteristic decision—one purportedly against the advice of his aide, 42-year-old Major Dwight Eisenhower—he chose to oversee the operations in the field with the troops. Military protocol called for a commanding officer to remain at headquarters. This was especially true for MacArthur, whose post was administrative rather than operational. So while he charged General Perry Miles with carrying out the eviction, MacArthur assumed the real responsibility. Although no other situation offers an exact comparison, MacArthur's action was as if General Maxwell Taylor, the head of the Joint Chiefs of

Staff in 1963, had led National Guard troops to the University of Alabama to confront Alabama Governor George Wallace.

Having driven the veterans from the downtown area, MacArthur had fulfilled his mission. But whether his blood was up, or he merely sensed a need to inflict a coup de grâce against the purported Communist element—an enemy he considered more insidious than disgruntled veterans—MacArthur did not rest on his laurels. He ordered his troops to advance upon the 11th Street bridge leading to Anacostia Flats. Someone, waving a white shirt as a flag of truce, came racing across to plea for time to evacuate the women and children. MacArthur granted an hour's reprieve.

Though accounts differ, the president now seemed suddenly to exhibit an untimely case of nerves. Fearing repercussions, he twice sent word that the Army was not to cross the bridge. MacArthur refused to listen, saying he hadn't time to be bothered by people coming down and pretending to bring orders. He sent the troops across against explicit instructions. Using more gas, the soldiers moved into Bonus City. Its occupants fled in terror, refugees rousted from their pitiful camp.

"One of the soldiers threw a bomb," said one woman hiding in a nearby house with her family. ". . . [W]e all began to cry. We got wet towels and put them over the faces of the children. About half an hour later my baby began to vomit. I took her outside in the air and she vomited again. Next day she began to turn black and blue and we took her to the hospital." Either veterans or soldiers torched the entire area—no one knows for sure. In the confusion, one baby was left behind, dead from gas inhalation.

Endeavoring to eliminate any doubt as to his motives, MacArthur next conducted an impromptu press conference—a job more appropriately left to civilian authorities. The conference allowed the general to expound on the claim that Reds had concocted the riot, the president's safety was at stake, and the government was threatened with insurrection. Describing the mob, MacArthur said: "It was animated by the essence of revolution. They had come to the conclusion, beyond a shadow of a doubt, that they were about to take over in some arbitrary way either the direct control of the government or else to control it by indirect methods. It is my opinion that had the president let it go on another week the institutions of our government would have been very severely threatened." It was a masterful performance. In praising the president and war secretary, MacArthur nearly absolved himself of responsibility—perhaps a calculated move.

Hoover watched the red glow of the bonfire at Anacostia Flats from a White House window. If he had second thoughts, he didn't include them in his record of the event; and in any case, it was too late. MacArthur's boldness had boxed him into a corner. The president's best option now was to vigorously support the general.

"A challenge to the authority of the United States Government has been met, swiftly and firmly," Hoover said in a statement the next morning. "The Department of Justice is pressing its investigation into the violence which forced the call of army detachments, and it is my sincere hope that those agitators may be brought speedily to trial in the civil courts."

Hysteria colored much of Washington's official view of the Bonus Army. In defense of both men, MacArthur and Hoover seem to have genuinely believed that Communists controlled the organization, with Walter Waters merely serving as the Bonus Army's titular head. Hoover believed that veterans made up no more than 50 percent of Bonus Army members, while MacArthur set an even lower number—10 percent. Waters said that was a "damned lie." While Communist operatives certainly tried to infiltrate the ranks of the Bonus Army and instigate trouble, evidence indicates they had little real influence. The president and Army chief of staff's estimates were badly overstated. A postevent study conducted by the Veterans Administration revealed that 94 percent of the marchers had Army or Navy service records. Nevertheless, the Communist Party was happy to take credit for what was billed as an uprising.

Events elsewhere help explain Hoover and MacArthur's state of mind. Students loudly interrupted the general's commencement address at the University of Pittsburgh that summer as he spoke against demonstrators protesting the government. More alarming, a union-inspired hunger march at a Detroit auto plant that spring had turned ugly. Police killed four civilians while trying to maintain control, injuring 60 others. Communist Party leaders retaliated, organizing a 6,000-man funeral procession, waving red banners and marching in cadence to the party's anthem, the "Internationale." Fearing a similar or worse result in Washington, Hoover and MacArthur acted with dispatch when confronted by a large group of disgruntled citizens. Throughout their lives, both officials clung stubbornly to the claim that subversive elements bent on destroying capitalism were behind the veterans. Neither man ever accepted the Bonus Army as primarily a group of destitute, desperate, hungry men trying to support their families.

The day's toll was three dead, 54 injured and 135 arrests. In the rush to point fingers, in addition to the Communist element, Congressman Patman and colleagues received their share of the blame. The *Chicago Tribune* editorialized that responsibility for the incident "lies chiefly at the door of men in public life who have encouraged the making of unreasonable demands by ex-service men and inflamed their mistaken sense of judgment." But Alabama Senator and future Supreme Court Justice Hugo Black directed his venom at a different target.

Arguing that Hoover had overreacted to the situation, Black said, "As one citizen, I want to make my public protest against this militaristic way of handling a condition which has been brought about by wide-spread unemployment and hunger." *The New York Times* hinted that other senators felt the same. Indeed, it was a common charge hurled by the opposition party during that fall's presidential election. Senator Hiram Johnson, speaking in Chicago a few days before the presidential vote, dubbed the incident "one of the blackest pages in our history." Hoping to evoke feelings of sympathy and patriotism, he continued, noting that the displaced veterans had been hailed as heroes and saviors only a decade earlier: "The president sent against these men, emaciated from hunger, scantily clad, unarmed, the troops of the United States army. Tanks, tear-bombs, all of the weapons of modern warfare were directed against those who had borne the arms of the republic."

The public soon followed Black's lead. Frustrated by Depression-era economics and in tune with Franklin D. Roosevelt's comparatively more aggressive assistance programs after he assumed the presidency, the public increasingly questioned the government's response to the plight of the Bonus Army. Many came to see it as callous and heavy-handed. Theater audiences reacted to Bonus Army newsreel footage with choruses of boos.

Ever conscious of his own place in history, MacArthur blinked. At least publicly the general would voice a more sympathetic view of the marchers he once routed. At first he had called them a "bad mob," but gradually time, or concern over public opinion, softened his expressed view. In his memoirs, MacArthur took credit for supplying the marchers with tents and rolling kitchens, and declared them a "vanguard of a starved band," remembering the whole affair as a "poignant episode."

If it was a purposeful attempt to improve his image, it failed. His reputation has remained forever scarred. MacArthur biographer William Manchester called his actions that day "flagrantly insubordinate" and "indefensible." Another historian, echoing Manchester's sentiment, said the general acted "with overzealous determination and reckless impulsiveness."

Likely influencing the judgment of historians was MacArthur's demonstrated knack for upsetting his superiors. Twenty years after the Bonus Army incident, President Harry Truman would relieve the general of his Korean command for perceived insubordination. In the end, the general's personality and ambition proved too great an obstacle for history to erase its view of his performance against the Bonus Army.

Along with MacArthur, two other soldiers who participated in the action would go on to write their names large in history—Eisenhower and Patton. Eisenhower would eventually undergo an even more dramatic transformation than his boss in describing the affair. Normally a frank diarist, Ike merely noted at the time that he "took part in Bonus Incident of July 28," and went on to say, "A lot of furor has been stirred up but mostly to make political capital." By the time he published *At Ease* 30 years later, Ike portrayed himself as a frustrated hero of sorts, claiming that he tried to dissuade MacArthur from personally leading the charge. He advised him that Communists held no sway over the marchers, and he reiterated the old claim that his boss ignored White House orders to halt operations. Interestingly, Ike waited until after MacArthur's death in 1964 to present this version. If it distorted history, MacArthur was not around to contest it.

It was a messy affair for everyone. Patton, a man who revered duty, had mixed emotions, calling it a "most distasteful form of service." Within months he criticized the Army's tactics, believing they violated every precept of how to handle civil unrest.

Still, he commended both sides: "It speaks volumes for the high character of the men that not a shot was fired. In justice to the marchers, it should be pointed out that had they really wanted to start something, they had a great chance here, but refrained." And while Patton was disgusted that "Bolsheviks" were in the mix, he considered most of the Bonus Army "poor, ignorant men, without hope, and without really evil intent." To his dismay, the routed marchers included Joseph Angelo, who 14 years earlier had saved the wounded Patton's life by pulling him to safety from a foxhole.

The episode would dog President Hoover in his attempt to win a second term of office in the fall of 1932. Presidents had called out federal troops before to suppress civil unrest, but this was the first time they had moved against veterans. It left a bad taste in the mouths of voters. A letter to the *Washington Daily News* expressed the sentiments of many. "I voted for Herbert Hoover in 1928," one disgusted woman wrote. "God forgive me and keep me alive at least till the polls open next November!"

Hoover's Democratic challenger in that fall's presidential election, Franklin D. Roosevelt, understood the political significance of the president's use of force. Like his opponent, the New York governor did not support payment of the bonus, but he found Hoover's tactics appalling. "He should have invited a delegation into the White House for coffee and sandwiches," Roosevelt told one aide as he perused the morning papers. Already confident of success, Roosevelt now felt victory was certain. This was a black eye no one could overcome. Roosevelt won decisively, capturing 42 states with 472 electoral votes compared to just 59 for his Republican rival.

Hoover had no illusions, but he could not help but feel bitter. Stopping just short of calling Roosevelt a liar, the former president later wrote of the campaign: "This whole Democratic performance was far below the level of any previous campaign in modern times. My defeat would no doubt have taken place anyway. But it might have taken place without such defilement of American life." The vision of Regular Army troops marching on veterans would provide propaganda for the Left for years to come.

Long before that, the remnants of the Bonus Army drifted home, stopping for a brief period in Johnson, Pa., until that community too urged them on. The government buried the two Bonus Army veterans slain by police at Arlington National Cemetery with full military honors. One year later, another contingent of veterans came to Washington to press the issue of the bonus payment. The new president was no more receptive than the last, but instead of the Army he sent his wife, Eleanor, to speak with the former servicemen. More important, he created the Civilian Conservation Corps, which offered the men employment. And three years later, Congress passed legislation over FDR's veto to complete the bonus payment, resolving one of the more disturbing issues in American politics.

From *American History*, by Wyatt Kingseed, June 2004, pp. 28–35. Copyright © 2004 by Weider History Group. Reprinted by permission.

A Monumental Man

FDR's chiseled features defined an American epoch.

GERALD PARSHALL

Franklin Roosevelt made no small plans—except for his own commemoration. The first Roosevelt memorial, now all but forgotten, was installed outside the National Archives building in 1965. A marble slab about the size of Roosevelt's desk, it was scaled to its subject's wishes. The new Roosevelt memorial now being completed in Washington is scaled to its subject's significance: Some 4,500 tons of granite went into it. Designer Lawrence Halprin laid out a wall that meanders over 7.5 acres, forming four outdoor rooms, each devoted to one of FDR's terms in the White House and each open on one side to a stunning vista of the Tidal Basin. Waterfalls, reflecting pools, and sculptures are set along what is likely to become one of the most popular walks in the nation's capital. The entry building contains a photograph of FDR in his wheelchair and a replica of the chair itself. The memorial's time line includes these words: "1921, STRICKEN WITH POLIOMYELITIS—HE NEVER AGAIN WALKED UNAIDED." But because no statue depicts him in his wheelchair, the dedication ceremony on May 2 faces a threatened protest by the disabled. Controversy often surrounded Roosevelt in life; his spirit should feel right at home.

the freshman's habit of tossing his head back and peering down his nose (on which he wore pince-nez like Theodore Roosevelt, a fifth cousin) and read in it a squire's disdain for grubby city boys. The quirk persisted but acquired a new meaning decades later, when FDR wrestled with unprecedented domestic and foreign crises. His upturned chin and eyes, along with his cigarette holder, itself tilted toward the heavens, became symbols of indomitable determination to triumph over adversity—his own and the country's.

It was, indeed, the face of a great actor, a living sculpture continuously reshaped by the artist. The knowing twinkle. The arched eyebrow. The eloquent grimace. Roosevelt was a master of misdirection. He could lie without blinking, disarm enemies with infectious bonhomie, and make a bore feel like the most fascinating fellow on Earth. Officials with rival agendas often came away from the Oval Office equally sure that they alone had the president's ear. "Never let your left hand know what your right is doing," FDR once confided to a cabinet member. Idealism and duplicity fused behind his smile, buttressing one another like the two sides of a Roosevelt dime.

The Power of His Smile

Today, we carry the face of Franklin Roosevelt in our pockets and purses—it is stamped on more than 18 billion dimes. From 1933 to 1945, Americans carried it in their hearts. It was stamped on their consciousness, looking out from every newspaper and newsreel, FDR's smile as bright as the headlight on a steam locomotive. Roosevelt's portrait hung in bus stations, in barber shops, in kitchens, in parlors, in Dust Bowl shacks—and in Winston Churchill's bedchamber in wartime London. It was the face of hope and freedom for the masses. Even among the "economic royalists," the haters of "that man in the White House," the portrait could stir emotion—as a dartboard.

In 1911, when the 28-year-old Roosevelt was newly elected to the New York Senate, the *New York Times* found him "a young man with the finely chiseled face of a Roman patrician" who "could make a fortune on the stage and set the matinee girl's heart throbbing with subtle and happy emotion." Tammany Hall Democrats, however, weren't swooning. They noted

The Warmth of His Words

He was one of the greatest orators of his time but suffered from stage fright. While he waited on the dais, Franklin Roosevelt fidgeted, shuffled the pages of his speech, chain-smoked, and doused the butterflies in his stomach with gulps of water. At last, they let him start—"My friends. . . ." In a New York minute, his nervousness was gone and the audience under his spell. His voice—languid one moment, theatrical the next—dripped with Groton, Harvard, and centuries of blue blood. Yet no president has ever communicated better with ordinary people.

A Roosevelt speech sounded spontaneous, straight from the heart, effortless—effects that took much effort to achieve. Some speeches went through a dozen drafts, with speech writers laboring at the big table in the Cabinet Room until 3 A.M. Roosevelt then revised mercilessly—shortening sentences, substituting words with fewer syllables, polishing similes—until his own muscular style emerged. Sometimes, he wrote a speech entirely by himself. He used a yellow legal pad to draft his first

Atlanta Chance—Franklin D. Roosevelt Library

Revisionist. FDR rewrote his speeches until they sang.

inaugural address, which rang with one of the most effective buck-up lines in history: "The only thing we have to fear is fear itself." He dictated to his secretary most of the Pearl Harbor message he delivered to Congress. He edited himself, changing "a date which will live in world history" to "a date which will live in infamy."

Roosevelt held two press conferences a week right in the Oval Office. Relaxed and jocular, he gently decreed what could and could not be printed. He talked to reporters, John Dos Passos remembered, in a fatherly voice "like the voice of a principal in a first-rate boy's school." Likewise, Roosevelt's "fireside chats" on the radio reverberated with paternal intimacy. He had a flair for homely analogies, such as equating Lend-Lease aid to Britan with loaning your neighbor a garden hose to put out a house fire. Who wouldn't do that? Speaking into the microphone, he gestured and smiled as if the audience would somehow sense what it could not see. Millions shushed the children and turned up the radio. They ached for leadership and "Doctor New Deal"—soon to become "Doctor Win the War"—was making a house call.

The Splendor of His Stride

At the 1936 Democratic National Convention, Franklin Roosevelt fell down as he moved across the podium to address the delegates. He was quickly pulled up again, his withered legs bruised but unbroken. No newspaper stories or radio reports mentioned this incident—and for good reason. It hadn't happened. America was in denial. Prejudice against "cripples" was widespread. The nation wanted no reminders that it was following a man who could not walk.

From the earliest days of the polio that ravaged his legs in 1921, denial had been Roosevelt's way of coping. He spoke of

his infirmity with no one, not even with members of his family. For seven years, almost every day, he took his crutches, tried—and failed—to reach the end of his Hyde Park driveway. He could not walk. But how he ran. Campaigning animatedly from open cars and the rear platform of trains, he was elected governor of New York twice and president of the United States four times. No crutches were seen and no wheelchair. His steel leg braces were painted black to blend with his socks; he wore extra long trousers. The Secret Service built ramps all over Washington, D.C., to give his limousine close access to his destinations. FDR jerkily "walked" the final distance by holding on to one of his sons with his left arm and supporting his right side with a cane. Newsreel cameras stopped; press photographers took a breather. If an amateur was spotted attempting to get a picture, the Secret Service swiftly closed in and exposed the film.

"FDR's splendid deception," historian Hugh Gallagher dubbed the little conspiracy in his book of that title. It worked so well that most Americans never knew of Roosevelt's disability, or they repressed what they did know. Such was the national amnesia, cartoonists even drew him jumping. FDR dropped the ruse for only one group. Military amputee wards were filled with men brooding about what fate had done to their futures. A high official sometimes came calling. The severely wounded GIs recognized the visitor immediately—no face was more famous—and his arrival brought an exhilarating revelation. Down the aisles came the nemesis of Hitler and Hirohito, his wheelchair in full view and looking like a royal chariot.

The Mainspring of His Mind

When the British monarch visited America in 1939, Franklin Roosevelt greeted him with unaccustomed familiarity. He served him hot dogs at a Hyde Park picnic and addressed him not as "your majesty" but as "George." "Why don't my ministers talk to me as the president did tonight?" an enchanted George VI remarked to a member of his entourage. "I felt exactly as though a father were giving me his most careful and wise advice." It was Roosevelt's genius to treat kings like commoners and commoners like kings. And both loved him for it.

His monumental self-assurance was bred in the bone. His mother, Sara, had reared him, her only child, to believe he had a fixed place in the center of the cosmos like other Roosevelts. She—and the example set by cousin Theodore—imparted another formative lesson: Privileged people have a duty to do good. Noblesse oblige, Christianity, and the golden rule made up the moral core of the aristocrat who became both the Democrat of the century and the democrat of the century.

Critics called him a socialist and a "traitor to his class." History would call him the savior of capitalism, the pragmatist who saved free enterprise from very possibly disappearing into the abyss and taking democracy with it. It seemed evident to him that only government could curb or cushion the worst excesses of industrialism. But, at bottom, he was less a thinker than a doer. Luckily, like gardeners and governesses, intellectuals could be hired. Roosevelt hired a brain trust and pumped it for ideas to which he applied this test: Will it work? If one program belly-flopped, he cheerfully tried another. "A second-class intellect," Justice Oliver Wendell Holmes pegged him. "But a first-class temperament."

For all his amiability, FDR knew with Machiavelli that self-seekers abound this side of paradise. Navigating perilous domestic and foreign waters by dead reckoning, he often felt compelled to be a shameless schemer. He hid his intentions, manipulated people, set aides to contrary tasks—all to keep control of the game in trustworthy hands (his own). Charm and high purposes palliated the pure ether of his arrogance. Franklin Roosevelt was hip-deep in the muck of politics and power, but his eyes were always on the stars.

When America Sent Her Own Packing

**Fueled by the Great Depression, an anti-immigrant frenzy
engulfed hundreds of thousands of legal American citizens
in a drive to 'repatriate' Mexicans to their homeland.**

STEVE BOISSON

A 9-year-old girl stood in the darkness of a railroad station, surrounded by tearful travelers who had gathered up their meager belongings, awaiting the train that would take her from her native home to a place she had never been. The bewildered child couldn't know she was a character in the recurring drama of America's love-hate relationship with peoples from foreign lands who, whether fleeing hardship or oppression or simply drawn to the promise of opportunity and prosperity, desperately strive to be Americans. As yet another act in the long saga of American immigration unfolds today, some U.S. citizens can recall when, during a time of anti-immigrant frenzy fueled by economic crisis and racism, they found themselves being swept out of the country of their birth.

Emilia Castañeda will never forget that 1935 morning. Along with her father and brother, she was leaving her native Los Angeles. Staying, she was warned by some adults at the station, meant she would become a ward of the state. "I had never been to Mexico," Castañeda said some six decades later. "We left with just one trunk full of belongings. No furniture. A few metal cooking utensils. A small ceramic pitcher, because it reminded me of my mother . . . and very little clothing. We took blankets, only the very essentials."

As momentous as that morning seemed to the 9-year-old Castañeda, such departures were part of a routine and roundly accepted movement to send Mexicans and Mexican-Americans back to their ancestral home. Los Angeles County-sponsored repatriation trains had been leaving the station bound for Mexico since 1931, when, in the wake of the Wall Street crash of 1929 and the economic collapse and dislocation that followed, welfare cases skyrocketed. The county Board of Supervisors, other county and municipal agencies and the Chamber of Commerce proclaimed repatriation of Mexicans as a humane and utilitarian solution to the area's growing joblessness and dwindling resources. Even the Mexican consul stationed in Los Angeles praised the effort, at least at the outset, thanking the welfare department for its work "among my countrymen, in helping them return to Mexico." The Mexican government, still warmed by the rhetoric of the 1910 revolution, was touting

the development of agricultural colonies and irrigation projects that would provide work for the displaced compatriots from the north.

By 1935, however, it was hard to detect much benevolence driving the government-sponsored train rides to Mexico. For young Castañeda's father, Mexico was the last resort, a final defeat after 20 years of legal residence in America. His work as a union bricklayer had enabled him to buy a house, but—like millions of other Americans—his house and job were lost to the Depression. His wife, who had worked as a maid, contracted tuberculosis in 1933 and died the following year. "My father told us that he was returning to Mexico because he couldn't find work in Los Angeles," Castañeda said. "He wasn't going to abandon us. We were going with him. When L.A. County arranged for our trip to Mexico, he and other Mexicans had no choice but to go."

Francisco Balderrama and Raymond Rodríguez, the authors of *Decade of Betrayal,* the first expansive study of Mexican repatriation with perspectives from both sides of the border, claim that 1 million people of Mexican descent were driven from the United States during the 1930s due to raids, scare tactics, deportation, repatriation and public pressure. Of that conservative estimate, approximately 60 percent of those leaving were legal American citizens. Mexicans comprised nearly half of all those deported during the decade, although they made up less than 1 percent of the country's population. "Americans, reeling from the economic disorientation of the depression, sought a convenient scapegoat," Balderrama and Rodríguez wrote. "They found it in the Mexican community."

During the early years of the 20th century, the U.S. Immigration Service paid scant attention to Mexican nationals crossing, the border. The disfavored groups among border watchers at the time were the Chinese, who had been explicitly barred by the Chinese Exclusion Act of 1882, criminals, lunatics, prostitutes, paupers and those suffering from loathsome and contagious diseases. In actuality, the Mexican immigrant was often a pauper, but he was not, in the law's language, "likely to become a public charge." Cheap Mexican labor was in great demand by a host of America's burgeoning industries. The railroads, mining companies and agribusinesses sent agents to greet immigrants at the border, where they extolled the rewards of their respective enterprises. Border officials felt no duty to impede the labor flow into the Southwest.

The Mexican population in the United States escalated during the years following 1910. By 1914, according to author Matt S. Meier, the chaos and bloodshed of the Mexican revolution had driven as many as 100,000 Mexican nationals into the United States, and they would continue to cross the border in large numbers legally and illegally. Immigration laws were tightened in 1917, but their enforcement at the border remained lax. While laws enacted in 1921 and 1924 imposed quotas on immigrants from Europe and other parts of the Eastern Hemisphere, quotas were not applied to Mexico or other Western nations. This disparity found its detractors, particularly East Texas congressman John C. Box, who was a vocal proponent of curtailing the influx from the south.

Though none of Box's proposals became law, his efforts drew favorable coverage in the *Saturday Evening Post* and other journals that editorialized against the "Mexicanization" of the United States. When a Midwestern beet grower who hired Mexican immigrants appeared at a House Immigration Committee hearing, Box suggested that the man's ideal farm workers were "a class of people who have not the ability to rise, who have not the initiative, who are children, who do not want to own land, who can be directed by men in the upper stratum of society. That is what you want, is it?"

"I believe that is about it," replied the grower.

Those who exploited cheap Mexican labor, argued Box and his adherents, betrayed American workers and imperiled American cities with invading hordes of mixed-blood foreigners. Those who railed against quotas should visit the barrios in Los Angeles, wrote Kenneth L. Roberts in the *Saturday Evening Post*, "and see endless streets crowded with the shacks of illiterate, diseased, pauperized Mexicans, taking no interest whatever in the community, living constantly on the ragged edge of starvation, bringing countless numbers of American citizens into the world with the reckless prodigality of rabbits."

Upon taking office in 1929, President Herbert Hoover had to face the raging debate. He resisted imposing the quotas demanded by Box and others, as Hoover probably feared they would rankle the Mexican government and thus threaten American business interests there. Instead, Hoover, hoping to appease the restrictionists, chose the less-permanent option of virtually eliminating visas for Mexican laborers and by bolstering the Immigration Service, which had grown from a minor government operation to a force that included a border patrol of nearly 800 officers.

After the Depression set in, the removal of foreigners who were taking jobs and services away from cash-strapped, struggling Americans seemed to be a salient solution, perhaps the only tangible recourse to the desperation that had swept the country. Under the direction of William N. Doak, Hoover's newly appointed secretary of labor, immigration officers dredged the country for illegal aliens. They raided union halls, dances, social clubs and other ethnic enclaves where people without papers might be found. Their tactics favored intimidation over legal procedure. Suspects were routinely arrested without warrants. Many were denied counsel, and their deportation "hearings" were often conducted in the confines of a city or county jail. Frightened and ignorant of their rights, many suspects volunteered to leave rather than suffer through deportation.

While Mexicans were not the only target in the drive against illegal aliens, they were often the most visible. This was certainly true in Los Angeles, which, at that time had some 175,000 inhabitants of Mexican descent, second only to Mexico City. In early 1931, Los Angeles newspapers reported on an impending anti-alien sweep led by a ranking immigration officer from Washington, D.C. Walter Carr, the federal Los Angeles district director of immigration, assured the press that no single ethnic group was under siege, but raids in the Mexican communities of El Monte, Pacoima and San Fernando belied that official line. The final show of force occurred with a raid on La Placita, a downtown Los Angeles park that was popular with Mexicans and Mexican-Americans. On February 26, an afternoon idyll on Olivera Street was shattered by an invasion of immigration agents and local police. Agents searched every person on the scene for proof of legal residence. Though hundreds were hauled off for questioning, few were ultimately detained. The message was in the bluster, not the busts.

As recounted in *Decade of Betrayal*, Labor Secretary Doak's efforts proved to be highly successful: Deportees outnumbered those who entered the United States during the first nine months of 1931. There were, however, some detractors. A subcommittee formed by the Los Angeles Bar Association found that Carr's tactics, such as inhibiting a suspect's access to counsel, fell outside the law. Cart dismissed these charges as nothing more than sour grapes over a lost client base and justified the deprivation of counsel on the grounds that lawyers merely sold false hopes in exchange for cash squeezed from needy immigrants.

Immigration officers raided union halls, dances, social clubs and other ethnic enclaves where people without papers might be found.

Investigations into the alleged abuses began on a national level, as well, by the National Commission on Law Observance and Enforcement, which was appointed by President Hoover in 1929. Named for its chairman, former U.S. Attorney General George W. Wickersham, the Wickersham Commission had made front-page news with its investigations into the rackets of Al Capone and others. Like the L.A. Bar Association, the commission also found the methods employed by Doak's underlings to be unconstitutional. Regardless of the legality or illegality of the practices, one thing was clear: Mexican immigrants were departing in great numbers. According to a report by Cart, by May 1931, "There have been approximately forty thousand aliens who left this district during the last eighteen months of which probably twenty percent [were] deportable." Even those who were here legally, he allowed, had been driven out by fear.

A child in 1932, Rubén Jiménez remembers, 'We were not a burden to the U.S. government or anybody.'

In retrospect, other options were available. The Registry Act of 1929, for example, ensured permanent residency status—a version of amnesty—to those who had been in the United States continuously since 1921 and had been "honest, law-abiding aliens." While this surely would have applied to many Mexicans, the act's provisions were utilized mostly by European or Canadian immigrants. In many cases, institutionalized hostility prevailed over legal rights. Anti-Mexican sentiments convinced the father of author Raymond Rodríguez to return to Mexico. His mother met with a local priest, who assured her that, as a mother of five American children and a legal resident, she could not be forced to leave. "So he left and we stayed," says Rodríguez, who never saw his father again.

Instead of driving Mexican aliens underground—as was often the result of raids and other scare tactics—it became apparent to anti-immigrant proponents that it was more expedient simply to assist them out of the country. "Repatriation" became a locally administered alternative to deportation, which was a federal process beyond the purview of the county and municipal officials. "Repatriation is supposed to be voluntary," says Francisco Balderrama, *Decade's* co-author. "That's kind of a whitewash word, a kind of covering up of the whole thing."

Some 350 people departed on the first county-sponsored repatriation train to leave Los Angeles in March 1931. The next month, a second train left with nearly three times as many people, of which roughly one-third paid for their own passage. The repatriates were led to believe that they could return at a later date, observed George F. Clements, manager of agriculture of the Los Angeles Chamber of Commerce. In a memo to the chamber's general manager, Arthur G. Arnoll, Clements, who wanted to keep the cheap labor, wrote, "I think this is a grave mistake because it is not the truth." Clements went on to state that American-born children leaving without documentation were "American citizens without very much hope of ever coming back into the United States."

Los Angeles later developed a highly efficient repatriation program under the direction of Rex Thomson, an engineer who had impressed members of the Board of Supervisors with his nuts-and-bolts know-how while advising them on the construction of the Los Angeles General Hospital. After the county welfare caseload nearly doubled from 25,913 cases during 1929–30 to 42,124 cases in 1930–31, the board asked the pragmatic Thomson to serve as assistant superintendent of charities. "It was one of the highest paying public jobs in California," Thomson recalled during an interview nearly 40 years later. Having lost a bundle in failed local banks, he continued, "I was interested in a job."

Thomson proved to be a tough administrator who excised bureaucratic fat and made welfare money work for the county. Men dug channels in the Los Angeles River in exchange for room and board. He put the unemployed to work on several local projects: building walls along Elysian Park, grading the grounds around the California State Building. When Thomson visited Congress in Washington, D.C., to seek funding for his public works program, he challenged the feds to "send out people to see if we aren't worthy of this federal help." By the end of the week, he later reported: "I'll be darned if they didn't agree. The government got the idea, and started this Works Progress [Administration], but they didn't always impose the discipline that was necessary."

Along with putting the unemployed to work on government-sponsored projects, repatriation would become another of Thomson's social remedies that would merit emulation. Thomson would later describe his program: "We had thousands of Mexican nationals who were out of work. I went to Mexico City and I told them that we would like to ship these people back—not to the border but to where they came from or where the Mexicans would send them if we agreed it was a proper place. We could ship them back by train and feed them well and decently, for $74 a family. So I employed social workers who were Americans of Mexican descent but fluent in the language, or Mexican nationals, and they would go out and—I want to emphasize offer repatriation to these people."

A child in 1932, Rubén Jiménez remembers one such social worker, a Mr. Hispana, who convinced Jiménez's father to exchange his two houses in East Los Angeles for 21 acres in Mexicali. "We were not a burden to the U.S. government or anybody," says Jiménez, whose father worked for the gas company and collected rental income on his property. Still, Hispana convinced the man that it was best for him to turn over his bungalow and frame house and depart with his family to Mexico, where their 21 acres awaited them. "We camped under a tree until Dad built a shack out of bamboo," Jiménez recalls. Since there was no electricity available, his parents traded their washing machine and other appliances for chickens, mules, pigs and other necessities for their new life.

In the clutches of the Depression's hard times, families sold their homes at low prices. In some cases, the county placed liens on abandoned property. "While there is no direct authority for selling the effects and applying their proceeds," a county attorney informed Thomson, "we fail to see how the county can be damaged by so doing."

"They are going to a land where the unemployed take all-day siestas in the warm sun," wrote the Los Angeles *Evening Express* in August 1931, which described children "following their parents to a new land of promise, where they may play in green fields without watching out for automobiles." The reality proved to be far less idyllic. Emilia Castañeda first glimpsed

Mexican poverty in the tattered shoes on the old train porter who carried her father's trunk. "He was wearing huaraches," she recalled. "Huaraches are sandals worn by poor people. They are made out of old tires and scraps." Along with her father and brother, Castañeda moved to her aunt's place in the state of Durango, where nine relatives were already sharing the one-room domicile. "There was no room for us," she said. "If it rained we couldn't go indoors." She quickly learned that running water and electricity were luxuries left back in Los Angeles. She took baths in a galvanized tub and fetched water from wells. The toilet was a hole in the backyard. "We were living with people who didn't want us there," Castañeda said. "We were imposing on them out of necessity." They left after her father found work. In time her brother would be working also and, to her great dismay, shuffling around in huaraches.

C ontrary to what was being propagated, Mexicans in Los Angeles did not impose a disproportionate strain on welfare services during the Depression. This is according to *Decade* and Abraham Hoffman, whose dissertation and subsequent book, *Unwanted Mexican Americans in the Great Depression,* examined repatriation from a Los Angeles perspective. Based on the county's own figures, Mexicans comprised an average of only 10 percent of those on relief. Nonetheless, repatriation was promoted and widely viewed as an effective means of diminishing welfare rolls, and Mexico's proclaimed plans for agricultural expansion conveniently complemented the movement. Indeed, Thomson traveled extensively throughout Mexico to survey proposed work sites and hold negotiations at various levels of the Mexican government, including the ministry of foreign affairs and the presidency. Some Mexican officials were so eager to get Thomson's repatriates, he later recalled, he was personally offered a bounty of land for each. "One time I was met by the governor of Quintaneroo. He offered me 17 and a half hectares (44 acres) for every repatriated individual I sent there to cut sisal and I said 'Absolutely no.'" Thomson claimed repatriates were in high demand across the border. "They brought across skills and industrial discipline," he said. "At that time, if you could repair a Model T Ford, that was quite an art."

Thomson's program—and its seemingly fantastic results—attracted the attention of state and local leaders from around the country, and his practice of engaging the Mexican government was copied as well. In the fall of 1932, Ignacio Batiza, the Mexican consul in Detroit, urged his compatriots to return home and "accept this opportunity which is offered them." While Batiza may have believed his country's promises of cooperation, others did not. A pamphlet circulated by a group called the International Labor Defense warned that thousands of workers choosing to return to Mexico would die of hunger. This was the end of 1932, and the feasibility of Mexico's grand plans was not yet widely challenged.

W ith a population of less than 15 million in the early years of the Depression, Mexico needed more workers to attain its goal of land transformation. Even as the Depression took hold, the Mexican government proceeded with its agricultural development plans, which would include repatriated nationals—especially those with farming skills. During that time, "They are proclaiming workers' rights," Balderrama explained. "If they're not accepting of the repatriates, that calls into question what they're all about." In the end, however, the government's post-revolutionary zeal eclipsed a hard reckoning of the facts. The returning mass of impoverished pilgrims from the United States would strain an already fragile economy. Officially, at least, the government welcomed the compatriots from the north, underscoring its proclamation of Mexicanism and support for workers rights.

Mexico struggled to cope with the deluge of new arrivals. Hungry and sick travelers crowded into border towns such as Ciudad Juárez and Nogales, where paltry food and medical supplies ensured a daily death count. There are many accounts of border towns crowded with people, as the train connections were not well organized. One repatriado reported: "Many that come here don't have any place to go. They don't have any idea of where they are going or what they'll do. Some families just stayed down at the railway station."

Forced relocation 'prevented me from completing my education and advancing for better employment.'

In an attempt to manage the crisis, Mexican governmental agencies joined several private organizations to create the National Repatriation Committee in 1933. The first colonization project undertaken by this august assembly was Pinotepa Nacional, located in a fertile tropical area of southern Mexico. Modern farming equipment and mules, along with food and other provisions, were made available to the farmers, who were to earn their equity through produce. And while the crops grew quickly, this highly touted proletarian collective proved to be a disastrous failure beset with complaints about mistreatment and meager food rations. The project's final undoing came from disease, as the land was rife with poisonous insects. Sixty people died within 20 days, according to a settler who had left after one month, taking his three small sons with him. "Some have families and can't leave very well," he told one researcher. "But my boys and I could. We walked to Oaxaca. It took us eight days."

Though the government welcomed repatriates, the general citizenry often did not. "Most of us here in Mexico do not look on these repatriates very favorably," remarked one Mexico City landlady. "They abandoned the country during the revolution, and after getting expelled from the north, they expected their old compatriots . . . to greet them with celebrations of fireworks and brass bands." Castañeda remembers children taunting her as a "repatriada." "The word was very offensive to me," she recalled. "It was an insult, as is calling someone a gringo or a wetback." As one Mexican ranch worker asked a repatriate in Torreón in the northeastern state of Coahuila: "What you doing here for? To eat the little bread we have?"

As news about the harsh conditions in Mexico traveled north, it became more difficult to convince people to leave the United States. President Franklin D. Roosevelt's New Deal provided work for some Mexicans, such as veterans of the U.S. military, and welfare was allotted to those who were barred from the work projects. But, back in Los Angeles, Thomson remained resolute in his efforts to repatriate Mexicans, eventually turning his attention to nursing homes and asylums in his desire to purge what he considered welfare leeches. In some cases, the bedridden were sent out on the back of a truck.

Many American children of repatriates never lost their desire for a true repatriation of their own. Emilia Castañeda, who had relocated 17 times while living in Mexico, decided to return to Los Angeles as her 18th birthday approached, some nine years after that dark morning in 1935. Her godmother in Boyle Heights forwarded Castañeda's birth certificate, along with money for the train ride. Ironically, this American citizen was again subjected to humiliation. At the border crossing, immigration officials asked to see her tourist card. "I had to pay for a tourist card because, according to them, I was a tourist. Can you imagine? Me, a tourist, for nine years." It was 1944, and the train was crowded with soldiers. "I sat on my suitcase in the aisle. The seats were reserved for servicemen, but some were kind and they offered me their seats. I spoke very little English by then. Here was this American girl coming back to the United States."

Castañeda relearned English in the same school she had attended as a child. As she would later admit, her forced relocation "prevented me from completing my education and advancing for better employment." Rubén Jiménez had attended school in Mexico, walking 12 miles a day to a one-room structure where six grades shared one teacher. When he returned to the States, the transition back into Los Angeles schools was difficult. A high school sophomore at age 17, Jiménez dropped out and joined the Army, serving as a radar operator during World War II. After several years, he completed college and eventually retired as a parole investigator.

While many American citizens who were caught up in the repatriation movement returned and struggled to readjust to their native country, thousands who had left without documentation had no legitimate proof of citizenship and were denied reentry. "We talked to one lady, part of her family came back, and part of it, unable to prove their residency, settled along the border so they could get together sometimes," recalls Rodríguez. "But the whole family was not able to make it back. And that was not an unusual circumstance."

In 1972 Hoffman noted that the history of Mexicans in the United States was largely ignored. "A case in point is that of the repatriation phenomenon," he said. "When I started working on it as a dissertation there was really nothing. Historians had neglected it as a topic, as they did essentially everything that today we call ethnic studies. I was interested in the topic because I was born in East L.A., and although I am not a Mexican American, I did have some concerns about what had been going on in an area where I had grown up."

Repatriates often tried to forget the experience, and they did not speak about it to their children. Many saw themselves as victims of local vendettas rather than scapegoats of a national campaign. "They really didn't understand the broad aspects," says Rodríguez. "They thought it was an individual experience. It wasn't something pleasant. It wasn't something they could be proud of."

The silence, however, did not dissuade a new generation from seeking answers. "I knew that my father had spent his childhood in Mexico, despite the fact that he was born in Detroit, and I always had questions about it," says Elena Herrada, a union official and activist in Detroit. While at Wayne State University in the '70s, Herrada and other students began collecting oral histories from elders in the community, a practice she continues today. "All we wanted to do was get the story told in our own families, and in our own communities, so that we would have a better understanding of why we don't vote, why we don't answer the census, why we don't protest in the face of extreme injustice. It just explains so many things for us."

In the summer of 2003, the subject of Mexican repatriation went beyond the confines of family and academic circles and returned to the scrutiny of government. A hearing was held in Sacramento, Calif., presided over by state Senator Joe Dunne, who had been inspired by *Decade of Betrayal*. The book's authors spoke at the session, and Rodríguez's voice faltered as he recalled his own father's flight to Mexico in 1936. Other scholars spoke, as did local politicians and two repatriates. A class action lawsuit on behalf of those who had been unfairly expelled from California was filed in July, with Castañeda as the lead plaintiff. The suit was eventually withdrawn, as two consecutive governors vetoed bills that would have funded research and expanded statutory limitations.

For a time, however, the civil action and the forgotten history behind it were national news. This, in a way, was the beginning of a more lasting restitution: an acknowledgement of the past. "My idea is for it to be in the history books," says Emilia Castañeda, "for children to learn what happened to American citizens."

Wings Over America

Each year the country's best pilots competed in the transcontinental Bendix Race, a top event during the period known as aviation's Golden Age. The 1936 contest, however, surprised the participants with a few unexpected twists.

RUTH MITCHELL

Late one night in August 1936, Louise McPhetridge Thaden received a phone call from her good friend Olive Ann Beech. Olive was married to Walter Beech of the Beech Aircraft Company, and she called to ask if Thaden wanted to fly in the Bendix Race, to be held in three weeks.

Women aviators Amelia Earhart and Jackie Cochran had both entered the Bendix the previous year, but Cochran didn't finish and Earhart had failed to distinguish herself. In an attempt to attract female pilots, Beech informed Thaden, the race organizers were once again offering a $2,500 bonus to the first woman to cross the finish line. If Thaden wanted to participate, Beech Aircraft had a plane she could use. Thaden said she'd think about it.

Flown annually since 1931 and sponsored by the Bendix Corporation of West Bend, Indiana, the race pitted aviation's best pilots in a transcontinental flight that ended at the site of the National Air Races, either in Cleveland or Los Angeles. The trophy itself was "a remarkable bronze statue of symbolic grace and beauty that has inspired two generations of airmen to struggle fiercely, and even to die, to possess it," wrote aviation historian Don Dwiggins. But the Bendix was more than a quest for glory. Aviation was making great technological advances in the years between the wars, and races such as the Bendix served as catalysts for change. As Dwiggins observed, such competitions "encouraged men of vision to rebuild American airpower from a shocking low in the Depression years of the 1930s to the new plateaus of speed, endurance, and reliability that helped crush the Axis powers in World War II."

Previous Bendix winners had included Jimmy Doolittle, colorful aviator Roscoe Turner, and Benjamin "Benny" Howard, who had won the 1935 race in an airplane he named *Mister Mulligan*. Women had first entered the race in 1933, and the 1936 contest—starting at New York's Floyd Bennett Field and ending at Los Angeles—would be the second for which the sponsors offered an additional incentive for the first woman to cross the finish line. Since no one thought a woman could actually come in first, the Bendix organizers called the $2,500 a "consolation prize."

The money must have helped, for the 1936 Bendix Race included an unprecedented number of women participants. Earhart was flying with copilot Helen Richey, who had become America's first woman airline pilot in 1934—but she resigned after the pilots' union refused to consider her application. ("If the practice of hiring women to pilot airliners continued, where would that leave the men?" the union asked the Department of Commerce.) Benny Howard's 23-year-old wife, Maxine "Mike" Howard, was *Mister Mulligan*'s copilot. Laura Ingalls was flying solo in a Lockheed Orion 9D, a low-wing monoplane she called *Auto-da-Fé,* French for "Act of Faith."

The race was more than a quest for glory. Aviation was making great advances, and such contests served as catalysts for change.

After mulling over Beech's invitation, Louise Thaden decided to enter the race, and she asked actress-turned-aviator Blanche Noyes to fly as her copilot. Thaden accepted Beech's offer of an airplane, a sleek blue model C17R biplane of the type known as the Staggerwing because its lower wing was in a staggered position in front of the upper. Walter Beech's company crafted its Staggerwings by hand and gave them powerful engines, retractable undercarriages, and smooth aerodynamics.

Despite the Staggerwing's qualities, and the addition of extra fuel tanks and some minor modifications for the Bendix, Thaden knew the odds were stacked against her. She was flying a modified business aircraft, and the race's only biplane at that, against *Mister Mulligan* and Roscoe Turner's Wedell-Williams ship, airplanes especially designed for racing. Still, Thaden thought she had a chance. As she wrote in her autobiography, *High, Wide and Frightened,* "I learned long ago from hard-earned experience in several long cross-country races that a race is not always won by the fastest plane; that good common sense in taking care of the engine and equipment sometimes proves the winning factor."

The period between the world wars is remembered as aviation's Golden Age, and Louise Thaden was one of many Americans swept away by the lure of the skies. "Since I can remember, from the time when I was seven and jumped off the barn under an oversized umbrella, I've wanted to fly," she once wrote. Born in Arkansas in 1905, Thaden displayed a mechanical aptitude while still a child and spent hours working on cars with her father. After only three years of high school she enrolled for a directionless education at the University of Arkansas in Fayetteville, then went to work in sales at the J.H.J. Turner Coal Company in Wichita, Kansas. Flying interested Thaden more than coal, and she spent so much time at the nearby Travel Air factory that her boss introduced her to its co-founder, Walter Beech. Impressed perhaps by the young woman's "insatiable curiosity," Beech hired her to work in Travel Air's San Francisco office. Her compensation included flying lessons, and Thaden soloed in 1927.

Thaden made a name for herself just two years later when she won the Women's Air Derby, the first women's cross-country air race (often called the "Powder-Puff Derby"). By then she had established women's records in endurance, speed, and altitude categories. Thaden gained more flight experience by working for the United States Bureau of Air Commerce, scouting sites for air-route landmarks that pilots could use as navigational aids, and as a sales representative for airplane manufacturers. She also experienced aviation's dangerous side, making her share of forced landings. One crash resulted in the death of her passenger.

In the meantime, Walter Beech had left Travel Air and started his own company in 1932, setting up shop in Wichita with the goal of making biplanes that were as fast as his competitors' monoplanes. The first Staggerwing appeared that year.

One by one the pilots in the 1936 Bendix Race headed toward the starting point at Floyd Bennett Field. On her way from Wichita, Thaden found that her Staggerwing's tail wheel wasn't unlocking and that the wheel-well covers wouldn't close when she retracted the main landing gear. Her airplane would need some work in New York.

Roscoe Turner had even worse luck. A flamboyant pilot who brought a showman's flare to the field of aviation, Turner had learned to fly in France during World War I. He later ran a flying circus, barnstormed at air shows and state fairs, and performed stunt flying in movies. Turner was always nattily attired in a uniform of his own design, and for a time he raced with a pet lion, Gilmore, as his copilot. (Turner's sponsor was the Gilmore Oil Company.) But all his attention-getting theatrics didn't hide the fact that he was a superb pilot. He had won the closed-circuit Thompson Trophy race in 1934 in the same Wedell-Williams racer he planned to fly to victory in the 1936 Bendix. But fate had other plans. On the way to New York from the West Coast,

Turner's engine failed over New Mexico. He managed to touch down in a field, but his wheels caught in a rut and the airplane went cartwheeling end over end for 50 yards before slamming to a halt. Turner walked away with only two cracked ribs, but his ship was knocked out of commission.

The night before the start of the race Thaden's worries kept her from sleeping.

With Turner out of the race, Benny Howard and *Mister Mulligan* became the clear favorite. A skinny beanpole of a man, Howard was a high-school dropout who had designed and built a series of airplanes he designated DGAs, for "Damn Good Airplane." Howard's early DGAs were small but fast craft with names like *Pete, Mike,* and *Ike,* but *Mister Mulligan*—DGA-6— was something different. It was a high-wing monoplane with a large Pratt & Whitney Wasp engine capable of delivering 830 horsepower and powering *Mister Mulligan* up to 287 mph. *Mister Mulligan* had won the Bendix and Thompson races in 1935.

Amelia Earhart was the most prominent woman in the race. She had earned her pilot's license in 1921 and had become famous seven years later as the first woman to fly across the Atlantic Ocean—although she made the flight only as a passenger. Frustrating as Earhart found that situation, the achievement did provide her with the fame she needed to further the cause of aviation and of women flyers. In 1932 she made a nonstop, solo flight across the Atlantic that established her as one of aviation's greats. She also made the first solo transcontinental flight by a woman, from Los Angeles to Newark, New Jersey, and the first ever solo flight from Hawaii to the United States mainland. In addition Earhart was a founding member (along with Thaden) of the women's pilot organization, the Ninety-Nines, and a visiting professor and counselor at Purdue University. Purdue had purchased the twin-engine Electra that Earhart was piloting in the Bendix.

George Pomeroy, William Gulick, and Joe Jacobson were the race's other contenders. Pomeroy had a lumbering Douglas DC-2 airliner, Gulick was flying a low-wing Vultee V1 A, and Jacobson was at the controls of a Northrop Gamma. All were sturdy and dependable craft, but none could compete with *Mister Mulligan*'s speed.

According to race rules, contestants could depart New York anytime after midnight on September 3, but had to reach Los Angeles before 6:00 P.M. Pacific Standard Time the same day. Thaden and Noyes planned to start at first light to avoid crossing the treacherous Allegheny Mountains in darkness. The night before the start Thaden's worries kept her from sleeping, and she listened as a racer took off. "Soon there was a louder din as Amelia and Helen Richey got away, the two Wasp engines splitting their throats pulling the overloaded Lockheed up into the air. Hopping out of bed, I padded into Blanche's room.

"'Let's get out of here,' I said. 'I can't stand this.'" The two women dressed and arrived at the airport around 3:00 A.M. Louise's husband, Herbert von Thaden, an experienced pilot and engineer himself, warmed up the plane for them. The aviators stopped for breakfast at the airport café, but the place was so busy they ended up leaving without even a cup of coffee.

It was a cold but clear morning as Thaden and Noyes climbed into the Staggerwing. "Herb stood near the wing tip, disheveled, two days' growth of beard unable to hide deep lines of fatigue." Over the sound of the engines he yelled, "Good luck! I think you have a darned good chance of placing second or third if you don't get lost."

Once cleared for takeoff, Thaden checked the magnetos, oil temperature, pressure, trim, and mixture control. The starter dropped a handkerchief, which quickly blew away. Thaden released the brakes, and the Staggerwing rolled down the runway. They were off. "My fast beating heart gave up trying to suffocate me and settled into normal rhythm as we lined out on our course, airspeed reading 120 mph as we gained altitude at 850 feet per minute." Around dawn, the Alleghenies came into sight, their tops just pushing through the fog. "I could picture vividly an enormous light blue pottery bowl half filled with the stiffly beaten white of eggs," Thaden wrote.

Forced to fly by means of dead reckoning because of static on the radio, the women hoped the sun would burn through the fog. Within 90 minutes they were somewhere over Ohio and Noyes spotted an air marker on a barn roof, one that Thaden herself had helped place while working for the Bureau of Air Commerce.

Thaden and Noyes were making good ground speed of better than 210 mph—on a conservative power setting. They didn't think much of their chances of beating Benny Howard, but they had a shot at the $2,500 prize. Despite a turbulent, dust bowl-driven storm near St. Louis that streaked the windshield with mud, they reached their refueling stop at Wichita without incident. There they found Walter Beech waiting with food and beverages, as well as the latest about the weather and competition. There was no news of Laura Ingalls. Benny and Mike had already refueled in Kansas City, while George Pomeroy's DC-2 had become stuck in the mud while taxiing at Wichita, losing precious time.

Eight minutes later the Staggerwing was ready to take off, but an army plane was approaching for a landing. Thaden didn't want to lose time—after all, in 1934 Benny Howard had edged out Roscoe Turner by less than 24 seconds—so she disregarded the rule that landing planes had the right of way and gunned the Staggerwing down the runway. Just as collision seemed inevitable, Thaden lunged into the air and veered left, her left wing tip clearing the ground by inches and the right wing missing the army plane by only a couple of feet.

As they headed toward Los Angeles, the two women still believed they had little chance of winning. Their hopes dropped further as they fought a headwind that lowered their airspeed to a discouraging 153 mph average. What they didn't know was that something far worse had befallen *Mister Mulligan*.

B enny Howard was confident and anticipated an uneventful flight. He didn't take off until 6:09 A.M. Less than five hours later he brought *Mister Mulligan* down in Kansas City to refuel. Howard kept the engine running during the 16 minutes it took the ground crew to fill the tanks, then took off and headed west toward Los Angeles.

In 1933 Roscoe Turner had crossed the country in 11 hours, 30 minutes. Mike studied the map and realized she and Benny had a good chance of beating that time. She turned to her husband and said, "We're way ahead of Roscoe Turner's record. They can't stop us now!" The words were barely out of her mouth when *Mister Mulligan* gave a violent tremor. Then there was a deafening explosion, and a propeller blade flew off the airplane. The plane slewed wildly, throwing Howard against the side of the cockpit and knocking him out cold. He struggled back to consciousness before the plane crashed and managed to land on a small clear spot. Despite his best efforts, the plane skipped and crashed into the side of a deep gully. The impact ripped the engine loose and threw it into the cockpit. As Benny lost consciousness again, he tried to remember if he had switched off the ignition to prevent fire.

Mister Mulligan had crashed in a Navajo Indian reservation 175 miles northwest of Albuquerque, New Mexico. Some time later, a lone tribal member discovered the wreck. Benny tried to signal to him, but the man disappeared. Howard thought he was going to die.

Help finally arrived, but it was eight hours after the crash before Benny and Mike were removed from the wreckage and driven in the back of a pickup truck to an infirmary 40 miles away. Mike survived the crash without permanent injury, but Benny's foot had to be amputated. By Christmas they were out of the hospital, and Howard was back at work for United Air Lines as chief research test pilot in May.

Joe Jacobson had his own near-fatal experience during the race. He had arrived at the airport late the night before the start, only to find there was no parachute in his plane. Feeling pressed for time, he decided to fly without one, but he ended up borrowing a parachute from a naval reserve unit. He was very glad he did. "There I was flying at five thousand over Stafford, 50 miles north of Wichita, when the plane suddenly exploded," Jacobson said later. "It felt like someone had hit me in the face. I was thrown clear. I pulled the ripcord of my parachute." Seconds passed as the line of Jacobson's parachute tangled. "After falling some distance the parachute opened, and I landed unhurt," Jacobson calmly reported. The reason for the explosion remains a mystery.

Thaden lunged into the air and veered left, missing the army plane by a couple of feet.

Amelia Earhart and Helen Richey narrowly escaped disaster after a hatch blew open over their heads. "The wind almost sucked us right out of the cockpit," Earhart recalled. Because of the slipstream, the two women had to fight with the hatch for two hours until they managed to tie it down with a rag. At Kansas City they wired the hatch shut, but by the time they took off again they had fallen far behind schedule.

Laura Ingalls' biggest problem was exhaustion. She had flown from Los Angeles to New York the night before and had left that morning without any sleep. Now she was flying alone and fighting to stay awake. Ingalls had discovered flying relatively late, having dabbled in ballet, nursing, and as a concert

The Staggerwing Museum

Few airplanes personify aviation's Golden Age better than the elegant Beech Staggerwing, the type of aircraft Louise Thaden flew to win the 1936 Bendix cross-country race. With its graceful, almost Art Deco curves and dramatically offset wings, the Beech Aircraft Company's Model 17 captures the romance and adventure of aviation in the years between the world wars.

Visitors to the Staggerwing Museum—founded in 1974 by fans and owners of the legendary aircraft and housed in the Beech Center at Tullahoma Airport in Tullahoma, Tennessee—can glimpse the plane's glamorous past. Among the museum's aircraft is SN#1, the first Staggerwing ever built. In addition, there are examples of each of the seven versions of the plane, plus a "naked" Staggerwing. Missing its outer skin, the plane gives visitors an inside look at its complex airframe. The museum also houses a growing collection of the Twin Beech monoplane, forerunner of today's twin-engine private planes, and has become curator of Beech's papers, although little of that memorabilia is displayed.

Aviation pioneer Walter Beech was born in Pulaski, Tennessee, in 1891; he learned to fly in 1914, and 10 years later he established the Travel Air Company with two other aviation pioneers—Clyde Cessna and Lloyd Stearman. The three partners eventually went their separate ways, and Beech set up his own company in 1932 in one of Cessna's empty buildings. The first Staggerwing, designed by Beech's Ted Wells, flew on November of that year. The Great Depression was hardly an auspicious time to introduce a new business airplane, but the Beech Aircraft Company was soon thriving. When Beech stopped production of the plane in 1946, the company had built some 800 Staggerwings, of which 200 survive.

The museum remembers Louise Thaden in a wing that displays newspaper clippings, awards, photographs, flying gear, and personal memorabilia that Thaden's family contributed. A small chapel connected to the museum's hangars is dedicated to Olive Beech, who first encouraged Thaden to enter the Bendix race.

Each October, owners of Staggerwings and other Beech classics fly into Tullahoma for a long weekend to celebrate the heyday of flight and the courage of trailblazers like Louise Thaden. The Staggerwing Museum is located off State Highway 55 at the Tullahoma Airport. It's open March 1 through November 30. There is an admission charge. You can get more information at www.staggerwing.com.

—Milton Bagby

pianist first, but then she embraced aviation with a vengeance. On one occasion she set a record by making 980 loops over Muskogee, Oklahoma. "The chamber of commerce paid me a dollar a loop, expecting me to make maybe fifty or sixty, so I just kept looping until I ran out of gas," she said. Despite her exhaustion, Ingalls had an uneventful flight to Wichita, but there she ran into a delay. "I had no one helping me, as the other girls did," she remembered. "I was strictly on my own; nobody warming up my engine, nobody plotting my course, nobody waiting with a fleet of gasoline trucks to help me refuel." After a fruitless attempt to find someone who would help her get fuel, Ingalls had to do it herself. The lost time cost her dearly.

Pomeroy and the crew of the DC-2 had the most uneventful flight, despite their problem with the Wichita mud. The crew played cards as the plane plodded westward. Gulick and his Vultee had no emergencies to report, although, like Ingalls, his refueling stop at Wichita cost him valuable time.

Thaden and Noyes flew over the Continental Divide, and the rest of the trip remained incident free. For a time the headwind had them worried that they would not arrive in Los Angeles by the 6:00 P.M. deadline. Squinting into the glare of the setting sun, they finally spotted the airport, but Thaden overshot the finish line and ended up crossing it from the wrong direction. "Normally when completing such a cross-country race, competing planes stop in front of the grandstands," Thaden wrote. "But we figured no one would be interested in an 'also ran.'" As they slowed to a stop, Thaden and Noyes were puzzled by the reactions of the crowd that gathered around their plane. "Everyone kept jumping up and down and making unintelligible ges-ticulations, shouting something we couldn't understand." Thaden turned to Noyes. "I wonder what we've done wrong now," she said.

What they had done was win the Bendix Race, with a never-to-be broken record for the contest's slowest winning speed of 165.3 mph. The flight took them 14 hours and 55 minutes, and they won both the $4,500 first prize and the $2,500 "consolation" money. Laura Ingalls took second place, with Gulick and Pomeroy coming in third and fourth and Earhart last. Although it was a triumphant moment for the women pilots, Thaden and Noyes noticed that the Bendix sponsors appeared a little disappointed that the men had been beaten. Olive Beech, who met Thaden and Noyes at the finish line, had no such reservations. "So a woman couldn't win, eh?" she said to Thaden with tears in her eyes.

RUTH MITCHELL is a freelance writer who specializes in history, travel, home, art, and lifestyles. She is also the author of *Arkansas Heritage*, a history text for elementary education.

From *American History*, by Ruth Mitchell, August 2002, pp. 45–51. Copyright © 2002 by Weider History Group. Reprinted by permission.

Labor Strikes Back

What was good for General Motors wasn't always good for GM workers. Sit-down strikes at the company's Michigan plants sparked a wave of similar actions in workplaces across the country.

R OBERT S HOGAN

'Sitting-down has replaced baseball as a national pastime.'

The Detroit News, 1937

It was the height of the Saturday shopping rush in the big F.W. Woolworth's five-and-ten-cent store in the heart of downtown Detroit. Customers thronged the aisles surveying the vast array of hair combs and knitting needles, lampshades and face creams, nearly everything on sale for only a nickel or a dime. The clerks stood by their counters as usual. All seemed normal. But this was February 27, 1937, more than seven years deep into the Great Depression, and what had once passed for normal had long since vanished from the American workplace. Suddenly, the bargain-hunting shoppers were startled by the screech of a whistle blown by a union organizer. The 150 women clerks knew just what to do. All of them, the lunch counter brigade in their white short-sleeved uniforms, and the others in their long, fitted skirts and knitted tops, stepped back from their counters and folded their arms, halting work in unison. "The jangle of cash registers stopped," reported the *Detroit News,* "and bewildered customers found themselves holding out nickels and dimes in vain."

The intrepid Woolworth clerks held their ground day and night for an entire week, taking command of the store. Confounded, the company rewarded the strikers with a 20 percent raise and gave their union a say in hiring.

The locally organized work stoppage in Woolworth's was only one of many examples of the potency of a novel weapon—the sit-down strike—that thousands of workers were taking up and using against their bosses across the land. The strikers demanded and frequently won higher wages, shorter working hours and, most commonly, recognition for their unions. Sparked by the signal triumph of the upstart United Auto Workers' (UAW) sit-down strike against General Motors in December 1936, "sit-downers" were causing Americans to take organized labor more seriously than ever before.

Entrenched corporate interests, the indifference of lawmakers and the outright opposition of the courts had combined to beat back the organizing campaigns of labor unions for years. The Great Depression and the launching of President Franklin Roosevelt's New Deal offered unions hope for contending against big business on a more level playing field. But Roosevelt's key legislative act in support of labor, a federal guarantee of collective bargaining, was torpedoed by the U.S. Supreme Court along with the rest of the National Recovery Administration (NRA), the centerpiece of FDR's reform program. The high court held that the NRA represented an unconstitutional grant of power over the economy to the executive branch of government. Meanwhile, the nation's great corporations continued to use every weapon at their disposal to throttle and disrupt the union movement.

Workers were growing desperate. And nowhere was despair deeper than in the auto industry, particularly at General Motors, then the nation's largest corporation. The pressure of the assembly line had always been a point of contention for autoworkers. But it became even harder to bear when GM stepped up the tempo to take advantage of the boost in the economy achieved by the early New Deal programs. Workers complained about what they considered the assembly line's unbearable pace, which some claimed made them ill or so dizzy that when they left the plant, they could not remember where they had parked their cars.

Well aware that such conditions made its factories a breeding ground for labor unions, GM did all it could to crush any such movement before it could start. Since the beginning of 1934, the automaker had spent about $1 million for private detectives to spy on union activities. A Senate committee, probing interference with union organizing efforts, called GM's espionage operation "a monument to the most colossal super-system of spies yet devised in any American corporation."

Spurred by unrest among the rank and file, UAW leaders on December 16, 1936, sought a meeting with General Motors to discuss working conditions. The company declined to meet with the union. Frustrated and angry, the workers were attracted to the sit-down idea, with its guerrilla war motif. A song composed by a UAW leader caught the mood of the workers:

When they tie the can to a union man, Sit down! Sit down!
When they give him the sack they'll take him back, Sit down! Sit down!
When the speed up comes, just twiddle your thumbs, Sit down! Sit down!
When the boss won't talk don't take a walk, Sit down! Sit down!

As auto industry national union strategists, led by the head of the Committee of Industrial Organizations (CIO), United Mine Workers president John L. Lewis, were still mulling over when to call a strike, the rank-and-file workers and their local leaders took the decision into their own hands. The catalyst was GM's plan for relocating the dies—the cutting tools used to shape the bodies of Chevrolets and Oldsmobiles—from the Fisher Body plant No. 1 in Flint, Mich., to other plants that were relatively free from UAW penetration.

On the night of December 30, 1936, the local UAW leaders sounded the alarm to their assembled workers at a hastily called lunch break meeting by alerting them to GM's plans for transferring the dies. The response was unanimous and swift. "Them's our jobs!" one worker cried out about the crucial equipment. "Shut her down, shut the goddamn plant down!" another worker shouted. Others took up the call and began sitting down at their machinery, just as the starting whistle was set to blow. Within an hour the production line had shut down. "She's ours!" one striker yelled. For good measure, sit-downers also seized control of the much smaller Fisher Body plant No. 2 nearby.

Sit-downs were by no means a brand-new tactic. As early as 1906, General Electric workers sat down at a Schenectady, N.Y., factory, and European workers staged various forms of sit-ins after World War I. But it was during the hard times and frustration of the Depression years that sit-downs caught on and mushroomed as never before.

As the Flint strike soon proved, the sit-down strategy offered great advantages to labor. It made it possible for a relatively small number of workers to completely shut down a huge factory. No more than 1,000 took over Fisher No. 1, and fewer than half that number controlled the smaller No. 2 plant. But their presence, standing guard at the machinery, was enough to keep management from using strikebreakers to reopen plants. While companies could get a court injunction against strikers, enforcing the order would mean driving the sit-downers out of the plant they controlled, a move that was hard to do without the violence and bloodshed that politicians wanted to avoid.

Grasping the sit-down's potential, Lewis and the CIO plunged into the fray, hoping to get a foothold in mass production industries such as autos, which had resisted the efforts of the craft-based American Federation of Labor. A hulking figure of a man, with a personality to match, Lewis saw the unplanned sit-down of the Flint UAW as a golden opportunity. On New Year's Eve 1936, barely 24 hours after the Flint sit-downs started, Lewis went on the radio to bolster the strikers' cause and to demand the help of President Roosevelt, to whose reelection the CIO had been a major contributor.

For GM the stakes were just as high as they were for Lewis, the CIO and the New Deal. The automaker could not ignore the fact that the strike was metastasizing across its vast empire.

In the week following the seizure of the Flint plants, UAW sit-downs and walkouts had closed the other GM plants throughout the Midwest. But none of those were as menacing to the company's profit margin as the sit-down at the Flint Fisher Body plants, the biggest producers of bodies and parts for all of GM.

Sit-downs made it possible for a small number of workers to completely shut down a huge factory.

On January 11, 1937, the 12th day of the strike, GM staged an assault on Fisher No. 2, the more lightly held of the two UAW bastions. A platoon of company guards rushed a group of workers handing food in through the main gate of the plant, overpowering them and slamming the gate shut. At the same time, with the outdoor temperature at just 16 degrees above zero, GM turned off the heat in the plant.

Union headquarters was alerted, and hundreds of workers rushed to the scene, reinforcing the union picket line outside the plant. To bolster the outnumbered company guards, Flint police soon arrived, brandishing revolvers and tear gas guns, laying siege to the plant. But the strikers inside dragged fire hoses to the windows and drenched the "bulls," as they called the company agents and police, while bombarding them with tools and hardware, including two-pound car door hinges. To make matters worse for the police, strong winds blew the tear gas they had fired at the strikers back into their faces, forcing them to call off their attack.

Their victory in the "Battle of the Running Bulls," as the union forces dubbed the confrontation, energized the strikers and buttressed their support among autoworkers in Flint and elsewhere. Just as important, the fracas at Fisher No. 2 brought Michigan's newly elected pro-labor Governor Frank Murphy into the picture. His interest carried with it the promise of an even more important development—the potential for increasing involvement on the part of President Roosevelt, Murphy's political patron as well as the beneficiary of union leader Lewis' largesse during his 1936 reelection campaign.

Murphy mobilized the National Guard and vowed to preserve order. But he also made clear that he did not intend to use the Guard to evict the strikers, but only to quell violence that the local police could not control.

For their part, the strikers organized themselves into committees to deal with food, sanitation and health, safety and entertainment. Every worker had a specific duty for six hours a day, which he performed in two three-hour shifts. Every night at 8, the strikers' six-piece band—three guitars, a violin, a mouth organ and a squeezebox—broadcast over a loudspeaker for the strikers and the women and children outside. Spirituals and country tunes made up most of their repertoire, but they always closed with "Solidarity Forever," the anthem of the labor movement, sung to the tune of "The Battle Hymn of the Republic," taking heart from its rousing chorus: "Solidarity forever, for the union makes us strong."

The sit-downers themselves were all men, but women played a major role in the effort. Wives came to the plant windows to distribute food, which went immediately into the general commissary, and clean laundry. Women were not allowed to enter, but children were passed through the windows for brief visits with their fathers.

The tenacity of the strikers and their families made it possible, within a month after the Battle of the Running Bulls, for the UAW to celebrate an even more significant victory. Facing an imminent collapse of its production schedule for the entire year, GM, prodded by Roosevelt and bulldozed by Lewis, came to an agreement with the UAW that paved the way for the long-term, quasi-partnership role the union would ultimately play in the auto industry.

The UAW's triumph inspired an epidemic of sit-down strikes the likes of which neither the United States, nor any other country, had ever seen. Shipyards and textile mills, college campuses and even coffin factories all were hit in one town or another. The number of sit-downs, which had nearly doubled from 25 in January 1937 to 47 in February, made a quantum leap in March to 170. This figure was more than three times the total for 1936, and represented strikes involving nearly 170,000 workers. In Detroit, the center of the storm, "sitting-down has replaced baseball as a national pastime," the *Detroit News* reported, "and sitter-downers clutter the landscape in every direction."

Sit-downs were by no means confined to the workplace. At penitentiaries in Pennsylvania and Illinois, inmates sat down to get better treatment—but failed. In Zanesville, Ohio, housewives occupied the office of the director of public services, protesting against a dusty neighborhood street.

The spree had its lighter side. In the town of Neponset, Ill., schoolchildren sat down in the local drugstore demanding free candy—until a generous resident resolved their grievance with a $5 check to the storeowner. A divorced woman sat down in her ex-husband's apartment demanding that he pay the back alimony he owed her. And in New York's Madison Square Garden, the New York Rovers amateur hockey team kept 15,000 fans waiting for half an hour while they sat down in their dressing room because they had been denied the free tickets promised them.

But most strikes were in deadly earnest, sometimes accompanied by violence. In the Fansteel Metallurgical Corp. plant south of Waukegan, Ill., a two-hour battle raged with more than 100 sit-downers beating back a like number of police and deputy sheriffs who tried to drive them out of their plant. The police and deputies then besieged the plant, sent for reinforcements and a few days later launched another attack. This time they forced the strikers to evacuate.

Nevertheless, the pace of sit-downs continued to quicken. On one single day, March 8, 1937, 300 members of the United Electrical Workers sat down at the Emerson Electric plant in St. Louis, while in Springfield, Ohio, 300 workers at the Springfield Metallic Casket Company stopped production, and in Pittsburgh 200 workers at the American Trouser Company refused to work. The union demanded a return to the 1929 wage scale of $16 a week for a 40-hour week and intended to organize all 700 pants makers in the city.

Later in the same week, 215 strikers sat down at four stores of the H.L. Green department store chain in New York City. They presented the company with a 22-point program calling for union recognition, a 40-hour workweek and a minimum weekly wage of $20. While negotiations went forward, the union's food distribution system provided workers at the largest of the stores in Manhattan with 85 pounds of veal, which they cheerfully made into goulash. At night a nearby Greek restaurant sent in dinner.

But the major battleground continued to be the starting point for the year's imbroglios—Michigan and the auto industry. This time the principal target of the United Auto Workers was Chrysler, then the second largest of the auto companies. The struggle between the union and Chrysler soon reached the bitter intensity of the previous battle with GM.

The UAW's victory over GM had led to concrete gains—pay raises, the rehiring of fired workers, the retiming of jobs to eliminate the speed-up—all of which helped fuel the UAW drive against Chrysler. The leaders of the Chrysler strike had sent observers to Flint and learned from the sit-down there. But so had Chrysler. When 6,000 strikers took over eight Chrysler plants in the Detroit area, the company lost no time in getting an injunction, giving the workers two days to evacuate.

The UAW's friend, Michigan Governor Murphy, was on the spot. While vowing to support the law, he was reluctant to bring force to bear against the strikers, and with good reason. Neither police nor sheriff's deputies were up to the job, and to call on the National Guard would result in a bloody battle.

So the sit-downs continued, appearing to some to threaten chaos, not only in Detroit but also in other major cities. On March 16, 1937, the same day the Chrysler strikers defied the courts and challenged their governor, taxicab drivers battled strikebreakers and police in the heart of Chicago's Loop as thousands watched from office windows. A mounted policeman who rode into the mob was pulled from his horse and beaten; nearby another officer chased away strikers by leveling a shotgun at them. The strikers stopped cabs driven by scab drivers, threw passengers into the street and in one case set a cab on fire.

In New York City, perhaps inspired by their peers' success with their strike in Detroit, Woolworth clerks caught the sit-down fever. At a downtown Manhattan store of the five-and-ten-cent chain, union supporters clambered up onto a second-story ledge above the store entrance, opened windows and threw food, blankets and other provisions to the strikers inside, while private police tried in vain to stop them. The sit-downers sent a cablegram rebuking the Woolworth heiress Barbara Hutton Mdivani

Haugwitz-Reventlow, whose extravagant lifestyle had become an embarrassment to the company's executives. "Babs," as the tabloids called her, had just recently bought $2 million worth of jewelry, two Rolls Royces, a 157-foot yacht and a mansion in London. The strikers condemned her profligacy in the face of the Depression-driven hunger and poverty that prevailed in New York and elsewhere in the country.

In Clifton, N.J., 150 employees of the Pacific Slipper Company sat down to demand higher wages and, among other things, cleaner toilets. The company appealed to the state's governor, Republican Harold Hoffman, who had previously likened sit-down strikers to "gangsters" and vowed to crush any such outbreaks in his state with force. But Hoffman, like Democrat Murphy, was not eager to back up his words with actions. Dealing with sit-down strikes, he declared, was a matter best left to the courts.

But in the U.S. Senate, some decided that the time for dithering had passed. On March 17, 1937, with Chrysler under siege and smaller companies beset everywhere by sit-down strikes, one of the Senate's aging lions, California Republican Hiram Johnson, called the outbreak of sit-downs "the most ominous thing in our national economic life today." If public officials permit the strikes to go on, he declared, "then the warning signals are out, and down that road lays dictatorship." Democrat James Hamilton Lewis of Illinois picked up on that theme, warning, "In every hour such as this there awaits another Hitler and there lurks in the shadows another Mussolini."

Other voices joined the chorus in the chamber until Arkansas' venerable Joseph Robinson, the Democratic majority leader of the Senate, unable to find any other way to silence the critics of the sit-down, adjourned the Senate. But adjournment came too late to erase the impact of the anti-sit-down oratory. The next day's front page of *The New York Times* carried, along with more news of the continued Chrysler strike in Detroit and other sit-downs, a streaming headline that declared "SIT-INS HOTLY DENOUNCED IN SENATE," with even more alarming subheads: "CHAOS IS FORESEEN" and "FASCISM HELD POSSIBLE."

Labor's friends in the Senate tried to counterattack by blaming the U.S. Supreme Court. The high court's conservative majority had bedeviled Roosevelt, leading him to shock the nation with his controversial "court-packing" scheme. This would have allowed FDR to blunt the anti–New Deal thrust of the court by appointing six more justices, one for each of the present justices over age 70. Noting that the court had so far failed to rule on the constitutionality of the Wagner Act, which had been passed to reestablish the protections for union organizing that had been voided earlier by the Supreme Court, Democratic Senator Sherman Minton of Indiana quipped, "Apparently there is a sit-down strike over there."

But such lame sarcasm was drowned out by the crash of events. In Detroit on March 19, city police broke up sit-down strikes in seven downtown shoe stores, smashing the glass doors to gain entrance when the strikers refused to leave. And as the Chrysler strike dragged on, sit-downers warned that if an attempt were made to evict them, they would meet force with force. Roosevelt privately fretted to his confidant, Interior Secretary

Harold Ickes, that the political storm stirred by the sit-down strikes might add to the difficulties facing his already beleaguered plan to overhaul the Supreme Court. He had more reason for anxiety on March 26, when a group of New England civic and business leaders, headed by Harvard University's president emeritus, A. Lawrence Lowell, wired Vice President John Nance Garner demanding an end to what newspaper headlines were now calling the "sit-down revolt." If such defiance of established authority and property rights continued, the distinguished group warned, "then freedom and liberty are at an end, government becomes a mockery, superseded by anarchy, mob rule and ruthless dictatorship."

In Garner, who promised he would present the statement to the Senate at its next session, the Lowell group could not have found a more enthusiastic messenger. Though typically he did not speak out publicly on issues, he made no secret of his views within the administration's inner councils. The sit-down strikes, he told Roosevelt's erstwhile campaign manager, Jim Farley, were "mass lawlessness" and "intolerable" and would lead to "great difficulty if not destruction." Garner was so frustrated about Roosevelt's failure to lambaste the sit-down strikers, as Garner thought he should, that he let his feelings erupt during a Cabinet meeting. The vice president stood behind Labor Secretary Frances Perkins and berated her for being insufficiently rigorous in opposing such outbreaks, causing the nation's first woman Cabinet secretary to weep.

Meanwhile, Lewis and other union leaders were not deaf to the outcry against the sit-downs. Fearful his political allies might desert him, Lewis went along with a compromise offered by Governor Murphy that ultimately led to a union agreement with Chrysler similar to the UAW's landmark deal with General Motors.

In mid-April 1937, the Supreme Court at last handed down its ruling on the Wagner Act, upholding the rights the new law granted to union organizing efforts. The decision was a stunning reversal of the court's previous labor decisions. Writing in his diary, Roosevelt's Attorney General Homer Cummings called the ruling "amazing," and court watchers speculated that the justices, already under pressure from Roosevelt's court-packing scheme, had decided to do what they could to ease the labor turmoil roiling the nation.

By the fall of 1937, 70 percent of Americans disapproved of sit-downs.

That same April, sit-down strikes began to decline for the first time that year. With the backing of the Wagner Act, workers were now finding the drastic action of the sit-down less necessary, and at the same time much riskier because of increased public resentment. Public opinion pollster George Gallup found that by the fall of 1937 about 70 percent of Americans disapproved of sit-downs, a negative view that colored overall public attitudes toward labor unions in general. By December, the sit-downs declined from their all-time high to a mere four, involving only a handful of workers.

In 1939 the Supreme Court put an end to the tactic by finding it illegal. Ruling on a case stemming from the 1937 sit-down at the Fansteel metallurgical factory in Illinois, the court ruled that although the company had violated provisions of the Wagner Act in dealing with its employees, the sit-down staged by its workers was "a high handed proceeding without shadow of a legal right."

But for labor, it was a great ride while it lasted. In a few stormy months in 1937, the sit-down strikers wrote a new chapter in the annals of American labor. They helped John L. Lewis fulfill his vision of industrial unionism, gaining the opportunity for unions to participate in decision-making within the American economy for decades to come. Just as important, they emboldened individual workers in their struggle for a living wage, the right to organize and a voice in working conditions.

The passion that infused the sit-down strikers faded over the years as the gains they helped to achieve came to be taken for granted by workers. Today some critics blame those gains for contributing to the decline and threatened financial ruin of the great auto giants of the past—GM, Ford and Chrysler. But, as organized labor once again faces stiff challenges from a combination of forces and foes, including a more competitive global economy, others feel that it is time for the union movement to recall the faith expressed in the opening verse of Ralph Chaplin's theme song for the sit-down strikers, "Solidarity Forever":

When the union's inspiration through the workers blood shall run,
There can be no power greater anywhere beneath the sun.
Yet what force on earth is weaker than the feeble strength of one,
But the union makes us strong.

This article is adapted from **ROBERT SHOGAN'S** new book, *Backlash: The Killing of the New Deal*, published by Ivan R. Dee.

From *American History*, by Robert Shogan, December 2006, pp. 36–42. Copyright © 2006 by Weider History Group. Reprinted by permission.

World War II: 1941 to 1945

ROGER J. SPILLER

Those Yanks of World War II are white-haired now. Great-grand children play about their feet. The grand parades and great commemorations are over. Only a few monuments to their achievements are yet to be built. But we can still see them as they were, striking the casual pose, caps and helmets tilted toward the big adventure, cigarettes dangling from a smile. The picture is all innocence. And then later: the hours and days of fatigue piled one on top of the other, "for the duration," eyes that have seen too much and will see more, bandages and blankets on the bloody cots, empty helmets, the wreckage of faith. We can see them like this too, and all in between, in the high councils of state and command, on the high seas and miles above, and in holes that turn into graves in an instant. In all the time since the Yanks were young, you see, history has been erecting its own monuments.

The Second World War may be the most thoroughly recorded and studied war in all military history. By now we might think our picture of the war is almost finished. Far from it. History never stops rearranging itself. But every modern war has created its own historical and literary reflection, a blurred image that gradually passes through stages, growing sharper each year. Just after the last shot come the hot-off-the-press first drafts of history. Memoirs and novels march out next, followed soon enough by stories of the war's bestknown events, battles, personalities, and policies. Only much later do the grand histories appear, seasoned by years of study, broad of scope and learning. Inevitably, however, revisions and counter-interpretations will challenge conventional wisdom to defend itself. Controversies great and small will compete for our opinions. Eventually the war's reflection assumes a familiar, mature form, perhaps stable for a time before the reinterpretations begin anew.

If the literature of World War II has indeed reached such a place, one might think it simple to choose the best books about the war. That, however, depends on what one expects from such a list. Those who think proportionality is more important than perspective, for instance, might like a list that represents the war by military service, with equal parts for the Army, Navy, Marines, Air Corps, Merchant Marine, and Coast Guard, not to mention the WAVES and WACS. They would quickly find themselves overwhelmed with books but no idea of how to make sense of the part the services contributed to the whole war. The same would be true if one were organizing a list around the weapons used. One might learn everything about armored warfare without knowing much of anything about the war in which it was used. That would be putting the tank before the horse, and as we all know, many more horses fought in World War II than tanks. All this is why I have made this list as though it were for me, many years ago, when I knew less than nothing about the war but wanted to learn. If I had read my way through these books, I would have known more, sooner and more systematically, than I did. They have added immeasurably to my understanding of this most important of modern wars.

I think the key to reading about America's part in the war, and thus America's role in it, is to realize that America's was not the only part—a salient fact all too often glossed over in literature and film ever since. This means that one must begin learning about America's part by seeing the war as a whole, in its vast scope and in its unending complexity. The book that best captures the war's totality is Gerhard L. Weinberg's monumental global history *A World at Arms: A Global History of World War II* (1994; Cambridge), which draws upon the wealth of archival and historical work that has appeared since the war and fuses the whole into an intelligible historical picture of that cataclysmic era. No one, scholars included, should presume to know about the Second World War if they have not read this book.

At more than a half-century's remove from the war, it is useful to remind ourselves that the Allied victory was not preordained. The Allies could have lost. No Olympian judge sat with history book on lap, dictating the war develop in this way or that. So, how were the Axis powers defeated? Richard Overy, for one, will not accept the casual, fashionable notion of recent years that the Axis lost the war and that the Allies simply enjoyed the results of their enemy's mistakes. Overy's analytical history, *Why the Allies Won* (1995; Norton), explains how the Allies won a victory that was far from inevitable. "The Allies did not have victory handed to them on a plate," he writes; "they had to fight for it."

And it is the fighting—or more exactly the human beings doing the fighting—that most interest Paul Fussell in *Wartime: Understanding and Behavior in the Second World War* (1989; Oxford), a thoroughly bad-tempered, unforgiving, and brilliant analysis of "the psychological and emotional culture" produced by the war. Fussell's war was not the war the statesmen or the generals or even the 90-day wonders wanted to contemplate, but the real war that belonged to Fussell and his comrades. As an angry infantryman turned distinguished professor of literature, Fussell is most interested in the war's "actuality," the war that will "never get in the books." He writes that "for the past fifty years, the Allied war has been sanitized and romanticized almost beyond recognition. I have tried to balance the scales." When you read Wartime, turn your Norman Rockwell print toward the wall.

Well before Pearl Harbor, American strategists had decided that in the event of a two-front war against Germany and Japan, the defeat of Germany would be America's primary strategic objective. But for nearly the first half of the war, America's fight against Japan took center stage. The war across the Pacific was a part of a struggle so different it could almost be seen as another war altogether. The Pacific Theater was the largest and most complex of all the operational theaters, requiring unprecedented, novel combinations of ground, air, and naval force, directed inventively against a skilled, desperate enemy. Some strategists at the time argued that the Pacific war was so important it should be America's only war. For all that, the Pacific campaign is still less well represented by history than the one in Europe. By seeing this particular war through the expert and comprehensive analysis in Ronald H. Specter's Eagle Against the Sun: The American War With Japan (1985; Vintage), readers can begin to appreciate not only how it was fought but just how critical it was to the outcome of the whole war.

One of the defining features of the Pacific war was the bitter racism that suffused both sides' conduct in the war. No corner of Allied or Japanese strategy, campaigns, operations, or minor tactics was beyond the reach of racism's poisonous effect. John W. Dower's prizewinning War Without Mercy: Race & Power in the Pacific War (1986; Pantheon) is the most thoroughly researched and balanced investigation into the sources of the Pacific war's viciousness. No one should journey into this region of the war without Dower's guiding hand.

For every one of the combatant nations in this war, some single campaign, battle, or event has assumed a symbolic power that outshines all others. For Americans, the D-day invasion of Normandy on June 6, 1944, is the iconic battle of the war. That is partly why the Normandy campaign has attracted so many able historians and inspired so many memoirists over the years. Carlo D'Este's Decision in Normandy (1983; William S. Konecky Assoc.), however, portrays the war from the vantage point of those who bore the responsibility of conceiving, planning, and executing the D-day campaign—a campaign that took the Allies to victory as no other operation could have done. After spending time with Decision in Normandy, the reader will have an idea of how the professionals plan and command modern war.

And then, at some point in one's reading, the shooting starts. The greatest challenge for any student of any war is to come to an understanding of the world of combat, for combat alone is the essence of war. Without the threat of combat, the dread of it, the act of it, or the sorrow of it, war itself would collapse. War has never held out the secrets of combat for historians to see.

This best-studied of all wars has produced very few histories that come directly to grips with war's fundamental nature. It is true, as it has long been true, that fiction and the literature of memory deal with the act of combat more effectively than any other forms of literature.

History will have to go some way, therefore, to equal Eugene B. Sledge's classic memoir of his war in the Pacific, With the Old Breed: At Peleliu and Okinawa (1981; Oxford). Fighting with the 1st Marine Division in 1944 and 1945, Sledge's company suffered 64 percent casualties during the savage battle for Peleliu. And then, on Okinawa, the fighting was worse. Only much later was Sledge able to reflect on what he had seen and done and lost during his war. An understanding of war is impossible without an understanding of combat; the reader is advised to pay attention to the lessons Sledge and his friends paid such a high price to learn.

Sledge's book has been justly praised since its first appearance. A much less well-known memoir depicts the vastly different experience of combat miles above the earth at the controls of a heavy bomber. John Muirhead fought with the 301st Bomb Group, first out of North Africa and then out of Italy, against Axis targets, one of which was Romania's infamous Ploesti oil field. Like Sledge, Muirhead returned to a quiet life after the war and did not sit down to his memoirs until much later, finally publishing Those Who Fall in 1986 (Random House; out of print). No American heavy bomber pilot had ever before published an account of his wartime experiences. Military memoirs are not usually noted for their literary quality, but Muirhead's book is distinguished by a style so fine the reader finds himself wishing the writer had made a life in letters. When these qualities are combined with his authoritative rendering of the Allied bomber offensive from the pilot's perspective, Those Who Fall must take its place on the shelf alongside Sledge's With the Old Breed as one of the two best memoirs of the Second World War.

Those Who Fall will eventually find the wider audience it deserves. Norman Mailer's World War II novel, The Naked and the Dead (Picador), found its wider audience as soon as it was published, in 1948. Drafted less than a year after graduating from Harvard, Mailer spent the last two years of the war as an enlisted man in the Army. His experiences as a rifleman in the Philippines inspired him to begin writing. The Naked and the Dead was published two years after he returned home. His dark rendition of the war from the conflicting perspectives of command and soldier defied the triumphal, sanitized version of the war then being retailed by dozens of instant histories. Remarkably, a war-weary American public kept Mailer's book at the top of the bestseller lists for 11 weeks. The work has had many imitators since, but The Naked and the Dead still stands at the top of the list of novels produced by the Second World War.

Despite their different ambitions, all these writers hold fast, unflinchingly, to the fundamental human nature of war. Each of these books in its own way shows the reader how war calls forth the best and the most terrible human qualities. That is why the last title on this shelf of World War II books may be the most important. Richard Rhodes's The Making of the Atomic Bomb (1986; Simon & Schuster) is an exquisitely rendered history of the most terrible of all weapons from its theoretical beginnings to its first use at Hiroshima and Nagasaki. The war made the bomb, and for the next generation the world struggled to control what the war had made. The Making of the Atomic Bomb is a masterly work of history, therefore, that also tilts its head in the direction of the future. That is where all the best history should aim. Armed with these books, and the wisdom they contain, we may see a future in which the term world war belongs to an ever-receding past.

The Biggest Decision: Why We Had to Drop the Atomic Bomb

ROBERT JAMES MADDOX

On the morning of August 6, 1945, the American B-29 Enola Gay dropped an atomic bomb on the Japanese city of Hiroshima. Three days later another B-29, *Bock's Car,* released one over Nagasaki. Both caused enormous casualties and physical destruction. These two cataclysmic events have preyed upon the American conscience ever since. The furor over the Smithsonian Institution's *Enola Gay* exhibit and over the mushroom-cloud postage stamp last autumn are merely the most obvious examples. Harry S. Truman and other officials claimed that the bombs caused Japan to surrender, thereby avoiding a bloody invasion. Critics have accused them of at best failing to explore alternatives, at worst of using the bombs primarily to make the Soviet Union "more manageable" rather than to defeat a Japan they knew already was on the verge of capitulation.

By any rational calculation Japan was a beaten nation by the summer of 1945. Conventional bombing had reduced many of its cities to rubble, blockade had strangled its importation of vitally needed materials, and its navy had sustained such heavy losses as to be powerless to interfere with the invasion everyone knew was coming. By late June advancing American forces had completed the conquest of Okinawa, which lay only 350 miles from the southernmost Japanese home island of Kyushu. They now stood poised for the final onslaught.

Okinawa provided a preview of what an invasion of the home islands would entail. Rational calculations did not determine Japan's position.

Rational calculations did not determine Japan's position. Although a peace faction within the government wished to end the war—provided certain conditions were met—militants were prepared to fight on regardless of consequences. They claimed to welcome an invasion of the home islands, promising to inflict such hideous casualties that the United States would retreat from its announced policy of unconditional surrender. The militarists held effective power over the government and were capable of defying the emperor, as they had in the past, on the ground that his civilian advisers were misleading him.

Okinawa provided a preview of what invasion of the home islands would entail. Since April 1 the Japanese had fought with a ferocity that mocked any notion that their will to resist was eroding. They had inflicted nearly 50,000 casualties on the invaders, many resulting from the first large-scale use of kamikazes. They also had dispatched the superbattleship *Yamato* on a suicide mission to Okinawa, where, after attacking American ships offshore, it was to plunge ashore to become a huge, doomed steel fortress. *Yamato* was sunk shortly after leaving port, but its mission symbolized Japan's willingness to sacrifice everything in an apparently hopeless cause.

The Japanese could be expected to defend their sacred homeland with even greater fervor, and kamikazes flying at short range promised to be even more devastating than at Okinawa. The Japanese had more than 2,000,000 troops in the home islands, were training millions of irregulars, and for some time had been conserving aircraft that might have been used to protect Japanese cities against American bombers.

Reports from Tokyo indicated that Japan meant to fight the war to a finish. On June 8 an imperial conference adopted "The Fundamental Policy to Be Followed Henceforth in the Conduct of the War," which pledged to "prosecute the war to the bitter end in order to uphold the national polity, protect the imperial land, and accomplish the objectives for which we went to war." Truman had no reason to believe that the proclamation meant anything other than what it said.

Against this background, while fighting on Okinawa still continued, the President had his naval chief of staff, Adm. William D. Leahy, notify the Joint Chiefs of Staff (JCS) and the Secretaries of War and Navy that a meeting would be held at the White House on June 18. The night before the conference Truman wrote in his diary that "I have to decide Japanese strategy—shall we invade Japan proper or shall we bomb and blockade? That is my hardest decision to date. But I'll make it when I have all the facts."

Truman met with the chiefs at three-thirty in the afternoon. Present were Army Chief of Staff Gen. George C. Marshall, Army Air Force's Gen. Ira C. Eaker (sitting in for the Army Air Force's chief of staff, Henry H. Arnold, who was on an inspection tour of installations in the Pacific), Navy Chief of Staff Adm. Ernest J. King, Leahy (also a member of the JCS), Secretary of the Navy James Forrestal, Secretary of War Henry L. Stimson, and Assistant Secretary of War John J. McCloy. Truman opened the meeting, then asked Marshall for his views. Marshall was the dominant figure on the JCS. He was Truman's most trusted military adviser, as he had been President Franklin D. Roosevelt's.

Marshall reported that the chiefs, supported by the Pacific commanders Gen. Douglas MacArthur and Adm. Chester W. Nimitz, agreed that an invasion of Kyushu "appears to be the least costly worthwhile operation following Okinawa." Lodgment in Kyushu, he said, was necessary to make blockade and bombardment more effective and to serve as a staging area for the invasion of Japan's main island of Honshu. The chiefs recommended a target date of November 1 for the first phase, code-named Olympic, because delay would give the Japanese more time to prepare and because bad weather might postpone the invasion "and hence the end of the war" for up to six months. Marshall said that in his opinion, Olympic was "the only course to pursue." The chiefs also proposed that Operation Cornet be launched against Honshu on March 1, 1946.

Leahy's memorandum calling the meeting had asked for casualty projections which that invasion might be expected to produce. Marshall stated that campaigns in the Pacific had been so diverse "it is considered wrong" to make total estimates. All he would say was that casualties during the first thirty days on Kyushu should not exceed those sustained in taking Luzon in the Philippines—31,000 men killed, wounded, or missing in action. "It is a grim fact," Marshall said, "that there is not an easy, bloodless way to victory in war." Leahy estimated a higher casualty rate similar to Okinawa, and King guessed somewhere in between.

King and Eaker, speaking for the Navy and the Army Air Forces respectively, endorsed Marshall's proposals. King said that he had become convinced that Kyushu was "the key to the success of any siege operations." He recommended that "we should do Kyushu now" and begin preparations for invading Honshu. Eaker "agreed completely" with Marshall. He said he had just received a message from Arnold also expressing "complete agreement." Air Force plans called for the use of forty groups of heavy bombers, which "could not be deployed without the use of airfields on Kyushu." Stimson and Forrestal concurred.

Truman summed up. He considered "the Kyushu plan all right from the military standpoint" and directed the chiefs to "go ahead with it." He said he "had hoped that there was a possibility of preventing an Okinawa from one end of Japan to the other," but "he was clear on the situation now" and was "quite sure" the chiefs should proceed with the plan. Just before the meeting adjourned, McCloy raised the possibility of avoiding an invasion by warning the Japanese that the United States would employ atomic weapons if there were no surrender. The ensuing discussion was inconclusive because the first test was a month away and no one could be sure the weapons would work.

In his memoirs Truman claimed that using atomic bombs prevented an invasion that would have cost 500,000 American lives. Other officials mentioned the same or even higher figures. Critics have assailed such statements as gross exaggerations designed to forestall scrutiny of Truman's real motives. They have given wide publicity to a report prepared by the Joint War Plans Committee (JWPC) for the chiefs' meeting with Truman. The committee estimated that the invasion of Kyushu, followed by that of Honshu, as the chiefs proposed, would cost approximately 40,000 dead, 150,000 wounded, and 3,500 missing in action for a total of 193,500 casualties.

That those responsible for a decision should exaggerate the consequences of alternatives is commonplace. Some who cite the JWPC report profess to see more sinister motives, insisting that such "low" casualty projections call into question the very idea that atomic bombs were used to avoid heavy losses. By discrediting that justification as a cover-up, they seek to bolster their contention that the bombs really were used to permit the employment of "atomic diplomacy" against the Soviet Union.

Myth holds that several of Truman's top military advisers begged him not to use the bomb. In fact, there is no persuasive evidence that any of them did.

The notion that 193,500 anticipated casualties were too insignificant to have caused Truman to resort to atomic bombs might seem bizarre to anyone other than an academic, but let it pass. Those who have cited the JWPC report in countless op-ed pieces in newspapers and in magazine articles have created a myth by omitting key considerations: First, the report itself is studded with qualifications that casualties "are not subject to accurate estimate" and that the projection "is admittedly only an educated guess." Second, the figures never were conveyed to Truman. They were excised at high military echelons, which is why Marshall cited only estimates for the first thirty days on Kyushu. And indeed, subsequent Japanese troop buildups on Kyushu rendered the JWPC estimates totally irrelevant by the time the first atomic bomb was dropped.

Another myth that has attained wide attention is that at least several of Truman's top military advisers later informed him that using atomic bombs against Japan would be militarily unnecessary or immoral, or both. There is no persuasive evidence that any of them did so. None of the Joint Chiefs ever made such a claim, although one inventive author has tried to make it appear that Leahy did by braiding together several unrelated passages from the admiral's memoirs. Actually, two days after Hiroshima, Truman told aides that Leahy had "said up to the last that it wouldn't go off."

Neither MacArthur nor Nimitz ever communicated to Truman any change of mind about the need for invasion or expressed reservations about using the bombs. When first informed about their imminent use only days before Hiroshima, MacArthur responded with a lecture on the future of atomic warfare and even after Hiroshima strongly recommended that the invasion go forward. Nimitz, from whose jurisdiction the atomic strikes would be launched, was notified in early 1945. "This sounds fine," he told the courier, "but this is only February. Can't we get one sooner?" Nimitz later would join Air Force generals Carl D. Spaatz, Nathan Twining, and Curtis LeMay in recommending that a third bomb be dropped on Tokyo.

Only Dwight D. Eisenhower later claimed to have remonstrated against the use of the bomb. In his *Crusade in Europe,* published in 1948, he wrote that when Secretary Stimson informed him during the Potsdam Conference of plans to use the bomb, he replied that he hoped "we would never have to use such a thing against any enemy," because he did not want the United States to be the first to use such a weapon. He added, "My views were merely personal and immediate reactions; they were not based on any analysis of the subject."

Eisenhower's recollections grew more colorful as the years went on. A later account of his meeting with Stimson had it taking place at Ike's headquarters in Frankfurt on the very day news arrived of the successful atomic test in New Mexico. "We'd had a nice evening at headquarters in Germany," he remembered. Then, after dinner, "Stimson got this cable saying that the bomb had been perfected and was ready to be dropped. The cable was in code . . . 'the lamb is born' or some damn thing like that." In this version Eisenhower claimed to have protested vehemently that "the Japanese were ready to surrender and it wasn't necessary to hit them with that awful thing." "Well," Eisenhower concluded, "the old gentleman got furious."

T he best that can be said about Eisenhower's memory is that it had become flawed by the passage of time. Stimson was in Potsdam and Eisenhower in Frankfurt on July 16, when word came of the successful test. Aside from a brief conversation at a flag-raising ceremony in Berlin on July 20, the only other time they met was at Ike's headquarters on July 27. By then orders already had been sent to the Pacific to use the bombs if Japan had not yet surrendered. Notes made by one of Stimson's aides indicate that there was a discussion of atomic bombs, but there is no mention of any protest on Eisenhower's part. Even if there had been, two factors must be kept in mind. Eisenhower had commanded Allied forces in Europe, and his opinion on how close Japan was to surrender would have carried no special weight. More important, Stimson left for home immediately after the meeting and could not have personally conveyed Ike's sentiments to the President, who did not return to Washington until after Hiroshima.

On July 8 the Combined Intelligence Committee submitted to the American and British Combined Chiefs of Staff a report entitled "Estimate of the Enemy Situation." The committee predicted that as Japan's position continued to deteriorate, it might "make a serious effort to use the USSR [then a

neutral] as a mediator in ending the war." Tokyo also would put out "intermittent peace feelers" to "weaken the determination of the United Nations to fight to the bitter end, or to create inter-allied dissension." While the Japanese people would be willing to make large concessions to end the war, "For a surrender to be acceptable to the Japanese army, it would be necessary for the military leaders to believe that it would not entail discrediting warrior tradition and that it would permit the ultimate resurgence of a military Japan."

Small wonder that American officials remained unimpressed when Japan proceeded to do exactly what the committee predicted. On July 12 Japanese Foreign Minister Shigenori Togo instructed Ambassador Naotaki Sato in Moscow to inform the Soviets that the emperor wished to send a personal envoy, Prince Fuminaro Konoye, in an attempt "to restore peace with all possible speed." Although he realized Konoye could not reach Moscow before the Soviet leader Joseph Stalin and Foreign Minister V. M. Molotov left to attend a Big Three meeting scheduled to begin in Potsdam on the fifteenth, Togo sought to have negotiations begin as soon as they returned.

American officials had long since been able to read Japanese diplomatic traffic through a process known as the MAGIC intercepts. Army intelligence (G-2) prepared for General Marshall its interpretation of Togo's message the next day. The report listed several possible constructions, the most probable being that the Japanese "governing clique" was making a coordinated effort to "stave off defeat" through Soviet intervention and an "appeal to war weariness in the United States." The report added that Undersecretary of State Joseph C. Grew, who had spent ten years in Japan as ambassador, "agrees with these conclusions."

Some have claimed that Togo's overture to the Soviet Union, together with attempts by some minor Japanese officials in Switzerland and other neutral countries to get peace talks started through the Office of Strategic Services (OSS), constituted clear evidence that the Japanese were near surrender. Their sole prerequisite was retention of their sacred emperor, whose unique cultural/religious status within the Japanese polity they would not compromise. If only the United States had extended assurances about the emperor, according to this view, much bloodshed and the atomic bombs would have been unnecessary.

A careful reading of the MAGIC intercepts of subsequent exchanges between Togo and Sato provides no evidence that retention of the emperor was the sole obstacle to peace. What they show instead is that the Japanese Foreign Office was trying to cut a deal through the Soviet Union that would have permitted Japan to retain its political system and its prewar empire intact. Even the most lenient American official could not have countenanced such a settlement.

T ogo on July 17 informed Sato that "we are not asking the Russians' mediation in *anything like unconditional surrender* [emphasis added]." During the following weeks Sato pleaded with his superiors to abandon hope of Soviet intercession and to approach the United States directly to find out what peace terms would be offered. "There is . . . no alternative but immediate unconditional surrender," he cabled on July 31, and he bluntly informed Togo that "your way of looking at things and the actual situation in the Eastern Area may be seen to be absolutely contradictory." The Foreign Ministry ignored his pleas and continued to seek Soviet help even after Hiroshima.

"Peace feelers" by Japanese officials abroad seemed no more promising from the American point of view. Although several of the consular personnel and military attachés engaged in these activities claimed important connections at home, none produced verification. Had the Japanese government sought only an assurance about the emperor, all it had to do was grant one of these men authority to begin talks through the OSS. Its failure to do so led American officials to assume that those involved were either well-meaning individuals acting alone or that they were being orchestrated by Tokyo. Grew characterized such "peace feelers" as "familiar weapons of psychological warfare" designed to "divide the Allies."

Some American officials, such as Stimson and Grew, nonetheless wanted to signal the Japanese that they might retain the emperorship in the form of a constitutional monarchy. Such an assurance might remove the last stumbling block to surrender, if not when it was issued, then later. Only an imperial rescript would bring about an orderly surrender, they argued, without which Japanese forces would fight to the last man regardless of what the government in Tokyo did. Besides, the emperor could serve as a stabilizing factor during the transition to peacetime.

There were many arguments against an American initiative. Some opposed retaining such an undemocratic institution on principle and because they feared it might later serve as a rallying point for future militarism. Should that happen, as one assistant Secretary of State put it, "those lives already spent will have been sacrificed in vain, and lives will be lost again in the future." Japanese hard-liners were certain to exploit an overture as evidence that losses sustained at Okinawa had weakened American resolve and to argue that continued resistance would bring further concessions. Stalin, who earlier had told an American envoy that he favored abolishing the emperorship because the ineffectual Hirohito might be succeeded by "an energetic and vigorous figure who could cause trouble," was just as certain to interpret it as a treacherous effort to end the war before the Soviets could share in the spoils.

There were domestic considerations as well. Roosevelt had announced the unconditional surrender policy in early 1943, and it since had become a slogan of the war. He also had advocated that peoples everywhere should have the right to choose their own form of government, and Truman had publicly pledged to carry out his predecessor's legacies. For him to have formally *guaranteed* continuance of the emperorship, as opposed to merely accepting it on American terms pending free elections, as he later did, would have constituted a blatant repudiation of his own promises.

Nor was that all. Regardless of the emperor's actual role in Japanese aggression, which is still debated, much wartime propaganda had encouraged Americans to regard Hirohito as no less a war criminal than Adolf Hitler or Benito Mussolini. Although Truman said on several occasions that he had no objection to retaining the emperor, he understandably refused to make the

first move. The ultimatum he issued from Potsdam on July 26 did not refer specifically to the emperorship. All it said was that occupation forces would be removed after "a peaceful and responsible" government had been established according to the "freely expressed will of the Japanese people." When the Japanese rejected the ultimatum rather than at last inquire whether they might retain the emperor, Truman permitted the plans for using the bombs to go forward.

Reliance on MAGIC intercepts and the "peace feelers" to gauge how near Japan was to surrender is misleading in any case. The army, not the Foreign Office, controlled the situation. Intercepts of Japanese military communications, designated ULTRA, provided no reason to believe the army was even considering surrender. Japanese Imperial Headquarters had correctly guessed that the next operation after Okinawa would be Kyushu and was making every effort to bolster its defenses there.

General Marshall reported on July 24 that there were "approximately 500,000 troops in Kyushu" and that more were on the way. ULTRA identified new units arriving almost daily. MacArthur's G-2 reported on July 29 that "this threatening development, if not checked, may grow to a point where we attack on a ratio of one (1) to one (1) which is not the recipe for victory." By the time the first atomic bomb fell, ULTRA indicated that there were 560,000 troops in southern Kyushu (the actual figure was closer to 900,000), and projections for November 1 placed the number at 680,000. A report, for medical purposes, of July 31 estimated that total battle and non-battle casualties might run as high as 394,859 *for the Kyushu operation alone.* This figure did not include those men expected to be killed outright, for obviously they would require no medical attention. Marshall regarded Japanese defenses as so formidable that even after Hiroshima he asked MacArthur to consider alternate landing sites and began contemplating the use of atomic bombs as tactical weapons to support the invasion.

By late July the casualty projection of 31,000 that Marshall had given Truman at the June 18 strategy meeting had become meaningless.

The thirty-day casualty projection of 31,000 Marshall had given Truman at the June 18 strategy meeting had become meaningless. It had been based on the assumption that the Japanese had about 350,000 defenders in Kyushu and that naval and air interdiction would preclude significant reinforcement. But the Japanese buildup since that time meant that the defenders would have nearly twice the number of troops available by "X-day" than earlier assumed. The assertion that apprehensions about casualties are insufficient to explain Truman's use of the bombs, therefore, cannot be taken seriously. On the contrary, as Winston Churchill wrote after a conversation with him at Potsdam, Truman was tormented by "the terrible responsibilities that rested upon him in regard to the unlimited effusions of American blood."

ome historians have argued that while the first bomb *might* have been required to achieve Japanese surrender, dropping the second constituted a needless barbarism. The record shows otherwise. American officials believed more than one bomb would be necessary because they assumed Japanese hard-liners would minimize the first explosion or attempt to explain it away as some sort of natural catastrophe, precisely what they did. The Japanese minister of war, for instance, at first refused even to admit that the Hiroshima bomb was atomic. A few hours after Nagasaki he told the cabinet that "the Americans appeared to have one hundred atomic bombs . . . they could drop three per day. The next target might well be Tokyo."

Even after both bombs had fallen and Russia entered the war, Japanese militants insisted on such lenient peace terms that moderates knew there was no sense even transmitting them to the United States. Hirohito had to intervene personally on two occasions during the next few days to induce hard-liners to abandon their conditions and to accept the American stipulation that the emperor's authority "shall be subject to the Supreme Commander of the Allied Powers." That the militarists would have accepted such a settlement before the bombs is farfetched, to say the least.

Some writers have argued that the cumulative effects of battlefield defeats, conventional bombing, and naval blockade already had defeated Japan. Even without extending assurances about the emperor, all the United States had to do was wait. The most frequently cited basis for this contention is the *United States Strategic Bombing Survey,* published in 1946, which stated that Japan would have surrendered by November 1 "even if the atomic bombs had not been dropped, even if Russia had

not entered the war, and even if no invasion had been planned or contemplated." Recent scholarship by the historian Robert P. Newman and others has demonstrated that the survey was "cooked" by those who prepared it to arrive at such a conclusion. No matter. This or any other document based on information available only after the war ended is irrelevant with regard to what Truman could have known at the time.

What often goes unremarked is that when the bombs were dropped, fighting was still going on in the Philippines, China, and elsewhere. Every day that the war continued thousands of prisoners of war had to live and die in abysmal conditions, and there were rumors that the Japanese intended to slaughter them if the homeland was invaded. Truman was Commander in Chief of the American armed forces, and he had a duty to the men under his command not shared by those sitting in moral judgment decades later. Available evidence points to the conclusion that he acted for the reason he said he did: to end a bloody war that would have become far bloodier had invasion proved necessary. One can only imagine what would have happened if tens of thousands of American boys had died or been wounded on Japanese soil and then it had become known that Truman had chosen not to use weapons that might have ended the war months sooner.

ROBERT JAMES MADDOX teaches American history at Pennsylvania State University. His *Weapons for Victory: Hiroshima Fifty Years Later* is published by the University of Missouri Press (1995).

From *American Heritage,* May/June 1995, pp. 71–74, 76–77. Copyright © 1995 by American Heritage, Inc. Reprinted by permission.

UNIT 5

From the Cold War to 2007

Unit Selections

Key Points to Consider

- What was the Marshall Plan and why did US policymakers believe it was necessary? How effective was it in trying to restore European nations to prosperity?

- "Rosie the Riveter" was a popular symbol during World War II. She was depicted in countless posters as a muscular young woman who worked in a factory to further the war effort. When the war ended and the men came home, she was supposed to exchange her working clothes for an apron. What was wrong with this scenario?

- What lessons did the American Civil Rights movement have for peoples in other parts of the world? What struggles abroad in turn influenced American activists in this movement?

- President John F. Kennedy placed great emphasis on the scientific achievements that a massive space program would provide. What were his real motives in supporting this costly enterprise?

- Discuss Bill Clinton's presidency. What did he accomplish, which of his objectives eluded him? How did his personal failings destroy his presidency?

- Discuss the President Bush/Karl Rove strategy to achieve a permanent Republican majority? Why did it fail?

Student Web Site

www.mhcls.com/online

Internet References

Further information regarding these Web sites may be found in this book's preface or online.

Coldwar
  http://www.cnn.com/SPECIALS/cold.war
The American Experience: Vietnam Online
  http://www.pbs.org/wgbh/amex/vietnam/
The Gallup Organization
  http://www.gallup.com/
STAT-USA
  http://www.stat-usa.gov/stat-usa.html
U.S. Department of State
  http://www.state.gov/

President Franklin D. Roosevelt sought to build a working relationship with Soviet leader Josef Stalin throughout World War II. Roosevelt believed that the wartime collaboration had to continue if a lasting peace were to be achieved. At the Yalta Conference of February 1945, a series of agreements were made that FDR hoped would provide the basis for continued cooperation. Subsequent disputes over interpretation of these agreements, particularly with regard to Poland, raised doubts in Roosevelt's mind that Stalin was acting in good faith. Roosevelt died on April 12, 1945, and there is no doubt that he was moving toward a "tougher" position during the last weeks of his life.

Harry S. Truman assumed the presidency with little knowledge of Roosevelt's thinking. Truman had not been part of the administration's inner circle and had to rely on discussions with the advisers he inherited and his own reading of messages passed between FDR and the Soviets. Aside from an ugly encounter with Soviet Foreign Minister V. M. Molotov at the White House only eleven days after Roosevelt's death, Truman attempted to carry out what he believed were Roosevelt's intentions: be firm with the Soviets, but continue to seek accommodation. He came to believe that Foreign Minister V. M. Molotov was trying to sabotage US-Soviet relations and that the best way to reach agreements was to negotiate directly with Stalin. This he did at the Potsdam Conference during the summer of 1945, and left the talks believing that Stalin was a hard bargainer but one who could be trusted.

Events during the late summer and early autumn eroded Truman's hopes that the Soviets genuinely wanted to get along. Disputes over Poland and other Eastern European countries, the treatment of postwar Germany, and a host of other issues finally persuaded Truman that it was time to stop "babying" the Soviets. A militant public speech by Stalin, which one American referred to as the "declaration of World War III," appeared to confirm this view. Increasingly hostile relations led to what became known as the "Cold War," during which each side increasingly came to regard the other as an enemy rather than merely an adversary.

Meanwhile the United States had to cope with the problems of conversion to a peacetime economy. Demobilization of the armed forces proved especially vexing as the public clamored to have service men and women, stationed virtually all over the world, brought home and discharged as quickly as possible. When the administration seemed to be moving too slowly, the threat "no boats, no votes" became popular. Race riots, labor strife, and inflation also marred the postwar period.

Relations with the Soviets continued to deteriorate. Perceived Soviet threats against Greece and Turkey led to promulgation of the "Truman Doctrine" in 1947, which placed the United States on the side of those nations threatened with overt aggression or internal subversion. That same year Secretary of State George C. Marshall sketched the outlines of what would become known

as the "Marshall Plan," an even more ambitious effort to prevent economic chaos in Europe. "Dollar Diplomacy: How Much Did the Marshall Plan Really Matter?" evaluates this program that has been described as "among the most noble experiences in human affairs."

How had things gotten to such a sorry state only a few years after the dragons of fascism and Japanese militarism had been slain? Some people began alleging that, as dangerous as the Soviet Union was, internal subversion was an even greater problem. Opponents of Roosevelt's "New Deal" and Truman's "Fair Deal" cited various allegations of spying on the part of former government officials to bolster their claims that Democrat administrations had been shot-through with subversion. Liberals cried frame up. Some of these allegations have been shown to be true, but what became known as "McCarthysim" (after a Wisconsin senator who was a prominent "Commie hunter") cast a pall of suspicion over the society.

In 1950, a scant five years after the end of World War II, the United States found itself at war again. The North Korean invasion of the South in June of that year appeared to American leaders as a Soviet-inspired probe to test Western resolve. Failure to halt aggression there, many believed, would embolden the Soviets to strike elsewhere just as Hitler had done in the 1930s. President Truman's decision to send American troops to Korea was almost universally applauded at first, but discontent arose as the war dragged on. Americans were not used to fighting "no win" wars.

Domestically, the 1950s offered a mixed bag. Social critics denounced the conformity of those who plodded up the corporate latter, purchased tract homes that all looked alike, or who had no greater ambition than to sit in front of their television sets every night. Both "From Rosie the Riveter to the General Assembly Line: American Women on the World Stage" and "The Civil Rights Movement in World Perspective" show that beneath the veneer of tranquility there were stirrings over civil rights and liberties that would erupt into prominence during the 1960s. At the same time, anti-New Deal conservatism began to grow, fueled in part by fears that Communism was taking over the world. "The Rise of Conservatism Since World War II" describes how this movement eventually took over the Republican Party.

The election of John F. Kennedy to the presidency in 1960 appeared to many as a turning point in American history. His charm and good looks, as well as his liberal agenda, provided a marked contrast to the Eisenhower era. Kennedy did sponsor some significant legislation and moved hesitantly on civil rights, but his assassination in 1963 leaves us only to speculate on what he might have accomplished had he served his full term and perhaps a second. Recent historians have given mixed grades to his presidency. They point to the Bay of Pigs fiasco and to the fact that he was the one to first send combat troops to Vietnam. "The Dark Side of the Moon" argues that Kennedy's commitment to the space program was motivated almost completely by his desire to use it as a Cold War tool against the Soviet Union rather than as a quest for scientific achievement.

Three other articles deal with presidential conduct. "Soft Power: Reagan the Dove" argues that in spite of his militant rhetoric against the Soviets, Ronald Reagan played a key role in ending the Cold War because of his commitment to peace. "The Tragedy of Bill Clinton" treats this extremely talented but flawed president. Author Gary Wills believes it would have been better for him and for his programs had he resigned from office. "The Rove Presidency" contends that President George W. Bush's key adviser, Karl Rove, had "the plan, the power, and the historic chance to remake American politics." This seemed especially true after 9/11. The vision of creating a permanent Republican majority dissipated through a series of blunders. "Bush will leave behind a legacy long on ambition," the author writes, "and short on positive results."

At this writing the second war against Iraq grinds on. "From Saigon to Desert Storm" tells how the United States Army reformed itself after the quagmire of Vietnam into an extremely capable fighting force. This was demonstrated dramatically in "Desert Storm," as the first campaign against Iraq in 1991 was called. Unfortunately, according to author Max Boot, the reforms that made the army so formidable in conventional warfare did not prepare it for the aftermath of the second war against Saddam Hussein. The U.S. military, he writes, was "superbly configured for a dash through the desert," but was "ill suited for waging irregular warfare against shadowy enemies who did not present easy targets for smart bombs and Abrams tanks."

Dollar Diplomacy

How much did the Marshall Plan really matter?

NIALL FERGUSON

It was "the most generous act of any people, anytime, anywhere, to another people," its chief administrator declared. It was "among the most noble experiences in human affairs," its representative in Europe said. It was "the most staggering and portentous experiment in the entire history of our foreign policy," the young Arthur Schlesinger, Jr., who served on its staff, wrote. Foreigners concurred. It was "like a lifeline to sinking men," according to the British Foreign Secretary Ernest Bevin. It "saved us from catastrophe," a manager at Europe's largest tire factory declared. Sixty years after Secretary of State George C. Marshall outlined the need for economic aid to stimulate European recovery, in a speech at Harvard University's commencement on June 5, 1947, the plan named after him continues to be fondly remembered in donor and recipient countries alike. In our own time, liberal internationalists have periodically called for new Marshall Plans. After the collapse of Communism, some economists maintained that the former Soviet Union was in need of one. More recently, there has been desultory talk of Marshall Plans for Afghanistan, Iraq, and even the West Bank and Gaza. When critics lament the allegedly modest sums currently spent by the American government on foreign aid, they often draw an unfavorable contrast with the late nineteen-forties. Yet some people, at the time of its inception and since, have questioned both the Marshall Plan's motivation and its efficacy. Was it really so altruistic? And did it really avert a calamity?

More popular history is written about war than about peace, and very little concerns itself with economics. Greg Behrman's "The Most Noble Adventure: The Marshall Plan and the Time When America Helped Save Europe" (Free Press; $27) is admirable for bringing to the potentially arid story of America's biggest aid program all the literary verve and drama one associates with the best military and diplomatic history. Behrman's approach recalls that of Margaret MacMillan in her recent book "Paris 1919," about the Paris Peace Conference after the First World War. Like "Paris 1919," "The Most Noble Adventure" is an account in which individual actors predominate over economic calculations. But, whereas MacMillan's book had few, if any, unalloyed heroes, Behrman's has a surfeit. I counted five.

There is Marshall himself, truly a titan among public servants. As Chief of Staff of the U.S. Army during the war, he had been, in Churchill's phrase, the "organizer of victory," and, as Secretary of State, he approached Europe's postwar reconstruction with the same sangfroid and self-discipline. There is William Clayton, the Under-Secretary of State for Economic Affairs, a Southerner who had made his fortune in cotton and his political reputation in wartime procurement. Clayton was another formidable workhorse, whose only weakness was his demanding wife, Sue, who hated his absence on government business and vetoed a succession of more senior appointments he was offered. (To crown it all, she divorced him a year after he retired, only to remarry the hapless fellow two months later.) A third hero is Arthur H. Vandenberg, a leading Republican in the Senate, who had been converted from isolationism to internationalism by the experience of war. Without him, Behrman suggests, the Marshall Plan might have been stymied by Republican opposition. The fourth member of Behrman's quintet is W. Averell Harriman, the imperious tycoon who, as Commerce Secretary, headed the President's Committee on Foreign Aid and then became the European Recovery Program's Special Representative in Europe. His contribution was to broker the diplomatic deals within Europe, whereby aid was subtly tied to other American objectives. Finally, there is Paul Hoffman, the indefatigable automobile salesman and president of Studebaker, whom Truman press-ganged into the job of Marshall Plan administrator. It was Hoffman, more than anyone else, who sold the Plan to Americans. (Richard Bissell, whom Hoffman summoned from M.I.T. to act as his chief economist, comes close to being a sixth hero—something of a rehabilitation for a figure now mostly recalled as one of the C.I.A. men behind the Bay of Pigs invasion.)

Flitting across this crowded stage are some better-known figures: Harry Truman, who declined to call the program the "Truman Plan" not out of modesty but for fear of riling Republican opponents; Josef Stalin, whose aggressive action toward Czechoslovakia greatly helped Vandenberg to overcome congressional resistance; Ernest Bevin, the overweight, ebullient, and ineffably proletarian British Foreign Secretary, who was the Plan's biggest fan; and the diarist and wit Harold Nicolson, whose condescending characterization of the United States ("a giant with the limbs of an undergraduate, the emotions of a spinster, and the brain of a pea-hen") now reads like postimperial sour grapes. The United States in 1945 was a giant, all right, but with the wealth of a Harriman, the altruism of a Marshall, and the sheer dedication of men like Clayton, Vandenberg, Hoffman, and Bissell, it was surely a benign colossus.

What, exactly, was Marshall's plan? To answer that question, as Behrman's diligent research shows, we need to go back to the speech at Harvard. More than two years after the end of the Second World War in Europe, Marshall bluntly informed his audience that "the rehabilitation of the economic structure of Europe" would "require a much longer time and greater effort than had been foreseen." The division of labor between town and country was "threatened with breakdown" in Europe because "town and city industries are not producing adequate goods to exchange with the food-producing farmer." Consequently, European governments were obliged to import essentials from the United States, using precious hard-currency reserves that would be better spent on capital goods for reconstruction. Marshall declared:

> The truth of the matter is that Europe's requirements for the next three or four years of foreign food and other essential products—principally from America—are so much greater than her present ability to pay that she must have substantial additional help or face economic, social, and political deterioration of a very grave character.

The alternative to intervention was "hunger, poverty, desperation, and chaos." The aim of the United States, then, should be to restore "the confidence of the European people in the economic future of their own countries and of Europe as a whole." But it was left up to the Europeans to decide whether or not to accept the offer of American aid and for what purposes they would like it to be used. "The initiative must come from Europe," Marshall stated. This new policy (Marshall himself did not use the word "plan") was "directed not against any country or doctrine." However, "any government which maneuvers to block the recovery of other countries" would be denied American assistance. And any political parties or groups that sought to "perpetuate human misery" for their own nefarious political purposes would "encounter the opposition of the United States."

Four things are especially striking about Marshall's speech, which he read (Behrman tells us) in a barely audible monotone from a seven-page typescript. The first is its economic premise: Europe urgently needed American aid so that urban consumers could be fed without exhausting hard-currency reserves, but the longer-term objective should be to restore European confidence, productivity, and self-sufficiency. The second is its disavowal of unilateralism: this was an invitation to Europeans to specify the help they needed. The third is the European scope of the speech: victors and vanquished were henceforth to be regarded as an integral unit. The fourth is Marshall's thinly veiled allusion to the Soviet Union and to Communism: anyone who opposed this new policy would get short shrift.

Even at the time, not everyone in the United States was convinced. "We are through being 'Uncle Sap,' " Senator Alexander Wiley, of Wisconsin, declared. To Senator Homer Capehart, of Indiana, the Marshall Plan was "state socialism." To congressman Frederick Smith, of Ohio, it was "outright communism." Not to be outdone, Senator Joseph McCarthy, of Wisconsin, later called it a "massive and unrewarding boondoggle" that had turned the United States into "the patsy of the modern world." The very fact of McCarthy's denunciation could be taken as a powerful argument in the Plan's favor, and it is tempting, at this distance, to see such critics as blinkered isolationists, partisan hacks, or incurable xenophobes. But a significant number of eminent economic historians—notably, the British scholar Alan Milward—have questioned just how vital Marshall Aid really was for Europe's postwar recovery. According to Milward, recovery was under way well before the advent of the Marshall Plan, and reconstruction of damaged infrastructure was far advanced before the funds reached Europe. The program was also too small to have a significant effect on Europe's capital stock. The total aid package was equivalent to less than three per cent of the recipient countries' combined national income, and it represented less than a fifth of their gross investment.

To gauge the true importance of the Marshall Plan, it is crucial to get a sense of the amounts involved. Behrman writes, "From June 1947 to its termination at the end of 1951, the Marshall Plan provided approximately $13 billion to finance the recovery . . . of Western Europe." This was less than half the Europeans' initial request and four billion dollars less than President Truman's initial proposal to Congress, but it was still serious money. Behrman computes that, in today's dollars, "that sum equals roughly $100 billion, and as a comparable share of U.S. Gross National Product it would be in excess of $500 billion." That's actually an understatement. In fact, the total amount disbursed under the Marshall Plan was equivalent to roughly 5.4 per cent of U.S. gross national product in the year of Marshall's speech, or 1.1 per cent spread over the whole period of the program, which, technically, dated from April, 1948, when the Foreign Assistance Act was passed, to June, 1952, when the last payment was made. A Marshall Plan announced today would therefore be worth closer to seven hundred and forty billion dollars. If there had been a Marshall Plan between 2003 and 2007, it would have cost five hundred and fifty billion. By comparison, actual foreign economic aid under the Bush Administration between 2001 and 2006 totalled less than one hundred and fifty billion, an average of less than 0.2 per cent of G.D.P.

Yet even these calculations understate the magnitude of the Marshall Plan. There had been American economic assistance to Europe before, through the United Nations Relief and Rehabilitation Administration, which spent about $2.5 billion, and ad-hoc measures like the loan of $3.75 billion to Britain that was negotiated in 1946. But none of these expedients addressed the fundamental problem of the "dollar gap"—the fact that an exhausted Europe could not earn the foreign exchange it needed to pay for indispensable U.S. imports. As Behrman demonstrates, Marshall Aid solved this problem. A French farmer who needed an American-manufactured tractor would buy it with French francs. The Economic Cooperation Administration (the Plan's executive arm) would then vet the transaction in consultation with the French government. If it was approved, the U.S. tractor manufacturer would be paid out of Marshall Plan funds. The French farmer's francs, meanwhile, would go to the French central bank, enabling the French government to spend the money on reconstruction. Marshall Aid thus did "double duty," relieving the pressure on the French balance of payments while at the same time channelling money into the French government's own recovery plan. It thereby had a "multiplier effect," a term borrowed from John Maynard Keynes. According to one contemporary, each dollar of Marshall cash stimulated four to six dollars' worth of additional European production.

This positive reassessment echoes the argument advanced in the early nineties by Brad DeLong and Barry Eichengreen (in an article that is absent from Behrman's bibliography). Marshall Aid was indeed vital, but more in terms of political economy than macroeconomics. It helped get the European economies through a balance-of-payments crisis, to be sure. More important, though, it helped European governments balance budgets and reduce inflation. It forced them to shift from wartime controls to free-market mechanisms. And it played an important part in moving Europe from a dysfunctional system of labor relations based on strike action and class conflict to one based on wage restraint and productivity growth. In all of this, the Marshall Plan resembled the "structural adjustment programs" the International Monetary Fund imposed on borrowers in the developing world during the nineties, but on a larger scale and with much better public relations. As Marshall had foreseen, tackling the food bottleneck was beneficial both materially and psychologically. One Dutch baker displayed a sign that read, "More than half of your daily bread is baked with Marshall wheat." Wherever the red-white-and-blue Marshall shield could be seen, its motto resonated: "For European Recovery: Supplied by the United States of America." The most important strings attached to such supplies were the ones tying Europe to the new American model of managerial capitalism.

Behrman goes still further, however. He also sees the Marshall Plan as having been instrumental to the process of European economic integration, presaging today's European Union in the Organization for European Economic Cooperation. And he accepts the claim that the Marshall Plan defused potentially revolutionary situations in Western Europe and helped prevent a Communist tide from engulfing West Berlin, Italy, and perhaps even France. He has no interest in the once fashionable arguments of Cold War revisionists that the Plan was—in the memorable phrase of Stalin's economic adviser Yevgeny Varga—"a dagger pointed at Moscow." If the Soviets chose to decline Marshall Aid for themselves and their clients, more fools they. The notion that Marshall and his colleagues aimed at "economic and political subjugation of European countries to American capital," to quote another Soviet source, is presented as unworthy of serious consideration.

This is a timely book, reminding us of the good things that the United States has achieved within living memory. Not for nothing do economists call aid payments "unrequited transfers." It is also useful to recall just how poisonously partisan Washington was after 1947, as Joseph McCarthy's witch hunt gathered momentum. This was no golden age of cross-party consensus.

Yet there is a need for caution. Historians have a duty to immerse themselves in contemporary testimony, as Behrman has clearly done. But they must also beware of uncritically accepting contemporary judgments.

One way of avoiding this is to pose counterfactual questions. "What would it cost not to aid Europe?" one congressman asked. That remains the key question. If there had been no Marshall Plan, would Western Europe's economies have failed to recover from the postwar crisis? It would seem not (though there would probably have been more currency volatility and more labor unrest). Under the Marshall Plan, grants and loans were received by sixteen different countries. Britain received more than twice the amount given to West Germany. Yet no European economy performed more dismally in the postwar period than Britain's. A crucial difference between the two was the success of the German currency reform of 1948, which saw the birth of the enormously successful Deutsche Mark, compared with the ephemeral stimulus of the British devaluation of 1949, the first of several vain attempts to revive the U.K. economy by cheapening exports.

If there had been no Marshall Plan, would Western Europe have remained economically fragmented? No, because the Europeans did not need America to come up with their own plan for a six-nation Coal and Steel Community, the decisive first step toward economic integration. By comparison, the American-sponsored O.E.E.C. was a cul-de-sac. Notice, too, that among the recipients of Marshall Aid were a number of countries that even today remain outside the European Union: Iceland, Norway, and Turkey. And no amount of American pressure could persuade the British to participate in the first wave of European integration. As one British official complained, "We are being asked to join the Germans, who started two world wars, the French, who had in 1940 collapsed in the face of German aggression, the Italians, who changed sides, and the Low Countries, of whom not much was known but who seemed to have put up little resistance to Germany."

If there had been no Marshall Plan, would American industry have enjoyed less access to European markets? Again, no: European recovery did not especially benefit American manufacturers, for whom domestic markets were vastly more important. In 1953, Britain still accounted for only 5.2 per cent of U.S. exports and Germany for just 2.3 per cent. As a whole, exports represented a modest share of U.S. G.D.P.—about three per cent even at the end of the nineteen-fifties, compared with roughly seven per cent today. Similarly, the French Communist paper *L'Humanité* exaggerated the threat of "Coca-colonization" of Europe by American capital. In fact, the volume of U.S. direct investment in Europe was relatively modest in the years following 1947.

Finally, if there had been no Marshall Plan, would Stalin have brought some or all of Western Europe into the Soviet imperium? Again, no; the principal deterrent to Stalin was not American dollars but American firepower. By the time the Plan had run its course, soft power was increasingly yielding to hard power in the struggle between the superpowers, particularly after the Soviet-sponsored North Korean invasion of South Korea. True, some Marshall Plan funds were channelled into the C.I.A.'s Office of Policy Coordination (a euphemism for covert operations). But these amounts were trivial compared with the sums being spent on more overt methods of containment. Ultimately, the North Atlantic Treaty mattered more than the Marshall Plan in checking the Soviet advance.

In all likelihood, then, Western Europe could have pulled through without the Marshall Plan. But it certainly could not have pulled through without the United States. At the time that Marshall made his speech in Harvard Yard, no one could be sure that all would turn out for the best in postwar Western Europe. No one could even be sure that the United States would deliver on Marshall's pledge. All people could remember was the sad sequence of events that had followed the previous World War, when Western Europe was swept by general strikes and galloping inflation, while the United States Senate reneged on Woodrow Wilson's "plan" for a new order based on collective security. The Marshall Plan was not the only difference between the two postwar eras, but, to West Europeans struggling to make ends meet, it was the most visible manifestation of American good will—and a mirror image of the Soviet policy of mulcting Eastern Europe. This, more than its macroeconomic impact, explains its endurance in the popular imagination. At a time when, according to the Pew Research Center, only thirty-nine per cent of Frenchmen and thirty per cent of Germans have a positive view of the United States, that is something worth remembering, and pondering.

First published in *The New Yorker,* August 27, 2007. Copyright © 2007 by Niall Ferguson. Reprinted by permission of The Wylie Agency on behalf of the author.

From Rosie the Riveter to the Global Assembly Line

American Women on the World Stage

LEILA J. RUPP

In 1939, shortly after the outbreak of war in Europe, American pacifist and feminist Emily Greene Balch wrote from Geneva to colleagues in the Women's International League for Peace and Freedom (WILPF) about their plight. "Ringed around by a wall of violence, we draw closer together."[1] It was a hopeful statement about organizational and gender solidarity in the face of impending doom, but it can perhaps also serve as a foreshadowing of the ways that, in the more than half century since the end of World War II, women across the continents have at times been able to make connections across national differences to confront common problems, including gendered violence. From a twenty-first century vantage point, we can look back over the decades and see how intimately connected the changes in American women's lives have been with events unfolding on the world stage and how little of what happens to women in the United States is unconnected to larger global forces.

The magnitude of the worldwide conflict that ended in 1945 with the surrender of Germany and Japan, the liberation of the concentration camps, and the unleashing of the atomic bomb had brought American women, like women elsewhere, into areas of the labor force previously reserved for men. Like Rosie the Riveter, the symbol of American women patriotically taking up factory jobs previously reserved for men, women in all of the combatant countries went to work as men left to fight. Women even made inroads into the armed forces, although not, in the United States, as combatants. Spared the devastation of bombed-out cities and the massive losses suffered by the peoples of Europe and Asia, Americans set about reestablishing "normal life," although in a vastly reconfigured global context. Men returning home sought both their jobs and the comforts of a wife at home, if they could afford it. Although many women who had moved from poorly paid service jobs into more financially rewarding factory jobs preferred to remain, employers moved to restore the prewar sexual division of labor. In fact, even as increasing numbers of white middle-class women were entering the paid labor force in the postwar years, the goal of returning women to the home became a hallmark of American life, in contrast to the Soviet-bloc countries, where women were encouraged to combine paid work and motherhood. Equally striking was the fact that the American occupation authorities in both Germany and Japan, assuming that women could serve as the foundation of democratic governments, insisted that those countries' new constitutions grant women equal rights, while the Equal Rights Amendment at home languished in congressional committees.

In the context of the Cold War that followed closely on the heels of the end of hostilities, differences between the Soviet employment of women, especially in factory labor, and American domesticity took on political and diplomatic importance. Symbolic of this cultural clash was the famous "kitchen debate" between U.S. vice president Richard Nixon and Soviet premier Nikita Khrushchev in 1959 at the opening of the American National Exhibition in Moscow. Nixon praised capitalism for providing U.S. housewives with an array of consumer goods and the choice of brands of appliances while Khrushchev, although also touting domesticity, boasted about the productivity of Soviet women workers. It was a debate that laid bare the ideological and economic differences between the two systems as they competed for dominance in the world system.

One way that rivalry played out was in competition for the hearts and minds of what came to be known as the "Third World." Just as the two superpowers raced to try to make over in their own image countries newly independent of colonial rule so, too, transnational women's organizations from each bloc sought to bring developing countries into their fold. The new Women's International Democratic Federation (WIDF), launched out of the Communist-led resistance movements of World War II and dominated by the Soviet Union, challenged the traditional transnational women's organizations such as the International Council of Women, the International Alliance of Women, and the WILPF and competed with them at the United Nations over who really represented the world's women. The older organizations, dedicated to women's rights and peace, had long sought to make their membership "truly global" but remained dominated in terms of membership and leadership by women from western and northern Europe and the United States. The WIDF, in contrast, although founded in Paris and supported from the Soviet

Image courtesy of the National Archives and Records Administration.

During World War II, women, like "Rosie the Riveter," could do a man's work while maintaining their femininity.

Union, won adherents throughout the Third World through its commitment to "win and defend national independence and democratic freedoms, eliminate apartheid, racial discrimination and fascism."[2] In the United States, organizations associated with the WIDF found themselves accused of Communist affiliations in the postwar crackdown.

The decade of the 1950s has indeed gone down in American history as Nixon depicted it to Khrushchev—a period of prosperity, conformity, domesticity, and suburbanization. Retreating from the disruptions of war and threatened by Soviet expansion and Chinese revolution without and Communist subversion within, Americans, according to the conventional story, clung to home and family life. White men, taking advantage when they could of mortgages and college educations made possible by the G.I. Bill, became "organization men" loyal to their corporate employers and took up "do-it-yourself" projects in their suburban homes on the weekends. White women stayed home in the expanding suburbs, giving birth to more children and drinking coffee with their neighbors. Such prosperity depended on U.S. domination of the world economy in the aftermath of the war. Suburban mothers chastised children reluctant to clean their plates to "think of the starving children in Europe;" with European economic recovery, the line shifted to the starving children in Africa. When Michael Harrington published *The Other America* in 1962, the fact that poverty existed at home came as something of a shock to those not experiencing deprivation themselves. A decade later, the revelation of the "feminization of poverty" both in the United States and globally called attention to the economic impact of discrimination against women, the sexual division of labor, the wage gap between women and men, and women's responsibility for rearing children.

Just as the reality of poverty underlay American prosperity in the 1950s, so too the domesticity and tranquility of the 1950s was far more apparent than real. In the burgeoning civil rights movement, African American women and men organized their communities and launched determined protests against segregation and discrimination, taking heart from national liberation movements in Africa and elsewhere. From the group of mostly mothers whose challenge to the segregated school system of Topeka, Kansas, contributed to the Supreme Court decision declaring segregation inherently unequal in *Brown* v. *Board of Education* (1954) to Rosa Parks, who refused to move to the back of the bus in 1955 and helped launch the Montgomery bus boycott, black women played critical roles in calling the attention of the country and the world to the second-class status of African Americans. In the West, Mexican American working-class women and men also took up civic activism on the local level, like African Americans inspired by nationalist movements in the Third World. Within the beleaguered union movement, in the peace movement, in the remnants of the women's movement, in the vilified Communist Party, in the homophile movement that sought acceptance for lesbian and gay Americans, women fought for social change despite the proclaimed contentment of the era.

The recognition that a great deal was going on beneath the surface calm of the 1950s goes a long way toward helping us understand the origins of the explosive decade of the 1960s. The social protest movements of the 1960s had their roots in the tensions and contradictions of the 1950s. But they also occurred in a global context, as national liberation movements increasingly freed former colonies from the grip of imperialism. Transnational connections can be glimpsed in Martin Luther King Jr.'s embrace of Gandhian nonviolence, while Gandhi himself used tactics in the Indian struggle for independence inspired by militant British women fighting for the right to vote. Or in the anthem of the civil rights movement, "We Shall Overcome," with origins in the "sorrow songs" of slaves brought from. Africa, then sung by striking tobacco workers in the 1940s, and then sung in Arabic by Palestinians, in Spanish by members of the United Farmworkers, and, in a sense going home, in the South African antiapartheid movement.

Social upheavals occurring across the globe made the year 1968 synonymous with struggles for social justice. It was in 1968, when French students threw up barricades in the Left Bank quarter and protesting Mexican students were gunned down by the government, that a group of feminists gathered in Atlantic City to protest the objectification of women in the Miss America Pageant. In what has become a legend in the history of the resurgence of feminism—and what gave rise to the mistaken notion that feminists burned their bras—feminists dumped bras, corsets, and hair rollers into a "freedom trash can" and crowned a sheep Miss America.

The turmoil of the 1960s sparked renewed activism by women all around the globe, although feminist movements almost everywhere had roots reaching back to earlier struggles by women for education, civil and political rights, employment opportunities, and other legal and social changes. Sometimes, as in the United States, women in male-dominated social justice movements began to adapt class or national or racial/ethnic critiques to their own situation as women, particularly if they found themselves pushed aside or relegated to second-class citizenship after fighting alongside men for freedom and justice. Although women's movements took on different shapes in various parts of the world—liberal feminism calling for the extension of the rights of men to women, socialist feminism advocating revolutionary change, radical feminism challenging the devaluing of women and the exploitation of women's sexuality and reproductive capacity—feminist movements growing from indigenous roots and influenced as well by a transnational exchange of ideas and strategies flourished. Feminism as a world view emphasizing the equal worth of women and men, a recognition of male privilege, an understanding of the ways that gender intersects with race, class, ethnicity, sexuality, ability, and other forms of difference, and a commitment to work for social justice found footholds everywhere. In different contexts, women organized and fought for access to education and employment, for control of their bodies, and against various forms of violence against women, including in wartime.

In the United States, African American, Latina, Asian American, and Arab American women, often angered by the white, middle-class assumptions of women's movement groups, connected their struggles to those of women in the Third World, taking on the term "Third World women" to describe themselves. Under the auspices of the United Nations, which included the principle of equality between women and men in its charter from its founding, women from across the globe came together in a series of conferences. A meeting in celebration of International Women's Year in Mexico City in 1975 gave rise to the UN's "Decade for Women," marked by a gathering in Copenhagen in 1980, and Nairobi in 1985, followed up by a fourth international conference in Beijing in 1995. From the beginning, conflicts erupted among women. In Mexico City, Domitila Barrios de Chungara, representing an organization of Bolivian tin miners' wives, expressed shock at discussions of such issues as prostitution, lesbianism, and male abuse of women, arguing that women in her group sought to work with men to change the system so that both women and men would have the right to live, work, and organize. In these meetings, the diverse lives of women came to light and made clear the need to broaden the definition of what counted as a "women's issue."

These international meetings brought together not only official government representatives but, more productively, auxiliary forums of nongovernmental organizations. There debates about the impact of development policies, poverty, welfare systems, population policies, imperialism, and national liberation movements on women raised consciousness among women in the United States and other industrialized nations. Women from the global South voiced criticism of the narrowly defined interpretation of gender interests often articulated by women from the affluent North in a way that resonated with the critiques of women of color in the United States. What difference does the "glass ceiling" that keeps U.S. women from reaching the top rungs of their professions make to women who have

no right to land and cannot feed their families? And perhaps more troubling, who is making the clothing worn by professional women in the industrialized countries, who is cleaning their houses and caring for their children, and under what conditions? The United Nations nongovernmental gatherings helped to articulate the multiple ways that the experiences of women of different nations were intertwined, from Asian and Latin American women producing clothing and electronic products on the global assembly line for purchase by U.S. women to the international sex trade that makes prostitution and the "entertainment industry" a major employer of women in a number of Asian countries, to the immigration of women from the Philippines, Mexico, and Latin America to work in U.S. and European homes as maids and nannies while forced to leave behind their own children.

As the twentieth century drew to a close and the Cold War ended, the world had come a long way from the "kitchen debate" of 1959. By the dawn of the new millennium, the divisions between the global North and South had superceded the old political rivalries, and the question of globalization's impact on women came to the fore. What happens to women's traditional work in agriculture or trade when international lending agencies require a country to gear its economy for the world market? Where does "surplus" female labor go? Connecting such questions to the employment of women in sweatshops, as domestics, and in the sex tourism industry makes clear the impact of large-scale forces on women's lives and the ties that bind women in developing countries to those in wealthy industrialized ones like the United States. The pressing questions for women all around the world are what kinds of work they do, how much they are paid, what kinds of opportunities are open to them, who does the housework and takes care of the children, how much control they have over their sexuality and reproductive capacity, who makes decisions for the family and nation. These are the questions with which transnational feminism grapples. All point to the interconnections of gender, class, race, ethnicity, sexuality, ability, and nation. In a world in which we are still, as Emily Greene Balch lamented, "ringed around by a wall of violence," hope lies in the connections American women can make with each other and with women around the globe.

Notes

1. Emily Greene Balch to International Executive Meeting, November 21, 1939, WILPF papers, reel 4.
2. WIDF Constitution, quoted in Cheryl Johnson-Odim and Nina Emma Mba, *For Women and the Nation: Funmilayo Ransome-Kuti of Nigeria* (Urbana, IL: University of Illinois Press, 1997), 137.

Sources

Dublin, Thomas and Kathryn Kish Sklar. "Women and Social Movements in the United States, 1775–2000." <http://www.womhist.binghamton.edu.> Website on the history of women's involvement in a variety of forms of activism throughout U.S. history.

Evans, Sara M. *Tidal Wave: How Women Changed America at Century's End.* New York: Free Press, 2003. An examination of the U.S. women's movement that emphasizes the diversity of participants, the geographical spread of activism, and the continuity of struggle.

Ferree, Myra Marx and Beth B. Hess. *Controversy and Coalition: The New Feminist Movement Across Four Decades of Change.* 3rd edition. New York: Routledge, 2000. A comprehensive sociological survey of the U.S. women's movement, tracing its development over time and its changing structure and strategies.

Freedman, Estelle B. *No Turning Back: The History of Feminism and the Future of Women.* New York: Ballantine Books, 2002. An analysis of the women's movement in global perspective, surveying the emergence of feminist movements, their varied approaches to work, family, sexuality, politics, and creativity, and the diversity of views and participants that ensures the continuation of feminist struggle.

Jayawardena, Kumari. *Feminism and Nationalism in the Third World.* London: Zed, 1986. A classic work on the history of women's political struggles in Asia and the Middle East since the late nineteenth century, arguing that feminism has indigenous roots throughout the Third World.

Johnson-Odim, Cheryl and Nina Emma Mba. *For Women and the Nation: Funmilayo Ransome-Kuti of Nigeria.* Urbana, IL: University of Illinois Press, 1997. A biography of a Nigerian activist involved with women's issues in her own country and transnationally through the Women's International Democratic Federation.

May, Elaine Tyler. *Homeward Bound: American Families in the Cold War Era.* New York: Basic Books, 1988. An analysis of the ways that the Cold War affected all aspects of American women's lives in the 1950s, from sexuality and reproduction to consumerism and family life.

Meyerowitz, Joanne, ed. *Not June Cleaver: Women and Gender in Postwar America, 1945–1960.* Philadelphia: Temple University Press, 1994. A collection of essays on diverse women's activities in the United States in the 1950s that explodes the myth of domesticity and contentment.

Miller, Francesca. *Latin American Women and the Search for Social Justice.* Hanover, NH: University Press of New England, 1991. A history of women's organizing in Latin America that includes Latin American women's involvement in international women's movements.

Naples, Nancy A. and Manisha Desai, eds. *Women's Activism and Globalization: Linking Local Struggles and Transnational Politics.* New York: Routlege, 2002. A collection of essays dealing with contemporary women's activism in opposition to the consequences of globalization.

Richardson, Laurel, Verta Taylor, and Nancy Whittier, eds. *Feminist Frontiers.* 6th ed. New York: McGraw-Hill, 2004. A women's studies text that includes articles detailing diverse women's experiences with appearance, socialization, work, family life, sexuality, reproduction, violence, politics, and the women's movement.

Rosen, Ruth. *The World Split Open: How the Modern Women's Movement Changed America.* New York: Viking, 2000. A comprehensive study, based on oral histories and archival research, of the women's movement and its impact on American society.

Rupp, Leila J. *Worlds of Women: The Making of an International Women's Movement.* Princeton, NJ: Princeton University Press, 1997. A history of the first wave of transnational organizing among women from the 1880s to 1945, focusing on the International Council of Women, the International Alliance of Women, and the Women's International League for Peace and Freedom.

Smith, Bonnie G., ed. *Global Feminisms Since 1945.* London: Routledge, 2000. A collection of essays focusing on women's movements in different parts of the world.

United Nations Division for the Advancement of Women. *Women Go Global: The United Nations and the International Women's Movement, 1945–2000.* CD-ROM. United Nations, 2000. An interactive CD-ROM on the events that have been shaping the international agenda for women's equality since the founding of the UN.

LEILA J. RUPP is a professor and chair of Women's Studies at the University of California, Santa Barbara. A historian by training, her teaching and research focus on sexuality and women's movements. She is coauthor with Vena Taylor of *Drag Queens at the 801 Cabaret* (2003) and *Survival in the Doldrums: The American Women's Rights Movement, 1945 to the 1960s* (1987) and author of *A Desired Past: A Short History of Same-Sex Sexuality in America* (1999), *Worlds of Women: The Making of an International Women's Movement* (1997), and *Mobilizing Women for War: German and American Propaganda, 1939–1945* (1978). She is also completing an eight-year term as editor of *The Journal of Women's History.*

From *OAH Magazine of History*, July 2004, pp. 53–57. Copyright © 2004 by Organization of American Historians. Reprinted by permission of Organization of American Historians.

The Civil Rights Movement in World Perspective

KEVIN GAINES

The Mighty Sparrow, a calypso performer from Trinidad, sang in 1963, at a perilous juncture during the civil rights movement, "I was born in the USA but because of my color I'm suffering today." "The white man preaching democracy but in truth and in fact it's hypocrisy," Sparrow continued, warning that he was "getting vexed." His proposed solution was the song's up-tempo refrain: "So—we want Martin Luther King for President!" Sparrow put his irreverent humor to deadly serious purpose, his song indicting both temporizing U.S. officials during the Birmingham crisis and a nation far from ready to elect a black president. Recorded for Caribbean audiences, including immigrants to the U.S., Sparrow's topical song reminds us, along with a number of recent studies, that the activities of King and the civil rights movement were keenly observed by audiences from all over the world.

Until quite recently, U.S. historians were accustomed to thinking of the civil rights movement within a domestic U.S.-based framework. But in its time, the movement had global dimensions that were abundantly clear to many contemporaries, including Sparrow, King, and many others, as this essay will show. Recent scholarship has engaged the ways in which the consciousness of civil rights leaders and black activists was in fact a *worldview*, a framework linking local and global events and perspectives. At the same time, that scholarship has yet to make a discernible impact in college and secondary school U.S. history textbooks. If the civil rights movement is covered in undergraduate surveys or high school classes (and sadly, we should not assume that even the most basic history of the movement is routinely taught), its story often remains a nation-based account of the response of presidential administrations to southern racial upheavals, with King as the movement's main protagonist.

That our understanding of the movement should emphasize a domestic U.S. narrative is not surprising. The violence that confronted civil rights demonstrators in Birmingham, Selma, Mississippi and other battlegrounds jolted the conscience of many throughout the nation. The sacrifices of those who died, and the traumas borne by their survivors, should never be forgotten. That said, viewing the civil rights movement within an international frame need not displace the memory of those who fought to end racial segregation on U.S. soil. Historians who examined the conditions that led many unsung local people in the South to risk their lives and livelihoods in opposing Jim Crow have learned that global events often informed the outlook and aspirations of activists.[1] Black World War II veterans, energized by the global struggle against fascism, were at the vanguard of postwar demands for voting rights in the South. They and others were also inspired by national independence struggles in Africa and Asia. One of those veterans, Medgar Evers, the director of the NAACP branch in Jackson, Mississippi, admired the Kenyan nationalist leader Jomo Kenyatta.[2] The Freedom Singers, a vocal ensemble made up of Student Nonviolent Coordinating Committee (SNCC) activists working to organize black Mississippians to demand voting rights despite the constant threat of vigilante terror, paid tribute to the armed resistance employed by Kenyan nationalists.[3] Such examples remind us that the local and the global are not antithetical. Rather, they complement each other.

By viewing the black freedom movement within a global frame, scholars and teachers may gain an enhanced appreciation of the motivations of those who challenged the racial status quo. Such a recontextualization also enables us to comprehend the limits, as well as the achievements, of civil rights strategies and reforms. In his discussion of the movement's mixed legacy, Thomas Holt has noted that South African and Brazilian freedom movements during the 1960s consciously aligned themselves with organized labor, while the U.S. civil rights movement severed its partnership with labor, a strategy that crucially limited the forms of freedom and citizenship that were imaginable in the U.S. context.[4] In addition to prompting a reconsideration of the movement's tactics, an engagement with the global context of decolonization, the emergence of new African and Asian nations from European colonial rule during the 1950s and 1960s, reveals a wider spectrum of political consciousness and debate among black activists. Within that wider world of black movement activism, even as student sit-ins and nonviolent direct action campaigns spread throughout the South during the early 1960s, northern urban black activists were fighting discrimination in employment and housing, and had been doing so since World War II.[5] Here again, the local and the global were inseparable. Activists based in New York, Chicago and other cites followed the decolonization of Africa just as avidly as they demanded equality on the local and national level. Their outlook was reflected in the views of such prominent figures as James Baldwin, Lorraine Hansberry, and Malcolm X, all of whom faulted the federal government for its failure to enforce and implement civil rights law.

Viewing the black freedom movement within the context of decolonization and African national liberation movements goes beyond acknowledging the origins of the movement's tactic of nonviolent direct action in the Gandhian philosophy of Satyagraha employed by Indian nationalists' struggle against British colonialism. Such a global reframing highlights the tension between U.S. conceptions of civil rights reforms, understood in terms of color blindness, or formal civil and political equality, and an evolving postwar international discourse of human rights, whose definitions of rights potentially embraced broader social needs such as income, housing, and health care. Arguably, this broader conception of social rights contained within human rights discourse partially informed Malcolm X's attempt, after he was forced out of the Nation of Islam, to substitute an internationalist rhetoric of human rights for that of civil rights.

To reconsider the U.S. black freedom movement within an international arena of political change is to discover that the status of African Americans in U.S. society has long been, and remains relevant for U.S. foreign affairs.[6] It could not be otherwise, given America's superpower status since World War II. From the global war against fascism to the Cold War, to the present U.S. occupation of Iraq, the situation of African Americans has often symbolized, for Americans and overseas audiences, depending on one's perspective, either a color-blind American dream of racial progress, or a nightmare of exclusion mocking the nation's democratic ideals. More recently, a global perspective of a different sort found expression after the U.S. government's abandonment of African Americans stranded in New Orleans by Hurricane Katrina. That debacle led many Americans and overseas observers to compare the federal government's feckless performance to that of a third world country, the chronic conditions of poverty, ill-health, and official neglect exposed by the storm suggest the limits of triumphalist accounts of the civil rights movement in the U.S., and likewise, claims of victory in the Cold War. Arguably, the destruction of much of New Orleans can be attributed in part to the diversion of manpower and resources needed—for maintaining the levee system before the storm and emergency management after—to the wars in Iraq and Afghanistan, wars that have their roots in the Cold War policy of arming proxies to fight such enemies as the Soviet Union.[7] The conjuncture of the Cold War and America's aspirations for global hegemony, the U.S. civil rights movement, and the decolonization of Africa was a momentous one. For Thomas Borstelmann, it led to a paradoxical divergence between domestic and foreign policy; while the Johnson administration could credit itself for passing landmark civil rights and voting rights legislation, its indulgent policy toward repressive white minority governments in southern Africa paved the way for substantial U.S. financial investments in those latter-day colonial societies.[8] The debacle of the Vietnam War justifiably looms large in our

assessment of LBJ's foreign policy, but the civil rights era also saw the subversion of African nationalist aspirations by the U.S. and other Western powers. Following such civil rights activists as Robert Moses, who linked the cause of black freedom in the U.S. with opposition to the Vietnam War, our account of the era must accommodate not only the sacrifices of the many who braved jail, beatings, and death in civil rights struggles at home, but also, the catastrophic toll of African and Asian victims of carpet bombing, "low intensity" proxy wars, and covert operations of U.S. foreign policy. A global approach to the civil rights movement fundamentally challenges us to ponder what is at stake in the teaching and writing of this history. Studying the black freedom movement within a global perspective can better prepare students to understand contemporary global affairs, helping them draw connections between postwar U.S. history and the histories of Africa, Asia and the Middle East.

The joint enterprise of teachers and students to "connect the dots" between ostensibly disparate histories—of labor and civil rights, and domestic and foreign policy—becomes more palpable when we adopt, as the wartime examples above suggest, the perspective of what Jacquelyn Hall has called "the long civil rights movement," marking the genesis of the movement well before the landmark events of the 1954 *Brown* decision and the Montgomery bus boycott a year later, and emphasizing the movement's evolution from reformist goals to an agenda of radical social change under King's leadership.[9] As Patricia Sullivan has shown, during the 1930s, federal New Deal reform and relief programs shifted the balance of power away from southern "states' rights" ideology, creating an opening in that region for labor organizing, civil rights activism and demands for voting rights.[10] During World War II, civil rights and labor organizations joined hands as struggles for equality in the South and nationwide attacked segregation in housing, the workplace, and at the polls.[11] African Americans supported the Fair Employment Practices Commission (FEPC), a federal agency mandated to safeguard African American rights in the workplace, the FEPC was established in 1941 by President Franklin D. Roosevelt's Executive Order 8802, as a concession to the pressure brought by A. Philip Randolph's March on Washington Movement. In addition, blacks in civilian life and the armed forces championed the Double V campaign publicized by African American newspapers and civil rights organizations, which insisted that victory at home against Jim Crow segregation was essential for victory in the global war against fascism.

As evidenced by the Double V campaign, the movement itself responded to, and was shaped by, world events. During the war, African American civil rights leaders and organizations rhetorically anchored their cause to the global momentum of decolonization, as newly independent nation-states emerged from European colonial rule in Asia and Africa. But the postwar world, and the fortunes of emergent Asian and African nations, as well as those of the civil rights movement, came increasingly under the sway of the Cold War struggle between the U.S. and the Soviet Union. The Cold War did not simply influence the rhetoric of the movement. By stifling domestic criticism and dissent, the Cold War also limited the range of possibilities for social reform, restricting the goals of the movement to formal civic and political equality. Although the March on Washington demanded jobs along with freedom, the movement's goals maintained an exclusive focus on obtaining federal legislation to ban racial discrimination in civic and political life.

The Cold War held a double-edged significance for the civil rights movement. In declaring segregation in public schools unconstitutional, the Court's unanimous decision in *Brown* enshrined the Cold War understanding that racial equality at home was a vital component of U.S. foreign policy and national security. But segregationists could and did marshal Cold War anticommunism to discredit the movement and its leadership. In their reliance on the federal government as an ally to secure civil rights legislative reforms, King and other leaders of the mainstream civil rights organizations maintained a discreet silence on U.S. foreign policy and the deepening U.S. war in Vietnam. By 1967, having achieved the hard won legislative victories of the civil rights and voting rights acts, King set about restoring the link between civil rights and economic justice. King could no longer refrain from criticizing the Vietnam War, which squandered resources needed to combat poverty and the effects of discrimination in the workplace and housing in the urban North and nationwide. The Vietnam War and opposition to it on a global scale had contributed to King's transformation from reformer to revolutionary.

The very fact that the world was watching the civil rights movement during the 1950s and 1960s ensured the responsiveness of otherwise reluctant U.S. policymakers to the demands of the black freedom movement. Throughout the modern civil rights movement, spanning the administrations of Truman, Eisenhower, and Kennedy, U.S. State Department officials endorsed civil rights, seeking to convince foreign audiences of the nation's commitment to eradicating systemic barriers to the full participation of African Americans in public life. Yet news media accounts of all too frequent incidents of racism broadcast to foreign audiences throughout the 1950s and early 1960s were a chronic headache for U.S. foreign policy makers. Whether from acts of discrimination against African diplomats traveling Route 40, the corridor between New York and Washington, or from the full-scale unrest ignited by the violence unleashed by authorities upon nonviolent civil rights demonstrators throughout the Jim Crow South, as was the case in Birmingham, such racial upheavals, U.S. officials feared, undermined their assertions that the U.S. was the leader of the "Free World." The persistence of racism was America's Achilles' heel in its competition with the Soviet Union for the allegiance of new nations having recently emerged from European colonial empires.

Sparrow's identification with King and African Americans' struggle for equality was also part of a tradition of black internationalism dating back to the interwar years, as peoples of African descent forged solidarities across geographical and historical divides. The example of New Negro radicalism in the United States during the 1920s, especially the mass movement led by the Jamaican-born Marcus Garvey, had inspired the anticolonial movements in Africa and the Caribbean that had shaped Sparrow's worldview. That internationalist consciousness was energized throughout the black world by Italy's invasion of the sovereign African nation of Ethiopia in 1935.[12] As World War II accelerated the collapse of European empires in Asia and Africa, African American civil rights and civic organizations lent support to African anticolonial movements, espousing what Penny Von Eschen has called a vibrant "politics of the African diaspora" that linked demands for equality in the U.S. with African national liberation movements.[13] Throughout the 1950s and 1960s, such prominent African Americans as the singer and actor Paul Robeson, the scholar W.E.B. Du Bois, the boxing champion Joe Louis, and later, of course, Martin Luther King, Jr., were household names among people of African descent worldwide. Likewise, many black Americans avidly followed in the black press the political exploits of Kwame Nkrumah, leader of the nationalist movement in the British Gold Coast Colony, Jawaharlal Nehru, the first Prime Minister of India, and Jomo Kenyatta of Kenya.

As the Cold War transformed the Soviet Union from wartime ally to postwar nemesis, a wartime black popular front alliance of African American civil rights organizations, the labor movement, and African nationalist parties came under official suspicion. African Americans' advocacy of African anticolonial movements and their democratic aspirations clashed with U.S. foreign policy makers bent on extending their influence over Africa's labor and raw materials. The allied victory over global fascism was not accompanied by the demise of Jim Crow segregation in the U.S. South, as most African American civic leaders, journalists, and soldiers had hoped. The political backlash of the Cold War led some, like the novelist and ex-communist Richard Wright, to relocate to France in 1946, where he could speak, write, and work with West Indian and African nationalists beyond the reach of House Un-American Activities Committee (HUAC) investigations.

The Cold War and its loyalty investigations had served as a warning to actual or potential critics. But if U.S. officials sought to keep internal dissent from overseas audiences, news coverage of violent outbursts by white southerners could not so easily be embargoed. U.S. officials sought a propaganda counteroffensive that would help audiences abroad view outbreaks of racial unrest as aberrations within a narrative of steady progress in race relations. *Brown,* the product of a protracted legal struggle waged by civil rights attorneys against Jim Crow "separate but equal" doctrine, was crucial for this narrative. But while it allowed U.S. foreign policy makers to proclaim to critics abroad that desegregation was the law of the land, *Brown* offered no plan for implementation.

Without an official federal strategy for integration, mass activism would be needed to desegregate public life in the Jim Crow South. The mobilization of African Americans in the Montgomery Movement had desegregated that city's public transportation system, and catapulted its leader, Martin Luther King, Jr., to national prominence. But King and other civil rights leaders seemed to falter in the face of white southern resistance, and an Eisenhower administration unwilling to enforce *Brown.* When Ghana (formerly the British-controlled Gold Coast Colony) achieved its independence in March of 1957, its Prime Minister, Kwame Nkrumah, invited King and other civil rights leaders and African American dignitaries as a show of support for the struggle for equality in the U.S. In doing so, Nkrumah also acknowledged African American leaders' support for nationalism in the Gold Coast and throughout Africa. Many attended, including A. Philip Randolph, Adam Clayton Powell, and Ralph Bunche. In Ghana, ironically enough, King achieved the high level contact with the Eisenhower administration that he and other civil rights leaders had vainly sought back home when he encountered Vice President Richard Nixon, head of the U.S. delegation. With his wife Coretta, King lunched with Nkrumah, and upon their return, King linked Ghana's independence to their own struggles: "Ghana tells us that the forces of the universe are on the side of justice . . . An old order of colonialism, of segregation, discrimination is passing away now. And a new order of justice, freedom and good will is being born."[14] King informed his audience that Nkrumah encouraged African Americans to move to Ghana and contribute to building the new nation. Over the 1950s and 1960s, some 300 African Americans did so, establishing an expatriate community whose destiny was closely tied to the political fortunes of Ghana under Nkrumah's leadership.

King's understanding of the cause of civil rights as a global issue, if not his optimism, was reinforced by the turmoil in Little Rock, Arkansas, in 1957, as menacing white mobs gathered outside that city's Central High School to prevent the enrollment of nine African American youths, thus desegregating the school. President Eisenhower hesitated to intervene, prompting an angry condemnation by jazz musician Louis Armstrong of the president and the state's segregationist governor Orval Faubus, for inflaming the situation. Amidst damaging worldwide press coverage of the crisis, Eisenhower finally sent in federal troops to restore order, and to allow the students to attend school. The international implications of the civil rights issue were on King's mind when he announced plans for the Pilgrimage for Prayer in Washington, where a crowd of 20,000 assembled at the Lincoln Memorial in May 1957 to demand federal enforcement of *Brown*. "[T]he hour is getting late," King warned, "[f]or if America doesn't wake up, she will one day arise and discover that the uncommitted peoples of the world will have given their allegiance to a false communistic ideology." King insisted that civil rights was not some "ephemeral, evanescent domestic" matter to be exploited by segregationists for immediate political gain, but an "eternal moral issue" that would determine the outcome of the Cold War. Vice President Nixon used similar logic, warning that continued discrimination against African Americans undermined U.S. influence in Africa, which he regarded a crucial terrain of the superpower struggle against international communism.

Not everyone subscribed to such stark visions of Cold War conflict, nor did others feel compelled, as King and his advisors did, to promote the image of Christian piety to deflect charges of communist influence on the movement. Several prominent African American intellectuals and artists viewed the U.S. black struggle for equality within the changing global order of decolonization, including sociologist E. Franklin Frazier, the expatriate novelists Richard Wright and James Baldwin, the playwright Lorraine Hansberry and others. How might African Americans redefine themselves and their relation to modern political change in America and Africa? Would they become

unhyphenated Americans, or in gaining formal equality, would they enact their U.S. citizenship in solidarity with African peoples and promote a broader definition of socioeconomic justice at home and abroad, that might contribute to the democratization of American society?[15]

Frazier, Hansberry, Baldwin, and increasingly, the Nation of Islam minister and national spokesman Malcolm X were voicing in their respective ways the frustration of African Americans in the urban North, where, since World War II, local civil rights activists had opposed discrimination in housing, labor unions, and the workplace, making little headway against white-controlled municipal governments, police departments, school systems, neighborhood associations and labor unions. The plight of northern urban African Americans mired in slum conditions while wealth, opportunity and the American dream lay beyond their reach, led many to look to Africa as the foundation for their identity, rather than an American nation still largely defined by the indignities and brutality of Jim Crow. As an alternative to what some regarded as the Scylla of integration and the Charybdis of separatism, black radical writers, artists and activists, including Hansberry, Maya Angelou, Julian Mayfield, Amiri Baraka (then Leroi Jones) and others advocated a new Afro-American nationalism, defined by an independent critique of Cold War liberalism, a sense that integration would not address the plight of northern urban blacks, and an anti-imperialist critique of U.S. foreign policy consonant with that of the Afro-Asian bloc in the United Nations. That emergent Afro-American nationalism had its most dramatic expression in the demonstration in February 1961 in the gallery of the United Nations Security Council by African Americans, including Angelou and Baraka, following the announcement of the death of Patrice Lumumba, the democratically elected prime minister of the Congo, whose independence from Belgium was marred by civil disorder fomented by Belgium. The demonstrators were outraged that Lumumba's ouster, disappearance, and murder occurred with the apparent complicity of the UN peacekeeping mission. The assassination of Lumumba, who had traveled to Washington and to the U.N. in a vain appeal for diplomatic support, would remain a decisive event for those northern urban black militants and radicals whose political consciousness had been shaped by the decolonization of Africa.

Malcolm X would become the most prominent spokesman for those northern blacks sympathetic to Afro-American nationalism. The demonstration at the U.N., the most prominent of many protests condemning Lumumba's death throughout the United States and worldwide, would become a defining moment for Malcolm and his generation. In the near term, U.S. officials regarded the demonstration as proof that those involved and others were susceptible to the influence of international communism. The secular Afro-American radicals involved in the demonstration could not have been further in temperament from the organization that most effectively tapped the disaffection of urban blacks, the Nation of Islam (NOI). Under the leadership of Elijah Muhammed, born Elijah Poole in rural Georgia, the NOI diverged from orthodox Islam, capitalizing on America's racial divide. The NOI's view that whites were devils made sense to those mired in the endemic poverty and exclusion of Jim Crow segregation in the urban North. Muhammed urged NOI members to eschew political activism, but Malcolm, his leading spokesman, intensified his criticism of the Kennedy administration during the Birmingham crisis of 1963. Malcolm's harsh rhetoric—he dismissed the March on Washington for Jobs and Freedom as a public relations event stage-managed by the Kennedys—had garnered headlines and FBI surveillance.

Malcolm's notoriety and his apparent disregard for the NOI's apolitical stance had opened a breach between him and Muhammed, along with those rival ministers who considered themselves Muhammed's rightful heirs. Instructed by Muhammed to refrain from public comment on the death of President Kennedy, Malcolm told a New York audience that Kennedy had fallen victim to the violence his administration had unleashed throughout the world. Calling the assassination a matter of "chickens coming home to roost," Malcolm's provocative claim led to his ouster from the NOI. Malcolm spent much of the eleven months remaining to him traveling throughout Africa and the Middle East. His travels and discussions with members of diplomatic corps and African heads of state informed his rejection of the idea of innate white racism. Malcolm addressed audiences throughout Europe, Africa and the U.S., his analyses focusing on institutionalized racism at home and abroad, and positing a universal moral standard of justice and human rights. Though unable to live down his media reputation as an extremist, Malcolm's critical posture would help shape African American leadership and civil rights organizations' attempts to influence U.S. foreign policy in Africa. At the Oxford Debate Union in December 1964, Malcolm condemned the recent military offensive by Belgium, backed with U.S. air support, against Congolese nationalists. That mission, described in the press as the humanitarian rescue of European hostages seized by Congolese rebels against the Belgian-controlled central government, resulted in the slaughter of some 3,000 Congolese civilians. The Belgium-U.S. intervention in the Congo was widely condemned by African officials at the United Nations. African American civil rights leaders, including King, A. Philip Randolph, Roy Wilkins, James Farmer, Whitney Young and Dorothy Height, pressed the Johnson administration to withdraw its support for the Congolese central government. For its part, the administration refused to meet with these prominent civil rights leaders who comprised the American Negro Leadership Conference on Africa. A White House memorandum of January 1965 referred to LBJ's desire to "discourage emergence of any special Negro pressure group (a la the Zionists) which might limit [the administration's] freedom of maneuver."[16] For Johnson, the achievement of civil rights reforms in the U.S. seemed to require the acquiescence of black leadership on African and foreign affairs.

At Oxford, Malcolm condemned the "cold-blooded murder" of Congolese civilians and linked that use of organized violence to the unredressed violence wielded by white extremists in Mississippi, where charges against the accused killers of three civil rights workers (James Chaney, Andrew Goodman, and Michael Schwerner) the previous summer had recently been dropped. Aided by fellow activists in Harlem, Malcolm founded the Organization of Afro-American Unity a secular organization whose agenda for liberation sought to address

local conditions within an internationalist framework. Malcolm also sought a *rapprochement* with civil rights organizations, sharing platforms with SNCC activists in Harlem and Selma, Alabama. In East Africa, Malcolm held court with SNCC activists including John Lewis. Upon his return, Malcolm, the son of Garveyite parents, told a Harlem audience that although a physical "return" to Africa was impractical, Afro-Americans should migrate "spiritually, culturally, and philosophically" to Africa. By this he meant that for African Americans, a sense of black and "African" cultural identification was essential for the achievement of equal citizenship. Malcolm's death in 1965 at the hands of assassins incited by NOI death threats brought a swift end to that fledgling organization.

Though unable to build an organization that remotely matched the influence of the NOI, black movement activists increasingly followed Malcolm's example in envisioning an international terrain of black struggle and liberation. As if emulating Malcolm's pilgrimage, SNCC activists, including Robert Moses and Fannie Lou Hamer, toured Africa, nursing their disillusionment at the defeat, as they perceived it, of their attempt to unseat the all-white Mississippi delegation at the 1964 Democratic Convention. While the sight of black officials exercising power and leadership in black majority societies was inspiring, they, like Malcolm, were dismayed by the reach of U.S. propaganda, whose rosy portrayals of progress clashed with their experience of violent resistance to their demands for voting rights in Mississippi and elsewhere throughout the South.[17]

As SNCC became bogged down in disputes over organizational structure and ideology, Moses gravitated toward the burgeoning anti-Vietnam war movement.[18] Here, it is crucial to note that antiwar statements by Moses, and later, King, were matters of sharp disagreement and conflict within the civil rights movement. A world of political differences may have separated youthful SNCC militants from the gray eminences of the civil rights establishment, but members of both camps could voice strong objection to criticism from the likes of Moses and King against U.S. foreign policy. In their view, antiwar statements at such a crucial juncture were diversions from the steadfast pursuit of freedom at home. The realities of a movement under siege and the urgent cause of voting rights, justified to some black activists reticence on matters of U.S. foreign policy.

Given the unwillingness of the Johnson administration to countenance an independent African American critique of U.S. foreign policy, it seems fitting to recall an assessment of global affairs by Richard Wright in his novel *The Outsider* (1953) that uncannily speaks to our present condition. Casting a pox on both houses of American capitalism and Soviet communism as totalitarian systems of exploitation, Wright, in the guise of his protagonist, claimed that those systems contained the seeds of the destruction of Western progress and modernity. The few hundred years of "freedom, empire-building, voting, liberty, democracy" would yield to a "more terrifyingly human" future. "There will be . . . no trial by jury, no writs of habeas corpus, no freedom of speech, of religion—all this is being buried, and not by Communists or Fascists alone, but by their opponents as well. All hands are shoveling clay onto the body of freedom before it even dies, while it lies breathing its last."[19] Those secular Cold War belief systems would be undermined by greed, corruption and cynicism, and would be rejected by much of the world's population, replaced by the rise of new forms of religious fundamentalism.

In this, and other writings, Wright seems to have sensed that civil rights—integration and formal equality envisioned solely within the U.S. terrain, would not be enough. Wright helps us to understand how devastating the eclipse of the movement's abandoned vision of socioeconomic justice that King had tried to restore was. Yet this was more than a matter of the lack of an alliance between labor unions and the black freedom movement. The liberating impact of the civil rights movement was limited, as well, by the Cold War's containment by the U.S. and Western powers of the democratic aspirations of the formerly colonized world, and the eclipse of an expansive international democratic vision of freedom emanating from the civil rights movement from such powerful exponents as King and Malcolm. The death of those figures, and the ideological defeat of their global vision of liberation, with its religious underpinnings, resulted in the moral and political vacuum left by the end of the Cold War, a vacuum ominously filled by religious fundamentalisms at home and abroad. And so it is at the end of 2006 that as the Roberts Court is poised to interpret the *Brown* decision in a manner that undermines the pursuit of integration, the global and the local merge once again in the return of the bodies of U.S. servicemen and women killed in Iraq and Afghanistan to their hometowns.

Notes

1. Stuart Burns, ed., *Daybreak of Freedom: The Montgomery Bus Boycott* (Chapel Hill: UNC Press, 1997) frames that event in the context of the national independence struggle in the Gold Coast, West Africa.

2. John Dittmer, *Local People: The Struggle for Civil Rights in Mississippi* (University of Illinois Press, 1995).

3. "Oginga Odinga," a selection from The Freedom Singers album, *Freedom Now,* describes SNCC activists' meeting with the Kenyan nationalist leader and politician who had been brought to the U.S. by the State Department.

4. Thomas Holt, *The Problem of Race in the 21st Century (Cambridge, MA: Harvard University,* 2000), xx.

5. Martha Biondi, *To Stand and Fight: The Struggle for Civil Rights in Postwar New York City* (Cambridge: Harvard University Press, 2003); Matthew J. Countryman, *Up South: Civil Rights and Black Power in Philadelphia* (Philadelphia: University of Pennsylvania, 2006): and Jeanne Theoharis, Komozi Woodard and Matthew Countryman, eds., *Freedom North: Black Freedom Struggles Outside the South, 1940–1980* (New York: Palgrave Macmillan, 2003); Jeanne Theoharris and Komozi Woodard, eds., *Groundwork: Local Black Freedom Movements in America* (New York: New York University Press, 2005).

6. Gerald Horne, *Black and Red: W.E.B. Du Bois and the Afro-American Response to the Cold War, 1944–1963* (State University Press of New York, 1986): Brenda Gayle Plummer, *Rising Wind; Black Americans and U.S. Foreign Affairs, 1935–1960* (Chapel Hill: University of North Carolina Press, 1996); Penny M. Von Eschen, *Race Against Empire: Black Americans and Anticolonialism, 1937–1957* (Ithaca: Cornell University Press, 1997); Azza Salama Layton. *International Politics and Civil Rights Policies in the United States, 1941–1960* (Cambridge: Cambridge University Press, 2000); Mary L. Dudziak, *Cold War Civil Rights: Race and the Image of American Democracy* (Princeton: Princeton University Press, 2000); Carol Anderson, *Eyes Off the Prize: The United Nations and the African American Struggle for Human Rights* (Cambridge: Cambridge University Press, 2003).

7. Mahmood Mamdani, *Good Muslim, Bad Muslim: America, the Cold War and the Roots of Terror* (New York: Pantheon Books, 2004).

8. Thomas Borstelmann, *The Cold War and the Color Line: American Race Relations in the Global Arena* (Cambridge, MA: Harvard University Press, 2001).

9. Jacquelyn Dowd Hall, "The Long Civil Rights Movement and the Political Uses of the Past," *The Journal of American History* 91(March 2005): 1233–63.

10. Patricia Sullivan, *Days of Hope: Race and Democracy in the New Deal Era* (Chapel Hill: University of North Carolina Press, 1996).

11. Robert Korstad and Nelson Lichtenstein, "Opportunities Found and Lost: Labor, Radicals and the Civil Rights Movement," *Journal of American History* 75 (December 1988): 786–811; Robert Rodgers Korstad, *Civil Rights Unionism: Tobacco Workers and the Struggle for Democracy in the Mid-Twentieth Century South* (Chapel Hill: University of North Carolina Press, 2003); see also Biondi, *To Stand and Fight;* and Countryman, *Up South.*

12. Winston James, *Holding Aloft the Banner of Ethiopia: Caribbean Radicalism in Early Twentieth-Century America* (New York: Verso, 1999); James H. Meriwether, *Proudly We Can Be Africans: Black Americans and Africa, 1935–1961* (Chapel Hill: University of North Carolina Press, 2002).

13. Von Eschen, *Race Against Empire,* 1997.

14. Kevin K. Gaines, *American Africans in Ghana: Black Expatriates and the Civil Rights Era* (Chapel Hill: University of North Carolina Press, 2006), 83–84.

15. Kevin K. Gaines, "E. Franklin Frazier's Revenge: Anticolonialism, Nonalignment, and Black Intellectuals' Critiques of Western Culture," *American Literary History* 17 (2005): 506–529.

16. Gaines, *American Africans in Ghana,* 218.

17. Clayborne Carson, *In Struggle: SNCC and the Black Awakening of the 1960s* (Cambridge, MA: Harvard University Press, 1982).

18. Eric R. Burner, *And Gently He Shall Lead Them: Robert Parris Moses and Civil Rights in Mississippi* (New York: New York University Press, 1994).

19. Richard Wright. *The Outsider* (New York: Perennial Library Edition, 1965), 366.

Bibliography

Teaching the international dimensions of the civil rights movement through music offers a powerful means of exposing students to the immediacy and contingency of consciousness as it is lived. The album containing the Mighty Sparrow's "Martin Luther King for President" contains other topical songs, including a tribute to President Kennedy after his assassination, and commentary on Khruschev and the Cold War. These songs are found on a compilation album, "The Mighty Sparrow Sings True Life Stories of Passion, People, Politics," Scepter International SI-9001. The song "Oginga Odinga" can be found on the album "The Freedom Singers Sing of Freedom Now!" Mercury Records, MG 20924. In part due to her association with SNCC activists, during the 1960s Nina Simone's music reflected the militancy of many younger blacks, while also foregrounding issues of Afro-American nationalism and gender equality as well. Her music is widely available on compact disc reissues and the relevant selections are discussed in Ruth Feldstein, "'I Don't Trust You Anymore': Nina Simone, Culture, and Black Activism in the 1960s," *Journal of American History* 91 (March 2005): 1349–79.

Teachers of the civil rights movement in world perspective would do well to begin with the work of Brenda Gayle Plummer. Her book, *Rising Wind: Black Americans and U.S. Foreign Affairs, 1935–1960* (Chapel Hill: University of North Carolina Press, 1996) extensively details African Americans' involvement with international affairs from the Italian invasion of Ethiopia to the emergence of newly independent African nations at the dawn of the civil rights movement. Penny Von Eschen's *Race Against Empire: Black Americans and Anticolonialism, 1937–1957* (Ithaca: Cornell University Press, 1997) foregrounds the broad-based support among African Americans for anticolonial movements in Africa during World War II, with an emphasis on the black press as a forum for wide-ranging commentary on global affairs. Von Eschen argues that in response to Cold War strictures, civil rights leaders downplayed linkages with African nationalist movements. Instead, they increasingly argued that desegregation was essential for winning the Cold War.

Nikhil Pal Singh, *Black Is A Country: Race and the Unfinished Struggle for Democracy* (Cambridge, Mass: Harvard University Press, 2004) builds upon the work of Plummer and Von Eschen with his intellectual history of African American intellectuals' sustained engagement with issues of race and democracy in a global arena since the 1930s. Singh's introduction asks students to rethink the legacy and popular memory of Martin Luther King and the civil rights movement. Singh places the often forgotten radicalism and "world perspective" of Martin Luther King during the later phase of his career within the context of earlier efforts by W.E.B. Du Bois (and others) to bring a global perspective to bear on their critiques of American democracy, as Du Bois did in the coda to his 1935 study *Black Reconstruction,* positing the post-Reconstruction repression of African American citizenship rights and colonial systems of exploitation founded on white supremacy as a unitary historical phenomenon. The active role Du Bois sought in advancing a vision of equality in the U.S. and world order defined by self-determination for colonized peoples at the conference devoted to crafting the United Nations charter is detailed by David L. Lewis, *W.E.B. DuBois—the Fight for Equality and the American Century, 1919–1963* (New York: Henry Holt, 2000) in chapter 14 of the second volume.

Studies of local movements have probed the significance of international events on the perspective of movement activists. Besides Dittmer's *Local People: The Struggle for Civil Rights in Missouri* (Urbana: University of Illinois Press, 1994), there is Timothy B. Tyson's *Radio Free Dixie; Robert F. Williams and the Roots of Black Power* (Chapel Hill: University of North Carolina Press, 1999), a pathbreaking study of the North Carolina NAACP official who gained notoriety for advocating armed self-defense among blacks. Tyson is attentive to Williams's adept use of Cold War internationalism during the late 1950s in what became known as the "kissing case" (in which two African American boys were jailed on charges of rape for "playing house" with white female playmates) to pressure federal intervention by attracting

international condemnation on that travesty and to publicize other such crises facing African Americans. In *To Stand and Fight: The Struggle for Civil Rights in Postwar New York City* (Cambridge, Mass: Harvard University Press, 2001). Martha Biondi reminds us of the centrality of struggles against racial discrimination in labor and the workplace, and also notes that internationalism was part and parcel of the political vision of the black popular front. Her account notes the paradox of the intensification of racial segregation in the urban North at the very moment that legal racial barriers were being dismantled in the South. Eric Burner, *And Gently He Shall Lead Them: Robert Parris Moses and Civil Rights in Mississippi* (New York: New York University Press, 1994) provides an account of Moses's evolving internationalism and his incorporation of an antiwar position in his work for SNCC. *Lost Prophet: The Life and Times of Bayard Rustin* (New York: The Free Press, 2000). John D'Emilio's biography of the pacifist who served as an advisor to King during and after the Montgomery movement, notes the importance of his encounter with national independence movements in India and Africa. Rustin's involvement in nuclear disarmament protests in Africa was integral to his—and the movement's—vision of nonviolent direct action.

Also building on earlier work on African Americans and U.S. foreign relations, Mary Dudziak's study *Cold War Civil Rights: Race and the Image of American Democracy* established the importance of viewing the *Brown* decision as a legal event embedded in national and international diplomacy and geopolitics, and the civil rights movement as profoundly exposed to the political winds of the Cold War. *Brown* was a landmark, but its reliance on extrajudicial arguments such as the need to maintain the image of the U.S. as the leader of the "Free World" overseas illustrates that constitutional law cannot be separated from sociopolitical conditions. The subtitle of Dudziak's book is instructive for she extensively portrays U.S. policymakers as more concerned with defending the image of American democracy than enforcing federal desegregation laws.

Viewing the civil rights movement in world perspective necessitates a reperiodization of sorts. Just as our understanding of *Brown* as the genesis of the modern civil rights movement is called into question by the framework of "the long civil rights movement," and complicated further by the impact of the Cold War, so must we consider the extent to which African American consciousness and U.S. domestic and foreign policymakers were responding not only to the black freedom movement in the U.S., but also to the decolonization of Africa, including such events as what became known as the Congo Crisis. For Malcolm X, Lorraine Hansberry, Amiri Baraka and a generation of Afro-American nationalists, the death of Lumumba was as formative as any of the hallmark civil rights campaigns and crises that occurred in the South. James Meriwether's *Proudly We Can Be Africans: Black Americans and Africa, 1935–1961* (Chapel Hill: University of North Carolina Press, 2002) captures the mood of those who looked to the new Africa of modern nation-states as an important basis for American civic identity. The impact of the Congo Crisis is detailed in Plummer, Meriwether, and my recent study, *American Africans in Ghana: Black Expatriates and the Civil Rights Era* (Chapel Hill: University of North Carolina Press, 2006). Newsreel footage of the demonstration of African Americans in the gallery of the United Nations Security Council, can be seen in the documentary *Ralph Bunche: An American Odyssey* (William Greaves Productions). One of the participants in that demonstration, Maya Angelou, provided an account of the demonstration in her evocative, if not always historically accurate memoir, *The Heart of a Woman* (New York: Random House, 1981), which describes the transformative potential of the new Africa on African American identity. In *The Cold War and the Color Line,* (Cambridge, Mass.: Harvard University Press, 2001). Thomas Borstelmann provides an account of the Congo Crisis from the standpoint of U.S. officialdom. Borstelmann argues that Eisenhower officials' racial attitudes toward the besieged Congolese prime minister Patrice Lumumba were decisive in their refusal to extend political or military support. While silent on the administration's racial perceptions of Lumumba, Stephen E. Ambrose notes Eisenhower's approval of a CIA plot to assassinate Lumumba in *Eisenhower* (New York: Simon and Schuster, 1983).

My study *American Africans in Ghana* resituates such familiar figures as King and Malcolm X within the framework of decolonization in Africa. As one of several African American honored guests, King visited the nation of Ghana in 1957 for that former British colony's independence ceremonies. A valuable contemporary account of King's visit to Ghana is in Lawrence D. Reddick, *Crusader Without Violence: A Biography of Martin Luther King, Jr.* (New York: Harper, 1959). See also the relevant documents on King's visit to Ghana collected by Clayborne Carson, senior editor, *The Papers of Martin Luther King, Jr. volume 4, Symbol of the Movement January 1957-December 1958* (Berkeley: University of California Press, 2000), particularly King's sermon on the Birth of Ghana. While in Ghana, King met with Prime Minister Kwame Nkrumah and other Ghanaian nationalist leaders, as did Malcolm X, during his own visit in 1964. By 1964, the optimism of the moment of independence was a distant memory, shattered by violent repression of nationalists in the Congo and in South Africa. Ghana was under siege from internal and external opposition, and Nkrumah had eroded civil liberties with a repressive domestic security apparatus after two assassination attempts. And in the U.S. setting, African American liberals and radicals who sought to influence U.S. foreign policy toward Africa clashed with the U.S. liberal establishment over the very terms and content of African American political consciousness and citizenship. For teaching purposes, I recommend chapter 6 of my book, *American Africans in Ghana,* on Malcolm X's visit to Ghana, which details his ouster from the Nation of Islam, his engagement with African affairs, and the impact the latter had on his ideas for mobilizing U.S. blacks.

KEVIN GAINES is director of the Center for Afroamerican and African Studies and professor of history at the University of Michigan, Ann Arbor. His new book is *American Africans in Ghana: Black Expatriates and the Civil Rights Era* (UNC Press). He is also the author of *Uplifting the Race: Black Leadership, Politics and Culture During the Twentieth Century* (UNC Press, 1996).

The Rise of Conservatism Since World War II

DAN T. CARTER

In the 1964 presidential election, Republican presidential nominee Barry Goldwater suffered a decisive defeat at the hands of Lyndon Johnson. Goldwater, the dream candidate of his party's conservative wing, had offered a "choice not an echo" in his campaign and the American people seemed to have little doubt about *their* choice. Goldwater carried only his home state of Arizona and five Deep South states where opposition to the Civil Rights movement was at high tide. Johnson took the rest with sixty-one percent of the popular vote and his coattails increased the Democratic majority by thirty-eight House members and two new senators. By all the traditional measurements of American politics, the election of 1964 was a disaster for American conservatism. Not only was their choice decisively rebuffed by the voters, but the overwhelming Democratic victory gave Johnson the opportunity to enact his "Great Society" programs, collectively the most far-reaching liberal legislation since Franklin Roosevelt's New Deal.

If 1964 was a decisive political defeat for Barry Goldwater, it was only a temporary setback in the steady growth of a conservative movement which would reach new heights in the election of Ronald Reagan in 1980 and the creation of a Republican majority in both houses of Congress in 1994. The complex story of that conservative resurgence—centered politically in the Republican Party but extending throughout American society—is one of the most critical developments in the last half of the twentieth century.

The rise of this conservative movement had its roots in the three decades before the Goldwater campaign, drawing upon two powerful and interrelated impulses. The first was an unambiguous defense of laissez-faire capitalism. Such conservative ideas ran deep in American history, but they had been badly discredited during the 1930s by the fact that most Americans attributed the Depression to the excesses of the capitalist system in general and the rapacious greed of corporate and business interests specifically. During the 1930s, most Americans seemed to accept the argument that the federal government had an obligation to protect the American people against those whom Franklin Roosevelt described as "malefactors of great wealth" by regulating and controlling these financial interests. At the same time, the establishment of a limited national welfare system—symbolized most concretely by the Social Security Act of 1935—represented a new and expanded role for the national state.

Despite the popularity of these measures, a vocal and articulate minority of Americans maintained their hostility to the national government.[1] Apart from their complaint that the welfare state led to idleness and undermined the work ethic of its recipients, they argued that the heavy hand of government thwarted the wealth-producing force of individual entrepreneurs with its stifling red tape and burdensome taxes.

The second conservative impulse came from the linking of the "welfare state" (and the Democratic Party that created it) with fears of international communism. Since the Bolshevik Revolution, American conservatives warned of the threat of international communism, but in the aftermath of World War II, their arguments fell upon particularly receptive ears. Joseph Stalin's ruthless suppression of democratic governments in eastern Europe after World War II and their absorption behind the Iron Curtain, the Soviet Union's emergence as a nuclear power in 1949, and the victory of Mao Tse Tung's Communist forces China that same year stunned and alarmed Americans. At the same time, the disclosure that a number of Americans had spied and passed on nuclear and other defense secrets, launched the great Red Scare of the late 1940s and 1950s. Anticommunism—most dramatically reflected in the emergence of Senator Joseph McCarthy—was undoubtedly inflamed by politics. Although there were spies and homegrown subversives operating within the United States, the heated political context of the Cold War vastly exaggerated their numbers. By charging that the "liberal" administrations of Franklin Roosevelt and Harry Truman sheltered traitors and thus strengthened America's Cold War adversaries, conservatives could strike a blow at their political enemies.

But these arguments were more than simply crude political tools. In the decade from 1943 to 1953, conservative intellectuals—led by the Austrian born economist and social philosopher Frederick Hayek—argued that the flaws of "Rooseveltian" liberalism went far deeper than the question of spies or internal subversion. There was, argued Hayek, a *philosophical* affinity between any "collectivist" political movement (like the New

Deal) and the forces of totalitarianism. Communism and German National Socialism were simply the mature results of all forms of "collectivism." As he argued in his brief but influential 1944 book, *The Road to Serfdom,* any attempt to control the economic freedom of individuals inevitably led (as his title suggested) to serfdom and barbarism.[2] Hayek's book was one of several works that would prove to be critical in the thinking of a new generation of conservative intellectuals.[3]

Even more important in creating an intellectual foundation for the new conservatism was the creation of the *National Review* magazine under the editorial leadership of William F. Buckley Jr. Founded in 1964 and bankrolled by wealthy business conservatives, the new magazine soon became the crossroads through which most intellectual and political conservatives passed. In the years that followed, there would be other magazines and other conservative institutions created, but the *National Review* remained, in many ways, the "Mother Church" of this new movement.

Still, the arguments of intellectuals did not create an electoral majority anymore than either businessmen's distaste for government bureaucrats or the angry passions of McCarthyism. While Republicans won the presidency in 1952 and again in 1956, it was not with their longtime conservative standard-bearer, Robert Taft of Ohio, but with the soothing and distinctly moderate war hero, Dwight Eisenhower. To the despair (and disgust) of the conservative faithful, Eisenhower made little effort to challenge the basic contours of the national state created during the Roosevelt and Truman years. While Richard Nixon, the unsuccessful 1960 Republican nominee, was more strident in his anticommunist rhetoric, he also expressed little interest in rolling back the changes of the previous three decades.

If the foundation for a conservative resurgence was being laid for the future (even as the national political movement suffered repeated political setbacks through the 1950s), conservatives usually captured the attention of the media and academics only in its most bizarre and extreme forms. There were the dozens of fanatical anticommunist ideologues, many combining religious enthusiasm with their hatred of the "Red Menace." At the violent fringe could be found Robert Pugh's Minutemen, with their storehouses of automatic weapons and their plans for guerilla war once the communists who controlled the United States government had removed the mask of liberalism and shown their true face. And there were the marginally more respectable spokesmen for the new Right and their organizations: the Rev. Carl McIntire's Twentieth Century Reformation, Dr. Fred Schwarz's Christian Anti-Communism Crusade, the Rev. Billy James Hargis's Christian Crusade, Edgar Bundy's League of America, Dean Clarence Manion's American Forum, Texas oilman H.L Hunt's nationwide radio "Life Line" broadcasts and, of course, Robert Welch's John Birch Society. The title of three of the most influential works of this period give some sense of the perspective of what we might call "establishment" attitudes: *The Radical Right,* edited by Daniel Bell; Arnold Forster and Benjamin Epstein's *Danger on the Right;* and Richard Hofstadter's *The Paranoid Style in American Politics.*[4]

These groups were, however, the extreme right of a far broader movement that was often unnoticed or, in many instances, simply

described, indiscriminately as "extremist." One critical building block for that new conservative movement was laid in the burgeoning suburban development of postwar America. In her study of Orange County, California, historian Lisa McGirr has given us a portrait of this emerging constituency—the "Suburban Warriors" of the new conservatism. Mainline political pundits of the 1950s had often described these new political activists as "antimodern." While it is true that they often rebelled against what they saw as the excesses of change, they were in fact products of suburban prosperity, "winners" for the most part who had benefitted from the Cold War prosperity of the 1950s and 1960s. In the case of McGirr's subjects, many, in fact, worked in the burgeoning defense industries of southern California.

The new suburban communities that surrounded declining inner cities offered a safe and relatively secure launching pad of privatized civic culture to attack the secular humanists and liberal social engineers who demanded much, notably higher taxes, and offered little: the charmless attraction of unruly public spaces and expensive public programs for what these new conservatives called the "undeserving poor." In these new communities, there was little space for or interest in a "public sphere." Instead, conservative churches and a fierce political activism created a different kind of community of political and cultural activists dedicated to protecting the status quo.

The ideology of this New Right centered around the traditional conservative demands of the 1950s: rolling back communism abroad, rooting out "Reds" at home, and shrinking the welfare state. But there was also a distinctly religious and "traditionalist" aspect to these new "suburban warriors." The 1950s were a period of astounding religious resurgence; by one estimate, the number of Americans who described themselves as regular churchgoers increased more than seventy percent during the decade. Most of that growth could be attributed to evangelical and culturally conservative churchgoers, like Southern Baptists, who were profoundly unsettled over the social "liberalization" of society.[5]

In part, the reason for the invisibility of this movement lay in the fact that much of it took place at the community level. Suburbia became the setting for new forms of community mobilization as middle- and upper-middle-class conservatives organized neighborhood meetings, showed "anticommunist" movies, launched petition drives to block sex education in the local schools, elected school board members who would guarantee the adoption of "proAmerican" texts, and, in the case of Los Angeles, selected a school board superintendent who barred discussion of the United Nations in the classroom.

The opening that allowed the dramatic growth of American conservatism came in the 1960s. In part it was an almost inevitable response to the ambitious liberalism of Lyndon Johnson's Great Society programs. Although liberals would deride the timidity and limited nature of the Johnson agenda, it did mark a substantial step in the expansion of the New Deal welfare state. Even before the Johnson landslide of 1964, he had persuaded Congress to enact the Economic Opportunity Act of 1964, the first measure of what he called an "unconditional war on poverty." In 1965 and 1966, he was even more successful in pushing through dozens of measures ranging from expanded public housing to the creation of the National Endowments for the Arts and the Humanities, as well as education subsidies, consumer protection, and environmental preservation measures. The capstone of this sweeping legislative agenda was the creation of Medicare and Medicaid.

As one might expect, conservatives attacked the Great Society on both fiscal and philosophical grounds. It was too expensive, they charged, and it discouraged initiative by giving the poor "handouts" rather than forcing them to find work on their own. But Johnson's program was more than simply an expansion of traditional social welfare programs, it also plunged into the thicket of racial politics. The New Deal had seen a shift in the allegiance of African Americans. Traditionally stalwarts of the party of Abraham Lincoln, black voters had turned to Roosevelt and then in even greater numbers to Harry Truman after he backed a strong civil rights plank in the 1948 Democratic Party platform. While the support of black voters in key northern industrial states proved critical to Truman's reelection, it also led to the creation of the third party "Dixiecrat Movement" and laid the foundation for the future defection of white Democratic voters in the South who had often backed their party's "liberal" economic agenda, but were adamantly opposed to the efforts of northern liberals to end segregation.

Nor had that racial backlash been confined to white southern Democrats. As a growing number of African Americans migrated to northern industrial cities, white urban working class and white-collar voters often reacted with growing hostility to what they perceived as "threats" to their neighborhoods and to their jobs. Urban historians who have studied such cities have found a growing disaffection among these traditional white Democratic working-class and middle-class voters well before the 1960s.[6]

But it was during the 1960s that this white backlash proved critical in the conservative movement. During the early 1960s, "respectable" conservatives made a conscious decision to distance themselves from the more extremist elements in the movement, an action symbolized by William F. Buckley Jr.'s decision to condemn John Birch Society founder Robert Welch for his claim that Dwight Eisenhower had been a "dedicated, conscious agent of the Communist conspiracy. . . ."[7]

If leading conservatives also sought to distance themselves from the cruder forms of racism, there was broad opposition to the Civil Rights movement as it emerged in the 1950s and 1960s. The more "extremist" conservative organizations such as the John Birch Society, and most of the prominent "anticommunist" leaders constantly linked movement leaders such as Martin Luther King Jr. with the international Communist movement, but more respectable mainline conservative groups were equally hostile to any attempts to use the power of government to protect the civil rights of African Americans. In an unsigned editorial in the *National Review* in 1957, Buckley told his readers that whites in the Deep South were the "advanced race" and thus entitled to take "such measures [as] are necessary to prevail, politically and culturally. . . ." Besides, he added, the "great majority of the Negroes of the South who do not vote do not care to vote and would not know for what to vote if they could."[8] When Barry Goldwater announced his opposition to the Civil

Rights Act of 1964, it was the logical culmination of a decade of fairly consistent conservative opposition to any federal action designed to protect the rights of African Americans.[9]

Traditional antistatism, muscular anticommunism, a vague uneasiness over accelerating social change, and a hostility to federally supported civil rights may have furnished the foundations for the growth of conservatism, but it was the tumultuous and unsettling events of the 1960s that made millions of Americans more responsive to conservative arguments.

First, in the long hot summers of the mid-1960s, angry African American civil rights activists retreated into a militant "black power" movement and race riots erupted in dozens of American cities across the Northeast, Midwest, and West. Large scale upheavals in such cities as Newark, the Watts district of Los Angeles, Washington, and Detroit left dozens dead and thousands of shops and buildings burned and looted. At the same time, American involvement in the Vietnam War accelerated from peaceful "teach-ins" in the nation's college classrooms to angry street demonstrations and confrontations with police.

As the signs of public disorder accelerated, conservatives bitterly attacked the Johnson administration for failing to quell "lawlessness" in American cities at home or to crush the North Vietnamese and Vietcong guerrillas abroad. These public manifestations of disorder increasingly reflected (in the minds of conservatives) a general social decay. Rising crime rates, the legalization of abortion, the rise of "out-of-wedlock" pregnancies, the increase in divorce rates, and the proliferation of "obscene" literature and films undermined traditional cultural symbols of conservatism and unnerved millions of Americans, an uneasiness reinforced by the new medium of television. For most Americans, their own community, their own neighborhood, might be relatively calm, but through the "immediacy of television," they became angered and felt menaced. Who were these disrespectful and unpatriotic drug-crazed hippies angrily burning the American flag night after night on the flickering screen while American soldiers died in Vietnam for their country? Who were these armed black men in combat fatigues and dark sunglasses, exultantly brandishing their semi-automatic weapons as they marched out of college classrooms? Who were these brazen women, flaunting their sexuality, burning their bras and challenging traditional "family values." In another time, these threatening events, these threatening individuals, would have remained remote, even abstract. Now they came directly into America's living room in living color.[10]

The general political impact could be felt in a growing anti-Washington rhetoric, for the federal government now seemed complicit in these assaults on traditional American values. Conservatives charged that the United States Justice Department proposed that northern schools be integrated and that the federal courts "pandered" to criminals and banned state-sponsored prayer from the schools even as it opened the nation's bookstores to "filth and pornography." Spurred by fire-eating politicians and a powerful new communication network of right-wing talk show hosts, federal bureaucrats from Internal Revenue Service agents to forest rangers to Occupational Safety and Health Administration inspectors to Environmental Protection Agency enforcement officers to Bureau of Alcohol, Tobacco, and Firearms agents were increasingly depicted as power hungry, arrogant, jackbooted thugs intent on harassing honest taxpaying citizens with mindless and unnecessary red tape while diverting their hard-earned dollars to shiftless and lazy undeserving poor and predominantly black people.

Barry Goldwater's 1964 campaign marked the first major effort of post-New Deal conservatives to take the political high-ground. The boisterously crude 1968 campaign of Alabama Governor George Wallace reflected the tumult of the politics of the 1960s. Wallace had begun his national political career in 1964 on one issue: opposition to the Civil Rights Act of that year. When he launched his 1968 "American Independent" Party candidacy, Wallace couched his anti-civil rights message in a political rhetoric that avoided explicit racism, but his angry attacks on "bussing," "welfare abuse," and "civil rights professional agitators" skillfully exploited the growing hostility of many white Americans to what they saw as the excesses of the Civil Rights movement. At the same time, Wallace married his racial message to the "social" issues of the 1960s, calling for the curbing of constitutional rights for "street hoodlums" and dramatic reductions in welfare expenditures. From race to religion (Wallace was the first national politician to call for a constitutional amendment restoring school classroom prayers), Wallace articulated the new conservative agenda. Six weeks before the November election, more than twenty-one percent of America's voters told pollsters that Wallace was their choice for president. Although his final vote faded to fourteen percent, he came within an eyelash of throwing the election of 1968 into the House of Representatives.[11]

Richard Nixon had cautiously sought to exploit this growing conservative movement while depicting himself as a "centrist" candidate; he learned from his narrow escape. Between 1968 and 1972, guided by the advice of such advisers as Harry Dent of South Carolina and voter analyst Kevin Philips, Nixon worked to make certain that those voters who had supported Wallace moved from his third party candidacy into the Republican Party. He did so by taking conservative views on a number of issues, particularly such controversial questions as bussing. Nixon's "Southern Strategy" was a critical factor in the electoral shift away from Democratic (and liberal) dominance. But his role in this process was cut short by the Watergate scandal, allowing the election of Jimmy Carter in 1976.

The last building block of the conservative movement fell into place during the Carter administration. By the 1970s, conservative evangelicals built a powerful group of educational, publishing, and broadcasting institutions. During the 1960s, they became alarmed over what they saw as an increasing drift toward a liberal secularism that undermined "traditional" values in American society. The Supreme Court's decisions in 1962 and 1963 outlawing official school prayers were a key complaint, but the Carter administration's demand that church schools (because they were tax exempt) undertake affirmative efforts to secure minority students pushed many evangelicals into politics. After 1978, under the leadership of evangelical activists like Marion "Pat" Robertson and Jerry Falwell, religious conservatives mobilized around such hot-button issues as abortion, school prayer and the teaching of evolution, becoming critical partners in a new coalition of social, cultural and economic conservatives. Conservative Christians had become Christian conservatives.

In 1980, conservatives finally achieved the victory they had lost in 1964 as Ronald Reagan swept into the White House, decisively defeating incumbent Jimmy Carter by promising dramatic tax cuts, a rollback of the federal government, a dramatic rebuilding of American military might, and a return to "traditional" American values. The eight years of the Reagan presidency left many of the staunchest conservatives dissatisfied. As one prominent spokesman of the New Right concluded, he had given little but symbolism to religious and social conservatives who wanted a return to "traditional" American values; he had done even less to slow the growth of government. Domestically, his only accomplishment was to dramatically cut taxes primarily for the well-off, thus creating such an enormous public debt that liberals in the future would be stymied in proposing any new additional government initiatives. Paul Weyrich's gloomy assessment was correct in many respects, but he underestimated the extent to which Reagan—notoriously uninformed on specific issues—had managed to create an "aura" of confidence. By the end of the Reagan years, conservatives had created a powerful and well-financed national constituency of small businessmen, suburbanites hostile to increasing taxes, religiously conservative evangelicals and traditional Catholics, gun owners passionately opposed to any control over firearms, and white blue-collar workers angry at affirmative action. Conservatives had also moved from the fringe to parity in the television media and dominance in the influential world of talk radio.

The decade of the 1990s saw both victories and defeats for conservatives. The victory of Democrat Bill Clinton in 1992 and his ability to survive eight years in the White House was a source of deep disappointment to movement leaders. But the 1994 strong showing of Republican conservatives under the leadership of Newt Gingrich reflected the shift that had taken place in American politics. The failure of the Equal Rights Amendment, the defeat of welfare entitlement while the Democratic Clinton was in the White House, the gradual erosion of Affirmative Action and, in general, the increasing conservatism of the United States Supreme Court showed that the framework for shaping public policy had shifted further to the right through the 1980s and 1990s.

Still, it is not, at all clear that there is a clear conservative hegemony. George W. Bush won the 2000 presidential election not by promising ultraconservative values, but by appealing to the American voters in a distinctly moderate tone. And yet he still did not capture a majority of the votes cast. In fact, by a popular margin of fifty-two to forty-eight percent, Americans supported a more liberal Albert Gore and a decidedly more left-wing Ralph Nader. Conservatives today are united in their opposition to what they see as the excesses of American liberalism, but they remain divided between those who would emphasize libertarian approach to personal as well as economic behavior and those who believe it is the duty of the state to enforce strict standards of public morality and public order.

Finally, the conservative movement ultimately will be judged by the extent to which it creates a just as well as a free society. But the gap between rich and poor has grown steadily with the rise of American conservatism in the last quarter of the twentieth century. According to the statistics compiled by the Congressional Budget Office, the income of the poorest one-fifth of Americans fell twelve percent between the late 1970s and the end of the 1990s; the top twenty percent saw its income rise by nearly forty percent and the top one percent of Americans saw their after-tax income grow by one hundred twenty percent. (The income of Americans between the fortieth and eightieth percentiles changed very little). By the beginning of the twenty-first century, the United States had become the most unequal society in the industrialized West. Although that growing inequality has been fed by many sources, it has clearly been reinforced by conservative priorities that have emphasized reducing the progressive nature of the federal income tax while holding the line or cutting back public services for the poor.[12]

Not surprisingly, those who have benefited from these policies and priorities have responded by opening their pocketbooks and by voting early and often. By one estimate, voters in the top twenty percent of the electorate cast as much as thirty percent of the votes in general elections and even more in local and off-year elections. Conservatives have traditionally accepted economic inequality as the price that must be paid for encouraging competition and economic productivity. But implicit in this postwar movement was the promise that conservatives would create a just as well as a moral and free society. Conservatives will ultimately succeed only if they move beyond their contempt for American liberalism and, in the words of a historian of the movement, "offer a model of political freedom that would protect the citizen against blind, impersonal economic forces, in which one man's freedom would not be another's subjection".[13]

Notes

1. Gary Wills describes, from a critical perspective, this deep-seated antigovernment tradition in American culture in *A Necessary Evil: A History of American Distrust of Government* (New York: Simon & Schuster, 1999).

2. Frederick Hayek, *The Road to Serfdom* (Chicago: University of Chicago Press, 1944).

3. While any list would be somewhat arbitrary, most historians of American conservatism would probably add Ayn Rand's best selling novel *The Fountainhead* (Indianapolis, IN: The Bobbs Merrill Company, 1943); Richard Weaver, *Ideas Have Consequences* (Chicago: University of Chicago Press, 1948); and Russell Kirk, *The Conservative Mind, from Burke to Santayana* (Chicago: H. Regnery Co., 1953). For an overview of the role played by these and other writers and intellectuals see George H. Nash, *The Conservative Intellectual Movement in America Since 1945* (New York: Basic Books, 1976).

   Forster and Epstein, *Danger on the Right* (New York: Random House, 1964); and Hofstadter, *The Paranoid Style in American Politics and Other Essays* (New York: Alfred A. Knopf, 1965).

Hofstadter's essay, originally delivered as a lecture at Oxford University in the fall of 1963, was clearly triggered by the Goldwater movement.

4. Daniel Bell, ed., *The New American Right* (New York: Criterion Books, 1955).

5. This religious resurgence was not limited to evangelicals. One measure of the growth of the new piety may be gauged by the fact that the number of individuals entering the priesthood dramatically increased in the post-World War II era. See Winthrop S. Hudson, *Religion in America* (New York: Charles Scribner's Sons, 1965), 396; Phillip E. Hammond, *Religion and Personal Autonomy: The Third Disestablishment in America*, (Columbia, SC: University of South Carolina Press, 1992), 114; Barry A. Kosmin and Seymour P. Lachman, *One Nation Under God: Religion in Contemporary American Society*, (New York: Harmony Books, 1993), 4–7, 298–99.

6. Thomas J. Sugrue, "Crabgrass-Roots Politics: Race, Rights, and the Reaction against Liberalism in the Urban North, 1940–1964," *Journal of American History*, 82 (1995): 551–78.

7. While Buckley and most other mainstream conservatives disavowed Welch's assertion that Eisenhower was a communist agent, they did not attack the John Birch Society or other far-right groups. See Jonathan Schoenwald, *A Time for Choosing: The Rise of Modern American Conservatism* (New York: Oxford University Press, 2001), 71–73.

8. *National Review,* 24 August 1957.

9. See, for example, the articles of November 1964 in the *National Review* on race and the election.

10. Dan T. Carter, *The Politics of Rage: George Wallace, the Origins of the New Conservatism and the Transformation of American Politics,* (New York: Simon & Schuster, 1995), 375–77.

11. Dan T. Carter, *From George Wallace to Newt Gingrich: Race in the Conservative Counterrevolution, 1963–1994* (Baton Rouge: Louisiana State University Press, 1996), 19, 23, 35.

12. *New York Times,* 5 September 1999, 14; see also Frank Levy's *The New Dollars and Dreams: Americans Incomes and Economic Change* (New York: Russell Sage Foundation, 1998).

13. Godfrey Hodgson, *The World Turned Right Side Up: A History of the Conservative Ascendancy in America* (Boston: Houghton Mifflin, 1996), 315.

DAN T. CARTER is the Educational Foundation Professor of History at the University of South Carolina, where he teaches twentieth-century United States and Southern regional history. He is the author of *The Politics of Rage: George Wallace, the Origins of New Conservatism, and the Transformation of American Politics,* and *From George Wallace to Newt Gingrich: Race in the Conservative Counterrevolution.* He also won an Emmy in 2001 for Outstanding Individual Achievement in a Craft as a researcher for the PBS American Experience documentary based on his 1995 biography of Wallace, "George Wallace, Settin' the Wood on Fire."

The Spirit of '68

What really caused the Sixties.

John B. Judis

This year Bob Dylan's album *Time Out of Mind* won the Grammy for best popular record, and teenagers in my local video store were waiting in line to rent *Don't Look Back,* D.A. Pennebaker's 1967 documentary about the irreverent Dylan. The National Organization for Women, the Consumer Federation of America, the Environmental Defense Fund, and other organizations from the Sixties are still influential in American politics. On the other hand, a host of grumpy social critics and cultural commissars, from Robert Bork and William Bennett to John Leo and Hilton Kramer, have continued to make a career out of denouncing that climactic period of American politics and culture. According to these critics, the "Vietnam syndrome" ruined our foreign policy, and the spirit of permissiveness and "anything goes" corrupted our schools and youth and destroyed the nuclear family. "The revolt was against the entire American culture," Bork declared recently.

Why all the fuss? As a political era—one characterized by utopian social experiments, political upheaval, and dramatic reform—the Sixties ended sometime during Richard Nixon's presidency. But the era left an indelible mark on the decades that followed. It vastly expanded the scope of what citizens expect from their government—from clean air and water to safe workplaces, reliable products, and medical coverage in their old age. It also signaled a change in what Americans wanted out of their lives. During the Sixties, Americans began to worry about the "quality of life" and about their "lifestyle" rather than simply about "making a living." The Sixties unleashed conflicts within these new areas of concern—over affirmative action, abortion, homosexuality, drugs, rock lyrics, air pollution, endangered species, toxic waste dumps, and automobile safety. And the era raised questions about the purpose of America and its foreign policy that are still being debated. The Sixties have preoccupied late-twentieth-century America almost as much as the Civil War preoccupied late-nineteenth-century America.

The difficulty in understanding the Sixties lies partly in the sheer diversity of people, events, and institutions that defined it—from John Kennedy's New Frontier to the Weatherman "Days of Rage," from the Black Panther Party to the Ford Foundation, from Betty Friedan and Ralph Nader to Barry Goldwater and George Wallace. Many of the books and articles that purport to be about the Sixties focus on one aspect of the era to the exclusion of the others. Todd Gitlin's excellent book, for instance, has only a passing reference to Nader and to the Sierra Club's David Brower but multiple references to Carl Oglesby, Huey Newton, and Staughton Lynd.

The nature of the Sixties has also been clouded by conservative jeremiads. Much of what disturbs the critics of the Sixties—from the spread of pornography to the denigration of the work ethic—was not the product of radical agitators but of tectonic shifts in American capitalism. Many of those who complain most vociferously about the Sixties' counterculture, such as House Speaker Newt Gingrich, are themselves products of the period. They no longer carry signs, as Gingrich once did, proclaiming the right of campus magazines to publish nude pictures, but, even as they denounce the Sixties, they echo the decade's themes and vocabulary in articulating their own political objectives. Unable to come to terms with their own past, they sow confusion about one of the most important periods in our history.

Like most periods described by the name of a decade, the Sixties don't strictly conform to their allotted time span. You could make a good case that the Sixties began in December 1955, when Rosa Parks refused to give up her seat in a segregated Montgomery, Alabama, bus, and only ended in 1973 or 1974, when the New Left lost its fervor. You could also make a case for dividing the Sixties into two periods. The first period—running from 1955 to 1965—spans the rise of the Southern civil rights movement and of Martin Luther King, the founding of Students for a Democratic Society (SDS) in 1960, the passage of the civil rights bills and Medicare, and the initiation of the War on Poverty. The second period begins with the escalation of the war and the ghetto riots and goes through the rise of the black power and militant antiwar movements, the growth of the counterculture, the rapid development of environmental, consumer, and women's movements, and the major legislative achievements of Nixon's first term.

On the most visible level—the level at which most books about the period have dwelled—there is a pronounced shift in mood during the escalation of the war and the onset of the riots in the mid-'60s. The antiwar and black movements became violent and apocalyptic, and the country itself seemed on the verge of disintegration. But the sharp difference in tone between the two periods obscures important continuities. Most of the major movements that began in the Sixties—the consumer and environmental movements, the modern women's movement—started in the early years of the decade. And the roots of the counterculture go back well into the 1950s, if not before. These movements, as well as the counterculture, took root in Europe, too. In the United States, the simultaneous presence of massive antiwar demonstrations, riots, and demands for black power merely lent those movements and the counterculture a frenzy and an urgency that they might otherwise not have possessed.

The first period of the Sixties looks exactly like a belated continuation of the Progressive era and the New Deal. Just as in earlier periods of reform, political change was precipitated by an economic downturn. Successive recessions in 1958 and 1960 helped Democrats increase their margin in Congress and helped put Kennedy in the White House. In 1964, Johnson, benefiting from a buoyant economy and an impolitic opponent, Barry Goldwater, identified with Southern segregationists and with a trigger-happy foreign policy, won a landslide victory, and liberal Democrats gained control of Congress for the first time since 1936.

Just as before, reform was aided by an alliance of popular movements, elite organizations, and pragmatic business leaders. By the early '60s, the Southern civil rights movement enjoyed enormous support in the North, financial backing from the Ford Foundation and the Rockefeller Brothers Fund, and editorial support from the major media. Business leaders, encouraged by prosperity after having endured four recessions in a decade, accepted Johnson and the administration's major legislative initiatives with equanimity. They didn't oppose Medicare (only the American Medical Association lobbied against it), and they actively backed the Great Society and War on Poverty programs, which they saw, correctly, as creating demand for new private investment. When Johnson appointed a National Commission on Technology, Automation, and Economic Progress, the nation's most powerful businessmen joined labor and civil rights leaders in recommending a guaranteed annual income and a massive job-training program.

The spirit of the early '60s—epitomized in Johnson's vision of the Great Society—was one of heady, liberal optimism. Many of the key leaders of the period, including Martin Luther King Jr., George McGovern, Hubert Humphrey, and Walter Mondale, were raised on the Protestant Social Gospel's millennial faith in the creation of a Kingdom of God in America. The political-economic premise of this optimism, enunciated in Galbraith's *The Affluent Society* and in Michael Harrington's *The Other America,* was that American industry, which was becoming highly automated, was capable of producing great abundance, but archaic political and economic arrangements were preventing many Americans from enjoying its fruits. The goal of such programs as Medicare and the War on Poverty was to allow the poor, the aged, and the disadvantaged to share in this abundance.

This first phase of the Sixties was also marked by signs of a looming redefinition of politics that would differentiate it from early reform epochs. During the Progressive era and the New Deal, politics pivoted primarily on conflicts among different sectors of business and between business and labor. The great battles of the first five decades of the twentieth century had been over the trusts, the tariff, the banking system, the abolition of child labor, and government regulation of collective bargaining. No legislative struggle attracted so many lobbyists, was fought as fiercely, and had as much impact on presidential politics as the Taft-Hartley labor bill in 1947.

In the early '60s, new issues that didn't fit easily within this pattern began to emerge. Americans became concerned not merely with obtaining lower prices for goods but with government overseeing the safety, reliability, and quality of goods. President Kennedy announced a consumer bill of rights in 1962. That same year, over the strong objection of the clothing industry, Congress passed landmark legislation requiring flame-resistant fabrics in children's clothing. In 1964, Assistant Secretary of Labor Daniel P. Moynihan hired a young Harvard Law graduate, Ralph Nader, to research auto safety. Two years later, amidst the furor created by Nader's work, Congress passed the National Traffic and Motor Vehicle Safety Act.

In the early '60s, Americans also became concerned about the environment—not merely as a source of renewable resources or as a wildlife preserve but as the natural setting for human life. In 1962, Rachel Carson's *Silent Spring* became a best-seller. Congress passed its first Clean Air Act in 1963 and its first Clean Water Act in 1965. During the early '60s, American women also began to stir as a political force in their own right. In 1963, Betty Friedan published *The Feminine Mystique,* and, three years later, she and other feminists formed the National Organization for Women. While the older women's movement had focused on suffrage, the new movement reached into the workplace and the home and even into the private lives of men and women.

The new concerns about work, consumption, and personal life were part of a fundamental change in American culture that began to manifest itself clearly in the early '60s. During the nineteenth and early twentieth centuries, Americans had still adhered to the Protestant work ethic introduced by seventeenth-century English emigrants to America and memorialized in Benjamin Franklin's *Autobiography.* They viewed idleness and leisure as sinful and saw life and work as unpleasant prerequisites to a heavenly reward. By the early '60s, Americans had begun to abandon this harsh view for an ethic of the good life. They wanted to discover a "lifestyle" that suited them. They worried about the "quality of life," including the kinds of foods they ate, the clothes they wore, and the cars they drove.

This change was not the work of sinful agitators but reflected deep-seated changes that had taken place in American capitalism over the century. In the nineteenth century and early twentieth century, economic growth, and the growth of the working class itself, was driven by the expansion of steel, railroads, machine tools, and other "capital goods" industries. Workers' consumption was held down in order to free up funds that could be used to invest in these new capital goods. To prevent recurrent economic crises, American industrialists were always on the lookout—in China, among other places—for new outlets for investment in railroads and other capital goods. But, as the historian Martin J. Sklar has demonstrated, sometime around the 1920s, the dynamic of economic growth changed. The growth of capital goods industries became, ironically, a threat to prosperity.

It happened because American industry, like American agriculture, became too successful for its own good. The introduction of electricity and the assembly line made the modern factory so productive that it could now increase its output without increasing its overall number of employees. During the '20s, manufacturing output grew 64 percent, but the number of workers in capital goods industries fell by twelve percent. Expanding the production of capital goods no longer required the sacrifice of workers' consumption. By the same token, it imperiled prosperity by encouraging the production of more goods than those producing them—the workers—could purchase and consume.

During the '20s, Edward Filene and other far-seeing businessmen understood that the fulcrum of the economy had shifted from production to consumption and that, to avoid depressions, employers would have to pay higher wages and induce their workers, through advertising, to spend money on consumer goods. Filene advocated a different kind of "industrial democracy" centered on workers' freedom to consume. After World War II, businesses adopted Filene's ethic and his strategy. They paid higher wages and devoted growing parts of their budgets to advertising, which was aimed at convincing Americans to spend rather than to save. Advertising budgets doubled between 1951 and 1962. Businesses and banks also introduced the installment plan and consumer loans and, later, credit cards as inducements to buy rather than to save.

In search of profit, businesses also invaded the family and home. They sold leisure and entertainment on a massive scale; they produced not merely clothes but fashion; they processed exotic foods and established fast-food chains; they sold physical and psychological health; they filled the home with appliances and gadgets. They convinced Americans that they should care about more than just having food on the table, a house to live in, and clothes on their backs. They encouraged the idea that Americans could remake themselves—that they could create their own "look," their own personality. They encouraged the idea that sex was not merely a means to procreate but a source of pleasure and visual excitement.

The origins of the counterculture lay at the interstices of this new American culture of leisure and consumption that business helped to promote. The counterculture was a product of the new culture at the same time as it represented a critique of and a counter to it. It rejected Filene's suggestion that workers seek their freedom entirely in consumption rather than work. It held out for meaningful work, but not as defined by the nineteenth or early twentieth centuries. In 1960, when Paul Goodman, writing in *Growing Up Absurd,* complained that "there are not enough worthy jobs in our economy for average boys and adolescents to grow up toward," he was not complaining about the lack of jobs at General Motors or on Wall Street.

The counterculture also rejected TV dinners and cars with tail fins that the advertisers urged Americans to buy, but it did so on behalf of more discriminating standards of its own. The critique of consumerism—articulated in the '50s by Vance Packard's *The Waste Makers* and *The Hidden Persuaders*—led directly to the formation of the modern consumer and environmental movements. And the rejection of sex symbols and stereotypes did not lead to a celebration of abstinence but to a wider exploration into sexual pleasure and to a reevaluation of homosexuality and heterosexuality. In the early '60s, all these concerns became the subjects not merely of books and small artistic cults, but of political manifestos and platforms and embryonic social movements.

The movements initially took root among college students and recent college graduates. Students who entered college in 1960 had been born after the Depression—they had been, in the words of SDS's Port Huron Statement, "bred in at least

modest comfort." Living in a time of unprecedented prosperity, they could afford not to worry about whether they would be able to get a job. They were raised to think about the "quality of life" rather than the iron law of wages, even to scorn some elements of what was then called "materialism." By 1960, they had become a major social group, capable on their own of disrupting society and upsetting its politics.

The New Left movements of the early '60s attacked the new economy, but they, too, implicitly used the new standards and ideals it had fostered. SDS's Port Huron Statement condemned the "idolatrous worship of things" but called for "finding a meaning in life that is personally authentic"—a formulation that would have made no sense to an industrial worker in 1909. In Berkeley, the Free Speech Movement of 1964—aimed at reclaiming the rights of students to distribute political literature on campus—gave way the next year to the Filthy Speech Movement, aimed at defending students against literary and sexual censorship. Over the next decade, these two movements—political and cultural—would develop in tandem.

The second period of the Sixties began with the Watts riot and Lyndon Johnson's escalation of the Vietnam War in 1965. These events signified and helped to precipitate a darker, more frenzied and violent period of protest. By escalating the war, Johnson broke a campaign promise not to send "our American boys to do the fighting for Asian boys." The war's escalation also threw into question the purpose of American foreign policy. Students who entered college in the Sixties had been imbued with the idea that America's mission was to create a democratic world after its own image. But, in Vietnam, the United States was backing a corrupt dictatorship, which, at our urging, had ignored the 1954 Geneva agreements to hold elections in Vietnam. The seeming contradiction between U.S. intervention and American ideals, Johnson's dishonesty and betrayal, and the rising list of casualties on both sides of the war inspired a growing rage against Johnson and the government. The antiwar movement split into a moderate wing that sought a negotiated withdrawal and a violent pro-North Vietnamese wing that threatened to bring the war home." As the conviction grew that U.S. intervention was not an unfortunate blunder but reflected the priorities of American capitalism and its power elite, antiwar militants began to see the United States itself as the enemy. SDS, the leading student organization, imagined itself by 1969 to be the vanguard of a violent revolution *against* the United States.

The first ghetto riots took place in the summer of 1964 and then grew in size and strength over the next three summers. In the Watts riot of 1965, 1,072 people were injured, 34 were killed, 977 buildings were damaged, and 4,000 people were arrested. In July 1967, there were 103 disorders, including five full-scale riots. In Detroit, 43 people were killed, and 7,200 were arrested. 700 buildings were burned, and 412 were totally destroyed. The riots were spontaneous. but they were invariably triggered by black perceptions of unequal treatment, particularly at the hands of white police officers.

At the same time that the riots began, Martin Luther King Jr. attempted to take the civil rights movement northward to Chicago. Contrary to the fantasies of his current conservative admirers, King never saw political and civil equality as ends in themselves but as part of a longer struggle for full social and economic equality. King wanted to desegregate housing in the North (which was the key to de facto school segregation), improve city services for blacks, and gain higher wages and better jobs for blacks. He failed abysmally in Chicago. The combination of the ghetto riots and King's failure contributed to the radicalization of the black movement. By 1968, when King was assassinated in Memphis while trying to support striking black garbage-men, many in the black movement had turned toward insurrectionary violence. It saw the Northern ghettos as Third World colonies that had to be liberated from their white imperialist oppressors.

Both the radical antiwar and the black power movements espoused what they called "revolutionary politics." They saw themselves in the tradition of Marx, Lenin, Mao, Fanon, Castro, and even Stalin, but, by the late '60s, they had become unwitting participants in a much older American tradition of Protestant millennialism. As historian William G. McLoughlin argued in *Revivals, Awakenings and Reform,* the Sixties were part of a religious revival comparable to the great awakenings of the mid-eighteenth and early nineteenth centuries. At such times, the seeming discord between ideal and reality has inspired intense self-examination, the proliferation of new sects and schisms, and alternating visions of doom and salvation. While the first phase of the Sixties saw the revival of the post-millennial Protestant Social Gospel—the view that the world would end after the millennium—the second phase saw "pre-millennial" visions of the apocalypse and Armageddon occurring before the millennium.

The emergence of this pre-millennial vision was provoked by the war's escalation and the combination of rage and guilt (guilt at complicity in the slaughter of seeming innocents) that it inspired; the repeated visions of violence and destruction in Vietnam and in American cities, which reinforced an image of change as conflagration; the assassinations of John and Robert Kennedy and of Martin Luther King, Jr., and Malcolm X; the Republican advances in 1966 and Nixon's election in November 1968, which discouraged New Left activists who had believed they could achieve majority support for their revolutionary aspirations; and the apparent success of the North Vietnamese in the war and the onset of China's Cultural Revolution, which suggested that revolution in the United States would occur only after a global revolution against American imperialism had succeeded.

The New Left of the late '60s dreamed not of America's salvation but of its destruction. If socialism or the "good life" were to come to the United States, it would be only after Armageddon—after a victorious armed struggle that would lay waste to the United States. The Panthers referred to the United States as "Babylon." When the Weatherman group took over SDS in 1969, it changed the name of SDS's newspaper, *New Left Notes,* to *Fire.* The new revolutionaries steeled themselves for a life of sacrifice and eventually death in the service of world revolution. Huey Newton, the cofounder of the Panther Party, described its program as "revolutionary suicide." Hal Jacobs, a Weatherman sympathizer, wrote in the movement magazine *Leviathan:* "Perhaps the best we can hope for is that in the course of the struggle we can develop human social relations among ourselves, while being engulfed by death and destruction."

The vision of Weatherman or the Panthers perfectly matched that of the Millerites—the precursors of today's Seventh Day Adventists. They were preparing themselves to be saved in the face of an imminent Armageddon. Even their organization resembled that of earlier Christian sects. The Weatherman group abandoned any pretense of building a mass movement. Instead, it sought to establish "revolutionary Marxist-Leninist-Maoist collective formations" that, through "criticism—self-criticism," would convert its members to true revolutionaries. Under Weatherman leadership, SDS, which at one point boasted 100,000 members, dwindled to several hundred aspiring visible saints.

During the late '60s, many of the people in the New Left, myself included, got caught up in the debate over class struggle, imperialism, racism, and revolution as if it were a genuine discussion based on reasonable, if debatable, assessments of world conditions. But others sensed that something was deeply wrong. In his 1968 campaign as the Democratic antiwar candidate, Eugene McCarthy continually frustrated his own followers by counseling calm and "reasoned judgment." Said McCarthy, "It is not a time for storming the walls, but for beginning a long march." Paul Goodman, whose writings had inspired the New Left, realized by 1969 that the political movement had turned unworldly even while it pretended to speak of world revolution:

> If we start from the premise that the young are in a religious crisis, that they doubt there is really a nature of things and they are sure there is no world for themselves, many details of their present behavior become clearer. Alienation is a powerful motivation, of unrest, fantasy and feckless action. It can lead ... to religious innovation, new sacraments to give life meaning. But it is a poor basis for politics, including revolutionary politics.

At the time, however, these voices were largely ignored. The question wasn't whether it made any sense at all to talk of revolution, but when the revolution would come and who would be on what side of the barricades.

This turn toward violence and revolutionary fantasy alienated many Americans and led to the rise of Ronald Reagan in California and George Wallace's surprising showing in the 1968 presidential election. That year, Richard Nixon ran a subtle "law and order" campaign to exploit the unpopularity of the antiwar and black protesters. Yet these movements still wielded enormous influence over the nation's political and legislative agenda. By the early '70s, they had helped force the Nixon administration to withdraw from Vietnam and had provoked Congress and the administration into pouring money into cities and adopting a strategy of affirmative action in hiring and federal contracts. During Nixon's first term, spending on Johnson's Great Society programs and on welfare and Food Stamps dramatically increased, while spending on the military went down.

There were two reasons for the movements' remarkable success. First, the movements were large and unruly enough to pose a constant threat of disruption. The major riots stopped by 1969, but the threat of riots persisted—both in actual fact and in the rhetoric and behavior of the black activists. In the summer of 1970 alone, city officials reported that black and Chicano militants made over 500 attacks on police, resulting in the deaths of 20 policemen. The antiwar movement also became increasingly violent. During the fall semester in 1970, 140 bombings occurred; at Rutgers, classes had to be vacated 175 times because of bomb threats.

Second, these movements had either the support or sympathy of policy elites. Some members of the foreign policy elite, acting partly out of conviction and partly out of fear of further disruption, favored immediate negotiation with the North Vietnamese and later unilateral withdrawal from Vietnam. By 1968, these included *The New York Times* editorial board and prominent members of the Council on Foreign Relations. Foundations and policy groups responded to the antiwar movement and to the riots and the black power movement the same way elite organizations in the early 1900s had responded to the threat of socialist revolution. They sought to tame the militants by helping them achieve their more reasonable objectives.

The Ford Foundation, the wealthiest and most powerful of all the foundations, with assets four times that of the Rockefeller Foundation, was particularly important. In 1966, Henry Ford and foundation board chairman John McCloy desirous that the foundation play a more active role in national affairs, brought in former Kennedy national security adviser McGeorge Bundy as the new president. Bundy threw the foundation into the struggle for racial equality. He helped new groups get off the ground, including La Raza and the Mexican-American Legal Defense Fund. But he also embroiled the foundation in controversy. Money that Ford gave to the Congress of Racial Equality in Cleveland went to funding a voter registration drive that helped elect Democrat Carl Stokes as Cleveland's first black mayor—in seeming violation of the foundation's nonpartisan status. In New York, Bundy sold New York City Mayor John Lindsay on a plan for community control of schools that put local blacks in charge of their own schools, which ended up pitting the city's blacks against the predominantly Jewish teachers' union.

While the late '60s are remembered mainly for the violent antiwar and black power movements, their most enduring legacy was the establishment of the environmental, consumer, and women's movements. By the early '70s, the National Organization for Women had 200 local chapters and had been joined in effort by the National Women's Political Caucus, the National Association for the Repeal of Abortion Laws, and hundreds of small local and national women's organizations. The movement enjoyed remarkable success. In 1972, the year Ms. magazine was founded, Congress approved the Equal Rights Amendment to the Constitution, strengthened and broadened the scope of the Equal Employment Opportunity Commission, and included a provision in the new Higher Education Act ensuring equal treatment of men and women.

The consumer and environmental movements enjoyed equally spectacular success. Organizations like the Sierra Club, Wilderness Society, and the Audubon Society expanded their purview and quadrupled their membership from 1960 to 1969. They were also joined by new groups, including Environmental Action, the Environmental Defense Fund, and Friends of the Earth. The Consumer Federation of America, a coalition of 140 state and local groups, was founded in 1967, and Consumers Union, which had published a magazine since 1936, moved its office to Washington in 1969. These groups got the Nixon administration and Congress to adopt a raft of reforms from establishing the Environmental Protection Agency and the Consumer Product Safety Commission to major amendments to the Clean Air and Clean Water acts.

The key individual behind these movements was Nader. He used his fame and income from *Unsafe at Any Speed*—his best-selling book about auto safety—and his successful battle with General Motors to help build a consumer movement. Nader started hiring young lawyers called "Nader's Raiders" in 1968 and founded his first campus-based Public Interest Research Group in 1970. By the mid-'70s, he had founded eight new organizations, including the Center for Responsive Law, Congress Watch, and the Health Research Group, which played an important role in getting Congress to pass a mass of new legislation, including the Wholesome Poultry Products Act, the Natural Gas Pipeline Safety Act, and the Occupational Safety and Health Act.

If Nader was the key individual, the key institution was once more the Ford Foundation. The foundation stepped in when the Audubon Society, worried about its own contributors, balked at funding the Environmental Defense Fund, the first public interest law firm designed to force business and government to comply with the new environmental laws. Ford also gave generous grants to the Sierra Club Legal Defense Fund and to the Los Angeles-based Center for Law in the Public Interest. By 1972, Ford was providing 86 percent of the grants to groups practicing consumer and environmental public interest law.

Unlike the later antiwar and civil rights movements, the environmental and consumer movements enjoyed enormous popular support. Republican and Democratic politicians vied to sponsor environmental and consumer legislation. In 1970, Nixon and Edmund Muskie, who was planning to run for president in 1972, got into a bidding war for the movements support, with each championing successively tougher revisions to the Clean Air Act. Businesses might have fought environmental and consumer legislation, but, in these years, they were restrained by a combination of complacency and defensiveness. From February 1961 to September 1969, the United States enjoyed the longest consecutive boom on record. The economy grew by 4.5 percent a year, compared to 3.2 percent in the '50s. Secure in their standing, only 50 corporations had registered lobbyists stationed in Washington in the early '60s.

In the mid-'60s, as the country's mood darkened, the public's opinion of business began to fall precipitously, but, as David Vogel recounts in *Fluctuating Fortunes*, business's initial response was to stress corporate social responsibility and to accommodate the demands of the consumer and environmental movements. While the auto and tobacco companies took umbrage at regulations targeted at them, business as a whole thought it could adapt the new environmental and consumer legislation to its own ends just as it had done earlier with the Interstate Commerce Commission and the Federal Trade Commission. A Fortune survey in February 1970 found 53 percent of Fortune 500 executives in favor of a national regulatory agency and 57 percent believing that the federal government should "step up regulatory activities." In a spirit of social responsibility, 85 percent of the executives thought that the environment should be protected even if that meant "reducing profits."

In the second phase of the Sixties, the counterculture spread from Berkeley, Madison, Ann Arbor, and Cambridge to almost every high school and college in America. Teenagers from pampered suburban homes who had never read Allen Ginsberg or Nelson Algren nevertheless denounced the "rat race" and the "neon wilderness." In extensive polls and interviews conducted from 1968 to 1974, Daniel Yankelovich saw steadily growing "acceptance of sexual freedom," rejection of "materialism," opposition to the laws against marijuana, and questioning of "such traditional

American views as putting duty before pleasure [and] saving money regularly."

Like the other movements of the Sixties, the counterculture had its theorists, and its own millennial vision, which propounded a utopian version of consumer capitalism. Sociologist Theodore Roszak, ecologist Murray Bookchin, Yale Law School professor Charles Reich, and other post-millennialists foresaw a transformation in human nature and human arrangements that would subordinate work to play and science to art. The instrument of change would not be a political movement but the change in consciousness that had already begun among college students. Reich saw the essence of change in the new "freedom of choosing a lifestyle." Work would become an "erotic experience, or a play experience."

Reich attributed the new counterculture to capitalism—what he called the "machine." As capitalism became capable of producing more goods than it could sell, it was forced to devise ways to expand people's needs and wants. It had to transform people themselves, moving them from the work ethic of "Consciousness II" to the lifestyle ethic of "Consciousness III," where a human being could "develop the aesthetic and spiritual side of his nature."

Reich, Roszak, and other spokesmen for the counterculture did not exalt idleness but artistic expression. They didn't promote pornography but eroticism. Most of what their current critics like Bork and Kramer lay at their door was attributable to consumer capitalism rather than the counterculture. And, while much of their vision of the future appears daffy, they—in contrast to their latter-day critics—realized that America had turned a corner. What they didn't understand was exactly where it was headed.

As a political era, the Sixties came to a close around 1973. In January 1973, Nixon signed a peace accord with North Vietnam, which not only put an end to the antiwar movement but, in doing so, removed a major source of political mobilization and energy. In 1969, the booming war economy also began a six-year slowdown. This slowdown, aggravated by the energy crisis of 1973, put a damper on the counterculture. Students became focused on preparing for jobs and careers rather than discovering the meaning of life.

The downturn of the early '70s, combined with a wave of strikes that began in 1969 and with growing competition from Japan and Western Europe, made American business leaders lose their tolerance for new government intervention. They began to push hard to limit new consumer and environmental regulations. They began hiring lobbyists and establishing corporate offices in Washington and funding policy groups and think tanks, and by the mid-'70s, many business leaders were beginning to look fondly upon Republican conservatives who combined their opposition to the social movements of the Sixties with support for business's agenda of "deregulation." By 1978, these two groups were setting the nation's political and legislative agenda, even with Democrats in control of the White House and Congress.

What, then, is the legacy of the Sixties? It endures, for one thing, in Bill Clinton's passionate commitment to racial reconciliation and in Al Gore's ardent environmentalism. It also could be found in Clinton's mistaken belief after November 1992 that he could fashion a "new beginning," including a wildly ambitious health care plan. But the era also endures ironically in its most bitter opponents—Gingrich, Dick Armey, Phil Gramm, and many of the leaders of the religious right. Gingrich and Armey's fantastic belief that they had led a "revolution" in November 1994 was straight out of the late '60s. So, too, is Gingrich's futurism and his insistence that Americans should have the highest "range of choices of lifestyle." Within the religious right, Weatherman has been reincarnated as Operation Rescue, and the communards of the Sixties have become the home-schoolers of the 1990s.

The Sixties clearly bequeathed political conflicts that continue to seethe but also made lasting contributions that cannot easily be undone. Medicare and the environmental and consumer legislation of Nixon's first term have withstood furious attacks from conservatives and business. While the issues of urban poverty and decay that King addressed in the last years of his life remain unsettled, the premises of the Civil Rights Act of 1964 and the Voting Rights Act of 1965 are no longer open to question.

The Sixties enlarged the scope of politics by adding new issues and constituencies to the traditional mix created by business and labor, and they changed the way politics was conducted. A proliferation of new movements, interests, and interest groups—some of them funded door-to-door and others through the mail—shifted the struggle to change the country from the halls of Congress to the media and even to time streets. By the 1980s, business lobbyists were employing "grassroots" techniques developed by shaggy protesters from the Sixties.

Perhaps most important of all, America passed irreversibly during the Sixties from a culture of toil, sacrifice, saving, and abstinence to a culture of consumption, lifestyle, and quality of life. The agent of this change was not the counterculture but consumer capitalism, to which the counterculture, like the religious right, is a reaction. This new stage of capitalism has opened to the average American possibilities of education, leisure, and personal fulfillment that had been reserved in the past for the upper classes. It has also, of course, exalted consumption over production, razed redwoods, turned shorelines into boardwalks, flooded cyberspace with spam, used sex to sell detergents, and helped to transform many American teenagers into television zombies. If our cultural commissars would understand this distinction between the culture of capitalism and the counterculture, perhaps they would waste less of our time blaming the radicals of the Sixties for all of today's problems and turn their attention to the real causes.

This article draws from **JOHN B. JUDIS'S** book on twentieth-century American politics, *The Paradox of American Democracy* (Pantheon Books, 2000).

Soft Power
Reagan the Dove

Vladislav M. Zubok

Death, not surprisingly, has secured Ronald Reagan's place in history. In recent days, policy veterans, journalists, and scholars have placed him among the top ranks of twentieth-century presidents. In a *New York Times* op-ed written shortly after Reagan's death, Mikhail Gorbachev, the former Soviet leader, acknowledged Reagan's role in bringing about the end of the cold war. Reagan's conservative admirers go even further. They proclaim him the architect of "victory" against the USSR, citing his support of the anti-communist mujahedin in Afghanistan, of the anti-Soviet Solidarity movement in Poland, and, above all, his Strategic Defense Initiative (SDI). Former White House Chief of Staff Donald Regan told CNN seven years ago that Gorbachev's failure to convince President Reagan to give up SDI at the Reykjavik summit in 1986 meant it was "all over for the Soviet Union." A memorial plaque in the court of the Ronald Reagan Presidential Library in Simi Valley, California, flatly states that Reagan's SDI brought down Soviet communism.

Newly released Soviet documents reveal that Reagan indeed played a role in ending the cold war. Yet, it was not so much because of SDI or the support of anti-Soviet forces around the world. Rather, it was the sudden emergence of another Reagan, a peacemaker and supporter of nuclear disarmament—whom conservatives opposed—that rapidly produced a new U.S.-Soviet détente. This détente facilitated Gorbachev's radical overhaul of Soviet domestic and foreign policy—changes that brought the USSR crashing down and that would have been impossible had Reagan remained the hawk conservatives now celebrate.

In retrospect, it's hard to see SDI as anything but a bit player in the final act of the cold war. In 1983, the year Reagan announced the program to stop Soviet missiles in space (immediately dubbed "star wars"), the Soviet leadership convened a panel of prominent scientists to assess whether SDI posed a long-term security threat. The panel's report remains classified, but various leaks point to the main finding (one that mirrored the assessment of independent U.S. scientists): In the next decade or even beyond, SDI would not work. The rumor circulating in politburo circles was that "two containers of nails hurled into space" would be enough to confuse and overwhelm

U.S. anti-missile defenses. In a compromise decision between Kremlin leaders and military commanders reached by 1985, a number of R&D labs received limited funds to look into possible countermeasures to SDI. The budget of the Soviet "anti-SDI" program, a fraction of the huge allocations to the Soviet military-industrial complex, remained at the same modest level through the rest of the '80s.

Gorbachev feared SDI less for the military threat it posed to the USSR than for the practical threat it posed to his political agenda. The young general secretary belonged to a generation shaped by the denunciations of Stalinist crimes, the cultural liberalization of the 1960s, and East-West détente; this generation wanted to reform the Soviet Union and end the confrontation with the United States. But the reformists remained a minority and operated in a milieu of anti-American paranoia. As a result, Gorbachev was frustrated by the Reagan administration's hawkish actions—such as increased military assistance to Afghanistan, provocative naval exercises near Soviet coasts, and the CIA's unrelenting "spy war" against the KGB.

The Soviets interpreted SDI as an outgrowth of this renewed American aggressiveness, which made it harder for Gorbachev to push his reforms. As Boris Ponomarev, a Communist apparatchik, grumbled in early 1986, "Let the Americans change their thinking instead. . . . Are you against military strength, which is the only language that imperialism understands?" Gorbachev admitted in his memoirs that he was initially too cautious to resist this pressure. At the politburo, he adopted hard-line language, describing the American president as a "troglodyte" in November 1985.

Still, the early interactions between Gorbachev and Reagan revealed that there might be enough common ground between the two leaders to allow Gorbachev to press ahead: As it happened, both men were closet nuclear abolitionists. For all his outward toughness, Reagan connected nuclear threats to the prophecy of Armageddon and, under the influence of his wife, Nancy, who saw ending the cold war as an opportunity to save the president's legacy from the taint of Iran-Contra, wanted to be remembered as a peacemaker. Gorbachev, likewise, saw eliminating the danger of nuclear confrontation between the superpowers as his top priority. When Gorbachev participated in a strategic game simulating the Soviet response to a nuclear attack shortly after coming to power, he allegedly refused to press the nuclear button "even for training purposes."

Though the continuing U.S.-Soviet confrontation obscured the common anti-nuclear agenda for much of the '80s, the shared goal surfaced suddenly in a dramatic exchange at the Reykjavik summit in October 1986. Gorbachev proposed eliminating all ballistic missiles. When Reagan demurred, Gorbachev raised the ante. Both leaders then began proposing that more and more categories of weapons be abolished until they had agreed upon total disarmament. But Gorbachev refused to cut anything if SDI remained, prompting the frustrated Reagan to interject: "What the hell use will anti-ballistic missiles or anything else be if we eliminate nuclear weapons?" The Soviet leader held firm, at which point the summit collapsed and Reagan returned home feeling angry and cheated.

Though conservatives lauded Reagan for courageously avoiding what they saw as a Soviet trap, administration insiders were furious at the president for even broaching the idea of a nuclear-free world. They were right to be concerned. By the end of 1987, Reagan had begun to distance himself from the extreme hawks who opposed any negotiations (the most prominent of them, Secretary of Defense Caspar Weinberger, left the administration in 1987) and was relying increasingly on the pragmatic advice of Secretary of State George Shultz. In December 1987, the president and Gorbachev met in Washington to sign a treaty eliminating intermediate-range missiles. And, by June 1988, Reagan was kissing Russian babies in Red Square and had nonchalantly dropped the "evil empire" label he had affixed to the Soviet Union in 1983.

For his part, Gorbachev used the increasingly warm encounters with Reagan as capital for domestic reforms. Soviet journalists, as well as the entire international media, covered the summits, transforming Gorbachev into a TV star. Back home, millions of Soviets felt proud of their leader for the first time in years. Reykjavik, in particular, increased Gorbachev's domestic standing; the Soviet audience appreciated his tough talk with Reagan, but not as much as his "struggle for peace." This enhanced stature allowed Gorbachev to make a series of crucial changes in the aftermath of various U.S.-Soviet summits: the release of the Nobel Laureate and political prisoner Andrei Sakharov in December 1986 and the introduction of glasnost came on the heels of Reykjavik; the withdrawal of troops from Afghanistan in January 1988 came just after the Washington summit the previous December; the liberalization of the communist political system began with the announcement of parliamentary elections during the summer of 1988, just after Reagan's visit to Moscow.

It was perhaps inevitable that some of Reagan's former advisers would begin to rewrite his legacy using their hard-line script. Back in the '80s, however, this script produced nothing but new cold war crises, an accelerated arms race, and a huge budget deficit. With the notable exception of the support of Polish Solidarity, U.S. measures to "bleed" the Soviet Union only bred mutual fears of war. The most notorious symbol of U.S. "victory" in the cold war, SDI, still remains an unfulfilled promise 20 years later.

It is not clear how much vision regarding the end of Soviet communism Ronald Reagan had. What Reagan certainly had in abundance was luck and instinct. He was lucky that a new reformist leadership came to power in Moscow looking for a partner to end the cold war. He sensed a historic opportunity in his relationship with Gorbachev and finally seized on it. It was Reagan the peacemaker, not the cold warrior, who made the greatest contribution to history. One only wishes more Americans were aware of this paradox as they pay homage to their fortieth president.

VLADISLAV M. ZUBOK, a professor of history at Temple University, is the author of the forthcoming book *The Enemy That Went Home* (University of North Carolina Press).

From Saigon to Desert Storm
How the U.S. Military Reinvented Itself after Vietnam

MAX BOOT

It's hard to remember now, but the outcome of the 1991 Persian Gulf War stunned the world. Few people even at the Pentagon expected it to be as one-sided as it was. Before Operation Desert Storm, Iraq's armed forces were widely seen as a formidable adversary, hardened by years of war against Iran and supplied with the best equipment Saddam Hussein's oil riches could buy. Iraq had 900,000 soldiers—more than the U.S. Army—and they had had months to entrench themselves in Kuwait and southern Iraq. The Iraqis also had modern fighter planes, ballistic and cruise missiles, chemical stockpiles, and an elaborate air-defense network that would make Baghdad the most heavily defended city ever attacked from the air. Paeans to Iraqi combat prowess filled newspaper pages and television screens in the fall and winter of 1990.

And the U.S. armed forces? Weren't they the bumblers who had been defeated outright by the Vietnamese and humiliated by the Cambodians, Iranians, and Lebanese in, respectively, the Mayaguez, Desert One, and Beirut operations? Even isolated American successes against weak adversaries, such as those in Grenada (1983) and Panama (1989), had been marred by serious miscalculations that suggested to many the American military was not ready for a real war.

Yet Operation Desert Storm went more smoothly than even its most optimistic architects could have imagined. Three weeks of air attacks were followed by a mere 100 hours of ground war that drove the Iraqis from Kuwait. It was America's most impressive military victory since 1945. And it had been achieved with the loss of just 147 Americans killed in action and another 467 wounded, "the lowest cost in human life ever recorded for a conflict of such magnitude," according to the U.S. Army's official history.

How were the U.S. armed forces able to achieve such an unprecedented victory? The answer may be found in the wholesale transformation wrought in the 15 years since American soldiers had stumbled, dazed, defeated, and demoralized, out of the jungles of Vietnam.

The Human Material

One of the first priorities for post-Vietnam military reformers was increasing the quality of those in uniform. From Gen. H. Norman Schwarzkopf on down, all the senior American commanders in 1991 were veterans of the Vietnam War. They could vividly remember how, in the 1970s, the armed forces were racked by racial tensions, rampant drug use, and alcoholism. Many officers would not venture into enlisted men's barracks without a sidearm; between 1969 and 1971 there had been 800 "fraggings," or incidents in which soldiers attacked their own officers or NCOs. Things only got worse after the draft was abolished in 1973. Defense spending plummeted, and recruiting quotas could not be met. Half of the Marine Corps and Army came to be composed of high school dropouts.

This all began to change in 1979, when Maj. Gen. Maxwell Thurman took over the Army's Recruiting Command. A Vietnam veteran, a devout Catholic, and a lifelong bachelor who, in the words of one journalist, "approached each assignment in the Army with the fervor and devotion of a Trappist monk," Thurman pushed Congress to approve a major military pay increase as well as a new version of the GI Bill that would offer college scholarships to soldiers after they left the service, and he began to market the Army as a place to learn valuable skills, an approach crystallized in a new slogan he developed with a New York advertising agency, "Be All You Can Be," which helped spark a recruiting renaissance.

The other services followed Thurman while also working closely with Hollywood to help prepare pro-military movies like Top Gun (1986) and The Hunt for Red October (1990). As the armed forces began to rack up small victories, such as the invasion of Grenada, their popularity rose, and recruiters actually began to turn away low-quality applicants. By 1990, 97 percent of Army recruits were high school graduates. The glut of recruits allowed the military to raise standards and crack down on troublemakers. The Navy led the way in 1981 by instituting a zero-tolerance policy for drug use, backed up by random urinalysis tests, a policy soon emulated by the other services. The number of people in uniform using illicit drugs fell from 27.6 percent in 1980 to 3.4 percent in 1992.

At the same time, the military made a conscientious attempt to improve the integration of African-Americans and women. This was not always a smooth process, but through a combination of outreach, mentoring, and crackdowns on discrimination, the military proved largely successful in achieving racial and gender diversity. The symbol of this accomplishment was the elevation of Colin Powell, who became the first black chairman of the Joint Chiefs of Staff in 1989. "The military had given African-Americans more equal opportunity than any other institution in American society," Powell wrote in his autobiography.

Outnumbered

Yet, despite the growing quality of its soldiers, the U.S. armed forces, with 2.1 million active-duty personnel in 1982, remained badly outnumbered by their Communist counterparts. The U.S.S.R., which had not abolished the draft, could field a force of more than 3.5 million men in the 1970s, increasing to more than 5 million by the early 1980s. The Soviet advantage was equally great in tanks, artillery, and aircraft. Back in the 1950s and 1960s the United States could rely on its nuclear edge to deter Soviet aggression, but that had disappeared by the end of the 1970s.

It became increasingly clear to strategists in the Ford, Carter, and Reagan administrations that they would have to develop a new generation of conventional weapons to offset the Soviet numbers. It was at just about this time that microprocessors were revolutionizing the computer industry. The Soviet Union, of course, had no Silicon Valley of its own. Here was one advantage that the United States still had, and the Pentagon was intent on exploiting it.

Getting Smart

Since the dawn of the gunpowder age, projectiles had been on their own once they left a gun barrel or, later, an airplane bomb bay. No matter how carefully a gunner or bombardier might aim, once the trigger had been pulled he no longer had any control over where the munitions went. They were at the mercy of the laws of ballistics and gravity, and hence not very accurate.

That first began to change in World War II. The Germans took the lead; their Fritz X, a radio-controlled bomb, was used against the Allied landing fleet at Salerno, Italy, in 1943. But most of their efforts were not terribly successful; more than half the V-2 rockets aimed at London missed the metropolitan area altogether because of their primitive gyroscopic steering mechanisms. U.S. scientists didn't fare much better with their initial guided bombs in World War II and the Korean War, and the whole field languished in the 1950s and early 1960s.

The U.S. Air Force was the natural outlet for smart bombs, but until the mid-1960s its bomb development was delegated to the Army and Navy ordnance departments, making it a bureaucratic orphan. Who needed accurate munitions, anyway, if (as the working assumption had it) the bombs of the next war would be atomic? It took the Vietnam War to revive interest in precision-guidance technology and to spark a general renaissance in air warfare.

The U.S. Navy and Air Force, which had put all their energies into getting ready for nuclear conflict against the Soviet Union, were woefully ill prepared for the type of conventional combat they encountered in the skies over North Vietnam. Heavy jet fighters, such as the F-105 Thunderchief, were not agile enough to dogfight against Soviet-built MiG-17s and MiG-21s. They had even worse luck in dealing with ground fire, which had been revolutionized by the development of surface-to-air missiles after World War II. The Soviets supplied their North Vietnamese allies with SA-2 radar-guided batteries and radar-controlled flak guns, later supplemented by SA-7 shoulder-fired missiles. The U.S. Air Force and Navy, both of which operated aircraft over North Vietnam, initially had neither the equipment nor the tactics to deal with this menace. As the war went on, American pilots learned to avoid enemy batteries with evasive maneuvers and to disrupt them with radiation-seeking missiles and electronic jamming equipment, giving birth to the techniques that would be utilized with such success against Iraq decades later. The United States paid a heavy price for these lessons: More than 1,500 of its aircraft were downed in Indochina, 95 percent of them by ground fire.

Besides leading to the death or capture of many pilots, heavy ground fire disrupted bombing patterns and made it hard for U.S. aircraft to achieve their objectives during the Rolling Thunder campaign against North Vietnam from 1965 to 1968. Pilots were further handicapped by the fact that unlike in World War II or the Korean War, they could not simply undertake indiscriminate area bombing. The Johnson administration was sensitive to the political ramifications of "collateral damage" and enforced strict limitations on where and when U.S. aircraft could strike. But with bomb accuracy only slightly improved since World War II, U.S. aircraft lacked the capacity to execute pinpoint raids.

The solution did not come from an intensive Manhattan Project-style crash program of the kind that had produced the moon landing and the atomic bomb. Rather, a stroke of serendipity inspired the Air Force colonel Joe Davis, Jr., to set in motion the first laser-guided bomb project, in 1964. As deputy commander of an Air Force armaments laboratory at Eglin Air Force Base in Florida, Davis was dazzled by a demonstration of a laser invented in 1960 by the physicist Theodore Maiman. The scientists who showed off the device had no intention of using it to guide bombs, but that was the first thing Davis, a fighter ace in World War II and Korea, thought of. He even went aloft with a handheld movie camera to prove that a beam from a cockpit could be consistently directed at a fixed point on the ground. Using discretionary funds that did not need approval from the cumbersome Pentagon procurement bureaucracy, Davis awarded a $99,000 contract to Texas Instruments to develop a laser bomb-aiming system. The result was the Paveway, which initially required two aircraft to deliver—one to drop a bomb with small, movable wings, the other to aim a laser beam at its target. Eventually a single aircraft was equipped with both the laser-guidance pod and the bomb. As soon as the Paveway had proved its effectiveness, it was rushed to Vietnam.

It was later determined that 48 percent of Paveways dropped in 1972–73 around Hanoi and Haiphong achieved direct hits, compared with only 5.5 percent of unguided bombs dropped on the same area a few years earlier. The average Paveway landed within 23 feet of its target, as opposed to 447 feet for a "dumb" bomb. The leap in accuracy brought about primarily by laser guidance made it possible to take out tough objectives that had eluded earlier air raids. The most dramatic example was the Thanh Hoa Bridge, 70 miles south of Hanoi, a crucial supply artery for the North. Starting in 1965, U.S. pilots had flown 871 sorties against it, losing 11 planes without managing to put it out of commission. In 1972 the "Dragon's Jaw" bridge was attacked with Paveway bombs, and 14 jets managed to do what the previous 871 had not: send the span into the Red River.

The United States wound up employing 28,000 Paveways in Southeast Asia, more smart bombs than have been used in any conflict before or since. They did not save the United States from defeat, partially because they were introduced late in the war (only 0.2 percent of all munitions dropped were precision guided), but mainly because a guerrilla foe hiding in the jungles was not very vulnerable to air attack. Still, the Vietnam experience set the U.S. military on the path to future smart-bomb developments. Better microelectronics led to the invention of improved bombs and missiles with aiming systems utilizing radar, lasers, thermal sensors, satellite navigation, inertial guidance, and electro-optical sensors.

By the time of the Gulf War the most common ground-attack precision munitions in the U.S. arsenal were laser-guided Paveway III bombs, guided missiles like the Maverick and Hell-fire, and ship-launched cruise missiles directed by internal computers programmed with precise target coordinates. Though laser-guided bombs and cruise missiles were relatively few in number, they would have a disproportionate impact in the war's early days by hitting Iraq's best-protected targets with unprecedented accuracy. The journalist David Halberstam later paraphrased the airpower strategist John Warden: "During World War II, an average B-17 bomb during a bombing run missed its target by some 2,300 feet. Therefore, if you wanted a 90 percent probability of having hit a particular target, you had to drop some nine thousand bombs. That required a bombing run of one thousand bombers and placed ten thousand men at risk. By contrast, with the new weaponry one plane flown by one man with one bomb could have the same level of probability. That was an improvement in effectiveness of approximately ten-thousand-fold."

Stealth

The most revolutionary weapons system of all in 1991 was a stealth aircraft equipped with two 2,000-pound laser-guided bombs. Its genesis lay in Lockheed's famed Skunk Works, the top-secret research lab in Burbank, California, that had produced such revolutionary Cold War aircraft as the U-2 and SR-71 high-altitude spy planes. In the mid-1970s Skunk Works engineers figured out how an airplane could be made virtually invisible at night by using special composite materials and flat panels that absorbed rather than reflected radar emissions. President Carter's Defense Secretary, Harold Brown, a physicist by training, and his undersecretary for research and engineering, William Perry, another scientist, grasped the possibilities immediately and gave the project their enthusiastic support.

Because it was so highly classified, the stealth work (known initially as Project Harvey, after the invisible rabbit in the 1950 James Stewart movie) cut through normal Pentagon red tape. The prototype of the F-117A stealth fighter was ready to fly in 1977, and the first production-line model was delivered in 1981, a remarkably fast procurement cycle. In the Gulf War, F-117As

would fly only 2 percent of all attack sorties, but they hit 40 percent of Iraq's best-defended targets.

The stealth aircraft was only the most advanced of many new weapons systems that were developed in the 1960s and 1970s and joined the U.S. arsenal in the 1970s and 1980s. The Air Force procured two agile new fighter-bombers, the F-16 Fighting Falcon and F-15 Eagle, the B-1 Lancer bomber, and an aircraft for close support of ground forces, the A-10 Warthog. The Navy had its own superfighters, the F-14 Tomcat and F/A-18 Hornet, as well as Aegis guided-missile cruisers (the first was the Ticonderoga, commissioned in 1983), Los Angeles—class nuclear submarines, and Nimitz-class nuclear-powered aircraft carriers. The Army bought a main battle tank, the M1 Abrams; an armored personnel carrier, the M2/M3 Bradley Infantry Fighting Vehicle; a utility vehicle called the Humvee (high mobility multipurpose wheeled vehicle); the AH-64 Apache attack helicopter and the UH-60 Blackhawk utility helicopter; an air defense system called the Patriot; and a mobile surface-to-surface missile launcher, the M270 Multiple Launch Rocket System.

With the exception of the stealth aircraft, which remained a tightly guarded secret until 1988, every one of these systems was extremely controversial when it was in development. Virtually all were plagued by delays and cost overruns that led to embarrassing stories in the press. The journalist James Fallows, in his influential 1981 book National Defense, derided the Pentagon's "pursuit of the magic weapon" encumbered with "more and more complex computer systems, whether or not there is reason to think that computers will help on the battlefield, and often when there is reason to think they will hurt." Such criticisms were echoed by Congress's Military Reform Caucus, a bipartisan group of more than 100 lawmakers led by Sen. Gary Hart who pushed for simpler, cheaper weapons in greater numbers.

A Better Tank

Luckily the Pentagon did not follow their advice. If it had, the United States would have fought Iraq in 1991 with equipment roughly equivalent to the enemy's, instead of having weapons at least a full generation ahead.

What the reformers did not realize was that adding sophisticated electronics did not have to make weapons systems less reliable and harder to operate. Thanks to advances in solid-state electronics, new aircraft like the F-15 and F-16 were not only far more lethal than their predecessors but also easier to fly and less prone to malfunction. Far from being an encumbrance, advanced electronics gave such weapons a vital edge over less sophisticated adversaries.

Consider the M1A1 tank, built by General Dynamics starting in 1980. It had a gas turbine engine that allowed it to go nearly 45mph and Chobham ceramic armor (named for the British research center where it was developed) that could survive frontal hits from the Soviet-built T-72s in Iraq's arsenal. Its 120-mm main gun fired 45-pound sabot rounds tipped with depleted uranium (more than twice as dense as steel) that could penetrate a T-72 at two and a half miles, well outside the T-72's own range. But its true advantage lay in a fire-control system that employed laser range-finders, thermal and optical sights, and ballistics computers to let its main gun hit targets while on the move and in fog, night, or other conditions that would have rendered earlier tanks useless. In World War II the average tank needed 17 shots to kill an enemy tank; in the Gulf War, the Abrams would come close to achieving the ideal of one shot, one kill.

In the Night and the Sky

The M1A1's ability to operate at night was a key advantage shared by most U.S. weapons systems in 1991. Night-vision equipment had been developed by the U.S. Army starting in the 1950s. It came in two versions: image-intensifying devices that amplify small amounts of ambient light and thermal forward-looking infrared detectors that sense differences in temperature between an object and its environment. The former are generally carried by soldiers as goggles; the latter usually come in more cumbersome systems attached to vehicles and aircraft. Since Iraqis had few, if any, comparable devices, the U.S. military owned the night.

Complementing its night-vision devices, the military benefited from unrivaled electronic warfare and reconnaissance capabilities. The U.S. Air Force and Navy operated a variety of aircraft designed to keep an eye on the "battle space," the most famous of which was the AWACS, a Boeing 707-320B equipped with a huge rotating radar dome that could identify low-flying objects from more than 250 miles away. Onboard sat 13 to 19 mission specialists who could analyze information and coordinate air operations in real time, allowing hostile aircraft to be intercepted as soon as they were airborne and friendly aircraft to avoid either hitting or shooting at each other.

What the AWACS did for air operations, the E-8A JSTARS (Joint Surveillance Target Attack Radar System) did for the ground war. Also housed in a 707 airframe, the JSTARS synthetic-aperture radar, in a canoe-shaped appendage under the fuselage, could locate and track moving vehicles over more than 200 miles. It was still in the experimental stages when Iraq invaded Kuwait in August 1990, but two prototypes went to Saudi Arabia and they proved invaluable in locating Iraqi ground forces.

The AWACS and JSTARS were joined by numerous other aircraft designed to listen in on enemy communications (RC-135 Rivet Joint), jam enemy radars (EA-6B Prowler, EC-130H Compass Call), or photograph enemy positions (TR-1/U-2). High above all these planes a constellation of satellites monitored the battlefield from space. Their exact details remain shrouded in secrecy, but satellites are known to have performed myriad functions, including providing meteorological data, creating detailed maps, offering early warning of Scud missile launches, relaying communications, and spying on enemy forces.

The most novel and important use of satellites was to provide navigational help to coalition forces. The Global Positioning System was based on a simple premise, that a user could determine his exact location by timing how long it took a radio beam to travel from his position to several satellites in fixed orbit. Navstar GPS, begun in 1973 by the Pentagon, was designed

to orbit at least 24 satellites that would give anyone anywhere line-of-sight to at least 4 of them at one time—the minimum needed to get an accurate fix. Only 16 of the satellites had been deployed when the Gulf War began, so they did not provide continuous coverage. Another major limitation was the lack of GPS receivers. By the time Desert Storm began, following a last-minute shopping spree, the coalition had about 840 military GPS receivers and 6,500 commercial models. Even with its limited availability, however, GPS made possible much more accurate maneuvering and striking than ever before. Allied tank forces would not have been able to move through the vast deserts of Iraq without it.

Against this vast array of air and space sensors, the Iraqis had no satellites of their own and no way to fly air reconnaissance because of the Allies' domination of the skies. Nor could they buy satellite time from private firms; the United States had bought up all the available capacity. It was almost as if soldiers on horseback were fighting tanks; the disparity between Iraq and the United States was that profound.

The Training Revolution

Developing all this high-tech gadgetry was one thing. Learning to use it properly was another. The United States would not have done so well in the Gulf War had not its armed forces transformed their training and doctrine since the Vietnam War. The training revolution began in 1969 when the Navy, concerned about the poor showing of its aircraft over North Vietnam, established the Fighter Weapons School at Miramar Naval Air Station in San Diego. "Top Gun" offered pilots realistic training in dogfighting that significantly improved their combat performance.

The Air Force took note and in 1975 opened its own version of Top Gun. Red Flag exercises at Nellis Air Force Base in Nevada allowed pilots to compete against an "aggressor squadron" emulating the tactics and equipment of Soviet adversaries. Here a new generation of aviators learned how to put together elaborate "strike packages" designed to penetrate enemy air defenses. Experience showed that a pilot was most likely to be shot down while still green, during his first 10 combat sorties; Red Flag was designed to ensure that those missions occurred only on a training range.

The Army set up a realistic training center of its own at Fort Irwin, California, amid the barren scrubland of the Mojave Desert. Starting in 1981, mechanized battalions would travel to the National Training Center to fight a simulated engagement against a highly skilled "Opfor" (opposing force) modeled on a Soviet motorized rifle regiment. Lasers simulated the effects of actual gunfire, and computers kept track of the action for later analysis. Umpires delivered unsparing after-action reports on what went right and wrong. The visitors usually got whipped by the first-rate Opfor, but they learned a good deal from the experience.

At the start of previous wars, American soldiers had been thrown into battle without much combat experience or realistic training to draw on, and they usually paid a steep price for their inexperience. For instance, the First Armored Division was mauled by veteran German units at Kasserine Pass, Tunisia, in

February 1943, losing more than 6,000 men. That didn't happen this time. "Desert Shield and Desert Storm went so easily," wrote the Air Force general Chuck Horner, U.S. air commander, "because everyone had been there before."

It also went well because the armed forces had worked out a doctrine ideally suited for operations against a foe like Iraq. One of the U.S. Army's most important innovations after Vietnam was the creation in 1973 of the Training and Doctrine Command to fashion an intellectual renaissance. Its first commander was Gen. William DePuy, a veteran of World War II and Vietnam who proceeded to obliterate the traditional American approach toward war. In his first operations manual, which came out in 1976, DePuy noted that traditionally the United States was "accustomed to victory wrought with the weight of matériel and population brought to bear after the onset of hostilities." This had worked in the industrial age but it was no longer suitable for the dawning information age. Given the lethality of modern weapons, General DePuy did not think it was possible to lose the first battles and still push on to victory. "Today the U.S. Army must, above all else, prepare to win the first battle of the next war."

This was an important innovation that was eagerly greeted by the Army. So was DePuy's emphasis on realistic training, which led to the creation of the National Training Center. The actual strategy he ultimately crafted, known as Active Defense, was less popular. As its name implies, it was an essentially reactive approach that called for falling back in the face of a Soviet onslaught in Europe. Other ideas bubbled up at various military institutions; they included advanced schools devoted to the operational art, opened by the Army, Marines, and Air Force in the 1970s.

The eventual result was a new doctrine prepared by DePuy's successor, Gen. Donn Starry, and adopted in 1982. His approach, known as AirLand Battle, was anything but static. It was essentially a variant of the German blitzkrieg or Russian "deep battle," and a far cry from the attritional strategy utilized by U.S. forces in all of the country's major conflicts going back to the Civil War. AirLand Battle called for attacking Red Army rear echelons, seizing the initiative, outmaneuvering the enemy, and utilizing a variety of weapons simultaneously to produce a counteroffensive that would be "rapid, unpredictable, violent, and disorienting to the enemy." It was predicated on the assumption that the United States had superior weapons and superior personnel that could compensate for its inferiority in total numbers. The Air Force bought into this doctrine, and the Marine Corps came up with its own version, known as Maneuver Warfare.

This was, in essence, the strategy that America put to use in Desert Storm. Originally developed to counter Soviet tank armies on the plains of Europe, AirLand Battle proved ideally suited to fighting Soviet-style tank armies in the deserts of the Middle East.

"Jointness"

The final element necessary to produce U.S. victory in the Gulf War was having the right organizational structure in place. Chaotic operations such as the 1980 Iranian hostage rescue attempt had revealed the pitfalls of interservice rivalry. This gave a boost to military reformers on Capitol Hill who wanted to create a more

unified command structure. After several years of debate, Sen. Barry Goldwater, an Arizona Republican, and Rep. Bill Nichols, an Alabama Democrat, managed in 1986 to push through the most significant shakeup of the Pentagon since the creation of the Department of Defense in 1947.

The Goldwater-Nichols Defense Reorganization Act emphasized "jointness": The chairman of the Joint Chiefs of Staff was made principal military adviser to the President and the Defense Secretary, sidelining the individual service chiefs with their more parochial concerns. To assist him, the chairman was given a vice-chairman (another four-star general) and an expanded joint staff of more than 1,000 officers. Service on a joint staff became mandatory for any officer seeking promotion to flag rank.

This legislation also established a clear chain of command running from the President through the Secretary of Defense to a unified field commander. The entire world was broken up into five vast regions—Europe and Africa (European Command), the Atlantic, the Pacific, Latin America (Southern Command), and the Middle East, East Africa, and Central Asia (Central Command, or Centcom)—each placed under the command of a four-star general who had complete authority over all U.S. forces within his jurisdiction. (Other commands were established for responsibilities such as special operations and transportation; they transcended geographical boundaries.) The Goldwater-Nichols Act gave the combat commanders unprecedented authority within their domains. It was power that General Schwarzkopf, who took over as Centcom's third chief in 1988, used to marshal the forces that won the Gulf War.

Into the Storm

Viewers around the world were amazed by the spectacle that unfolded on their TV screens between January 17 and February 27, 1991. Video clips of bombs and missiles hitting with seemingly unerring accuracy obliterated once and for all the previous image of America's "hollow" army. In its place came a new vision of an unbeatable superpower.

Yet just as victories can grow out of defeats, so too can defeats grow out of victories. The very prowess displayed by the armed forces in 1991 made future foes wary of challenging this new Goliath on its own terms. In the future, America's enemies would use unconventional weapons—weapons like hijacked airliners and suicide bombers—to circumvent its dominance in conventional combat. And the U.S. military, superbly configured for a dash through the desert, would find itself ill suited for waging irregular warfare against shadowy enemies who did not present easy targets for smart bombs and Abrams tanks.

That weakness would come back to haunt the United States a decade after Desert Storm, following another flawless blitzkrieg against Iraq. In the years after the fall of Baghdad on April 9, 2003, soldiers and Marines suffered a growing number of casualties to terrorist bombings and ambushes. As one U.S. general complained, "Insurgents don't show up in satellite imagery very well." To defeat such an elusive foe requires very different skills from those cultivated in the years after the Vietnam War, skills such as knowledge of foreign languages and cultures, policing, intelligence, information operations, and civil affairs. All these areas were neglected by reformers of the 1970s and 1980s, who recoiled from the horrors of counterinsurgency warfare in Vietnam, but they were to prove an inescapable necessity in the global war on terrorism. Whether the United States can defeat Islamist terrorists and maintain its post-Cold War hegemony will rest in good part on whether its armed forces can pull off another metamorphosis of the kind that produced victory in the Gulf War.

This article is based on his new book, War Made New: Technology, Warfare, and the Course of History, 1500 to Today, just out from Gotham Books.

All the American commanders in 1991 were Vietnam veterans; they had known what needed changing in the military.

With the exception of the stealth aircraft which remained secret until 1988, every new weapons system was extremely controversial.

In World War II a tank needed 17 shots to kill an enemy tank; in the Gulf War the Abrams came close to the ideal of one shot, one kill.

The very prowess shown by the U.S. armed forces in 1991 made future foes wary of fighting this new Goliath on its own terms.

MAX BOOT is a senior fellow in national security studies at the Council on foreign Relations.

The Tragedy of Bill Clinton

GARRY WILLS

So far, most readers of President Clinton's book seem to like the opening pages best, and no wonder. Scenes of childhood glow from many memoirs—by Jean-Jacques Rousseau, Henry Adams, John Ruskin, John Henry Newman, and others. It is hard to dislike people when they are still vulnerable, before they have put on the armor of whatever career or catastrophe lies before them as adults. In fact, Gilbert Chesterton advised those who would love their enemies to imagine them as children. The soundness of this tactic is proved by its reverse, when people become irate at attempts to imagine the childhood or the youth of Hitler—as in protests at the Menna Meyjez film *Max*. So it is hard, even for his foes, to find Clinton objectionable as a child. Yet the roots of the trouble he later had lie there, in the very appeal of his youth.

Another reason we respond to narratives of childhood is that first sensations are widely shared by everyone—the ways we became aware of the world around us, of family, of school, of early friends. One might expect Clinton's pineywood world to be remote from people who did not grow up in the South. But since he experienced neither grinding poverty nor notable privilege, there is an everyman quality to what he is writing about. His relatives were not blue-collar laborers but service providers—as nurse (mother and grandmother), heavy equipment salesman (father), car dealer (first stepfather), hairdresser (second stepfather), food broker (third stepfather). This was no Dogpatch, as one can tell from the number of Clinton's childhood friends who went on to distinguished careers. (The daughters of one of his ministers became, respectively, the president of Wellesley and the ombudsman of *The Washington Post*.)

Admittedly, Clinton's family was notably fissiparous, with a litter of half-relatives filling the landscape—but even that is familiar to us in this time of frequent divorce and divided custodies. It may seem out of the ordinary for Clinton's father to have been married four times by the age of twenty-six, his first stepfather to have been married three times (twice to Clinton's mother), his second stepfather to have been married twice (with twenty-nine months in jail for fraud bridging the two). His mother, because of the mortality rate of her husbands, was married five times (though two of the times were to the same man). Clinton, who has had the gift of empathy throughout his life, remained astonishingly close to all the smashed elements of this marital kaleidoscope—even to his stepfather, whose abuse of his mother Clinton had to stop with physical interventions and

calls to the police. He took time from college to give his stepfather loving care at the end of his life. The most recurrent refrain in this book is "I liked him," and it began at home.

Clinton usually looked at the bright side. What the jumble of marriages gave him as a boy was just more relatives to charm and be cosseted by. Later the same people would be a political asset. The first time he ran for office, "I had relatives in five of the district's twenty-one counties." Later still, he could rely on "a big vote in south Arkansas, where I had lots of relatives." One might think he was already preparing for a political career when he got along so well with all his scattered families. But he was, even then, a natural charmer, with an immediate gratification in being liked, not looking (yet) for remoter returns from politics. Clinton won others' affection for a reason Aristotle famously gave—we enjoy doing things that we do well.[1]

Clinton claims that his sunny adaptability as a child was a front, that he lived a secret "parallel life" imposed on a "fat band boy" by his father's violence and alcoholism. He is preparing his explanation of the Monica Lewinsky affair as a product of this secret life. It is true that we all have a public self and several private ones. It is also true that childhood and adolescence prompt dark or lonely moments in most people. But the India-rubber-man resiliency of Clinton makes it hard to believe his explanation-excuse for later aberrations. "Slick Willie," the nickname he says he dislikes most, was always an unlikely brooder. The thing that would impress others about Clinton's later philandering, which long preceded the Monica stuff, was its lack of secrecy, its flamboyant risk-taking.

His attempt at a Dickensian shoe-black-factory childhood is therefore unconvincing. One of the afflictions he says he had to bear in silence was going to church in shoes his mother bought him; "pink and black Hush Puppies, and a matching pink suede belt." But since he shared his mother's idolatry of Elvis, his S-C (sartorially correct) attitude is probably retrospective. In fact, the "fat band boy" was very popular, with a wide circle of friends who stayed true to him (and he to them) ever after. His ability to enthrall others would become legendary, and one of the pleasures of his book is watching him get around obstacles by force of personality and cleverness:

—As a Yale law student organizing New Haven for the nascent McGovern campaign, Clinton goes to the city's Democratic boss,

Arthur Barbieri, who tells him he has the money and organization to crush the McGovern insurgency:

> I replied that I didn't have much money, but I did have eight hundred volunteers who would knock on the doors of every house in his stronghold, telling all the Italian mothers that Arthur Barbieri wanted to keep sending their sons to fight and die in Vietnam. "You don't need that grief," I said. "Why do you care who wins the nomination? Endorse McGovern. He was a war hero in World War II. He can make peace and you can keep control of New Haven."

Barbieri is struck by this law student—he and Matty Troy of New York are the only old-line bosses to endorse McGovern in the primary.

—Wanting to take Hillary Rodham to a special exhibit in the Yale art gallery for their first date, he finds the gallery locked, but talks his way in by telling the custodian that he will clean up the litter in the gallery courtyard if he lets them go through the exhibit.

—Fresh from law school, Clinton hears his application for a teaching job is turned down by the dean of the University of Arkansas Law School because he is too young and inexperienced, and he says those qualities are actually a recommendation:

> I'd be good for him, because I'd work hard and teach any courses he wanted. Besides, I wouldn't have tenure, so he could fire me at any time. He chuckled and invited me to Fayetteville for an interview.

He gets the job.

—After doing the whole Lamaze course to assist his wife when their first child is born; he learns that she must have a Caesarean section because the baby is "in breech." No one is allowed in the operating room during surgery. He pleads that Hillary has never been in a hospital before and she needs him. He is allowed to hold her hand during the delivery. Can no one say no to this man?

Persuasiveness on Clinton's scale can be a temptation. The ability to retrieve good will can make a person careless about taking vulnerable steps. Indeed, a certain type will fling himself over a cliff just to prove he can always catch a branch and crawl back up to the top. There is nothing, he begins to feel, for which he cannot win forgiveness. This kind of recklessness followed by self-retrieval is what led Clinton to think of himself as "the comeback kid" (the use of the word "kid" is probably more indicative than he intended). Famous charmers are fun to be around, but they are not people to depend on.

Washington

David Broder at his sniffiest declared that Clinton was a social usurper in Washington: "He came in here and he trashed the place, and it's not his place."[2] Clinton was simply "not one of us." But unlike Broder he had gone to school there. From the time he saw Washington as a high school member of Boys Nation and shook President. Kennedy's hand, Clinton wanted to get back there. His college placement counselor, Edith Irons, told me she urged him to apply to several colleges, not just one. But he filled out forms only for Georgetown—not because it was a Jesuit school, or a good school. Because it was in Washington. And so ingratiating was this Southern Baptist in a cosmopolitan Catholic school that he quickly became class president as a freshman and sophomore. He did not run for the office in his third year because by then he was an intern in Arkansas senator William Fulbright's office. He had to be given security clearance because he ran classified documents from place to place on Capitol Hill. Already he was a Washington insider.

Some of the freshest pages in the book register Clinton's impressions of the senators he observed. These were models against which he was measuring his future career, and the images were printed deep in him. He saw Carl Hayden of Arizona, whom a friend called "the only ninety-year-old man in the world who looks twice his age." The senior senator from his own state, John McClellan, had sorrows "drowned in enough whiskey to float the Capitol down the Potomac River." Clinton was especially interested in Senator Robert Kennedy, brother to his own fallen hero:

> He radiated raw energy. He's the only man I ever saw who could walk stoop-shouldered, with his head down, and still look like a coiled spring about to release into the air. He wasn't a great speaker by conventional standards, but he spoke with such intensity and passion it could be mesmerizing. And if he didn't get everyone's attention with his name, countenance, and speech, he had Brumus, a large, shaggy Newfoundland, the biggest dog I ever saw. Brumus often came to work with Senator Kennedy. When Bobby walked from his office in the New Senate Building to the Capitol to vote, Brumus would walk by his side, bounding up the Capitol steps to the revolving door on the rotunda level, then sitting patiently outside until his master returned for the walk back. Anyone who could command the respect of that dog had mine too.

One of Clinton's housemates at Georgetown worked in Robert Kennedy's office, and another was in Henry "Scoop" Jackson's office. A Georgetown girl he was dating hated Kennedy because she was working for his rival, Eugene McCarthy, whose lassitude Clinton compared unfavorably with Kennedy's energy. He especially admired his own boss, Senator Fulbright:

> I'll never forget one night in 1967 or '68. I was walking alone in Georgetown when I saw the Senator and Mrs. Fulbright leaving one of the fashionable homes after a dinner party. When they reached the street, apparently with no one around to see, he took her in his arms and danced a few steps. Standing in the shadows, I saw what a light she was in his life.

Oxford

Clinton not only worked for Fulbright in Washington but drove him around Arkansas. He sincerely admired his opposition to the Vietnam War—among other things it gave him an excuse for avoiding the war. The flap over Clinton's "draft dodging" looks quaint in retrospect. He first tried to do what George W. Bush did, join the National Guard, but he did not have the contacts to be accepted. The differences are that he, unlike Bush, did not support the war, and he is honest in saying that he was trying to avoid combat. He was in his first term as a Rhodes Scholar at Oxford, and a friend and housemate of his (Frank Aller) was defying the draft as a conscientious objector. Aller said Clinton should risk the draft in order to have a political career, though he could not do that himself.

A man much admired by his Oxford contemporaries but tortured by his scruples, Aller later committed suicide. Robert McNamara, who came to know of Aller's anguish, wrote Clinton when he was elected president:

> By their votes, the American people, at long last, recognized that the Allers and the Clintons, when they questioned the wisdom and morality of their government's decisions relating to Vietnam, were no less patriotic than those who served in uniform.

After Clinton failed to get into the National Guard, his uncle tried to get him into a navy program (which would involve less danger, and a delay in enlistment). Clinton's third try was as an ROTC law student at the University of Arkansas in Fayetteville, which would have given him three to four years' delay in actual service—but would have kept him from continuing at Oxford. Only when he drew a low number in the draft did he take his chances on staying in England rather than going to Fayetteville. The famous letter he wrote to explain why he was not going to show up for the ROTC spot was a typical act of ingratiation with the man who had admitted him into the program, Colonel Eugene Holmes. He said that he would "accept" the draft (he did not say he had been given a low number) only "to maintain my political viability within the [political] system." The ingratiation worked, at first. Colonel Holmes, when asked about Clinton's relations with ROTC, said for years that there was nothing abnormal about them. Only in the 1992 campaign did he write a letter denouncing Clinton as a draft dodger. Clinton suggests that Holmes may have had "help" with his memory from his daughter, a Republican activist in the Arkansas Bush campaign. Clinton's best biographer, David Maraniss, goes much further, and says that national officials of the Bush campaign "reviewed the letter before it was made public."[3]

C linton's time in Oxford led to many silly charges against him. He was said to have been a protester in Arkansas, at a time when he was in England—an accusation that came up in his campaigns for state office. Much was made of his confession that he tried marijuana but "did not inhale." *Could* not inhale would have been more truthful—his allergies had kept him from smoking any kind of cigarette, and the respected British journalist Martin Walker, who was with Clinton at the time, confirmed that he and others tried to teach Clinton to inhale, but he could not—he would end up "leaning his head out an open window gasping for fresh air." The problem with a reputation for being "slick" is that even the simple truth can look like a ploy.

Clinton's asthma and allergies stood in his way during his first political campaign, but charm overcame the problem when two local figures he wanted to campaign for him in Arkansas took him out from town in a truck, pulled out a pack of Red Man chewing tobacco, and said, "If you're man enough to chew this tobacco, we'll be for you. If not, we'll kick you out and let you walk back to town." Clinton hesitated a moment, then said: "Open the damn door." The two men laughed and became his campaigners for many years.

A more serious charge arising from his two years at Oxford came from his trip to Russia, which would later be called treasonous—a charge that the senior Bush's campaign tried to verify by breaking its own rules on passport and embassy reports. Clinton's interest in Russia came from the fact that his housemate and fellow Rhodes Scholar, Strobe Talbot, was already such an expert on the Russian language and history that he was translating the memoirs of Khrushchev, smuggled out to him by Jerry Schecter, the Moscow correspondent for *Time*. Clinton learned more about America than about either England or Russia during his time at Oxford, where his fellow Rhodes Scholars talked endlessly about their country and the war. Clinton gave up a third year and a degree in England to get back to the Yale Law School and antiwar activities, first in Joseph Duffey's failed Connecticut campaign for senator and then in McGovern's campaign for the presidency. In the latter cause, he had an ally in Hillary Rodham.

Yale

Clinton refers to various women he dated or traveled with in Europe, and he drops some indirect references to his reputation as a ladies' man—as inoculation, I suppose. He says he "had lived a far from perfect life," and carried "more baggage than an ocean liner." "The lies hurt, and the occasional truth hurt more." He even admits that when he proposed to Hillary, "nothing in my background indicated I knew what a stable marriage was all about." With women before Hillary, he was the one not seeking a commitment; but he pursued Hillary relentlessly. As law students, after they began living together, they traveled to Europe and the American West. He first proposed to her in England's Lake Country, but she said no. When she spent the summer of 1968 as an intern for a law firm in Oakland, California, he turned down an offer to organize the McGovern campaign in Miami and went with her to California for the whole summer. He was afraid he would lose her. What their marriage proves is that even a lecherous man can have the one great love affair of his life.

Lechery

In this book Clinton misleads not by equivocation but by omission. He gives a long account of his decision not to run for president in July of 1988—how he summoned friends with wide experience to Little Rock and weighed all the options. He admits that Gary Hart had withdrawn from the race two months earlier, and that "after the Hart affair, those of us who had not led perfect lives had no way of knowing what the press's standards of disclosure were." Clinton had to be paying close attention to the Hart campaign that year. He had worked closely with Hart on the McGovern team—in fact, Hart had rebuked him for paying too much attention to his "girl friend" (Hillary) during the campaign.[4] What Clinton leaves out of the account of his decision in 1988 is the brutal candor of the advice given him by his longtime aide, Betsey Wright. According to David Maraniss,

> Wright met with Clinton at her home on Hill Street. The time had come, she felt, for Clinton to get past what she considered his self-denial tendencies and face the issue squarely. For years, she told friends later, she had been covering up for him. She was convinced that some state troopers were soliciting women for him, and he for them, she said. Sometimes when Clinton was on the road, Wright would call his room in the middle of the night and no one would answer. She hated that part of him, but felt that the other sides of him overshadowed his personal weaknesses.
>
> . . . She started listing the names of women he had allegedly had affairs with and the places where they were said to have occurred. "Now," she concluded, "I want you to tell me the truth about every one." She went over the list twice with Clinton, according to her later account, the second time trying to determine whether any of the women might tell their stories to the press. At the end of the process, she suggested that he should not get into the race. He owed it to Hillary and Chelsea not to.[5]

No one who has seen Clinton with his daughter can doubt that he loves her deeply, and he does say that concern for her kept him out of the 1988 race, when she was eight years old. "Carl Wagner, who was also the father of an only daughter, told me I'd have to reconcile myself to being away from Chelsea for most of the next sixteen months." The same problem would arise, of course, four years later, when Chelsea would be twelve—yet he would run then. Wagner's advice is given a much different sense in his account to Maraniss. Wagner, who was a friend of Betsey Wright and had been given a job by her when he arrived in Little Rock, knew about her concerns, and shared them. After the conference with advisers, he stayed while the others left, to tell Clinton:

> When you reach the top of the steps, walk into your daughter's bedroom, look at her, and understand that if you do this, your relationship with her will never be the same. I'm not sure if it will be worse or better, but it will never be the same."[6]

Wagner was not worried about Clinton's absence from Chelsea, but about the presence of shadowy women in her young mind.

When Clinton ran in 1992, he admits that he anticipated trouble. A man in George H. W. Bush's White House, Roger Porter—with whom Clinton had worked on the President's "education initiative"—called him to say that "if I ran, they would have to destroy me personally."

He went on to say the press were elitists who would believe any tales they were told about backwater Arkansas. "We'll spend whatever we have to spend to get whoever we have to get to say whatever they have to say to take you out. And we'll do it early."

Of course, this is Clinton's version of the phone call; it has the ring of a Lee Atwater campaign, although it can even be interpreted as kindly meant. Clinton was being forewarned that he could not expect to get a free pass on his background. Clinton presents his decision to run despite this warning as a brave refusal to be blackmailed: "Ever since I was a little boy I have hated to be threatened."

On Gennifer Flowers, Clinton did resort to equivocation. In the famous post—Super Bowl interview on *60 Minutes,* Steve Kroft asked about "what she calls a twelve-year affair with you." Clinton said, "That allegation is false" (referring to the twelve-year aspect). So, said Kroft, "you're categorically denying that you ever had an affair with Gennifer Flowers?" Clinton answered, "I've said that before, and so has she." Both answers were technically correct, though six years later he would admit that they were "misleading"—he did have an affair. Most people forget that Clinton's trouble with women taping their phone calls did not begin with Monica Lewinsky. In 1992 Flowers was taping him, at a time when she was publicly denying claims of their affair. When he called her after defeating Sheffield Nelson for governor, Clinton mocked Nelson for denying that he had charged Clinton with infidelity: "I knew he lied. I just wanted to make his asshole pucker. But I covered you," Clinton said on a tape that became public.[7]

The Lewinskiad

Clinton claims that he does not offer excuses for his past life in this book. But he now says that he lied because he was confused, fatigued, and angry at being surrounded by bloodhound prosecutors, a hostile Congress, and a barking press: "And if there had been no Kenneth Star—if we had different kind of people, I would have just said, 'Here are the facts. I'm sorry. Deal with it however you please.' " Here all the contrived contrition is forgotten—it was Ken Starr who made him lie. But what was he lying about? For that he has another excuse, his "parallel life" in which he kept embarrassing things secret. Well, we all do that. But why did he do the reckless things with Lewinsky that he had to keep secret? With both Dan Rather and Charlie Rose he said: "I think I did something for the worst possible reason, just because I could. I think that's the most—just about the most morally indefensible reason that anybody could have for doing anything, when you do something just because you could." Here he is applying to himself what Newt Gingrich said to him when Clinton asked why the Republicans shut down the government in 1995. The answer: "Because we could." Later Clinton says the prosecutors hunted him "because they could."

As applied to him, the answer is nonsense. First of all, he *couldn't* do it, if that meant doing it with impunity—as he found out. Moreover, that is not the worst possible reason for doing anything. There are far worse reasons—hatred, revenge, religious fanaticism, sadism. He avoids saying that he did it because he wanted to, but that is the only honest answer. He did it from lechery. And the absurdity of it, the risk, just spiced the matter with danger. He was not withdrawing into a secret self but throwing himself outward in flamboyant bravado. Clinton, like his mother, is a gambler. He does not, as she did, play the ponies. He dares the lightning. He knew he had numerous hunters and trackers circling him about. He knew that he already had to cope with Gennifer Flowers, Paula Jones, and Kathleen Willey. The young woman he was adding to the list was not likely to be discreet—she boasted of earning her presidential kneepads, and wangled thirty-seven entrances to the White House, and snapped her thong, and preserved the candied semen. (DNA technology is still a comparatively young discipline, but it is not likely for some time to get a stranger exercise than testing the effluvia of presidential fellation.)

Flirting with ever greater peril, he repeatedly telephoned Lewinsky. He sent her presents (*Leaves of Grass* as Seducer's Assistant). He wore her present. He lied in risky forums. He put in jeopardy political efforts he cared about, as well as the respect and love of his wife and daughter. It was such a crazy thing to do that many of us could not, for a long time, believe he had done it. But Betsey Wright, from her long experience of the man, knew at once: "I was miserably furious with him, and completely unable to communicate with him from the time the Lewinsky stuff was unfolded on the national scene. This was a guy I had given thirteen years of my life to."[8]

Starr

Though Clinton's conduct was inexcusable, it does pale next to the deep and vast abuses of power that Kenneth Starr sponsored and protected. He is a deceptively sweet-looking fellow, a dimpled, flutily warbling Pillsbury Doughboy. But he lent himself to the schemes of people with an almost total disregard for the law. A man of honor would not have accepted his appointment by a right-wing judge to replace Robert Fiske, a Republican general counsel who was a distinguished prosecutor. Not only did Starr have no prosecutorial experience; he had already lent support to Paula Jones's suit against the President. He continued private practice for right-wing causes with right-wing funding. Five former presidents of the American Bar Association said that he had conflicts of interest for which he should recuse himself. At one point in his investigation, a *New York Times* editorial said he should resign. His own chosen ethics adviser, Sam Dash, left him in protest at his tactics. The American Civil Liberties Union had to bring an end to the "barbaric" conditions he imposed on the imprisoned Susan McDougal.[9]

Starr raised again the suspicion that Vince Foster was murdered, after his predecessor had disposed of that claim. This was a favorite cause of the man funding much of the right-wing pursuit of Clinton, Richard Mellon Scaife, who is a principal donor to Pepperdine College, where Starr now holds a chair. The list of Starr's offenses is long and dark. Congressman Barney Frank questioned him about the fact that he released his damning "sex report" on Clinton before the 1998 elections though he held findings that cleared Clinton of other charges—findings reached months earlier—until after the election. After Starr made several attempts at evading the question, Frank said, "In other words, you don't have anything to say [before an election] unless you have something bad to say."[10]

Starr prolonged his investigations as charge after charge was lengthily discredited, until the right-wing Rutherford Institute's lawyers, representing Paula Jones, could trap Clinton in a confession of his contacts with Monica Lewinsky, to which Starr then devoted his frenzied attention. The wonder is that Starr got away with all his offenses. For that he needed a complicit press, which disgraced itself in this period, gobbling up the illegal leaks that flowed from his office. The sniffy Washingtonians went so berserk over the fact that Clinton was Not One of Us that they bestowed on Starr an honorary Oneness with Usness. Sally Quinn wrote in *The Washington Post* that "Beltway Insiders" were humiliated by Clinton, and that "Starr is a Washington insider, too."[11]

Starr was one thing that made some people stay with Clinton, who says Starr's unfairness helped bring Hillary back to his side. Paul Begala admitted he was disgusted by what Clinton had done, but determined that he would not let Starr accomplish a "coup d'etat." That does not describe what a Starr success would have meant. Conviction on impeachment charges would not have brought in a Republican administration. Succession would have gone to Vice President Al Gore in Clinton's own administration. But Clinton agrees with Begala. He presents his fight with Starr as a defense of all the things the right wing disliked about him—his championship of blacks, and gays, and the poor. He works himself up to such a righteous pitch that he says his impeachment trial was a "badge of honor."

Honor

Actually, the honorable thing for Clinton would have been to resign. I argued for that in a *Time* magazine article as soon as he revealed that he had lied to the nation.[12] I knew, of course, that he wouldn't. He had thrown himself off the highest cliff ever, and he had to prove he could catch a last-inute branch and pull himself, improbably, back up. And damned if he didn't. He ended his time as president with high poll numbers and some new accomplishments, the greatest of the Kid's comebacks—so great that I have been asked if I still feel he should have resigned. Well, I do. Why? Partly because what Ross Perot said in 1996 was partly true—that Clinton would be "totally occupied for the next two years in staying out of jail." That meant he would probably go on lying. He tried for as long as possible to "mislead" the nation on Gennifer Flowers. He still claims that Paula Jones and Kathleen Willey made false charges. Perhaps they did, but he became unbelievable about personal behavior after lying about Flowers and Lewinsky. I at first disbelieved the story Paula Jones told because it seemed too bizarre; but the cigar-dildo described by Monica Lewinsky considerably extended the vistas of the bizarre.

Though Clinton accomplished things in his second term, he did so in a constant struggle to survive. Unlike the current president, his administration found in Sudan the presence of a weapon of mass destruction (the nerve gas precursor Empta) and bombed the place where it had existed—but many, including Senator Arlen Specter and the journalist Seymour Hersh, said that Clinton was just bombing another country to distract people from his scandal.[13] "That reaction," according to Richard Clarke, "made it more difficult to get approval for follow-up attacks on al Quaeda."[14] Even when Clinton was doing things, the appearance of his vulnerability made people doubt it. It was said in the Pentagon that he was afraid to seize terrorists because of his troubles; but Clarke rebuts those claims—he says that every proposal to seize a terrorist leader; whether it came from the CIA or the Pentagon, was approved by Clinton "during my tenure as CSG [Counterterrorism Security Group] chairman, from 1992 to 2001."

We shall never know what was not done, or not successfully done, because of Clinton's being politically crippled. He has been criticized for his insufficient response to the ethnic cleansing in Kosovo. Michael Walzer said of the bombing raids Clinton finally authorized that "our faith in airpower is . . . a kind of idolatry."[15] But Clinton was limited in what he could do by the fact that the House of Representatives passed a resolution exactly the opposite of the war authorization that would be given George W. Bush—it voted to deny the President the power to commit troops. Walzer says that Clinton should have prodded the UN to take action; but a Republican Congress was not going to follow a man it distrusted when he called on an institution it distrusted.

At the very end of Clinton's regime, did Arafat feel he was not strong enough in his own country to pressure him into the reasonable agreement Clinton had worked out and Ehud Barak had accepted? Clinton suggests as much when he says that Arafat called him a great man, and he had to reply: "I am not a great man. I am a failure, and you have made me one."

Clinton had a wise foreign policy. But in an Oval Office interview, shortly before he admitted lying to the nation, he admitted that he had not been able to make it clear to the American people. His vision had so little hold upon the public that Bush was able to discard it instantly when he came in. Clinton summed up the difference between his and Bush's approach for Charlie Rose by saying that the latter thinks we should "do what we want whenever we can, and then we cooperate when we have to," whereas his policy was that "we were cooperating whenever we could and we acted alone only when we had to." The Bush people are learning the difference between the two policies as their preemptive unilateralism fails.

Clinton claims that he was not hampered in his political activity by scandals. He even said, to Charlie Rose, that "I probably was more attentive to my work for several months just because I didn't want to tend to anything else." That is improbable a priori and it conflicts with what he told Dan Rather about the atmosphere caused by the scandal: "The moment was so crazy. It was a zoo. It was an unr—it was—it was like living in a madhouse."

Even if he were not distracted, the press and the nation were. His staff was demoralized. The Democrats on the Hill were defensive, doubtful, absorbed in either defending Clinton or deflecting criticism from themselves. His freedom to make policy was hobbled.

Clinton likes to talk now of his "legacy." That legacy should include partial responsibility for the disabling of the Democratic Party. There were things to be said against the Democratic Leadership Council (Mario Cuomo said them well) and the "triangulation" scheme of Dick Morris, by which Clinton would take positions to the right of most congressional Democrats and to the left of the Republican Party. But Clinton, as a Southerner, knew that the party had to expand its base back into sources of support eroded by the New Right. This was a defensible (in fact a shrewd) strategy as Clinton originally shaped it. He could have made it a tactical adjunct to important strategic goals. But after the scandals, all his maneuvering looked desperate—a swerving away from blows, a flurried scrambling to find solid footing. His very success made Democrats think their only path to success was to concede, cajole, and pander. Al Gore began his 2000 campaign unhappy about his association with Clinton but trying to outpander him when he opposed the return of the Cuban boy Elian Gonzalez to his father. There is a kind of rude justice in the fact that the election was stolen from Gore in the state where he truckled to the Cubans.

Clinton bequeathed to his party not a clear call to high goals but an omnidirectional proneness to pusillanimity and collapse. This was signaled at the very outset of the new presidency. The Democrats, still in control of the Senate, facing a president not even strong enough to win the popular vote, a man brought into office by linked chicaneries and chance (Kathleen Harris, Ralph Nader, Antonin Scalia), nonetheless helped to confirm John Ashcroft as attorney general. The senators knew Ashcroft well; they were surely not impressed by his acumen or wisdom.

A whole series of capitulations followed. While still holding a majority in the Senate, the Democrats did not use subpoenas and investigative powers to challenge Dick Cheney's secret drafting of energy policy with Enron and other companies. A portion of the Democrats would support the welfare-to-billionaires tax cut. They fairly stampeded to support the Patriot Act and the presidential war authorization—with John Kerry, John Edwards, and Hillary Clinton at the front of the pack. The party had become so neutered that Al From and others from the Democratic Leadership Council called Howard Dean an extremist for daring to say what everyone is now saying about the war with Iraq—that it was precipitate, overhyped, and underprepared, more likely to separate us from the friends needed to fight terrorists than to end terrorism.

What would have happened had Clinton resigned? Gore would have been given a "honeymoon" in which he could have played with a stronger hand all the initiatives Clinton had begun, unashamed of them and able to bring them fresh energy. That is what happened when Lyndon Johnson succeeded John Kennedy. Clinton himself may have reaped a redeeming admiration for what he had sacrificed to recover his honor. Before him would have lain all the opportunities he has now, and more. Hillary Clinton's support of him in this act of real contrition would have looked nobler. Clinton's followers were claiming that it was all and only about sex. Clinton could have said, "Since that is what it is about, I'll step aside so more important things can be addressed." All the other phony issues Starr had raised would have fallen of their own insubstantiality.

Of course, this is just one of many what-ifs about the Clinton presidency. By chance I saw a revival of Leonard Bernstein's musical *Wonderful Town,* just before getting my copy of the Clinton book. All through the 957 pages of it, a song from the show kept running through my head: "What a waste! What a waste!"

Notes

1. Aristotle, *Nichomachean Ethics* 1097–1098.
2. Sally Quinn, "Not in Their Backyard: In Washington, That Let Down Feeling," *The Washington Post,* November 2, 1998.
3. David Maraniss, *First in His Class: A Biography of Bill Clinton* (Simon and Schuster, 1995), p. 205.
4. Garry Wills, "Lightning Rod," *The New York Review,* August 14, 2003.
5. Maraniss, *First in His Class,* pp. 440–441.
6. Maraniss, *First in His Class,* p. 441.
7. Maraniss, *First in His Class,* p. 457.
8. Interview in the Harry Thomason and Nicholas Perry film *The Hunting of the President* (Regent Entertainment, 2004).
9. The despicable treatment of Susan McDougal is movingly presented in *The Hunting of the President,* a film that has many trivializing touches (like intercut clips of old Hollywood melodramas). McDougal's story is backed up by a very impressive woman, Claudia Riley, the wife of Bob Riley, the former Arkansas governor and college president, who stayed with McDougal through her ordeal and describes the bullying tactics she witnessed.
10. Sidney Blumenthal, *The Clinton Wars* (Farrar, Straus and Giroux, 2003), p. 512.
11. Quinn, "Not in Their Backyard: In Washington, That Let Down Feeling."
12. Garry Wills, "Leading by Leaving," *Time,* August 31, 1998.
13. See the important work by two former National Security Council antiterrorist directors, Daniel Benjamin and Steven Simon, *The Age of Sacred Terror: Radical Islam's War Against America* (Random House, 2002), pp. 352–360. See also Richard Clarke, *Against All Enemies: Inside America's War on Terror* (Free Press, 2004), pp. 146–147.
14. Clarke, *Against All Enemies,* p. 189.
15. Michael Walzer, *Arguing About War* (Yale University Press, 2004), p. 99.

The Rove Presidency

Karl Rove had the plan, the power, and the historic chance to remake American politics. What went wrong?

JOSHUA GREEN

With more than a year left in the fading Bush presidency, Karl Rove's worst days in the White House may still lie ahead of him. I met Rove on one of his best days, a week after Bush's reelection. The occasion was a reporters' lunch hosted by *The Christian Science Monitor* at the St. Regis Hotel in Washington, a customary stop for the winning and losing campaign teams to offer battle assessments and answer questions.

Kerry's team had glumly passed through a few days earlier. Afterward his chief strategist, Bob Shrum, boarded a plane and left the country. Rove had endured a heart-stopping Election Day (early exit polls indicated a Kerry landslide) but had prevailed, and plainly wasn't hurrying off anywhere. "The Architect," as Bush had just dubbed him, had spent the week collecting praise and had now arrived—vindicated, secure of his place in history—to hold court before the political press corps.

When Rove entered the room, everyone stood up to congratulate him and shake his hand. Washington journalism has become a kind of Cult of the Consultant, so the energy in the room was a lot like it might have been if Mickey Mantle had come striding into the clubhouse after knocking in the game-winning run in the World Series. Rove was pumped.

Before taking questions, he removed a folded piece of paper from his pocket and rattled off a series of numbers that made clear how he wanted the election to be seen: not as a squeaker but a rout. "This was an extraordinary election," Rove said. "[Bush won] 59.7 million votes, and we still have about 250,000 ballots to count. Think about that—*nearly 60 million votes!* The previous largest number was Ronald Reagan in 1984, sweeping the country with 49 states. We won 81 percent of all the counties in America. We gained a percentage of the vote in 87 percent of the counties in America. In Florida, we received nearly a million votes more in this election than in the last one." Rove was officially there to talk about the campaign, but it was clear he had something much bigger in mind. So no one missed his point, he invoked Franklin Roosevelt's supremacy in the 1930s and suggested that something similar was at hand: "We've laid out an agenda, we've laid out a vision, and now people want to see results."

The Early Birds

At dawn they start again, the early birds, as if they'd left some bitter things unsaid the day before. The sharp notes rise in thrids. I wake up knowing that I'll soon be dead, and that's no worse than justice, as is just. The kindest words are almost never meant. Most fond endearments fill us with disgust. To lie is sometimes all too eloquent; but, as I stumble toward that unknown date, even the lies may be inadequate.

—William Logan

William Logan's most recent book of essays and reviews, *The Undiscovered Country,* received the 2005 National Book Critics Circle Award in Criticism. His most recent book of poetry is *The Whispering Gallery* (2005).

One of the goals of any ambitious president is to create a governing coalition just as Roosevelt did, one that long outlasts your presidency. It's the biggest thing you can aim for, and only a few presidents have achieved it. As the person with the long-term vision in the Bush administration, and with no lack of ambition either, Rove had thought long and hard about achieving this goal before ever arriving in the White House, and he has pursued it more aggressively than anyone else.

Rove has always cast himself not merely as a campaign manager but as someone with a mind for policy and for history's deeper currents—as someone, in other words, with the wherewithal not just to exploit the political landscape but to reshape it. At the *Christian Science Monitor* lunch, he appeared poised to do just that. It was already clear that Social Security privatization, a longtime Rove enthusiasm, was the first thing Bush would pursue in his second term. When things are going well for Rove, he adopts a towel-snapping jocularity. He looked supremely sure of his prospects for success.

But within a year the administration was crumbling. Social Security had gone nowhere. Hurricane Katrina, the worsening war in Iraq, and the disastrous nomination of Harriet Miers to the Supreme Court shattered the illusion of stern competence that had helped reelect Bush. What surprised everybody was how suddenly it happened; for a while, many devotees of the Cult of Rove seemed not to accept that it had. As recently as last fall, serious journalists were churning out soaring encomiums to Rove and his methods with titles like *One Party Country* and *The Way to Win*. In retrospect, everyone should have been focusing less on how those methods were used to win elections and more on why they couldn't deliver once the elections were over.

The story of why an ambitious Republican president working with a Republican Congress failed to achieve most of what he set out to do finds Rove at center stage. A big paradox of Bush's presidency is that Rove, who had maybe the best purely political mind in a generation and almost limitless opportunities to apply it from the very outset, managed to steer the administration toward disaster.

Years from now, when the major figures in the Bush administration publish their memoirs, historians may have a clearer idea of what went wrong than we do today. As an exercise in not waiting that long, I spent several months reading the early memoirs and talking to people inside and outside the administration (granting anonymity as necessary), in Congress, and in lobbying and political-consulting firms that dealt directly with Rove in the White House. (Rove declined requests for an interview.) The idea was to look at the Bush years and make a first pass at explaining the consequential figure in the vortex—to answer the question, How should history understand Karl Rove, and with him, this administration?

Fifty years ago, political scientists developed what is known as realignment theory—the idea that a handful of elections in the nation's history mattered more than the others because they created "sharp and durable" changes in the polity that lasted for decades. Roosevelt's election in 1932, which brought on the New Deal and three decades of Democratic dominance in Washington, is often held up as the classic example. Modern American historians generally see five elections as realigning: 1800, when Thomas Jefferson's victory all but finished off the Federalist Party and reoriented power from the North to the agrarian South; 1828, when Andrew Jackson's victory gave rise to the modern two-party system and two decades of Jacksonian influence; 1860, when Abraham Lincoln's election marked the ascendance of the Republican Party and of the secessionist impulse that led to the Civil War; 1896, when the effects of industrialization affirmed an increasingly urban political order that brought William McKinley to power; and Roosevelt's election in 1932, during the Great Depression.

Academics debate many aspects of this theory, such as whether realignment comes in regular cycles, and whether it is driven by voter intensity or disillusionment. But historians have shown that two major preconditions typically must be in place for realignment to occur. First, party loyalty must be sufficiently weak to allow for a major shift—the electorate, as the political scientist Paul Allen Beck has put it, must be "ripe for realignment." The other condition is that the nation must undergo some sort of triggering event, often what Beck calls a "societal trauma"—the ravaging depressions of the 1890s and 1930s, for instance, or the North-South conflict of the 1850s and '60s that ended in civil war. It's important to have both. Depressions and wars throughout American history have had no realigning consequence because the electorate wasn't primed for one, just as periods of electoral unrest have passed without a realignment for lack of a catalyzing event.

Before he ever came to the White House, Rove fervently believed that the country was on the verge of another great shift. His faith derived from his reading of the presidency of a man most historians regard as a mediocrity. Anyone on the campaign trail in 2000 probably heard him cite the pivotal importance of William McKinley's election in 1896. Rove thought there were important similarities.

"Everything you know about William McKinley and Mark Hanna"—McKinley's Rove—"is wrong," he told Nicholas Lemann of *The New Yorker* in early 2000. "The country was in a period of change. McKinley's the guy who figured it out. Politics were changing. The economy was changing. We're at the same point now: weak allegiances to parties, a rising new economy." Rove was suggesting that the electorate in 2000, as in 1896, was ripe for realignment, and implying, somewhat immodestly, that he was the guy who had figured it out. What was missing was an obvious trigger. With the economy soaring (the stock-market collapse in the spring of 2000 was still months away) and the nation at peace, there was no reason to expect that a realignment was about to happen.

Instead, Rove's idea was to use the levers of government to create an effect that ordinarily occurs only in the most tumultuous periods in American history. He believed he could force a realignment himself through a series of far-reaching policies. Rove's plan had five major components: establish education standards, pass a "faith-based initiative" directing government funds to religious organizations, partially privatize Social Security, offer private health-savings accounts as an alternative to Medicare, and reform immigration laws to appeal to the growing Hispanic population. Each of these, if enacted, would weaken the Democratic Party by drawing some of its core supporters into the Republican column. His plan would lead, he believed, to a period of Republican dominance like the one that followed McKinley's election.

Rove's vision had a certain abstract conceptual logic to it, much like the administration's plan to spread democracy by force in the Middle East. If you could invade and pacify Iraq and Afghanistan, the thinking went, democracy would spread across the region. Likewise, if you could recast major government programs to make them more susceptible to market forces, broader support for the Republican Party would ensue. But in both cases the visionaries ignored the enormous difficulty of carrying off such seismic changes.

The Middle East failure is all too well-known—the vaulting ambition coupled with the utter inability of top administration figures to bring about their grand idea. What is less appreciated is how Rove set out to do something every bit as audacious with domestic policy. Earlier political realignments resulted from historical accidents or anomalies, conditions that were recognized and exploited after the fact by talented politicians.

Nobody ever planned one. Rove didn't wait for history to happen to him—he tried to create it on his own. "It's hard to think of any analogue in American history," says David Mayhew, a Yale political scientist who has written a book on electoral realignments, "to what Karl Rove was trying to do."

Rove's style as a campaign consultant was to plot out well in advance of a race exactly what he would do and to stick with it no matter what. But he arrived in the White House carrying ambitions at striking variance with those of a president whose stated aims were modest and who had lost the popular vote. The prevailing view of Bush at the time seems impossibly remote today. But the notion that he wanted nothing more than "to do a few things, and do them well," as he claimed, seemed sensible enough. Nothing suggested that radical change was possible, much less likely, and the narrow margins in Congress meant that any controversial measure would require nearly flawless execution to prevail.

And yet at first it appeared that Bush might be capable of achieving big things. His first initiative, the No Child Left Behind Act, unfolded as a model of how to operate in a narrowly divided environment. Bush had made education a central theme of his campaign, an unlikely choice given that the issue strongly favors Democrats. Accountability standards had been one of his signature accomplishments as governor of Texas, and he made a persuasive pitch for them on the campaign trail. Rove likes to point out that people who named education as their top issue voted for the Democrat over the Republican 76–16 percent in the 1996 presidential election, but just 52–44 in 2000. His point is that Bush moved the electorate.

As the top political adviser in the White House, Rove orchestrated the rollout of Bush's legislative agenda. In December, even before the inauguration, he put together a conference in Austin that included key Democrats who went on to support the education bills that sailed through Congress and became the first piece of Rove's realignment. At the time, everybody assumed this was how Bush would operate—"as a uniter, not a divider," his method in Texas, where he left behind a permanent-seeming Republican majority.

In retrospect, everyone should have been focusing less on how Rove's methods were used to win elections and more on why they couldn't deliver once the elections were over.

It's not clear why Bush abandoned the moderate style that worked with No Child Left Behind. One of the big what-ifs of his presidency is how things might have turned out had he stuck with it (education remains the one element of Rove's realignment project that was successfully enacted). What did become clear is that Rove's tendency, like Bush's, is always to choose the most ambitious option in a list and then pursue

it by the most aggressive means possible—an approach that generally works better in campaigns than in governing. Instead of modest bipartisanship, the administration's preferred style of governing became something much closer to the way Rove runs campaigns: Steamroll the opposition whenever possible, and reach across the aisle only in the rare cases, like No Child Left Behind, when it is absolutely necessary. The large tax cut that Bush pursued and won on an almost party-line vote just afterward is a model of this confrontational style. Its limitations would become apparent.

By late summer of his first year, the early burst of achievement had slowed and Bush's approval ratings were beginning to sag. Ronald Brownstein of *The Los Angeles Times* dubbed him the "A4 president," unable even to make the front page of the newspaper. He did not seem the likely leader of a realignment.

That September 11 was both a turning point for the Bush administration and an event that would change the course of American history was immediately clear. It was also clear, if less widely appreciated, that the attacks were the type of event that can instantly set off a great shifting of the geological strata of American politics. In a coincidence of epic dimensions, 9/11 provided, just when Rove needed it, the historical lever missing until then. He had been presented with exactly the sort of "societal trauma" that makes realignment possible, and with it a fresh chance to pursue his goal. Bob Woodward's trilogy on the Bush White House makes clear how neoconservatives in the administration recognized that 9/11 gave them the opening they'd long desired to forcefully remake the Middle East. Rove recognized the same opening.

After 9/11, any pretense of shared sacrifice or of reaching across the aisle was abandoned. The administration could demand—and get—almost anything it wanted, easily flattening Democratic opposition, which it did with increasing frequency on issues like the PATRIOT Act and the right of Department of Homeland Security workers to unionize. The crisis atmosphere allowed the White House to ignore what normally would have been some of its most basic duties—working with Republicans in Congress (let alone Democrats) and laying the groundwork in Congress and with the American public for what it hoped to achieve. At the time, however, this didn't seem to matter.

Rove's systematic policy of sharply contrasting Republican and Democratic positions on national security was a brilliant campaign strategy and the critical mechanism of Republican victory in the 2002 midterms. But he could not foresee how this mode of operating would ultimately work at cross-purposes with his larger goal. "What Bush went out and did in 2002," a former administration official told me, "clearly at Karl's behest, with an eye toward the permanent Republican majority, was very aggressively attack those Democrats who voted with him and were for him. There's no question that the president helped pick up seats. But all of that goodwill was squandered."

From the outset, Rove's style of pursuing realignment—through division—was in stark contrast to the way it had happened the last time. In *Franklin D. Roosevelt and the New Deal*, the historian William E. Leuchtenburg notes that Roosevelt mentioned the Democratic Party by name only three times in his entire 1936 reelection campaign. Throughout his presidency, Roosevelt had large Democratic majorities in Congress but operated in a nonpartisan fashion, as though he didn't. Bush, with razor-thin majorities—and for a time, a divided Congress—operated as though his margins were insurmountable, and sowed interparty divisions as an electoral strategy.

R ove never graduated from college. He dropped out of the University of Utah and campaigned for the chairmanship of the College Republicans, a national student organization whose leaders often go on to important positions in the party. He won, placing himself on a fast track to a career in politics. But he was and remains an autodidact, and a large part of his self-image depends on showing that his command of history and politics is an order of magnitude greater than other people's. Rove has a need to outdo everybody else that seems to inform his sometimes contrarian views of history. It's not enough for him to have read everything; he needs to have read everything and arrived at insights that others missed.

This aspect of Rove was on fuller-than-usual display during a speech he gave at the University of Utah, titled "What Makes a Great President," just after the Republicans swept the 2002 elections. The incumbent presidential party typically loses seats in the off-year election, so winning was a big deal to Rove, who actively involved himself in many of the campaigns. Overcoming historical precedent seemed to feed his oracular sense of himself, and during his speech and the question-and-answer period that followed he revealed a lot about how he thinks and where he imagined his party was going.

In his speech, he described a visit to the White House by the revisionist historian Forrest McDonald, who spoke about presidential greatness. Rove expressed delight at discovering a fellow McKinley enthusiast, and said that McDonald had explained in his talk, "Nobody knows McKinley is great, because history demanded little of him. He modernized the presidency, he modernized the Treasury to deal with the modern economy, he changed dramatically the policies of his party by creating a durable governing coalition for 40 years"—this last part clearly excited Rove—"and he attempted deliberately to break with the Gilded Age politics. He was inclusive, and he was the first Republican candidate for president to be endorsed by a leader in the Catholic hierarchy. The Protestant Anglo-Saxon Republicans were scandalized by his 1896 campaign, in which he paraded Portuguese fishermen and Slovak coal miners and Serbian iron workers to Canton, Ohio, to meet him. He just absolutely scandalized the country."

In this way of telling it, McKinley alone understood what everybody else was missing: A political realignment was under way, and by harnessing it, though it might "scandalize" conventional thinking, McKinley would not only carry the presidency but also bring about an unprecedented period of dominance for his party. The subtext seemed to be that Rove, too, recognized something everybody else had missed—the chance for a Republican realignment—just as he recognized the overlooked genius of William McKinley. He joked to the audience, "This tripled the size of the McKinley caucus in Washington—it was Bob Novak, me, and now Forrest McDonald."

After the speech a member of the audience asked a question that took as its premise the notion that America was evenly divided between Republicans and Democrats. Rove insisted this was not the case, pouring forth a barrage of numbers from the recent midterm elections that seemed to lay waste to the notion. "Something is going on out there," Rove insisted. "Something else more fundamental . . . But we will only know it retrospectively. In two years or four years or six years, [we may] look back and say the dam began to break in 2002."

Like his hero McKinley, he alone was the true visionary. Everyone else looked at the political landscape and saw a nation at rough parity. Rove looked at the same thing and saw an emerging Republican majority.

F rom Rove's vantage point after the 2002 elections, everything seemed to be on track. He had a clear strategy for achieving realignment and the historical conditions necessary to enact it. His already considerable influence within the administration was growing with the Republican Party's rising fortunes, which were credited to his strategy of aggressive divisiveness on the issues of war and terrorism. But what Rove took to be the catalyst for realignment turned out to be the catalyst for his fall.

September 11 temporarily displaced much of what was going on in Washington at the time. The ease with which Republicans were able to operate in the aftermath of the attacks was misleading, and it imbued Rove, in particular, with false confidence that what he was doing would continue to work. In reality, it masked problems—bad relationships with Congress, a lack of support for Bush's broader agenda—that either went unseen or were consciously ignored. Hubris and a selective understanding of history led Rove into a series of errors and misjudgments that compounded to devastating effect.

He never appreciated that his success would ultimately depend on the sustained cooperation of congressional Republicans, and he developed a dysfunctional relationship with many of them. This wasn't clear at first. Several of the administration's early moves looked particularly shrewd, one of them being to place the White House congressional liaisons in the office suite of the majority whip, Tom De Lay of Texas. At the time, DeLay was officially third in the Republican House leadership hierarchy, but as everyone knew, he was the capo of House Republicans and the man to see if you wanted to get something done.

Things never clicked. Republicans on the Hill say that Rove and DeLay, both formidable men who had known each other in Texas, had a less-than-amiable relationship. When I asked DeLay about their history, he let out a malevolent chuckle and told me that his very first race had pitted him against one of Rove's candidates. "They were nasty to me," DeLay recalled. "I had some payroll tax liens against me, as most small businessmen do, and I was driving a red Eldorado at the time. The taxes were paid, but they were running radio ads saying I was a deadbeat who didn't pay my taxes." DeLay still remembered the ad: "He wants to drive his red Cadillac to Washington on the backs of the taxpayers."

XYZ

The cross the fork the zigzag—a few straight lines
For pain, quandary and evasion, the last of signs.
                                                —Robert Pinsky

Robert Pinsky's new collection of poems, *Gulf Music*, will be published this fall. He served three terms as the United States poet laureate and currently teaches at Boston University.

DeLay made a point of saying he didn't hold a grudge. ("That wouldn't be Christian of me.") But he did allow that Rove had been extremely aggressive in trying to impose his ideas on Congress. "Karl and I are sort of the same personality," he explained, "so we end up screaming at each other. But in the end you walk out of the room with an agenda." DeLay insists he didn't mind Rove's screaming, but if that's true, he belongs to a truly Christian group.

Rove's behavior toward Congress stood out. "Every once in a while Rove would come to leadership meetings, and he definitely considered himself at least an equal with the leaders in the room," a Republican aide told me. "But you have to understand that Congress is a place where a certain decorum is expected. Even in private, staff is still staff. Rove would come and chime in as if he were equal to the speaker. Cheney sometimes came, too, and was far more deferential than Rove—and he was the vice president." Other aides say Rove was notorious for interrupting congressional leaders and calling them by their first name.

Dick Armey, the House Republican majority leader when Bush took office (and no more a shrinking violet than DeLay), told me a story that captures the exquisite pettiness of most members of Congress and the arrogance that made Bush and Rove so inept at handling them. "For all the years he was president," Armey told me, "Bill Clinton and I had a little thing we'd do where every time I went to the White House, I would take the little name tag they give you and pass it to the president, who, without saying a word, would sign and date it. Bill Clinton and I didn't like each other. He said I was his least-favorite member of Congress. But he knew that when I left his office, the first schoolkid I came across would be given that card, and some kid who had come to Washington with his mama would go home with the presidents autograph. I think Clinton thought it was a nice thing to do for some kid, and he was happy to do it." Armey said that when he went to his first meeting in the White House with President Bush, he explained the tradition with Clinton and asked the president if he would care to continue it. "Bush refused to sign the card. Rove, who was sitting across the table, said, 'It would probably wind up on eBay," Armey continued. "Do I give a damn? No. But can you imagine refusing a simple request like that with an insult? It's stupid. From the point of view of your own self-interest, it's stupid. I was from Texas, and I was the majority leader. If my expectations of civility and collegiality were disappointed, what do you think it was like for the rest of the congressmen they dealt with? The Bush White House was tone-deaf to the normal courtesies of the office."

Winning the 2002 elections earned Rove further distinction as an electoral strategist. But it didn't change the basic dynamic between the White House and Congress, and Rove drew exactly the wrong lesson from the experience, bringing the steamroller approach from the campaign trail into his work in government. Emboldened by triumph, he grew more imperious, worsening his relations with the Hill. With both houses now in Republican hands, he pressed immigration reform and Social Security privatization. A congressional aide described a Republican leadership retreat after the midterms where Rove whipped out a chart and a sheaf of poll numbers and insisted to Republican leaders that they pursue a Social Security overhaul at once. Making wholesale changes to a beloved entitlement program in the run-up to a presidential election would have been a difficult sell under the best of circumstances. Lacking goodwill in Congress and having laid no groundwork for such an undertaking, Rove didn't get a serious hearing on the issue—or on immigration, either.

A revealing pattern of behavior emerged from my interviews. Rove plainly viewed his standing as equal to or exceeding that of the party's leaders in Congress and demanded what he deemed his due. Yet he was also apparently annoyed at what came with his White House eminence, complaining to colleagues when members of Congress called him to consult about routine matters he thought were beneath his standing—something that couldn't have endeared him to the legislature.

When Bush revived immigration reform this past spring and let it be known that Rove would not take part in the negotiations, the president seemed to have belatedly grasped a basic truth about congressional relations that Armey summed up for me like this: "You can't call her ugly all year and expect her to go to the prom with you."

Another important misjudgment by Bush, prodded by Rove, was giving Rove too much power within the administration. This was partly a function of Rove's desire to control policy as well as politics. His prize for winning the reelection campaign was a formal role and the title of deputy chief of staff for policy. But his power also grew because the senior policy staff in the White House was inept.

In an early scene in Ron Suskind's book *The Price of Loyalty*, Treasury Secretary Paul O'Neill, not yet alive to the futility of his endeavor, warns Dick Cheney that the White House policy process is so ineffectual that it is tantamount to "kids rolling around on the lawn." Had O'Neill lasted longer than he did (he resigned in 2002), he might have lowered his assessment. Before she left the White House in humiliation after conservatives blocked her nomination to the Supreme Court, White House Counsel Harriet Miers had also served as deputy chief of staff for policy. The president's Domestic Policy Council was run by Claude Alien, until he, too, resigned, after he was caught shoplifting at Target.

Rove was and remains an autodidact, and a large part of his self-image depends on showing that his command of history and politics is an order of magnitude greater than other people's.

The weakness of the White House policy staff demanded Rove's constant involvement. For all his shortcomings, he had clear ideas about where the administration should go, and the ability to maneuver. "Where the bureaucracy was failing and broken, Karl got stuff done," says a White House colleague. "Harriet was no more capable of producing policy out of the policy office she directed than you or I are capable of jumping off the roof of a building and flying to Minneapolis."

As a result, Rove not only ran the reelection campaign, he plotted much of Bush's second-term agenda, using the opportunity to push long-standing pet issues—health-savings accounts, Social Security privatization—that promised to weaken support for Democrats, by dismantling Medicare and Social Security. But this also meant committing the president to sweeping domestic changes that had no public favor and had not been a focus of the 2004 campaign, which had centered almost exclusively on the war.

Bush's reelection and Rove's assumption of a formal policy role had a bigger effect than most of Washington realized at the time. It is commonly assumed (as I assumed) that Rove exercised a major influence on White House policy before he had the title, all the time that he had it, and even after it was taken away from him in the staff shake-up last year that saw Josh Bolten succeed Andrew Card as chief of staff.

Insiders don't disagree, but say that Rove's becoming deputy chief of staff for policy was still an important development. For the purposes of comparison, a former Bush official cited the productiveness of the first two years of Bush's presidency, the period that generated not just No Child Left Behind but three tax cuts and the Medicare prescription-drug benefit. At the time, Bolten was deputy chief of staff for policy, and relations with Congress had not yet soured. "Josh was not an equal of Karl's with regard to access to the president or stature." says the official. "But he was a strong enough intellect and a strong enough presence that he was able to create a deliberative process that led to a better outcome." When Bolten left to run the Office of Management and Budget, in 2003, the balance shifted in Rove's favor, and then shifted further after the reelection. "Formalizing [Rove's policy role] was the final choke-off of any internal debate or deliberative process," says the official. "There was no offset to Karl."

Rove's greatest shortcoming was not in conceptualizing policies but in failing to understand the process of getting them implemented, a weakness he never seems to have recognized in himself. It's startling that someone who gave so much thought to redirecting the powers of government evinced so little interest in understanding how it operates. Perhaps because he had never worked in government—or maybe because his standing rested upon his relationship with a single superior—he was often ineffective at bringing into being anything that required more than a presidential signature.

As the September 11 mind-set began to lose its power over Washington, Rove still faced the task of getting the more difficult parts of his realignment schema through Congress. But his lack of fluency in the art of moving policy and his tendency to see the world through the divisive lens of a political campaign were great handicaps. There was an important difference between the administration's first-term achievements and the entitlement overhauls (Social Security and Medicare) and volatile cultural issues (immigration) that Rove wanted to push through next. Cutting taxes and furnishing new benefits may generate some controversy in Washington, but few lawmakers who support them face serious political risk. (Tax cuts get Republicans elected!) So it's possible, with will and numbers alone, to pass them with the barest of majorities. Rove's mistake was to believe that this would work with everything.

Entitlement reform is a different animal. More important than reaching a majority is offering political cover to those willing to accept the risk of tampering with cherished programs, and the way to do this is by enlisting the other side. So the fact that Republicans controlled the White House and both houses of Congress after 2002—to Rove, a clinching argument for confrontation—actually *lessened* the likelihood of entitlement reform. Congressional Republicans didn't support Rove's plan in 2003 to tackle Social Security or immigration reform because they didn't *want* to pass such things on a party-line vote. History suggested they'd pay a steep price at election time.

Rove's idea was to use the levers of government to create a realignment—to force an effect that ordinarily occurs only in the most tumultuous periods in American history.

To understand this, Rove need not have looked back any farther than the last Republican president who had attempted something on this order. Before he was president, Ronald Reagan talked about letting people opt out of the Social Security system, a precursor of the plan Rove favors. In 1981, in the full tide of victory, Reagan proposed large cuts—and the Republican Senate refused even to take them up. The mere fact that they had been put forward, however, was enough to imperil Republicans, who took significant losses in 1982.

The following year, Reagan tried again, this time cooperating with the Democratic speaker of the House, Tip O'Neill. He now understood that the only way to attain any serious change on such a sensitive issue was for both parties to hold hands and jump together. To afford each side deniability if things fell apart, the two leaders negotiated by proxy. O'Neill chose Robert Ball, a widely respected Social Security commissioner under three presidents, while Reagan picked Alan Greenspan, the future chairman of the Federal Reserve. Key senators in both parties were looped in.

As Ball and Greenspan made headway, it was really O'Neill and Reagan who were agreeing. To assure both sides political cover, the negotiations were an all-or-nothing process. The plan that was eventually settled on addressed the solvency problem by raising the retirement age (which pleased Republicans) and taxing Social Security benefits for the first time (which pleased Democrats). Unlike in 1981, Republicans in Congress weren't left exposed. Democrats couldn't attack them for raising the retirement age, because Tip O'Neill had signed on. Republicans couldn't complain about higher taxes, because Democrats had supported Ronald Reagan's plan.

At the *Christian Science Monitor* lunch just after the reelection, Rove, then at the apogee of his power, had no time for nostrums like bipartisanship or negotiation. Armed with his policy title and the aura of political genius, he pressed for the Social Security changes so far denied him. In many ways, this decision was the fulcrum of the Bush presidency. Had Bush decided not to pursue Social Security or had he somehow managed to pursue it in a way that included Democrats, his presidency might still have ended up in failure, because of Iraq. But the dramatic collapse of Rove's Social Security push foreclosed any other possibility. It left Bush all but dead in the water for what looks to be the remainder of his time in office.

Rove pursued his plan with characteristic intensity, running it out of the White House from the top down, like a political campaign, and seeking to enlist the network of grassroots activists that had carried the Bush-Cheney ticket to a second term. Bush gave Social Security prominence in his State of the Union address, then set out on a national road show to sell the idea. But after an election fought over the war, Social Security drew little interest, and in contrast to the effect Bush achieved on education in the 2000 campaign, public support didn't budge. (It actually worsened during his tour.)

Unlike Reagan, Bush did not produce a bill that could have served as a basis for negotiation—nor did he seriously consult any Democrats with whom he might have negotiated. Instead, Rove expected a bill to emerge from Congress. The strategy of a president's outlining broad principles of what he'd like in a bill and calling on Congress to draft it has worked many times in the past. But Rove had no allies in Congress, had built no support with the American public, and had chosen to undertake the most significant entitlement reform since Reagan by having Bush barnstorm the country speaking before handpicked Republican audiences with the same partisan fervor he'd brought to the presidential campaign trail—all of which must have scared the living daylights out of the very Republicans in Congress Rove foolishly counted upon to do his bidding. The problems buried for years under the war and then the presidential race came roaring back, and Bush got no meaningful support from the Hill. He was left with a flawed, unpopular concept whose motive—political gain—was all too apparent.

Within months it was clear that the Social Security offensive was in deep trouble and, worse, was dragging down Bush's popularity at a time when he needed all the support he could muster for Iraq. Every week, the political brain trust in the Bush White House gathers under Rove for what is known as the "Strategery Meeting" (an ironic nod to Bush's frequent malapropisms) to plot the course ahead. What transpires is usually a closely held secret. But two former Bush officials provided an account of one meeting in the late spring of 2005, in the middle of the Social Security push, that affords a remarkable glimpse of Rove's singularity of purpose.

He opened the meeting by acknowledging that the Social Security initiative was struggling and hurting the president's approval ratings, and then announced that, despite this, they would stay the course through the summer. He admitted that the numbers would probably continue to fall. But come September, the president would hit Democrats hard on the issue of national security and pull his numbers back up again. Winning on Social Security was so important to Rove that he was evidently willing to gamble the effectiveness of Bush's second term on what most people in the White House and Congress thought were very long odds to begin with. The gamble didn't pay off. Even before Hurricane Katrina hit New Orleans on the morning of August 29, what slim hope might have remained for Social Security was gone.

Hurricane Katrina clearly changed the public perception of Bush's presidency. Less examined is the role Rove played in the defining moment of the administration's response: when Air Force One flew over Louisiana and Bush gazed down from on high at the wreckage without ordering his plane down. Bush advisers Matthew Dowd and Dan Bartlett wanted the president on the ground immediately, one Bush official told me, but were overruled by Rove for reasons that are still unclear: "Karl did not want the plane to land in Louisiana." Roves political acumen seemed to be deserting him altogether.

An important theme of future Bush administration memoirs will be the opportunity cost of leading off the second term with the misguided plan to overhaul Social Security. "The great cost of the Social Security misadventure was lost support for the war," says a former Bush official. "When you send troops to war, you have no higher responsibility as president than to keep the American people engaged and maintain popular support. But for months and months after it became obvious that Social Security was not going to happen, nobody—because of Karl's stature in the White House—could be intellectually honest in a meeting and say, 'This is not going to happen, and we need an exit strategy to get back onto winning ground.' It was a catastrophic mistake."

It strains belief to think that someone as highly attuned as Rove to all that goes on in politics could have missed the reason for Bush's reelection: He persuaded just enough people that he was the better man to manage the war. But it's also hard to fathom how the master strategist could leave his president and his party as vulnerable as they proved to be six months into the second term. The Republican pollster Tony Fabrizio says, "People who were concerned about the war, we lost. People who were concerned about the economy, we lost. People who were concerned about health care, we lost. It goes on and on. Any of those things would have helped refocus the debate or at least put something else out there besides the war. We came out of the election and what was our agenda for the next term? Social Security. There was nothing else that we were doing. We allowed ourselves as a party to be defined by—in effect, to live and die by—the war in Iraq."

That Rove ignored a political reality so clear to everyone else can be explained only by the immutable nature of his ambition: Social Security was vital for a realignment, however unlikely its success now appeared. At the peak of his influence, the only person who could have stopped him was the one person he answered to—but the president was just as fixated on his place in history as Rove was on his own.

Moments of precise reckoning in politics are rare outside of elections. Snapshot polls don't tell you much about whole epochs. Even voter identification can be a misleading indicator. In 1976, the post-Watergate Republican Party would have appeared to be in existential peril, when in fact it was on the verge of setting the agenda for a generation. So the question of where exactly things stand right now is more complicated than it might appear.

As he nears the end of his time in government. Rove has been campaigning for the notion that Bush has been more successful than he's being credited for. But the necessity of adopting history's longer perspective to make his argument says a great deal. Of the five policies in his realignment vision, Social Security and immigration failed outright; medical-savings accounts and the faith-based program wound up as small, face-saving initiatives after the original ambitions collapsed; and the lone success, No Child Left Behind, looks increasingly jeopardized as it comes up for renewal in Congress this year, a victim of Bush's unpopularity. Rove no longer talks about realignment—though the topic is now very popular with Democrats, who have a good shot at controlling both houses of Congress and the presidency after the next election. On the face of things, the Republican Party is in trouble. In a representative example, voters in a recent NBC-*Wall Street Journal* poll preferred that the next president be a Democrat by 52–31 percent, and delivered the most negative assessment of the Republican Party in the surveys two-decade history. In 2002, Americans were equally split along partisan lines. A recent Pew study shows that 50 percent of the public identifies as Democratic or leaning that way, while just 35 percent identifies with the GOP.

Rove is a great devotee of the historian Robert H. Wiebe, who also emphasizes the pivotal quality of the 1896 election. Wiebe thought industrialization had launched a great sorting-out process in the 1880s and '90s that reached a dramatic culmination in 1896. He argues in his book *The Search for Order, 1877–1920* that "a decade's accumulated bitterness ultimately flowed into a single national election."

It seems highly unlikely, though not impossible, that historians will one day view 2000 or 2004 as the kind of realigning election that Rove so badly wanted. Ken Mehlman, a protégé of Rove's and one of the sharper minds in the Republican Party, is adamant that the analysis that led Rove to believe realignment was at hand remains fundamentally correct. "If you look back over the last few decades, an era of politics has run its course," Mehlman told me. "Both parties achieved some of their highest goals. Democrats got civil rights, women's rights, the New Deal, and recognition of the need for a cleaner environment. Republicans got the defeat of the Soviet Union, less violent crime, lower tax rates, and welfare reform. The public agrees on this. So the issues now become: How do you deal with the terrorist threat? How do you deal with the retirement of the Baby Boomers? How do you deliver health care with people changing jobs? How do you make sure America retains its economic strength with the rise of China and India? How that plays out is something we don't know yet." As far as what's happened since 2000, Mehlman says, "the conditions remain where they were."

In this view, America is still in the period of great churn, and the 1896 election hasn't happened yet.

Rove has no antecedent in modern American politics, because no president before Bush thought it wise to give a political adviser so much influence.

Premised as it is on the notion that the past seven years have been a wash, Mehlman's analysis has a self-justifying tinge. At least for now, Republicans have measurably fallen behind where they were in 2000. It's hard to sift underlying political views from temporary rage against Bush, or to anticipate what effect his presidency will have on the Republican Party's fortunes once he's gone. But the effect does seem certain to be less pronounced—less disastrous—than it is now. Considered in that context, Mehlman's analysis rings true.

When I asked Mark Gersh, one of the Democrats' best electoral analysts, for his view of how the political landscape has shifted, he basically agreed with Mehlman, and offered his own perspective on Rove's vision of realignment. "September 11 is what made them, and Iraq is what undermined them, and the truth lies in between the two—and that is that both parties are at parity," Gersh told me. "There was never any indication that the Republicans were emerging as the majority party. What was happening was that partisanship was actually hardening. Fewer people in both parties were voting for candidates of the other party." Gersh added that he doesn't believe Democrats are the majority party, and he gives Republicans "at worst a 4-in-10 chance" of holding the presidency in 2008. Even if Rove didn't create a generational shift to the Republican Party, so far at least he does not appear to have ushered in a Democratic one, either.

Nonetheless, certain painful, striking parallels between the presidencies of George Bush and William McKinley can't have been lost on Rove, even if he would be the last to admit them. Both originally campaigned almost exclusively on domestic issues, only to have their presidencies dominated by foreign affairs. Neither distinguished himself. *Policy inertia* is the term the historian Richard L. McCormick uses to characterize McKinley's presidency. David Mayhew, the political scientist, writes in his skeptical study *Electoral Realignments,* "Policy innovations under McKinley during 1897–1901 [McKinley was assassinated in 1901] probably rank in the bottom quartile among all presidential terms in American history." Both sentiments could be applied to Bush.

Perhaps the strangest irony is the foreign adventure that consumed much of McKinley's presidency. Though he lacked Bush's storm-the-barricades temperament, McKinley launched the Spanish-American War partly at the urging of his future vice president, Teddy Roosevelt, and other hawks. As the historian Eric Rauchway has pointed out, after American forces defeated the Spanish navy in the Philippines, the U.S. occupation encountered a bloody postwar insurgency and allegations of torture committed by U.S. troops. Roosevelt, who succeeded

McKinley, was hampered by questions about improper force size and commitment of troops and eventually came to rue his plight. "While I have never varied in my feeling that we had to hold the Philippines," he wrote in 1901, "I have varied very much in my feelings whether we were to be considered fortunate or unfortunate in having to hold them."

To understand Rove's record, it's useful to think of the disaster as being divided into foreign and domestic components. Rove had little say in foreign policy. Dick Cheney understood from decades of government experience how to engineer a war he'd pressed for, and still the administration failed to reshape the Middle East. More than anyone outside the Oval Office, Rove was responsible for much of what went wrong on the domestic front—partly because he had never served in government, and he lacked Cheney's skill at manipulating it. Both men came in believing they had superior insights into history and theoretical underpinnings so strong that their ideas would prevail. But neither man understood how to see them through, and so both failed.

Rove has proved a better analyst of history than agent of historical change, showing far greater aptitude for envisioning sweeping change than for pulling it off. Cheney, through a combination of stealth and nuance, was responsible for steering the Bush administration's policy in many controversial areas: redirecting foreign policy, winning a series of tax cuts, weakening environmental regulations, asserting the primacy of the executive branch. But his interests seldom coincided with Rove's overarching goal of realignment. And Rove, forever in thrall to the mechanics of winning by dividing, consistently lacked the ability to transcend the campaign mind-set and see beyond the struggle nearest at hand. In a world made new by September 11, he put terrorism and war to work in an electoral rather than a historical context, and used them as wedge issues instead of as the unifying basis for the new political order he sought.

Why did so many people get Rove so wrong? One reason is that notwithstanding his pretensions to being a world-historic figure, Rove excelled at winning elections, which is, finally, how Washington keeps score. This leads to another reason: Journalists tend to admire tactics above all else. The books on Rove from last year dwell at length on his techniques and accept the premise of Republican dominance practically on tactical skill alone. A corollary to the Cult of the Consultant is the belief that winning an election—especially a tough one you weren't expected to win—is proof of the ability to govern. But the two are wholly distinct enterprises.

Rove's vindictiveness has also cowed his critics, at least for the time being. One reason his standing has not yet sunk as low as that of the rest of the Bush administration is his continuing ability to intimidate many of those in a position to criticize him. A Republican consultant who works downtown agreed to talk candidly for this article, but suggested that we have lunch across the river in Pentagon City, Virginia. He didn't want to be overheard. Working with Rove, he explained, was difficult enough already: "You're constantly confronting the big, booming voice of Oz."

In ways small and large, Rove has long betrayed his lack of understanding of Washington's institutional subtleties and the effective application of policy, even for the rawest political objectives. The classic example is Rove's persuading the president in 2002 to impose steep tariffs on foreign steel—a ploy he believed would win over union workers in Rust Belt swing states, ordinarily faithful Democrats, in the next presidential election. This was celebrated as a political masterstroke at the time. But within a year the tariffs were declared illegal by the World Trade Organization and nearly caused a trade war. The uproar precipitated their premature and embarrassing removal.

"It is a dangerous distraction to know as much about politics as Karl Rove knows," Bruce Reed, the domestic-policy chief in Bill Clinton's administration, told me. "If you know every single poll number on every single issue and every interest group's objection and every political factor, it can be paralyzing to try to make an honest policy decision. I think the larger, deeper problem was that they never fully appreciated that long-term success depended on making sure your policies worked."

Rove has no antecedent in modern American politics, because no president before Bush thought it wise to give a political adviser so much influence. Rove wouldn't be Rove, in other words, were Bush not Bush. That Vice President Cheney also hit a historic high-water mark for influence says a lot about how the actual president sees fit to govern. All rhetoric about "leadership" aside, Bush will be viewed as a weak executive who ceded far too much authority. Rove's failures are ultimately his.

Bush will leave behind a legacy long on ambition and short on positive results. History will draw many lessons from his presidency—about the danger of concentrating too much power in the hands of too few, about the risk of commingling politics and policy beyond a certain point, about the cost of constricting the channels of information to the Oval Office. More broadly, as the next group of presidential candidates and their gurus eases the current crew from the stage, Rove's example should serve as a caution to politicians and journalists.

The Bush administration made a virtual religion of the belief that if you act boldly, others will follow in your wake. That certainly proved to be the case with Karl Rove, for a time. But for all the fascination with what Rove was doing and thinking, little attention was given to whether or not it was working and why. This neglect encompasses many people, though one person with far greater consequences than all the others. In the end, the verdict on George W. Bush may be as simple as this: He never questioned the big, booming voice of Oz, so he never saw the little man behind the curtain.

JOSHUA GREEN is a senior editor of *The Atlantic*.

UNIT 6

New Directions for American History

Unit Selections

Key Points to Consider

- Analyze the war in Iraq. Why, after such a quick victory over Iraq's conventional forces, has it been so difficult to defeat terrorist groups? What are the prospects of ending the conflict in the foreseeable future? Discuss the methods used by the United to interrogate prisoners, what this has done to our image abroad.

- Is global warming a genuine threat, or merely a case of crying wolf? If it is a threat, which nations are more likely to be affected? What should we be doing about it?

- What are "Baby Boomers?" Discuss the conditions under which they came to maturity, and how this has affected their attitudes toward the future?

- A long time goal in the United States has been to achieve "equal opportunity" for people regardless of race, gender, or economic status. Universities were seen as a place where merit would count for more than family income or connections. Why have universities, especially elite ones, remained "bastions of privilege?" What factors stand in the way of reforming this situation?

Student Web Site

www.mhcls.com/online

Internet References

Further information regarding these Websites may be found in this book's preface or online.

American Studies Web
http://www.georgetown.edu/crossroads/asw/
National Center for Policy Analysis
http://www.public-policy.org/web.public-policy.org/index.php
The National Network for Immigrant and Refugee Rights (NNIRR)
http://www.nnirr.org/
STANDARDS: An International Journal of Multicultural Studies
http://www.colorado.edu/journals/standards
Supreme Court/Legal Information Institute
http://supct.law.cornell.edu/supct/index.html

U.S. Air Force photo by Master Sgt. Efrain Gonzalez

The breakup of the Soviet Union and the end of the Cold War could only be welcomed by those who feared a great power confrontation might mean all-out nuclear conflict. One scholar proclaimed that the collapse of Communism as a viable way of organizing society (only a few small Communist states remain and China is Communist in name only) in effect signaled "the end of history." By that he meant that liberal democracy has remained as the only political system with universal appeal. Not so, argued another scholar. He predicted that the "clash of cultures" would engender ongoing struggles in the post-Cold War era. At the time of this writing, the United States is enmeshed in a war against Iraq, the ostensible goals of which are to bring democracy to that unfortunate nation and to counter terrorism.

Evan Thomas and Eve Conant's "Refusing to Lose," analyzes the war in Iraq, which has now lasted longer than United States participation in World War II. The Bush administration claims, as it as long claimed, that real progress is being made and that victory will come if only Americans persevere. Critics have argued that we have become bogged down in a hopeless struggle, but have been unable to suggest viable solutions and are susceptible to charges that they "do not support the troops." "Pssst . . . Nobody Loves a Torturer," claims that revelations of torture at Abu Ghraib and elsewhere did more than anything else to turn the people of Iraq against the United States. President Bush and other administration officials deny the United States has employed torture. They prefer to use the euphemism "stress techniques."

The death of Rosa Parks in 2005 elicited an outpouring of testimonials to her courage in resisting segregation. She became a symbol in the civil rights movement after refusing to relinquish her seat to a white man on a Montgomery, Alabama bus in 1955. Author Ellis Cose, in "A Legend's Soul Is Rested," provides a tribute to this brave woman. Unfortunately, he writes, today's "softer" forms of segregation are more difficult to fight. He points out the alarming fact that segregation in our schools actually is increasing and "remains a fundamental American reality."

Two articles focus on the environment. "The Threatening Storm" argues that the damage wrought on New Orleans by hurricane Katrina was not a "natural disaster," it was a "man-made disaster" caused by faulty engineering and other failures. He warns that the same thing might happen again. "Global Warming: Who Loses—and Who Wins" predicts that this phenomenon could cause a "broad-based disruption of the global economy" unparalleled by any event since World War II. Gregg Easterbrook points out that in all likelihood global warming will do the most damage to those nations already mired in poverty and might actually benefit the more affluent ones.

The final two essays in this volume pertain to domestic issues. "Boomer Century" refers to that generation born between 1946 and 1964, a period when the national birthrate skyrocketed. Baby Boomers were raised in a period of unprecedented prosperity, but now have to cope with a situation of more limited resources and diminished American power. Boomers, author Joshua Zeitz points out, have "long been defined by a vain search for satisfaction." Ross Douthat, in "Does Meritocracy Work," reveals that although universities have greatly increased minority enrollments since the 1960s, socioeconomic status still exerts a dominant influence. "Through boom and recession, war and peace," he writes, "the proportion of the poorest Americans obtaining college degrees by age twenty-four has remained about six percent."

Refusing to Lose
The Iraq War

EVAN THOMAS ET AL.

The Secretary of State was cordial, but forceful and insistent. Wait until September, Condoleezza Rice told Sen. Susan Collins of Maine over the phone last week. Wait until the commanders on the ground can report their progress. "It was a strong plea for me not to join in any calls for a change of mission in Iraq," Collins recalled to NEWSWEEK. But Collins, a Republican, was thinking of her recent trip to Iraq, where she claims that both Iraqi Prime Minister Nuri al-Maliki and American commanders told her that a surge in troops in the end would not be the answer. On a more visceral level, she recalled visiting a Maine soldier recuperating at Walter Reed. The soldier was trying to decide whether to have his foot amputated. "There's a 5 percent chance his foot might be saved if he waits, but he could also lose his entire leg if he doesn't amputate now," said Collins. "I thought, 'Here is this 19-year-old with this crushing decision to make.' And I have a crushing decision to make, too."

Collins seemed fed up. She says she told Rice "that the fact that Iraqi politicians still appear to be going on vacation in August, while our men and women are out there dying, doesn't make me think we're going to see any more progress by September," when Gen. David Petraeus delivers his report on the war. Collins sighed. "It's just that my patience with the administration's strategy is exhausted." The senator introduced a bipartisan amendment to immediately wind down combat operations and instead have troops focus on counterterrorism, border security and training Iraqi troops. Collins believes her plan—broadly similar to others floating around Congress—will result in a "significant drawdown of our troops." Maybe. But military experts whom NEWSWEEK interviewed (among them senior officers serving in Iraq) suggest that for such a combination of missions to be done effectively, there would be little allowance for any reduction in troops. Given political realities, of course, adding troops is a nonstarter.

How do you manage the process of losing a war? Americans don't like the word "defeat"; certainly, President George W. Bush won't be caught using it. He continues to talk of victory in Iraq, to insist that anything less is unacceptable. But his circle of true believers seems to be getting ever smaller. It may be limited to Vice President Dick Cheney, maybe a military commander or two and a few diehard senators. For everyone else in a position of authority over the war effort, there seems to be a grim recognition that Iraq is a lost cause, or very nearly so. The real question is not whether America can win, but rather how to get out.

It is a dilemma without a right answer. Pull out now and abandon thousands of Iraqis to their deaths. Stay in and doom a smaller but still-significant number of American troops, while probably just postponing the day of reckoning, the seemingly inevitable bloodbath as Iraq collapses into full-scale civil war. And what, exactly, would withdrawal look like? Americans still remember the desperate images of the fall of Saigon—the iconic helicopter on the roof. Would Iraqis who cast their lot with the American "liberators" be seen clinging to tanks as they pull out of Baghdad?

This no-win reality is behind the current round of posturing on Capitol Hill. Some Democrats offer resolutions calling for the withdrawal of U.S. troops within a few months—knowing that there's no real chance of the measure's passing and the president's accepting it. Some Republicans argue strongly to stay the course, while others (especially the ones up for re-election) look for a middle ground—a gradual drawdown of troops by March. There's no strong evidence that a partial withdrawal would be an effective end-game, but the president probably has, at the outside, until next spring to show that his surge plan can provide the security for Iraq's fractious politicians to mend their differences. By that time, President Bush may have no choice but to cut his troop force in Iraq for the simple reason that the U.S. Army is on the verge of breaking under the strain of a war that has lasted longer than World War II.

Politicians talk; votes are cast; Washington fiddles while Iraq slowly burns. Nothing definitive is likely to happen any time soon. But the pressure will grow on the White House to face political reality: that the American people will not support an open-ended war to save a country that seems incapable of saving itself. In the new NEWSWEEK Poll, 54 percent said they were not willing to give the president until spring before making troop cutbacks and 65 percent said they were not confident that the Iraq government could control the violence after a U.S. pullout.

The White House is not in panic mode, say two White House aides not authorized to speak on the record. The aides were trying to tamp down speculation after *The New York Times* reported serious internal divisions over what to do in Iraq. But at a Senate lunch Cheney attended last week, Collins said she detected an unusual note of urgency. "The vice president comes to our lunch frequently, but he speaks rarely," Collins tells NEWSWEEK. This time, however, Cheney spoke up to second Sen. John McCain's pitch to stay the course. "There is a real step-up of activity in the White House," says Collins. "I think they are extremely worried, and they should be. There is a steady erosion of support for their policies."

Publicly, the president was defiant. "I don't think Congress ought to be running the war," he told reporters before the House voted, largely on party lines, to require that the United States withdraw most combat troops by April 1, 2008. "I think they ought to be funding the troops." Privately, however, he was more reflective. Talking to Sen. Gordon Smith of Oregon about another matter, the president got on to the subject of burying dead kids, a highly personal topic for Smith, whose 21-year-old adopted son committed suicide in 2003. Smith says he told the president that his opposition to the war was based in part on "knowing what it's like as a parent to bury a child." Smith pointedly added: "And we're doing a lot of that in this country now." Bush responded, "I understand, because I've talked to several thousand families." Smith tells NEWSWEEK: "He didn't say this, but I know that's the hardest part of his job, and I know how personally this all grieves him."

Yet Bush's personal anguish does not seem to have altered his calculations, Smith says. "His formula is, 'We'll stand down while they stand up.' I've come to believe that is a mirage," says Smith, who calls Iraqi Prime Minister Maliki a "weak reed." Smith has company: at the heart of the Republican rebellion on the Hill is disgust with Maliki and the Iraqis. Part of the idea behind pushing a troop drawdown is to force Maliki and other Iraqi leaders to settle their sectarian feuds. "My conclusion is that Iraqi political leaders won't reach honorable compromises until they have their skin in the game. Not their soldiers', but their own," says Smith. There are signs that the White House is also losing patience with Maliki & Co. The White House is seriously considering a plan to lock Maliki and the others in a room until they come up with compromises on vexing issues like sharing oil revenues, says a White House official who asked for anonymity speaking about a sensitive matter. Whether the Iraqis would go along with this scheme is another question.

To overcome a presidential veto, at least 18 Republicans will have to join with the Democrats to vote for legislation changing course on Iraq. As of now, fewer than a dozen Republicans are ready to bolt. Many eyes are on Sen. John Warner of Virginia. A genteel, preppy type who wore a kilt to his own wedding (his third), Warner is regarded as a mainstream pillar of the establishment. But Warner is also adaptable. "Watch John Warner," an aide to a Republican senator, who wasn't authorized to speak on the record, recalls being told by his boss. "He's not going to end up on the wrong side of anything." Last week Warner joined Sen. Richard Lugar, another senior statesman, to nudge the administration to prepare to head for the exits. The bill would require the administration to draw up a plan to pull out

or redeploy forces by mid-October—in other words, soon after General Petraeus presents his progress report on the surge. (An interim report released last week showed some military gains but no political progress.) As Warner swept out of his Senate office last Friday, a NEWSWEEK reporter asked him if this proposal meant that he was "defecting" from the administration on Iraq. "I do not consider this a defection, I certainly do not!" Warner exclaimed.

From Iraq, General Petraeus is watching the Washington political dance with misgivings. "I can think of few commanders in history who wouldn't have wanted more troops, more time or more unity among their partners," Petraeus told military analyst Ralph Peters last week. "However, if I could only have one, at this point in Iraq it would be more time." Petraeus, who is sympathetic to the problems faced by Iraqi leaders, has often talked ruefully of Washington time versus Baghdad time. Insurgencies (like those in Northern Ireland and the former Yugoslavia) take a long time to burn out, he has noted, and suggested that this one could go on for another decade.

The much-vaunted surge of 30,000 troops that began back in January did not actually crest until June. Only in the past month has the operational chief in Iraq, Lt. Gen. Raymond Odierno, been able to throw a pair of armed rings around Baghdad to cut off the movement of insurgents and munitions from the countryside. American forces often, it seems, play whack-a-mole—they can pacify an area, but as soon as they leave, the insurgents come back. At the same time, however, American forces are making some progress. A plan to surround and cut off Baqubah, an Al Qaeda in Iraq stronghold, seemed to fizzle in June when the insurgents fled before the troops arrived. But last week American forces got a tip from a local resident that insurgents from the group were hiding in the small town of Sherween. This time, using American planes to bomb bridges and deploying Iraqi soldiers (aided by U.S. Special Forces) on the ground, the Americans were able to cut off escape and kill or capture about 40 insurgents.

Cutting the number of troops or changing their mission, as Senator Collins and other lawmakers suggest, may not be so straightforward. A senior officer with a command role in Iraq operations, who requested anonymity to maintain his relationship with Congress, scoffed at the assumptions held by lawmakers who want to draw down forces. Concentrating on counterterrorism, stopping terrorists or munitions from coming over the border and training and equipping Iraqis are missions that in total could require more, not fewer, troops. "This isn't Harry Potter," says the official. "You can't just wave a wand." Many lawmakers want to implement the suggestions of the Iraq Study Group from last December. The Baker-Hamilton report suggested embedding U.S. troops with Iraqi units. "That's a prescription for getting American soldiers killed," says retired Gen. Barry McCaffrey.

If American soldiers start dying in ever-larger numbers, political pressure will grow to pull out of Iraq altogether. Pentagon officials wary of seeming to undercut the president decline to discuss it on the record; but Gen. Peter Pace, chairman of the Joint Chiefs, has ordered up "staff estimates"—rough cuts—of what several contingencies might entail. One sobering conclusion: withdrawal would take at least nine months and possibly as long as two years. The nine-month scenario would be "if we were told to leave quickly," and would be "under combat conditions," says a military official who also didn't want to undercut the president on the record. Translation: the U.S. military would have to fight its way out. General McCaffrey predicts a "nightmare" of ambushed convoys and a tidal wave of desperate refugees. Getting out of Iraq, it seems, would be just as horrendous as staying in.

A Legend's Soul Is Rested

Rosa Parks, 1913–2005

ELLIS COSE

For most of America, she was not quite real—more an icon than a full-fledged human being. And Rosa Parks understood that better than anyone. "I understand I am a symbol," Parks wrote in 1992. She died last Monday at the age of 92; but she ascended to the realm of legend long ago. A weary seamstress on a bus in Montgomery, Ala., in 1955 refused to stand so a white man could sit, ushering in the age of equality. So goes the "children's version of the civil-rights movement," in the words of author Diane McWhorter. The complete story is considerably less child friendly. It would include at least a reference to Thomas Edward Brooks, a 21-year-old black soldier who got on a Montgomery bus in 1950. Brooks made the mistake of entering through the front door instead of the back. For that, as authors Donnie Williams and Wayne Greenhaw relate in "The Thunder of Angels," a policeman bashed him on the head with a billy club and shot him dead. At least two other black men were similarly killed in the years leading up to Parks's act of civil disobedience. Parks's quiet protest coincided with the NAACP's search for the perfect test case. Her courage led to the creation of the Montgomery Improvement Association, headed by Martin Luther King Jr., chosen in part because he was an outsider and thereby less subject to reprisals. The Montgomery Bus Boycott made history—and heroes out of both King and Parks. But the fame did not lead to fortune.

She and her husband lost their jobs and moved to Detroit, where they struggled financially. "I always thought it was a mistake for them [the black leadership] to let her leave Montgomery. I always thought Rosa Parks should have left this earth from the city she loved most and helped to make sacred," said the Rev. Fred Shuttlesworth, another civil-rights icon.

In 1964, Parks endorsed a young Detroit lawyer for Congress. And after John Conyers won, he hired her as a receptionist and assistant. "I didn't do it out of sympathy for her," said Conyers. She was a living connection to the civil-rights movement who happened to add a bit of celebrity cachet to the place. "People came to my office to see her," Conyers recalled, and they invariably left impressed with her humility and grace. "She was one of the most approachable heroes you could ever encounter," said Betty DeRamus, a columnist for The *Detroit*

News. Parks retired in 1988 and stayed largely out of the public eye until 1994, when she was attacked in her home and robbed by a crack user. Following that assault, fellow Detroiters saw to it that she was moved to a high rise on the Detroit River.

In the twilight of her life, Parks struggled with a range of woes, including poor health and dementia. She never ceased being a symbol of the epic battle for human rights; and she never claimed victory in the larger war. "I try to keep hope alive, but that's not always the easiest thing to do," she wrote in 1992. As *The Detroit News* observed after her death, her adopted home "is today the most segregated metropolitan area in the nation." And segregation remains a fundamental American reality.

In the newly published "The Shame of the Nation," Jonathan Kozol sheds a book's length of tears over segregation in schools. He cites research that shows segregation is worsening and notes that three fourths of black and Latino children attend schools with no or relatively few whites. It is a daunting task to convince poor, minority kids they can learn "when they are cordoned off by a society that isn't sure they really can," writes Kozol.

'I try to keep hope alive, but that's not always the easiest thing to do,' Parks wrote.

In their study of the Montgomery boycott, authors Williams and Greenhaw quote a white woman who, as a 13-year-old, witnessed the murder of the black soldier on the bus. The world has forgotten, she said, "about the white children who grew up in that society. They forgot that we suffered, too. I had nightmares for years, and I still can't get it off my mind sometimes."

It's easy looking back some 50 years to see the insanity of the old Southern system. It is much more difficult to see (or become outraged about) the harm in today's softer form of segregation. For despite the damage it may do psychologically, economically, and to the social fabric of our collective community, it doesn't generally leave dead bodies sprawled on the ground. But it's far from the brotherhood Rosa Parks dreamed of and spent her life trying to create.

Ending the Fool's Game
Saving Civilization

DOUGLAS MATTERN

"A fool's game" is how retired General George Lee Butler, former head of the U.S. Strategic Command, refers to nuclear weapons. He says that these weapons offer no security and their complete elimination is "the only defensible goal."

A fool's game, indeed—and the United States is the biggest fool for allowing the power elite to maintain a stockpile of over thirty thousand nuclear weapons more than a decade after the end of the Cold War.

The ultimate absurdity is that thousands of U.S. and Russian nuclear warheads remain on hair-trigger alert and could be launched on a few minutes' notice, potentially destroying both countries in less than an hour. As Bruce Blair, head of the Center for Defense Information (CDI) and a former Minuteman Missile Launch officer states, "Both sides are cocked on hair-triggers . . . and both sides can retarget a missile in seconds—just a few strokes on a keyboard."

The result is that the United States continues to be under the daily threat of nuclear incineration whether initiated by an accidental missile launch, miscalculation, or design. Regarding miscalculation, the United States and Soviet Union had come frighteningly close to nuclear war over the years, with mere luck playing a major role in averting disaster.

Robert McNamara, secretary of defense in the Kennedy and Johnson administrations, acknowledges that during the Cuban missile crisis "we came within a hairbreadth of nuclear war without realizing it." He said, "It's no credit to us that we missed nuclear war—at least we had to be lucky as well as wise."

It can only be guessed how many other close calls there have been over the years but here are a few documented examples:

1979: A CNN Cold War program reported that a technician at the North American Air Defense Command mistakenly placed a training tape into the main systems at NORAD's Cheyenne Mountain Complex in Colorado. The tape caused NORAD's early-warning system computer to respond that the United States was undergoing a massive Soviet missile attack. NORAD officials were alerted but within minutes the error was discovered, ending the threat of launching U.S. missiles in retaliation. This incident was one of five missile warning system failures that occurred over an eight-month period.

1980: In the August 14, 1983, issue of *Parade,* Jack Anderson reports that on November 19, 1980, two Air Force missile officers were conducting a drill of a simulated missile launch of their Titan missile at McConnell Air Force Base near Wichita, Kansas. When Captain Henry Winsett and First Lieutenant David Mosley turned the keys for the simulated launch, something went wrong. They received a message of "Launch Sequence Go," which means the real missile launch sequence is underway. Fortunately, Winsett had the good sense to shut the missile down before it could be launched. Mosley said it couldn't be determined whether the missile's guidance system would have steered the missile to a target in Russia, which would assuredly have resulted in Soviet retaliation. But, he said, it would have gone somewhere "north." This close call still gives him tremors.

1984: As reported on the CNN Cold War program, in August 1984 a low-ranking officer at Soviet Pacific fleet headquarters in Vladivostok broadcast a war alert to Soviet forces at sea. For thirty minutes, until it was determined that the alert was false, Soviet ship commanders sent back urgent inquiries about the alert as they prepared for combat. In the meantime, U.S. and Japanese forces also went to a higher alert status.

1995: The Center for Defense Information (CDI) and several other reliable sources report that in 1995 the monitors of the Russian Strategic Rocket Force at the Olengrosk early-warning radar site registered the launch of a U.S.-Norwegian research missile probe of the upper atmosphere. To the Russians, the missile's trajectory looked like a U.S. Trident missile, which carries multiple nuclear warheads. This set off alarms at the Russian nuclear weapons command, which notified President Boris Yeltsin, who reportedly activated his "nuclear briefcase." For a few minutes perhaps the fate of the United States—and Western civilization—hung on Yeltsin's judgment.

All of these incidents constituted alarmingly close calls. Blair believes that the closest the Americans and Soviets ever came to accidental nuclear war, however, was the 1983 incident involving Soviet Lieutenant Colonel Stanislav Petrov. His story has been reported by the BBC, on *NBC Dateline* and *NOVA,* and in the *London Daily Mail* and other sources and is perhaps the most dramatic of all the reported close calls, other than the Cuban Missile Crisis. This story could rightly be called "A Forgotten Hero of Our Time."

The story of Stanislav Petrov is perhaps the most dramatic of all the reported close calls, other than the Cuban Missile Crisis.

On September 26, 1983, Petrov was in charge of two hundred men, mostly officers, operating the Russian early-warning bunker just south of Moscow. Petrov's job that fateful night was to lead a staff monitoring incoming signals from satellites. He reported directly to the Russian early-warning system headquarters which reported directly to the Soviet leader on the possibility of launching a retaliatory attack.

It's important to note that this was a period of very high tension between the United States and the Soviet Union. U.S. President Ronald Reagan was continually referring to the Soviets as "the evil empire." The Soviet military had shot down a Korean passenger jet just three weeks prior to this incident and the United States and North Atlantic Treaty Organization were organizing a military exercise that centered on using tactical nuclear weapons in Europe. Some Soviet leaders were worried the West was planning a nuclear attack.

In an interview with the *Daily Mail,* Petrov recalled that night, when computer screens were showing an attack launched by the United States. He said, "I felt as if I'd been punched in my nervous system. There was a huge map of the States with a U.S. base lit up, showing that the missiles had been launched."

For several minutes Petrov held a phone in one hand and an intercom in the other as alarms blared, red lights blinked, and computers reported that U.S. missiles were on their way. In the midst of this horrific chaos and terror—the prospect of the end of civilization itself—Petrov made a historic decision not to alert higher authorities, somehow believing that, contrary to what all the sophisticated equipment was reporting, the alarm was an error.

"I didn't want to make a mistake," Petrov said. "I made a decision and that was it." As the *Daily Mail* states, "Had Petrov cracked and triggered a response, Soviet missiles would have rained down on U.S. cities. In turn, that would have brought a devastating response from the Pentagon."

As agonizing minutes passed, Petrov's decision proved correct. A computer error had falsely signaled the U.S. attack. In the *Daily Mail* interview, Petrov said, "After it was over, I drank half a liter of vodka as if it were only a glass and slept for 28 hours." He commented, "In principle, a nuclear war could have broken out. The whole world could have been destroyed."

In increasingly superficial modern societies that praise celebrities and all manner of fools as role models, many legitimate heroes go unnoticed and without reward. In the case of Petrov, he was dismissed from the army on a pension that in succeeding years would prove nearly worthless. Petrov's superiors were reprimanded for the computer error and all in the group were subjected to the same treatment.

The *Daily Mirror* report found Petrov's health destroyed by the enormous stress of the incident. His wife died of cancer and he lives alone in a second-floor flat in a small town about thirty miles from Moscow. "Once I would have liked to have been given some credit for what I did," said Petrov. "But it is too long ago and today everything is emotionally burned out inside me. I still have a bitter feeling inside my soul as I remember the way I was treated."

In a November 12, 2000, interview with Petrov, *Dateline* reporter Dennis Murphy said, "I know you don't regard yourself as a hero, Colonel, but, belatedly, on behalf of the people in Washington, New York, Philadelphia, Chicago, thank you for being on duty that night."

The twentieth anniversary of this incident revealed, once again, how little has changed with the thousands of nuclear warheads still on hair-trigger alert. The utter madness of this situation was demonstrated in a recent report by the BBC that some scientists and military people are worried that a small asteroid passing close to the Earth could accidentally trigger a nuclear war if mistaken for a missile strike.

The greatest terrorism by far is that each day the people of the world continue to be under the threat of nuclear incineration whether by an accidental missile launch, a computer error, or design.

This dark scenario is exacerbated by President George W. Bush's nuclear weapons policy. Most ominous is National Security Presidential Directive 17, signed by Bush. This document declares that the United States reserves the right to respond with overwhelming force—including nuclear weapons—to the use of weapons of mass destruction against the United States, its forces abroad, friends, and allies. Military analyst William Arkin writes that the Bush administration's war planning "moves nuclear weapons out of their long-established special category and lumps them in with all the other military options."

The Bush team is also determined to build a new generation of tactical nuclear weapons designed to attack hardened underground bunkers. The United States has, for the first time in fourteen years, resumed production of plutonium parts for nuclear bombs. The Energy Department announced that plans are underway for a factory that could produce parts of hundreds of nuclear weapons a year. Congress gave the Bush team funding for this production—and just about everything it requested in the massive 2004 military budget of $401 billion. The CDI reports that U.S. military spending is equal to the military spending of the next twenty countries combined.

Blair reports that both the United States and Russia remain preoccupied with preparing to fight a large-scale nuclear war with each other. U.S. spy planes monitor the Russian coast and

U.S. submarines still trail Russian submarines as soon as they leave port.

As the nuclear crisis escalates with scant reporting by the media, the words of General Douglas McArthur in a speech to the Congress of the Republic of the Philippines on July 5, 1961, seem appropriate:

> But this very triumph of scientific annihilation—this very success of invention—has destroyed the possibility of war's being a medium for the practical settlement of international differences. . . . Global war has become a Frankenstein to destroy both sides. . . . If you lose you are annihilated. If you win, you stand only to lose. No longer does it possess even the chance of the winner of a duel. It contains now only the germs of double suicide.

The nuclear policymakers have known the "double-suicide" consequences of nuclear weapons for decades. In the 1960s, McGeorge Bundy, assistant to President John F. Kennedy, said, "In the real world even one hydrogen bomb on one city would be a catastrophe; ten bombs on ten cities would be a disaster beyond history. A hundred, or even less, would be the end of civilization."

Today, in this fourth year of the new millennium, thirty thousand nuclear weapons remain stockpiled, while the nuclear club has expanded to include India, Israel, Pakistan, and possibly North Korea. And a recent International Atomic Energy Commission report states that up to forty other countries may be capable of building nuclear weapons.

Terrorism is a burning problem that the United States must counter. But the greatest terrorism by far is that each day the people of the world continue to be under the threat of nuclear incineration whether by an accidental missile launch, a computer error, or design.

An intelligent visitor from another world might conclude that Euripides was correct in saying, "Whom the gods would destroy they first make mad." Certainly the present nuclear condition is a madness created by those in power. It must be ended before it is too late, as Kennedy stated in his speech before the United Nations General Assembly on September 25, 1961:

> Every man, woman and child lives under a nuclear sword of Damocles, hanging by the slenderest of threads, capable of being cut at any moment by accident or miscalculation or madness. The weapons of war must be abolished before they abolish us.

We cannot count on a Petrov to always be on duty, or on the luck that has played a big role in averting nuclear war to this date. We can only count on ourselves to have the intelligence and the respect for humanity and life on this planet to mobilize with an unyielding determination to apply a constant pressure on world governments—particularly the United States as the leading culprit in the new escalation—until these weapons are abolished "before they abolish us."

The starting point is for all nuclear warheads to be removed from hair-trigger alert, placed in storage, and constantly inspected by representatives of the United States, Russia, and the United Nations. This would eliminate the possibility of a nuclear exchange starting by an accidental missile launch or computer error.

Beyond this first step, the goal that can never be compromised is the total elimination of nuclear weapons from the face of the Earth. Only then will humanity be liberated from the "fool's game" and the nuclear nightmare that began with the mushroom cloud over the obliterated city of Hiroshima, Japan, on August 6, 1945.

DOUGLAS MATTERN is president of the Association of World Citizens, a San Francisco-based international peace organization with branches in over thirty countries and nongovernmental organization status with the United Nations, including consultative status with the UN Economic and Social Council.

Pssst . . . Nobody Loves a Torturer

Ask any American soldier in Iraq when the general population really turned against the United States and he will say, "Abu Ghraib."

FAREED ZAKARIA

As President Bush's approval ratings sink at home, the glee across the globe rises. He remains the most unpopular political figure in the world, and newspapers from Europe to Asia are delighting in his troubles. Last week's protests in Mar del Plata were happily replayed on televisions everywhere. So what is the leader of the free world to do? Well, I have a suggestion that might improve Bush's image abroad—and it doesn't require that Karen Hughes go anywhere. It would actually help Bush at home as well, and it has the additional virtue of being the right thing to do. It's simple: end the administration's disastrous experiment with officially sanctioned torture.

We now have plenty of documents and testimonials that make plain that the administration created an atmosphere in which the interrogation of prisoners could lapse into torture. After 9/11, high up in the administration—at the White House and the Pentagon—officials and lawyers were asked to find ways to bend and stretch the traditional rules of war. Donald Rumsfeld publicly declared that the Geneva Conventions did not apply to the war against Al Qaeda. Whether or not these legalisms were correct, their most important effect was the message they sent down the chain of command: "Push the envelope."

For example, when Rumsfeld read a report documenting some of the new interrogation procedures at Guantanamo in November 2002, including having detainees stand for four hours, he scribbled a note in the margin, "Why is standing limited to 4 hours? . . . I stand for 8 hours a day." (Rumsfeld probably does not stand for eight hours, scarcely clad and barely fed, with bright lights, prison guards and attack dogs trained on him.) The signal Rumsfeld was sending was clear: "Get tougher." No one at the top was outlining what soldiers should not do, which lines they should not cross, which laws they should remember to adhere to strictly. The Pentagon's own report after investigating Abu Ghraib, by Gen. George Fay, speaks of "doctrinal confusion . . . a lack of doctrine . . . [and] systemic failures" as the causes for the incidents of torture. In a 2 million-person bureaucracy, such calculated ambiguities will inevitably lead to something like Abu Ghraib.

And the incidents clearly go well beyond Abu Ghraib. During the past few months, declassified documents and testimony from Army officers make abundantly clear that torture and abuse of prisoners is something that has become quite widespread since 9/11. The most recent evidence comes from autopsies of 44 prisoners who have died in Iraq and Afghanistan in U.S. custody. Most died under circumstances that suggest torture. The reports use words like "strangulation," "asphyxiation" and "blunt force injuries." Even the "natural" deaths were caused by "Arteriosclerotic Cardiovascular disease"—in other words, sudden heart attacks.

Sen. John McCain has proposed making absolutely clear in law that the United States does not permit the torture of prisoners—returning America to the position it had taken for five decades. McCain's amendment, endorsed by Colin Powell, passed the Senate last month by 90 to 9 in a stunning rebuke of administration policy. But Republicans in the House are trying to kill it. Vice President Cheney is making great exertions to gut it with loopholes. The White House has threatened to veto the entire defense budget, to which McCain's proposal was originally attached, unless his ban is removed. White House spokesmen don't answer questions about the bill plainly, and Cheney simply refuses to explain his views at all. (As the writer Andrew Sullivan has noted, someone needs to remind the vice president that he is an elected and accountable public servant, not a monarch.)

This is a case of more than just bad public relations. Ask any soldier in Iraq when the general population really turned against the United States and he will say, "Abu Ghraib." A few months before the scandal broke, Coalition Provisional Authority polls showed Iraqi support for the occupation at 63 percent. A month after Abu Ghraib, the number was 9 percent. Polls showed that 71 percent of Iraqis were surprised by the revelations. Most telling, 61 percent of Iraqis polled believed that no one would be punished for the torture at Abu Ghraib. Of the 29 percent who said they believed someone would be punished, 52 percent said that such punishment would extend only to "the little people."

America washes its dirty linen in public. When scandals such as this one hit, they do sully America's image in the world.

But what usually also gets broadcast around the world is the vivid reality that the United States forces accountability and punishes wrongdoing, even at the highest levels. Initially, people the world over thought Americans were crazy during Watergate, but they came to respect a rule of law so strong that even a president could not break it. But today, what angers friends of America abroad is not that abuses like those at Abu Ghraib

happened. Some lapses are probably an inevitable consequence of war, terrorism and insurgencies. What angers them is that no one beyond a few "little people" have been punished, the system has not been overhauled, and even now, after all that has happened, the White House is spending time, effort and precious political capital in a strange, stubborn and surely futile quest to preserve the option to torture.

Global Warming
Who Loses—and Who Wins?

Climate change in the next century (and beyond) could be enormously disruptive, spreading disease and sparking wars. It could also be a windfall for some people, businesses, and nations. A guide to how we all might get along in a warming world.

GREGG EASTERBROOK

Coastal cities inundated, farming regions parched, ocean currents disrupted, tropical diseases spreading, glaciers melting—an artificial greenhouse effect could generate countless tribulations. ¶ If Earth's climate changes meaningfully—and the National Academy of Sciences, previously skeptical, said in 2005 that signs of climate change have become significant—there could be broadbased disruption of the global economy unparalleled by any event other than World War II.

Economic change means winners as well as losers. Huge sums will be made and lost if the global climate changes. Everyone wonders what warming might do to the environment—but what might it do to the global distribution of money and power?

Whether mainly natural or mainly artificial, climate change could bring different regions of the world tremendous benefits as well as drastic problems. The world had been mostly warming for thousands of years before the industrial era began, and that warming has been indisputably favorable to the spread of civilization. The trouble is that the world's economic geography is today organized according to a climate that has largely prevailed since the Middle Ages—runaway climate change would force big changes in the physical ordering of society. In the past, small climate changes have had substantial impact on agriculture, trade routes, and the types of products and commodities that sell. Larger climate shifts have catalyzed the rise and fall of whole societies. The Mayan Empire, for instance, did not disappear "mysteriously"; it likely fell into decline owing to decades of drought that ruined its agricultural base and deprived its cities of drinking water. On the other side of the coin, Europe's Medieval Warm Period, which lasted from around 1000 to 1400, was essential to the rise of Spain, France, and England: Those clement centuries allowed the expansion of farm production, population, cities, and universities, which in turn set the stage for the Industrial Revolution. Unless greenhouse-effect theory is completely wrong—and science increasingly supports the idea that it is right—21st-century climate change means that sweeping social and economic changes are in the works.

To date the greenhouse-effect debate has been largely carried out in abstractions—arguments about the distant past (what *do* those 100,000-year-old ice cores in Greenland really tell us about ancient temperatures, anyway?) coupled to computer-model conjecture regarding the 22nd century, with the occasional Hollywood disaster movie thrown in. Soon, both abstraction and postapocalyptic fantasy could be pushed aside by the economic and political realities of a warming world. If the global climate continues changing, many people and nations will find themselves in possession of land and resources of rising value, while others will suffer dire losses—and these winners and losers could start appearing faster than you might imagine. Add artificially triggered climate change to the volatility already initiated by globalization, and the next few decades may see previously unthinkable levels of economic upheaval, in which fortunes are won and lost based as much on the physical climate as on the business climate.

It may sound odd to ask of global warming, What's in it for me? But the question is neither crass nor tongue-in-cheek. The ways in which climate change could skew the world's distribution of wealth should help us appreciate just how profoundly an artificial greenhouse effect might shake our lives. Moreover, some of the lasting effects of climate change are likely to come not so much from the warming itself but from how we react to it: If the world warms appreciably, men and women will not sit by idly, eating bonbons and reading weather reports; there will be instead what economists call "adaptive response," most likely a great deal of it. Some aspects of this response may inflame tensions between those who are winning and those who are losing. How people, the global economy, and the international power structure adapt to climate change may influence how we live for generations. If the world warms, who will win? Who will lose? And what's in it for you?

Land

Real estate might be expected to appreciate steadily in value during the 21st century, given that both the global population and global prosperity are rising. The supply of land is fixed, and if there's a fixed supply of something but a growing demand, appreciation should be automatic. That's unless climate change increases the supply of land by warming currently frosty areas while throwing the amount of *desirable* land into tremendous flux. My hometown of Buffalo, New York, for example, is today so déclassé that some of its stately Beaux-Arts homes, built during the Gilded Age and overlooking a park designed by Frederick Law Olmsted, sell for about the price of one-bedroom condos in Boston or San Francisco. If a warming world makes the area less cold and snowy, Buffalo might become one of the country's desirable addresses.

At the same time, Arizona and Nevada, blazing growth markets today, might become unbearably hot and see their real-estate markets crash. If the oceans rise, Florida's rapid growth could be, well, swamped by an increase in its perilously high groundwater table. Houston could decline, made insufferable by worsened summertime humidity, while the splendid, rustic Laurentide Mountains region north of Montreal, if warmed up a bit, might transmogrify into the new Poconos.

These are just a few of many possible examples. Climate change could upset the applecarts of real-estate values all over the world, with low-latitude properties tanking while high latitudes become the Sun Belt of the mid-21st century.

Local changes in housing demand are only small beer. To consider the big picture, examine a Mercator projection of our planet, and observe how the Earth's landmasses spread from the equator to the poles. Assume global warming is reasonably uniform. (Some computer models suggest that warming will vary widely by region; for the purposes of this article, suffice it to say that all predictions regarding an artificial greenhouse effect are extremely uncertain.) The equatorial and low-latitude areas of the world presumably will become hotter and less desirable as places of habitation, plus less valuable in economic terms; with a few exceptions, these areas are home to developing nations where living standards are already low.

So where is the high-latitude landmass that might grow more valuable in a warming world? By accident of geography, except for Antarctica nearly all such land is in the Northern Hemisphere, whose continents are broad west-to-east. Only a relatively small portion of South America, which narrows as one travels south, is high latitude, and none of Africa or Australia is. (Cape Town is roughly the same distance from the equator as Cape Hatteras; Melbourne is about the same distance from the equator as Manhattan.) More specifically, nearly all the added land-value benefits of a warming world might accrue to Alaska, Canada, Greenland, Russia, and Scandinavia.

This raises the possibility that an artificial greenhouse effect could harm nations that are already hard pressed and benefit nations that are already affluent. If Alaska turned temperate, it would drive conservationists to distraction, but it would also open for development an area more than twice the size of Texas. Rising world temperatures might throw Indonesia, Mexico, Nigeria, and other low-latitude nations into generations of misery, while causing Canada, Greenland, and Scandinavia to experience a rip-roarin' economic boom. Many Greenlanders are already cheering the retreat of glaciers, since this melting stands to make their vast island far more valuable. Last July, *The Wall Street Journal* reported that the growing season in the portion of Greenland open to cultivation is already two weeks longer than it was in the 1970s.

And Russia! For generations poets have bemoaned this realm as cursed by enormous, foreboding, harsh Siberia. What if the region in question were instead enormous, temperate, inviting Siberia? Climate change could place Russia in possession of the largest new region of pristine, exploitable land since the sailing ships of Europe first spied the shores of what would be called North America. The snows of Siberia cover soils that have never been depleted by controlled agriculture. What's more, beneath Siberia's snow may lie geologic formations that hold vast deposits of fossil fuels, as well as mineral resources. When considering ratification of the Kyoto Protocol to regulate greenhouse gases, the Moscow government dragged its feet, though the treaty was worded to offer the Russians extensive favors. Why might this have happened? Perhaps because Russia might be much better off in a warming world: Warming's benefits to Russia could exceed those to all other nations combined.

Of course, it could be argued that politicians seldom give much thought—one way or the other—to actions whose value will become clear only after they leave office, so perhaps Moscow does not have a grand strategy to warm the world for its own good. But a warmer world may be much to Russia's liking, whether it comes by strategy or accident. And how long until high-latitude nations realize global warming might be in their interests? In recent years, Canada has increased its greenhouse-gas output more rapidly than most other rich countries. Maybe this is a result of prosperity and oil-field development—or maybe those wily Canadians have a master plan for their huge expanse of currently uninhabitable land.

Global warming might do more for the North, however, than just opening up new land. Temperatures are rising on average, but *when* are they rising? Daytime? Nighttime? Winter? Summer? One fear about artificially triggered climate change has been that global warming would lead to scorching summer-afternoon highs, which would kill crops and brown out the electric power grid. Instead, so far a good share of the warming—especially in North America—has come in the form of nighttime and winter lows that are less low. Higher lows reduce the harshness of winter in northern climes and moderate the demand for energy. And fewer freezes allow extended growing seasons, boosting farm production. In North America, spring comes ever earlier—in recent years, trees have flowered in Washington, D.C., almost a week earlier on average than a generation ago. People may find this creepy, but earlier springs and milder winters can have economic value to agriculture—and lest we forget, all modern societies, including the United States, are grounded in agriculture.

If a primary impact of an artificially warmed world is to make land in Canada, Greenland, Russia, Scandinavia, and the United States more valuable, this could have three powerful effects on the 21st-century global situation.

First, historically privileged northern societies might not decline geopolitically, as many commentators have predicted. Indeed, the great age of northern power may lie ahead, if Earth's very climate is on the verge of conferring boons to that part of the world. Should it turn out that headlong fossil-fuel combustion by northern nations has set in motion climate change that strengthens the relative world position of those same nations, future essayists will have a field day. But the prospect is serious. By the middle of the 21st century, a new global balance of power may emerge in which Russia and America are once again the world's paired superpowers—only this time during a Warming War instead of a Cold War.

Second, if northern societies find that climate change makes them more wealthy, the quest for world equity could be dealt a huge setback. Despite the popular misconception, globalized economies have been a positive force for increased equity. As the Indian economist Surjit Bhalla has shown, the developing world produced 29 percent of the globe's income in 1950; by 2000 that share had risen to 42 percent, while the developing world's share of population rose at a slower rate. All other things being equal, we might expect continued economic globalization to distribute wealth more widely. But if climate change increases the value of northern land and resources, while leaving nations near the equator hotter and wracked by storms or droughts, all other things would not be equal.

That brings us to the third great concern: If climate change causes developing nations to falter, and social conditions within them deteriorate, many millions of jobless or hungry refugees may come to the borders of the favored North, demanding to be let in. If the very Earth itself turns against poor nations, punishing them with heat and storms, how could the United States morally deny the refugees succor?

Shifts in the relative values of places and resources have often led to war, and it is all too imaginable that climate change will cause nations to envy each other's territory. This envy is likely to run both north-south and updown. North-south? Suppose climate change made Brazil less habitable, while bringing an agreeable mild clime to the vast and fertile Argentinean pampas to Brazil's south. São Paulo is already one of the world's largest cities. Would a desperate, overheated Brazil of the year 2037—its population exploding—hesitate to attack Argentina for cool, inviting land? Now consider the up-down prospect: the desire to leave low-lying areas for altitude. Here's an example: Since its independence, in 1947, Pakistan has kept a hand in the internal affairs of Afghanistan. Today Americans view this issue through the lens of the Taliban and al-Qaeda, but from Islamabad's perspective, the goal has always been to keep Afghanistan available as a place for retreat, should Pakistan lose a war with India. What if the climate warms, rendering much of Pakistan unbearable to its citizens? (Temperatures of 100-plus degrees are already common in the Punjab.) Afghanistan's high plateaus, dry and rocky as they are, might start looking pleasingly temperate as Pakistan warms, and the Afghans might see yet another army headed their way.

A warming climate could cause other landgrabs on a national scale. Today Greenland is a largely self-governing territory of Denmark that the world leaves in peace because no nation covets its shivering expanse. Should the Earth warm, Copenhagen might assert greater jurisdiction over Greenland, or stronger governments might scheme to seize this dwarf continent, which is roughly three times the size of Texas. Today Antarctica is under international administration, and this arrangement is generally accepted because the continent has no value beyond scientific research. If the world warmed for along time—and it would likely take centuries for the Antarctic ice sheet to melt completely—international jockeying to seize or conquer Antarctica might become intense. Some geologists believe large oil deposits are under the Antarctic crust: In earlier epochs, the austral pole was densely vegetated and had conditions suitable for the formation of fossil fuels.

And though I've said to this point that Canada would stand to become more valuable in a warming world, actually, Canada and Nunavut would. For centuries, Europeans drove the indigenous peoples of what is now Canada farther and farther north. In 1993, Canada agreed to grant a degree of independence to the primarily Inuit population of Nunavut, and this large, cold region in the country's northeast has been mainly self-governing since 1999. The Inuit believe they are ensconced in the one place in this hemisphere that the descendants of Europe will never, ever want. This could turn out to be wrong.

For investors, finding attractive land to buy and hold for a warming world is fraught with difficulties, particularly when looking abroad. If considering plots on the pampas, for example, should one negotiate with the current Argentinian owners or the future Brazilian ones? Perhaps a safer route would be the contrarian one, focused on the likelihood of falling land values in places people may leave. If strict carbon-dioxide regulations are enacted, corporations will shop for "offsets," including projects that absorb carbon dioxide from the sky. Growing trees is a potential greenhouse-gas offset, and can be done comparatively cheaply in parts of the developing world, even on land that people may stop wanting. If you jump into the greenhouse-offset business, what you might plant is leucaena, a rapidly growing tree species suited to the tropics that metabolizes carbon dioxide faster than most trees. But you'll want to own the land in order to control the sale of the credits. Consider a possible sequence of events: First, climate change makes parts of the developing world even less habitable than they are today; then, refugees flee these areas; finally, land can be snapped up at Filene's Basement prices—and used to grow leucaena trees.

Water

If Al Gore's movie, *An Inconvenient Truth,* is to be believed, you should start selling coastal real estate now. Gore's film maintains that an artificial greenhouse effect could raise sea levels 20 feet in the near future, flooding Manhattan, San Francisco, and dozens of other cities; Micronesia would simply disappear below the waves. Gore's is the doomsday number, but the scientific consensus is worrisome enough: In 2005, the National Academy of Sciences warned that oceans may rise between four inches and three feet by the year 2100. Four inches may not sound like a lot, but it would imperil parts of coastal Florida and the Carolinas, among other places. A three-foot sea-level rise would flood significant portions of Bangladesh, threaten the national survival of the Netherlands, and damage many coastal cities, while submerging pretty much all of the world's trendy beach destinations to boot. And the Asian Tigers? Shanghai and Hong Kong sit right on the water. Raise the deep a few feet, and these Tiger cities would be abandoned.

The global temperature increase of the last century—about one degree Fahrenheit—was modest and did not cause any dangerous sea-level rise. Sea-level worries turn on the possibility that there is some nonlinear aspect of the climate system, a "tipping point" that could cause the rate of global warming to accelerate markedly. One reason global warming has not happened as fast as expected appears to be that the oceans have absorbed much of the carbon dioxide emitted by human activity. Studies suggest, however, that the ability of the oceans to absorb carbon dioxide may be slowing; as the absorption rate declines, atmospheric buildup will happen faster, and climate change could speed up. At the first sign of an increase in the rate of global warming: Sell, sell, sell your coastal properties. Unload those London and Seattle waterfront holdings. Buy land and real property in Omaha or Ontario.

The Inuit believe they are ensconced in the one place in this hemisphere that the descendants of Europe will never, ever want. This could turn out to be wrong.

An artificial greenhouse effect may also alter ocean currents in unpredictable ways. Already there is some evidence that the arctic currents are changing, while the major North Atlantic current that moves warm water north from the equator maybe losing energy. If the North Atlantic current falters, temperatures could fall in Europe even as the world overall warms. Most of Europe lies to the north of Maine yet is temperate because the North Atlantic current carries huge volumes of warm water to the seas off Scotland; that warm water is Europe's weathermaker. Geological studies show that the North Atlantic current has stopped in the past. If this current stops again because of artificial climate change, Europe might take on the climate of present-day Newfoundland. As a result, it might depopulate, while the economic value of everything within its icy expanse declines. The European Union makes approximately the same contribution to the global economy as the United States makes: Significantly falling temperatures in Europe could trigger a worldwide recession.

While staying ready to sell your holdings in Europe, look for purchase opportunities near the waters of the Arctic Circle. In 2005, a Russian research ship became the first surface vessel ever to reach the North Pole without the aid of an icebreaker. If arctic sea ice melts, shipping traffic will begin transiting the North Pole. Andrew Revkin's 2006 book, *The North Pole Was Here*, profiles Pat Broe, who in 1997 bought the isolated far-north port of Churchill, Manitoba, from the Canadian government for $7. Assuming arctic ice continues to melt, the world's

cargo vessels may begin sailing due north to shave thousands of miles off their trips, and the port of Churchill may be bustling. If arctic polar ice disappears and container vessels course the North Pole seas, shipping costs may decline—to the benefit of consumers. Asian manufacturers, especially, should see their costs of shipping to the United States and the European Union fall. At the same time, heavily trafficked southern shipping routes linking East Asia to Europe and to America's East Coast could see less traffic, and port cities along that route—such as Singapore—might decline. Concurrently, good relations with Nunavut could become of interest to the world's corporations.

Oh, and there may be oil under the arctic waters. Who would own that oil? The United States, Russia, Canada, Norway, and Denmark already assert legally complex claims to parts of the North Pole seas—including portions that other nations consider open waters not subject to sovereign control. Today it seems absurd to imagine the governments of the world fighting over the North Pole seas, but in the past many causes of battle have seemed absurd before the artillery fire began. Canada is already conducting naval exercises in the arctic waters, and making no secret of this.

Then again, perhaps ownership of these waters will go in an entirely different direction. The 21st century is likely to see a movement to create private-property rights in the ocean (ocean property rights are the most promising solution to overfishing of the open seas). Private-property rights in the North Pole seas, should they come into existence, might generate a rush to rival the Sooners' settlement of Oklahoma in the late 1800s.

Whatever happens to our oceans, climate change might also cause economic turmoil by affecting freshwater supplies. Today nearly all primary commodities, including petroleum, appear in ample supply. Freshwater is an exception: China is depleting aquifers at an alarming rate in order to produce enough rice to feed itself, while freshwater is scarce in much of the Middle East and parts of Africa. Freshwater depletion is especially worrisome in Egypt, Libya, and several Persian Gulf states. Greenhouse-effect science is so uncertain that researchers have little idea whether a warming world would experience more or less precipitation. If it turns out that rain and snow decline as the world warms, dwindling supplies of drinking water and freshwater for agriculture may be the next resource emergency. For investors this would suggest a cautious view of the booms in China and Dubai, as both places may soon face freshwater-supply problems. (Cost-effective desalinization continues to elude engineers.) On the other hand, where water rights are available in these areas, grab them.

Much of the effect that global warming will have on our water is speculative, so water-related climate change will be a high-risk/high-reward matter for investors and societies alike. The biggest fear is that artificially triggered climate change will shift rainfall away from today's productive breadbasket areas and toward what are now deserts or, worse, toward the oceans. (From the human perspective, all ocean rain represents wasted freshwater.) The reason Malthusian catastrophes have not occurred as humanity has grown is that for most of the last half century, farm yields have increased faster than population. But the global agricultural system is perilously poised on the

A 401 (K) for a Warming World

Climate change could have a broad impact on industrial sectors, and thus help or hurt your stock investments and retirement funds. What types of equity might you want to favor or avoid?

Big Pharma. Rising temperatures might extend the range of tropical diseases such as malaria and dengue fever. A 2005 World Health Organization report suggested that global warming may already cause 150,000 deaths annually, mainly by spreading illnesses common to hot nations. If diseases of the poor, low-latitude regions of the world began to reach developed countries, large amounts of capital would flow into the Pharmaceuticals sector as the affluent began to demand protection—so it could prove profitable to be holding pharmaceutical stocks, although exactly which shares to buy would be influenced by laboratory discoveries that are impossible to predict. But consider the social upside: If malaria threatened the United States, this scourge might finally be cured.

Health-Care Service Providers. The contrarian view is that a warming world would, on balance, improve public health in high-latitude areas. Though hot regions in the developing world experience high rates of communicable diseases that scare us, people are still far more likely to die from the cold than from heat—overall death rates in winter are much higher than those in summer. Retirees living in Florida, for instance, have less reason to fear a hot summer than those living in Vermont have to fear a cold winter. If the cold areas of affluent nations became less cold, we would expect longevity to increase. That would be good for society, and also a reason to hold health-care (and pharmaceutical) stocks, since the elderly require far mare in the way of hospital services and drugs. The assisted-care industry might also be in for a long bullish run.

Electricity Producers. The World Energy Council has estimated that global demand for electricity will triple by 2050. The lion's share of the increased demand will be in developing nations, but the United States and the European Union nations will need more megawatts too—and that's even assuming increases in energy efficiency. It is all but certain that some form of greenhouse-gas regulation will come to the United States; many Fortune 500 CEOs already assume this. The result will be an electricity sector that's much more technology- and knowledge-sensitive than today's. Lots of brainpower and skill will be required to increase electricity generation and reduce greenhouse-gas emissions at the same time. It's reasonable to guess that power-production firms with a track record of innovation, such as Duke Energy (which pioneered many techniques to improve the efficiency of nuclear-power plants), will be the kind of energy-sector stocks to own. Don't be surprised if nuclear energy, which is nearly greenhousegas-free, enjoys a boom in coming decades. General Electric, Westinghouse, and Siemens are some of the leading producers of new "inherently safe" power reactors designed so they can't melt down even if all safety systems are turned off.

"Green" Energy. Renewable-energy industries—such as solar energy and biofuels—might seem like a promising place for 401 (k) chips, but bear in mind that no form of green energy is yet cost-competitive with fossil energy, and no one knows which may eventually win in the marketplace. Solar-cell production, for example, is an expanding sector, but nearly all large solar cells for residential and commercial applications are currently sold in California, Japan, or Germany, which heavily subsidize the installation of solar power. Many investors today are racing to ethanol, but wariness seems advisable. Bill Gates has already invested $84 million in a start-up called Pacific Ethanol; venture-capital firms have moved into the ethanol "space." If the smart money is already there, you're too late. Besides, BP and DuPont are now looking past ethanol to bet on butanol, a crop-derived petroleum substitute with superior technical properties.

Agriculture. Should growing seasons and rainfall patterns change quickly, genetic engineering of crop plants might become essential to society's future. DuPont, Monsanto, Syngenta, and other firms that are perfecting genetic improvement of crops—either through gene splicing or via natural crossbreeding aided by genetic analysis—could become even bigger players if there is significant climate change.

The Deus Ex Machina Industry. Be wary of start-ups and venture capitalists who may soon talk up "geoengineering." In theory, it could be possible to cause the seas to absorb more greenhouse gases, if oceans were fertilized with substances that encourage the growth of marine organisms that need carbon dioxide. In theory, the upper atmosphere could be seeded with shiny fleck-sized particles that bounce sunlight back into space, cooling the Earth. In theory, if volcanoes could be made more active, their emissions also would reduce global temperature by blocking some sunlight. (The sole exception to the last two decades of warm years resulted from the 1991 eruption of Mount Pinatubo, in the Philippines, which caused cool weather worldwide.) It's likely that some investors will be tempted by offers of early stakes in geoengineering enterprises. But it's unlikely that any government will ever approve an experiment involving the entire planet.

Want the profile of what seems the perfect large firm of the future? Think General Electric. The company builds nuclear-power reactors and is ready to build extremely efficient coal-fired power plants, which are likely to become more commonplace than nuclear reactors owing to lower cost and less political opposition. George W. Bush talks grandly of Future-Gen, a billion-dollar federal initiative for a prototype coal-fired power plant that emits hardly any greenhouse gases. But the FutureGen crash program doesn't even break ground until 2009. Meanwhile, GE has already completed the engineering work for an advanced coal-fired power plant able to operate with negligible greenhouse-gas emissions. If greenhouse-gas regulations are enacted, GE may be swamped with orders for its new coal-fired generating station. GE has also recently engineered jet engines, power turbines, and diesel locomotives that require less fuel, and hence release less greenhouse gas, than those now in use. The company has also made serious investments in wind turbines, photovoltaic cells, and other zero-emission energy forms. This big, profit-conscious corporation is at the cutting edge of preparation for a greenhouse world—which is likely to keep GE big and profitable.

—Gregg Easterbrook

assumption that growing conditions will continue to be good in the breadbasket areas of the United States, India, China, and South America. If rainfall shifts away from those areas, there could be significant human suffering for many, many years, even if, say, Siberian agriculture eventually replaces lost production elsewhere. By reducing farm yield, rainfall changes could also cause skyrocketing prices for commodity crops, something the global economy has rarely observed in the last 30 years.

Recent studies show that in the last few decades, precipitation in North America is increasingly the result of a few downpours rather than lots of showers. Downpours cause flooding and property damage, while being of less use to agriculture than frequent soft rains. Because the relationship between artificially triggered climate change and rainfall is conjectural, investors presently have no way to avoid buying land in places that someday might be hit with frequent downpours. But this concern surely raises a red flag about investments in India, Bangladesh, and Indonesia, where monsoon rains are already a leading social problem.

Water-related investments might be attractive in another way: for hydropower. Zero-emission hydropower might become a premium energy form if greenhouse gases are strictly regulated. Quebec is the Saudi Arabia of roaring water. Already the hydropower complex around James Bay is one of the world's leading sources of water-generated electricity. For 30 years, environmentalists and some Cree activists opposed plans to construct a grand hydropower complex that essentially would dam all large rivers flowing into the James and Hudson bays. But it's not hard to imagine Canada completing the reengineering of northern Quebec for hydropower, if demand from New England and the Midwest becomes strong enough. Similarly, there is hydropower potential in the Chilean portions of Patagonia. This is a wild and beautiful region little touched by human activity—and an intriguing place to snap up land for hydropower reservoirs.

Adaptation

Last October, the treasury office of the United Kingdom estimated that unless we adapt, global warming could eventually subtract as much as 20 percent of the gross domestic product from the world economy. Needless to say, if that happens, not even the cleverest portfolio will help you. This estimate is worst-case, however, and has many economists skeptical. Optimists think dangerous global warming might be averted at surprisingly low cost (see "Some Convenient Truths," September 2006). Once regulations create a profit incentive for the invention of greenhouse-gas-reducing technology, an outpouring of innovation is likely. Some of those who formulate greenhouse-gas-control ideas will become rich; everyone will benefit from the environmental safeguards the ideas confer.

Enactment of some form of binding greenhouse-gas rules is now essential both to slow the rate of greenhouse-gas accumulation and to create an incentive for inventors, engineers, and businesspeople to devise the ideas that will push society beyond the fossil-fuel age. *The New York Times* recently groused that George W. Bush's fiscal 2007 budget includes only $4.2 billion

for federal research that might cut greenhouse-gas emissions. This is the wrong concern: Progress would be faster if the federal government spent nothing at all on greenhouse-gas-reduction research—but enacted regulations that gave the private sector a significant profit motive to find solutions that work in actual use, as opposed to on paper in government studies. The market has caused the greenhouse-gas problem, and the market is the best hope of solving it. Offering market incentives for the development of greenhouse-gas controls—indeed, encouraging profit making in greenhouse-gas controls—is the most promising path to avoiding the harm that could befall the dispossessed of developing nations as the global climate changes.

Yet if global-warming theory is right, higher global temperatures are already inevitable. Even the most optimistic scenario for reform envisions decades of additional greenhouse-gas accumulation in the atmosphere, and that in turn means a warming world. The warming may be manageable, but it is probably unstoppable in the short term. This suggests that a major investment sector of the near future will be climate-change adaptation. Crops that grow in high temperatures, homes and buildings designed to stay cool during heat waves, vehicles that run on far less fuel, waterfront structures that can resist stronger storms—the list of needed adaptations will be long, and all involve producing, buying, and selling. Environmentalists don't like talk of adaptation, as it implies making our peace with a warmer world. That peace, though, must be made—and the sooner businesses, investors, and entrepreneurs get to work, the better.

Why, ultimately, should nations act to control greenhouse gases, rather than just letting climate turmoil happen and seeing who profits? One reason is that the cost of controls is likely to be much lower than the cost of rebuilding the world. Coastal cities could be abandoned and rebuilt inland, for instance, but improving energy efficiency and reducing greenhouse-gas emissions in order to stave off rising sea levels should be far more cost-effective. Reforms that prevent major economic and social disruption from climate change are likely to be less expensive, across the board, than reacting to the change. The history of antipollution programs shows that it is always cheaper to prevent emissions than to reverse any damage they cause.

For the United States, there's another argument that is particularly keen. The present ordering of the world favors the United States in nearly every respect—political, economic, even natural, considering America's excellent balance of land and resources. Maybe a warming world would favor the United States more; this is certainly possible. But when the global order already places America at No. 1, why would we want to run the risk of climate change that alters that order? Keeping the world economic system and the global balance of power the way they are seems very strongly in the U.S. national interest—and keeping things the way they are requires prevention of significant climate change. That, in the end, is what's in it for us.

GREGG EASTERBROOK is an *Atlantic* contributing editor, a visiting fellow at the Brookings Institution, and the author of *The Progress Paradox* (2003).

Boomer Century

What's going to happen when the most prosperous, best-educated generation in history finally grows up? (And just how special are the baby *boomers*?)

Joshua Zeitz

Just a matter of weeks from now, On December 31, as millions of Americans don party hats and pop champagne corks to usher in the New Year, Kathleen Casey, the Philadelphia-born daughter of a Navy machinist and his wife, will likely find her phone once again ringing off the hook. It happens every decade or so. Journalists and academics and earnest civic leaders, family and friends, all find their way to Casey's doorstep, hoping for just a few minutes of her time, eager to glean a little bit of wisdom about what it all means and where it's all going.

Kathleen Casey, you see, bears the unique distinction of having launched the baby boom.

Born at 12:01 A.M. on January 1, 1946, she was the first of 76 million Americans brought into the world between 1946 and 1964, when, in a sharp reversal of a steady century-long decline, the national birthrate skyrocketed, creating a massive demographic upheaval.

So this year the very first baby *boomer,* the vanguard of that endlessly youthful generation, turns 60. But hers is not like other generations. If its last, unrecorded member was born at 11:59 P.M. on December 31, 1964, he or she will just be turning 41. Certainly this person, the Unknown Boomer, will have encountered very different cultural signposts than did Kathleen Casey (say, Pat Boone vs. the Sex Pistols), but together the two of them bracket a group that, despite its immensity, is strangely unified, and whose influence today defines both the limits and the promise of American life—and will for years to come.

Last summer, 40 years after "(I Can't Get No) Satisfaction" climbed to the top of Billboard's singles chart and earned the Rolling Stones their first gold release in the United States, the Stones launched their 2005 World Tour at Boston's Fenway Park. For tens of thousands of *boomers* who came to see Mick Jagger and Keith Richards perform the greatest hits of yesteryear, age really is just a number.

Their kids might have been mortified to see these graying veterans of the 1960s filling a ballpark for one last great rock V roll show. But in many ways, it all makes sense. There is still no more fitting anthem for the baby-boom generation than the Stones' signature hit.

Raised in an era of unprecedented affluence and national omnipotence, but coming of age in a time that perceived more limited resources and diminished American power, the *boomers* have long been defined by a vain search for satisfaction. No matter how much they have, they can't ever seem to get enough. This quest for satisfaction has at times led to nadirs of narcissism and greed. As a generation the *boomers* have always seemed to want it all: cheap energy, consumer plenty, low taxes, loads of government entitlements, ageless beauty, and an ever-rising standard of living. They inherited a nation flush with resources and will bequeath their children a country mired in debt.

But their quest for personal satisfaction has also pushed the boundaries of civic life in radical and unusual directions. In their youth, black and white *boomers* took to the streets to tear down the walls of racial segregation. They strove toward greater equality of opportunity between men and women, made it harder for policymakers to choose war over peace without first convincing a skeptical electorate of its merits, and created a nation that was more accepting of diversity.

For all their faults and all their virtues, they remain exemplars of what Henry Luce called the American Century. The social commentators Neil Howe and William Strauss got it exactly right when they wrote that "from V-J Day forward, whatever age bracket *Boomers* have occupied has been the cultural and spiritual focal point for American society as a whole. Through their childhood, America was child-obsessed; in their youth, youth-obsessed; in their 'yuppie' phase, yuppie-obsessed." Maybe Luce had it wrong. It wasn't the American Century. It was the *Boomer* Century.

Scholars continue to marvel at the phenomenon known as the baby boom. It seemed then, and seems now, to fly in the face of modern demographic and social history. Between 1800 and 1920 the number of children borne by the average American woman fell by more than half, from roughly seven to three. As America transformed itself from a nation of small farmers into an urban, industrial behemoth, increasing numbers of parents no longer needed small armies of children to work the family farm. In this new world of machine and factory, surplus children were a liability. They required much in the way of food, clothing, and shelter but contributed very little in turn to the economic well-being of their families.

The national birthrate, long on the decline, bottomed out in the 1930s. With unemployment running as high as 25 percent, many young Americans, facing an uncertain economic future, decided to put off marriage and parenthood until better days.

When those better days finally arrived in 1940, courtesy of America's swift and total mobilization for war, most commentators expected only a temporary upsurge in births. The editors of Life magazine worried that by 1970 the Soviet Union's population would outstrip that of the United States, Britain, France, and Italy combined. They were taken completely by surprise at the magnitude and duration of what actually followed.

Beginning in 1942 with so-called furlough babies, taking off in May 1946—nine months after V-J Day—and peaking around 1947 or 1948, when an American child was born every eight seconds, the GI generation broke sharply with a century-long demographic trend toward smaller families. The population boom also hit Australia, Canada, and New Zealand, whose economies enjoyed a postwar expansion similar to (though not on scale with) America's, but not Europe, large portions of which lay in ruins. Little wonder, then, that a British visitor traveling in the United States in 1958 observed with something like amazement that "every other young housewife I see is pregnant. "

Though its causes continue to puzzle scholars, the baby boom probably grew from three distinct trends.

First, in the prosperous 1940s and 1950s, thirtyish Americans who had postponed marriage and children during the Great Depression were eager to make up for lost time and start building families. They crowded the field 10 years after they would normally have contributed their share of progeny to the national population.

Second, they were joined by a younger cohort, including many recently demobilized GIs who had come home to find economic prosperity, generous government assistance in the form of housing and educational benefits for veterans, and a general sense of optimism born of conquering global fascism. For these young victors, many still in their early twenties, it made little sense to put off marriage and family. Like their older brothers and sisters, they understood that the years of Depression scarcity and wartime sacrifice were over. Finally, and in a more subtle way, the general euphoria that drove up marriage and birth rates was soon complemented by Cold War-era anxieties over nuclear competition. In an uncertain world, the comforts of home and hearth could provide a salve against atomic angst, just as the stabilizing influence of marriage and parenthood offered a strategic advantage in the nation's struggle against communism.

Noting the dangers posed by the Cold War, two Harvard sociologists informed the Ford Foundation that the "world is like a volcano that breaks out repeatedly. . . . The world approaches this critical period with a grave disruption of the family system. . . . The new age demands a stronger, more resolute and better equipped individual. . . . To produce such persons will demand a reorganization of the present family system and the building of one that is stronger emotionally and morally." Ultimately, if Americans wanted to do their part in this new global war, they'd settle down, have lots of kids, and raise them to do well in school and well in life.

Even household architecture seemed to reinforce the relationship between Cold War worries and the cult of domesticity in which the baby boom prospered. The standard suburban ranch house favored by many young families in the 1950s was set back from the street and protected by a fence, and it had a low-slung roof and an attached carport, lending it a bit of the appearance of a well-fortified bunker.

Not just homes, but the children who were starting to crawl through them, formed a "defense—an impregnable bulwark" against the horrors of the atomic age, the social commentator Louisa Randall Church argued in 1946. Many Americans seemed to agree, and out of this vague combination of economic optimism and atomic unease, they were fruitful, and they multiplied.

Their children—the *boomers*—were necessarily a heterogeneous lot. America still suffered from deep racial and economic divisions. A country as large as the United States contained a host of distinctive regional folkways. Still, as the cultural critic Annie Gottlieb has observed, for all their differences, the baby *boomers* formed a distinctive "tribe with its roots in time, rather than place or race." By any measure, the America in which they grew up was more abundant, more powerful, and more enraptured with its own glory than ever before. When John F. Kennedy called on his countrymen to "explore the stars, conquer the deserts, eradicate disease, tap the ocean depths, and encourage the arts and commerce," he echoed the optimism that helped forge the new generation's outlook.

Part of this confidence grew out of America's total victory in World War II and the country's scientific and medical achievements, including Jonas Salk's discovery of a polio vaccine in the early 1950s. But most of it was due to the nation's dynamic economy. Between 1940 and 1960 our gross national product doubled; real wages—and real purchasing power—increased by 30 percent; the portion of owner-occupied homes climbed to 61 percent; four-fifths of American families kept at least one car in the driveway; average life expectancy rose by almost 11 percent; most employees of large firms enjoyed such new benefits as private health insurance, paid vacations, and retirement pensions; and the typical American house held seven times more gadgets and goods than in the 1920s. By 1957 the energy of the American economy led U.S. News & World Report to declare that "never had so many people, anywhere, been so well off." When Richard Nixon famously sparred with Nikita Khrushchev at the 1959 American National Exhibition in Moscow and proclaimed the superiority of the American suburban kitchen, with its sleek electric appliances in their myriad styles and models, he articulated a vague but popular sense that America's consumer abundance was a sure sign of its Cold War advantage.

For *boomer* children, this cornucopia translated into billions of dollars' worth of Hula-Hoops, Davy Crockett raccoon skin hats, Hopalong Cassidy six-shooters, bicycles and tricycles,

195

Slinkys, Silly Putty, and skateboards (and, in California, the shining lure of Disneyland). The writer Joyce Maynard remembered that when the Barbie doll made its debut in 1959, her world changed "like a cloudburst, without preparation. Barbie wasn't just a toy, but a way of living that moved us suddenly from tea parties to dates with Ken at the soda shoppe." Relatively speaking, to grow up a middle-class American kid in the 1950s meant wanting for nothing.

It also meant television. in just four years, between 1948 and 1952, the number of American households with TV sets jumped from 172,000 to 15.3 million. T. S. Eliot observed that television was "a medium of entertainment which permits millions of people to listen to the same joke at the same time, and yet remain lonesome," but for the millions of children raised on it, the new device offered up endless hours of entertainment in the form of family sitcoms like "The Adventures of Ozzie and Harriet," "Father Knows Best," and "Leave It to Beaver," all of which idealized the carefree, child-centered world of suburban America.

More popular still were the Westerns: "Gunsmoke," "Wyatt Earp," "Bonanza," "The Texan," "Wagon Train," "Cheyenne," "The Rifleman," "The Outcasts," "Wanted: Dead or Alive," "Have Gun, Will Travel." Together, these serial epics captured close to half of America's weekly television audience and, by the end of the decade, constituted 7 of the 11 most popular shows on the small screen. The programs mythologized the rugged individualism and physical strength of the American frontiersman, who tamed both his enemy (the Indian or outlaw standing in for the Soviet menace) and the natural environment. It was a genre well suited for a country confident of its ability to reach the stars, vanquish disease, and collapse the limits of time and space.

Complementing this message of abundance and conquest were new vogues in child rearing and pedagogy rooted in John Dewey's ideas about the merits of progressive education. They entered the mainstream in 1946, when Benjamin Spock published The Common Sense Book of Baby and Child Care. His book instructed the parents of the baby-boom generation to go light on punishment and heavy on reason and persuasion, and to bear in mind that their daughters' and sons' happiness was the paramount objective of child rearing. If Johnny steals someone's toy, don't hit him. Explain that stealing is wrong, and buy him the toy that he coveted. If Suzie misbehaves at the dinner table, don't worry. Table manners are overrated.

Spock was enormously influential. A study conducted in 1961 revealed that two-thirds of new mothers surveyed had read his book. He made permissive or child-centered parenting mandatory for millions of new postwar middle-class families. By the mid-1950s his message was routinely echoed in the pages of Parents magazine and found confirmation in countless sociological studies.

In later years critics would decry the effects of progressive child rearing, some of them crediting it with an entire generation's egotism. The iconoclastic historian Richard Hofstadter worried that America would be overrun by the "overvalued child." Writing of the typical GI generation mother, the novelist Lisa Alther lamented: "If anything had been drummed into

her in years of motherhood, it was that you mustn't squelch the young. It might squelch their precious development. Never mind about your own development."

Hyperbole aside, millions of **boomers** did grow up in prosperous, nurturing homes in which children formed the core of the family. Raised amid plenty, taught to value their needs and satisfy their wants, and imbued with a sense of national greatness and purpose, it would have been odd had they not entered young adulthood with at least some sense of entitlement.

In 1956, noting the connection between postwar vogues in Freudian analysis and progressive child rearing, the literary critic Alfred Kazin was bemused by the national "insistence on individual fulfillment, satisfaction and happiness." Years later the pollster Daniel Yankelovich observed that grown **boomers,** instead of asking themselves, "Will I be able to make a living?," as their parents, raised in the Depression years, often did, were more prone to wonder, "How can I find self-fulfillment?"

No American generation has been so intensely studied, so widely celebrated, and so roundly condemned as this one. Out of the cacophony of analysis, two standard criticisms—one from the left, the other from the right—stand out.

For contemporary liberals, popular films like The Big Chill and television series like "thirty-something" follow a familiar narrative line in which idealistic, socially committed children of the sixties grow into self-centered, blandly acquisitive adults. In the words of the former sixties activist Todd Gitlin, by the 1980s a generation that once raged against "banality, irrelevance, and all the ugliness which conspire to dwarf or extinguish the human personality" had graduated from "J'accuse to Jacuzzi."

Even when television **boomers** retained their fundamental goodness—think, for instance, of Michael J. Fox's parents, Elise and Steven Keaton, in the popular 1980s sitcom "Family Ties"—they remained painfully conscious of their generation's potential drift toward self-absorption.

To conservatives, on the other hand, the generation embodies the evils of secular liberalism. In Slouching Towards Gomorrah, Robert Bork credits the pampered baby-boom generation with virtually every insidious social trend in recent American history. "The dual forces of radical egalitarianism . . . and radical individualism (the drastic reduction of limits to personal gratification)," explains the book's back cover, have "undermined our culture, our intellect, and our morality."

Of course, traditionalists don't have to look far to make their case. **Boomers** are certainly more tolerant than their parents of looser personal mores. In 1983, 44 percent of them approved of cohabitation outside marriage, 29 percent supported legalizing marijuana, and 37 percent endorsed casual sex. Whereas only a quarter of Americans approved of premarital sex in the 1950s, by the 1970s that figure had climbed to three-quarters.

More recently, boomers from left and right have begun weaving a third critique. In an effort of historical revision that comes close to self-flagellation, they have begun to worship their parents' generation. That the "GI Generation" has become "the Greatest Generation" is evident everywhere—in popular television series like "Band of Brothers," in films like Saving Private Ryan, and in official tributes, such as the World War II memorial in Washington, D.C. Offered by the children of G.I. Joe and Rosie the Riveter, these accolades carry an implicit message: Try as we may, we will simply never measure up to our parents' self-sacrificing greatness.

The problem with all these critiques is that they ignore both the creative use to which the generation has sometimes put its terrific sense of entitlement and the continuities between sixties idealism and eighties excess.

In February 1960, when four black college students staged a sit-in at a Woolworth's lunch counter in Greensboro, North Carolina, sparking a national campaign and inaugurating a decade of youth-driven political activism, they were doing nothing so much as demanding access to the same entitlements that other children of the postwar era claimed as their American birthright. A sympathetic advertisement appearing in three Atlanta newspapers in March 1960 hit the nail on the head when it explained "the meaning of the sit-down protests that are sweeping this nation": "Today's youth will not sit by submissively, while being denied all of the rights, privileges, and joys of life." Raised on the same television advertisements and political rhetoric as their white peers, young black Americans were determined to get their piece of satisfaction.

In a country where happiness and dignity were so inextricably bound up with the individual's right to enjoy the blessings of the national wealth, this argument resonated. In his "Letter from Birmingham Jail," Martin Luther King, Jr., the father of young baby *boomer*s of his own, drove home this point. He spoke of finding your "tongue twisted and your speech stammering as you seek to explain to your six-year-old daughter why she can't go to the public amusement park that has just been advertised on television, and see tears welling up in her eyes when she is told that Funtown is closed to colored children."

The legions of junior high and high school students who heeded his call in Birmingham—who filled the jails, attended the prayer meetings, and drove King himself to embrace more radical tactics and demands—ultimately compelled the nation to confront long-standing inequities that "the Greatest Generation" had been content to ignore.

They were the shock troops of the 1960s rights revolution. Like their white peers, these *boomer* kids had seen an average of 500 hours of television advertisements by the age of 6 and over 300,000 commercials by the age of 21. (King's daughter had clearly seen an ad for Funtown.)

In the aftermath of the Newark riots of 1967, the black poet Amiri Baraka told a state investigatory commission that the "poorest black man in Newark, in America, knows how white people live. We have television sets; we see movies. We see the fantasy and the reality of white America every day." The schism between fantasy and reality could inspire a truly creative tension.

And so it went for other boomers as well. Young black activists influenced women, gays and lesbians, students, welfare recipients, Latinos, and American Indians to appreciate the gap between America's lofty democratic promise and its imperfect reality, and to work to narrow that gap.

By the 1970s *boomer* rights activists forced changes in credit laws, so that married women could have their own credit cards, and pushed for the enactment of Title IX, which broke down gender barriers in education and athletics. In forcing a new liberalization of sex and romance, they insisted on everyone's right to satisfaction and self-realization—not just married couples but also unmarried partners, no matter what their sexual orientation. They played an instrumental role in bringing down a U.S. President, Lyndon Johnson, and in making the Vietnam War increasingly untenable for his successor, Richard Nixon.

In other words, the generation raised on Spock, television, and abundance put its sense of privilege and entitlement to work for the better good. Today most scholars agree that the *boomers* will leave their children and grandchildren a country that's a little more just, a little more humane, and a little more inclusive than the one they inherited from their parents.

These accomplishments notwithstanding, it's small wonder that the generation has accumulated mixed reviews. The radical left is no happier with the *boomers* than is the reactionary right. In their youth they effected so massive an upheaval in politics and culture that they were bound eventually to fall in the public's esteem. Apostles of what Gitlin has called "the voyage to the interior," and what the late historian and social critic Christopher Lasch derided as a "culture of narcissism," they seemed after the 1960s to place an unusually high premium on self-discovery and personal satisfaction.

The generation that had raged against authority, vowing with Bob Dylan, "I ain't gonna work on Maggie's farm no more," was now swinging to Andrea True's refrain "More, more, more. How do you like it, how do you like it?" They bought minivans, microwaves, and self-help books, embraced transcendental meditation, embarked on various diets, visited tanning salons and fat farms, and filled their homes with more durable goods than their prosperous parents could ever have imagined.

Even their politics seemed to change. In 1980 it was an eleventh-hour swing among *boomer* voters that turned Ronald Reagan's razor-thin margin into a landslide victory. In fact, there was always more continuity than the critics liked to admit. Even in 1972, the first year that 18-year-olds were allowed to take part in national elections, fewer than half the eligible new voters bothered to show up at the polls, and just half of those who did cast their lot with the liberal antiwar Democrat George McGovern.

Popular memory notwithstanding, the sixties generation has never been a political monolith. Nor was it uniformly engaged by public issues. Only 20 percent of students who attended college in the late 1960s participated in marches or protests, and far fewer—2 or 3 percent—regarded themselves as activists.

The antiwar movement, which many liberal *boomers* fondly remember as embodying the altruistic, public spirit of the era, was always more self-interested than its veterans might wish to admit. Whereas virtually every able-bodied, draft-eligible man of the GI generation served in the military during World War II, only 10 percent of the 27 million draft-eligible *boomers* were in uniform while America fought the Vietnam War.

The rest, most of them white and middle-class, found creative ways to stay safe. They claimed medical dispensations and student deferments, became schoolteachers or entered defense industries, or married and had children before their local draft boards could sweep them up.

In opposing the war, which many activists did sincerely view as both immoral and unwinnable, protesters betrayed as much selfish entitlement as noble intent. They wanted the United States out of Southeast Asia, but they also wanted to keep themselves out of Southeast Asia. Richard Nixon understood this when he shifted the draft burden away from men in their twenties and back onto 18- and 19-year-olds. Suddenly college campuses quieted down. Why bother to protest once you're safely out of the woods?

In effect, for all their racial, economic, and cultural diversity, if the *boomers* shared anything, it was that perpetual search for satisfaction. In their best moments, and in their worst, they demanded that the country make good on the promises it had handed them in the 1950s. The problem was that when they began to come of age in the 1970s, the bottom fell out on the American economy. Even as they clamored for "more, more, more," what they found was less, less, less. Between the 1960s and 1980s the income of young men just entering the job market declined by 50 percent. This mostly was due to forces beyond anyone's control: Government expenditures for the Vietnam War caused runaway inflation; economic restructuring took a toll on manufacturing; oil shortages in the 1970s drove up energy costs and interest rates. The long slump also came from the gradual erosion of progressive tax policies and growth in entitlements like health insurance.

Ironically, the baby boom was itself a major cause of the nation's economic slide. So many young people seeking jobs drove down wages and accounted for as much as half of the unemployment rate during the 1970s and 1980s. So *boomers* made the necessary adjustments. To maintain a standard of living that reflected their upbringing, they, like their Depression-bred parents, postponed marriage and children. Though women's wages, once adjusted for changing education and skill levels, remained stagnant in the 1970s and 1980s, the proportion of young married women in the work force more than doubled, from roughly 30 percent to 70 percent. Two-earner households helped keep pace with the generation's material expectations, but at the expense of outsourcing Generation X to after-school daycare and sports programs.

Even these adjustments fell short. The generation that couldn't get no satisfaction could hardly be expected to live within its means. In 2002 baby *boomers* spent between 20 percent and 30 percent more money each year than did the average American consumer. In part, this was out of necessity. They had children to feed, houses to furnish, and college tuitions to pay. But the *boomers* have long stretched the limits of sound household economy. According to the economist Robert Samuelson, between 1946 and 2002 consumer debt climbed from 22 percent of household income to 110 percent. In other words, we've become a debtor nation, and the *boomers* have presided over this transition.

Now at the height of their political influence (the 2000 presidential election saw the first-ever race between two baby *boomers,* and the commentators Neil Howe and William Strauss estimate that *boomers* will hold a plurality in Congress until 2015) they are also presiding over the creation of a national debt that their children and grandchildren will be left to pay off in coming years.

In the end the boomers may be less culpable, less praiseworthy, and less remarkable than they, and everyone else, think. Their cohort was so big, arrived so suddenly, and has grown up so closely alongside the modern broadcast media that they have always struck us as standing apart from larger historical forces that drive the normal workings of states and societies. Yet much about this seeming exceptionalism just isn't new.

When the husband-and-wife sociologist team Robert and Helen Lynd visited Muncie, Indiana, in the early 1920s, they found many of the same traits popularly associated with the *boomers* already evident among Jazz Age youth. Their famous, pathbreaking book, Middletown: A Study in Modern American Culture, reported a younger generation in the thrall of movies and music, willing to stretch the limits of romantic and sexual propriety, obsessed with clothes and cosmetics, and eager to stake out shocking new degrees of personal autonomy.

And if the children of the 1950s were technically the first generation raised on Spock, they weren't the first generation raised on the ideas of Spock. By the mid-1950s upward of 75 percent of middle-class men and women were reading advice books that, more often than not, counseled unprecedented attention to the child. Most experts in the 1920s and 1930s had figured out Spock before Spock figured out Spock.

Nor were the *boomers* the first generation to make therapeutic self-discovery a competitive sport. In their parents' youth, in the twenties and thirties, Freud was already all the rage. Popular books of the day included The Psychology of Golf, Psychology of the Poet Shelley, and The Psychology of Selling Life Insurance. Bookstores and mail-order houses peddled new titles like Psychoanalysis by Mail, Psychoanalysis Self-Applied, Ten Thousand Dreams Interpreted, and Sex Problems Solved.

Long before the *boomers* arrived on the scene, Americans were drawn to a new cult of self-improvement that celebrated the mastery of one's deepest impulses and thoughts. In the 1920s millions followed the advice of the French wonder guru, Emile Coué, faithfully repeating the simple catechism "Day by day, in every way, I am getting better and better."

The explosion of self-help literature peaked in 1936 with the publication of Dale Carnegie's How to Win Friends and Influence People.

If the *boomers* weren't entirely original in their loosened sexual standards, emphasis on physical appearance and youth, or search for a therapeutic mind cure, neither were they all that unusual in their resistance to collective sacrifice. It hardly diminishes the decisive effort of the World War II generation to note that civilians traded on the black market, deeply resented rationing and wage and labor controls, and often worked in defense production as much for profit as for patriotism.

A *Boomer* Bookshelf

Given their central role in recent history, baby *boomers* figure prominently in many of the most important and illuminating books about postwar America. Here are 10 volumes that I found of particular interest.—J.Z.

TERRY H. ANDERSON The Movement and the Sixties: Protest in America From Greensboro to Wounded Knee (Oxford. 1995). Anderson, a Vietnam veteran and history professor at Texas A&M University, presents a comprehensive and balanced portrait of *boomer*-generation activism in the 1960s that avoids both the triumphal and condemnatory posturing typical of other works on this subject.

JAMES CARROLL An American Requiem: God. My Father, and the War That Came Between Us (Houghton Mifflin, 1996). Though Carrol l, a former priest and antiwar activist, was born in 1943, just barely missing the arbitrary jump-off for the baby boom, his memoir of growing up in the postwar years and coming to political consciousness during the Vietnam War era is a vital contribution to *boomer* literature.

STEVE M. GILLON *Boomer* Nation: The Largest and Richest Generation Ever and How It Changed America (The Free Press. 2004). In this engaging and informative book—written for a popular audience but with a professional's touch—Steve Gillon, of the University of Oklahoma and the History Channel, weaves together several lives to present a sweeping history of an entire generation.

DAVID HALBERSTAM The Children (Random House. 1998). Though almost 800 pages in length, Halberstam's history of the young black men and women who formed the Student Nonviolent Coordinating Committee and other organizations fighting for civil rights in the 1960s provides an exciting and accessible narrative of the *boomer* generation's most committed shock troops for justice.

JAMES T. PATTERSON Grand Expectations; The United States, 1945–1974 (Oxford, 1996) and Restless Giant: The United States From Watergate to Bush v. Gore (Oxford, 2005). A Bancroft Prize winner and professor emeritus at Brown University. Patterson has written the definitive two-volume history of America in the Cold War era. His work is essential for understanding the environment in which the *boomers* were raised and in which they grew to adulthood.

SUSAN FALUDI Backlash: The Undeclared War Against American Women (Crown, 1991) and Stiffed: The Betrayal of the American Man (William Morrow and Co., 1999). A prizewinning journalist and writer, Faludi has written two must-read volumes on the culture and politics of gender in recent American history. Her works are implicitly about the country the *boomers* inherited and made.

RICK ATKINSON The Long Gray Line: The American Journey of West Point's Class of 1966 (Houghton Mifflin, 1999). Atkinson, a Pulitzer Prize-winning journalist, presents a rich and complicated portrait of some of the first *boomers* to graduate from the U.S., Military Academy. As essential as understanding those *boomers* who protested the Vietnam War is appreciating those who fought it.

JONATHAN FRANZEN The Corrections (Farrar, Straus and Giroux, 2001). Most *boomer* literature focuses on the children of the 1960s, ignoring the younger half of the cohort that came of age in the 1970s and 1980s. Franzen's celebrated novel addresses this imbalance and offers a painfully honest glimpse at younger *boomers* approaching middle age.

Even the era's soldiers had mixed reasons for going to war. When The Saturday Evening Post ran a series of articles by American GIs entitled "What I Am Fighting For," readers learned that their sons and brothers were in Europe "for that big house with the bright green roof and the big front lawn," their "nice little roadster," pianos, tennis courts, and "the girl with the large brown eyes and the reddish tinge in her hair, that girl who is away at college right now, preparing herself for her part in the future of America and Christianity."

The same conflation of private and public interests drove home-front advertisers to pitch their wares as a just reward for wartime sacrifice—as in an ad promising that "when our boys come home . . . among the finer things of life they will find ready to enjoy will be Johnston and Murphy shoes. Quality unchanged."

None of this suggests that the *boomers* aren't a distinct category of Americans. If many of the character traits popularly assigned them were in evidence long before they were born—if the *boomers* were, in fact, walking along the arc of history rather than outside it—still, they have, for good and for ill, made a lasting imprint on the nation.

Social commentators have long been inclined to make sense of the world in generational terms. Writing about his travels in the United States in the 1830s, Alexis de Tocqueville argued that "among democratic nations each new generation is a new people." Roughly 100 years later the social scientist Karl Mannheim similarly observed: "Early impressions tend to coalesce into a natural view of the world."

The *boomers*—a generation born into national wealth and power, raised on the promise of their limitless potential and self-worth, reared on television and advertising, enthralled by the wonders of modern science and medicine—are, for all their differences, a most potent emblem of the long American Century.

Even today they remain characteristically unfulfilled. Looking for "more, more, more"—for that "satisfaction" that seems forever to elude them—they will, as they have since 1946, stretch the limits of America's possibilities and its resources.

In 2046 we'll still be appraising their work.

The *boomers,* said one critic, were a distinctive "tribe with its roots in time, rather than place or race." Relatively speaking, to grow up a middle-class American child m the 1950s meant wanting for nothing. A 1961 study revealed that two-thirds of all new mothers surveyed had read Dr. Spock. These students ultimately compelled the nation to confront inequities "the Greatest Generation" hadn't. The antiwar movement was always more self-interested than its veterans might wish to admit. They will continue to do what they have done since 1946—stretch the limits of America's possibilities.

Joshua Zeitz's book Flapper, about an earlier social revolution, will be published by Crown in April.

Does Meritocracy Work?

Not if society and colleges keep failing to distinguish between wealth and merit

Ross Douthat

For a parent drowning in glossy college mailings, a college admissions officer deluged with applications, or a student padding a résumé with extracurricular activities, it's easy to see applying to college as a universal American rite of passage—a brutal and ecumenical process that ushers each generation of stressed-out applicants into the anteroom of adulthood. But for many American teenagers the admissions process is something else entirely—a game that is dramatically rigged against them, if they even play it. In a country where a college degree is a prerequisite for economic and social advancement, rich and upper-middle-class students can feel secure about their chances. They may not have the grades or the good fortune to attend their first-choice schools, but they're still likely to be admitted to a college that matches their interests and ambitions reasonably well. For those further down the socioeconomic ladder, though, getting in is hard, and getting through can be even harder.

Native intelligence and academic achievement do lift many poor students into college. But especially where elite colleges are concerned, students from well-off families have a big advantage. The figures are stark. If you hope to obtain a bachelor's degree by age twenty-four, your chances are roughly one in two if you come from a family with an annual income over $90,000; roughly one in four if your family's income falls between $61,000 and $90,000; and slightly better than one in ten if it is between $35,000 and $61,000. For high schoolers whose families make less than $35,000 a year the chances are around one in seventeen.

This is not how the modern meritocracy was supposed to work. American higher education was overhauled in the middle years of the twentieth century to be a force for near universal opportunity—or so the overhaulers intended. The widespread use of the SAT would identify working-class kids with high "scholastic aptitude," as the initialism then had it (since 1994 the SAT has been for "scholastic assessment"), and give them the academic chances they deserved. Need-based financial aid and government grants would ensure that everyone who wanted a college education could afford one. Affirmative action would diversify campuses and buoy disadvantaged minorities.

Part of this vision has come to pass. Minority participation in higher education has risen since the 1960s, and college campuses are far more racially and ethnically diverse today than they were half a century ago. But the socioeconomic diversity that administrators assumed would follow has failed to materialize. It's true that more low-income students *enroll* in college now than in the 1970s—but they are less likely to graduate than their wealthier peers. Through boom and recession, war and peace, the proportion of the poorest Americans obtaining college degrees by age twenty-four has remained around six percent.

This is not something that most colleges like to discuss—particularly elite schools, which have long taken pride in their supposed diversity. But the idea that the meritocracy isn't working is gaining currency among observers of higher education. It's visible in recent high-profile changes in the financial-aid policies of such schools as Harvard, Princeton, and the University of Virginia; as a thread of disquiet running through the interviews this magazine has conducted with admissions officers over the past two years; and as the unpleasant but undeniable conclusion of a number of new studies.

The most prominent of these studies was headed by William Bowen, a former president of Princeton, who since leaving that office, in 1988, has produced a series of weighty analyses of college admissions—on the consequences of racial preferences, the role of athletics, and, most recently, the question of socioeconomic diversity. In the recently published book *Equity and Excellence in American Higher Education,* Bowen and his co-authors use detailed data from the 1995 entering class at nineteen selective schools—five Ivies, ten small liberal arts colleges, and four flagship state universities—to argue that elite universities today are as much "bastions of privilege" as they are "engines of opportunity." Only six percent of the students at these schools are first-generation collegians; only 11 percent of the graduates come from families in the country's bottom economic quartile. The picture is even worse in another recent study. The education expert Anthony Carnevale and the economist Stephen Rose surveyed 146 top colleges and found that only three percent of their students came from the bottom economic quartile of the U.S. population—whereas 74 percent came from the top one.

At the very least, the persistence of this higher-education gap suggests that the causes of the decades-old growth in economic inequality are deeper than, say, tax cuts or the ebb and flow of the stock market. Inequality of income breeds inequality of education, and the reverse is also true: as long as the financial returns on a college degree continue to rise, the upper and upper-middle classes are likely to pull further away from the working and lower classes.

Through boom and recession, war and peace, the proportion of the poorest quarter of Americans obtaining college degrees has remained constant, at around six percent.

The United States still leads most countries by a considerable margin in proportion of the population with a college degree (27 percent). But when the sample is narrowed to those between the ages of twenty-five and thirty-four, we slip into the pack of industrialized nations, behind Canada, Japan, and five others. Further, the U.S. college-age population is swelling (it will increase by about 3.9 million during this decade, according to one estimate), with much of the growth occurring among low-income Hispanics, one of the groups least likely to attend college. Educating this population is an enormous challenge—one that we are unprepared to meet.

The obvious culprits are the universities, which have trumpeted their commitment to diversity and equal access while pursuing policies that favor better-off students. Not only is admitting too many low-income students expensive, but it can be bad for a school's rankings and prestige—and in the long run prestige builds endowments.

The current arms race for higher rankings began in earnest in the early 1980s, when the post-Baby Boom dearth of applicants sent colleges, both public and private, scrambling to keep tuition revenue coming in. It has been sustained by anxious Boomer parents, by the increasing financial advantages of a college degree, by cutbacks in government aid, and by magazines eager to make money from ranking America's top schools. The rankings rely on statistics such as average SAT scores, alumni giving, financial resources, and graduation rates. Attracting students with high scores *and* high family incomes offers the biggest gains of all. (See Matthew Quirk's "The Best Class Money Can Buy," page 128.)

Meanwhile, the admissions process is strewn with practical obstacles for low-income students. Early-admissions programs, for instance, which James Fallows has discussed in these pages (see "The Early-Decision Racket," September 2001 *Atlantic*), offer many benefits to applicants, but they almost exclusively help wealthy students, whose parents and guidance counselors are more likely to have the resources to take advantage of them.

Poorer students are also less likely to know about the availability of financial aid, and thus more likely to let "sticker shock" keep them from applying in the first place. And a poor student put on a waiting list at a selective school is less likely than a well-to-do student to be accepted, because often a school has exhausted its financial-aid budget before it turns to the list.

In this scramble selectivity is "the coin of the realm," as one admissions officer put it to *The Atlantic* last year. More and more schools define themselves as "selective" in an effort to boost their position and prestige, and fewer and fewer offer the kind of admissions process that provides real opportunities for poorer students. As a result, those disadvantaged students who do attend college are less and less likely to find themselves at four-year schools. Among students who receive Pell Grants— the chief need-based form of federal assistance—the share attending four-year colleges fell from 62 percent in 1974 to 45 percent in 2002; the share attending two-year schools rose from 38 percent to 55 percent.

The advantage to well-off students is particularly pronounced at private colleges and universities. Over the course of the 1990s, for instance, the average private-school grant to students from the top income quartile grew from $1,920 to $3,510, whereas the average grant to students from the lowest income quartile grew from $2,890 to $3,460. And for all the worry of the middle class over rising tuition, increases in grant dollars often outstrip increases in tuition costs for middle- and upper-income students—but not for their poorer peers. In the second half of the 1990s, a study by the Lumina Foundation (a higher-education nonprofit) found, families with incomes below $40,000 received less than seventy cents in grants for every dollar increase in private-college tuition. All other families, including the richest, received more than a dollar in aid for every dollar increase in tuition.

It isn't just schools that have moved their aid dollars up the income ladder. State and federal governments have done the same. Since the 1980s public funds have covered a shrinking share of college costs, and with entitlements claiming an ever growing chunk of state and federal budgets, the chance of a return to the free-spending 1970s seems remote. But even when higher-education outlays have increased—they did during the 1990s boom years, for instance—government dollars have been funneled to programs that disproportionately benefit middle- and upper-income college students.

Both colleges and states have increasingly invested in "merit-based" scholarships, which offer extra cash to high-performing students regardless of need; these programs are often modeled on Georgia's HOPE scholarship, established in 1993 and funded by a state lottery, and thus amount to a form of regressive taxation. The federal government, meanwhile, has used tax credits to help parents defray the cost of college—a benefit that offers little to low-income families. Pell Grants have been expanded, but the purchasing power of individual grants hasn't kept pace with rising tuition.

Overall, American financial aid has gradually moved from a grant-based to a loan-based system. In 1980, 41 percent of all financial-aid dollars were in the form of loans; today 59 percent are. In the early 1990s Congress created a now enormous "noneed" loan program; it has been a boon for upper-income students, who can more easily afford to repay debts accrued during college. At the same time, the federal government allowed families to discount home equity when assessing their financial circumstances, making many more students eligible for loans that had previously been reserved for the poorest applicants. The burdens associated with loans may be part of the reason why only 41 percent of low-income students who enter four-year colleges graduate within five years, compared with 66 percent of high-income students.

All these policy changes have been politically popular, supported by Democratic and Republican politicians alike. After all, the current financial-aid system is good for those voters—middle-class and above—who already expect to send their kids to college, and who are more likely to take the cost of college into consideration when they vote. And though Americans support the ideal of universal educational opportunity, they also support the somewhat nebulous notion of merit and the idea that a high SAT score or good grades should be rewarded with tuition discounts—especially when it's their children's grades and SAT scores that are being rewarded.

But it's not enough to blame the self-interest of many universities or the pandering of politicians for the lack of socioeconomic diversity in higher education. There's also the uncomfortable fact that a society in which education is so unevenly distributed may represent less a failure of meritocracy than its logical endpoint.

That the meritocracy would become hereditary was the fear of Michael Young, the British civil servant who coined the term. His novel *The Rise of the Meritocracy* (1958)—written in the form of a dry Ph.D. thesis that analyzed society from the vantage point of 2034—envisions a future of ever more perfect intelligence tests and educational segregation, in which a cognitive elite holds sway until the less intelligent masses rise to overthrow their brainy masters. A scenario of stratification by intelligence was raised again in 1971, in these pages, by the Harvard psychologist Richard Herrnstein, and in 1994 by Herrnstein and Charles Murray, in their controversial best seller *The Bell Curve*. That book is now remembered for suggesting the existence of ineradicable racial differences in IQ, but its larger argument was that America is segregated according to cognitive ability—and there's nothing we can do about it.

Today Young's dystopian fears and *The Bell Curve's* self-consciously hardheaded realism seem simplistic; both reduce the complex questions of merit and success to a matter of IQ, easily tested and easily graphed. The role that inherited intelligence plays in personal success remains muddy and controversial, but most scholars reject the "Herrnstein Nightmare" (as the journalist Mickey Kaus dubbed it) of class division by IQ.

It doesn't really matter, though, whether our meritocracy passes on success genetically, given how completely it is passed on through wealth and culture. The higher one goes up the income ladder, the greater the emphasis on education and the pressure from parents and peers to excel at extracurricular achievement—and the greater the likelihood of success. (Even the admissions advantage that many schools give to recruited athletes—often presumed to help low-income students—actually tends to disproportionately benefit the children of upper-income families, perhaps because they are sent to high schools that encourage students to participate in a variety of sports.) In this inherited meritocracy the high-achieving kid will not only attend school with other high achievers but will also marry a high achiever and settle in a high-achieving area—the better to ensure that his children will have all the cultural advantages he enjoyed growing up.

Powerful though these cultural factors are, change is possible. The same studies that reveal just how class-defined American higher education remains also offer comfort for would-be reformers. Certainly, policies that strengthen families or improve elementary education undercut social stratification more effectively than anything colleges do. For now, however, numerous reasonably prepared students—300,000 a year, by one estimate—who aren't going to college could be. And many students who are less likely than their higher-income peers to attend the most selective schools would thrive if admitted.

The obvious way to reach these students is to institute some sort of class-based affirmative action—a "thumb on the scale" for low-income students that is championed by Bowen and by Carnevale and Rose in their analyses of educational inequality. Many elite universities claim to pursue such policies already, but Bowen's study finds *no* admissions advantage for poor applicants to the selective schools in the sample simply for being poor. In contrast, a recruited athlete is 30 percent more likely to be admitted than an otherwise identical applicant; a member of an under-represented minority is 28 percent more likely; and a "legacy" (alumni child) or a student who applies early is 20 percent more likely.

As an alternative Bowen and his co-authors propose that selective schools begin offering a 20 percent advantage to low-income students—a policy with "a nice kind of symbolic symmetry" to the advantage for legacies, they point out. By their calculations, this would raise the proportion of low-income students at the nineteen elite schools in their sample from 11 to 17 percent, without much impact on the schools' academic profiles.

Class-based affirmative action has an obvious political advantage: it's more popular with the public than race-based affirmative action. (Bowen envisions socioeconomic diversky as a supplement to racial diversity, not a replacement.) Increasing socioeconomic diversity might offer something to both sides of the red-blue divide—to a Democratic Party rhetorically committed to equalizing opportunity, and to a Republican Party that increasingly represents the white working class, one of the groups most likely to benefit from having the scales weighted at elite universities.

But however happy this may sound in theory, one wonders how likely schools are to adopt class-based preferences. As Carnevale and Rose put it, doing so "would alienate politically powerful groups and help less powerful constituencies"; Bowen notes that it would reduce income from tuition and alumni giving. A selective school might court backlash every time it admitted a poor kid with, say, a middle-range SAT over an upper-middle-class kid with a perfect score. It's doubtful that many colleges would be willing to accept the losses—and, for the more selective among them, the possible drop in *U.S. News* rankings.

Even the elite of the elite—schools like the nineteen examined in Bowen's book, which are best able to afford the costs associated with class-based affirmative action—seem more inclined to increase financial aid than to revamp their admissions policies with an eye toward economic diversity. In the past several years schools like Harvard, Princeton, and Brown have shifted financial-aid dollars from loans to grants, helping to ensure a free ride for the neediest students once they get in. Such gestures make for good public relations, and they do help a few students—but they don't make it easier for low-income students to gain admission.

The benefits and the limitations of moving from loans to grants can be observed in the "AccessUVa" program at the University of Virginia, one of the schools in Bowen's sample. In 2003 it had a typical entering class for an elite school—58 percent of the students came from families with annual incomes above $100,000—and in 2004 fewer than six percent of students came from families with incomes below $40,000. In 2004 Virginia announced that for students with family incomes below 150 percent of the poverty line it would eliminate need-based loans and would instead offer grants exclusively (the school has since raised the threshold to include families of four making less than 200 percent of the poverty line, or about $40,000). It would also cap the amount of debt any student could accrue, funding the rest of his or her tuition through grants. The school publicized its increased affordability, with large-scale outreach to poorer parts of the state. It's too early to judge the program's success, but the first year's results are instructive: the number of low-income freshmen increased by nearly half, or sixty-six out of a class of about 3,100. This is a praiseworthy if small step: those sixty-six brought the low-income total to 199, or about six percent of the class. But it does not solve the problem of unequal access to higher education.

Significant improvements in access, if and when they come, will probably have little to do with the policies at the most elite schools. In America access ultimately rests on what happens in the vast middle rank of colleges and universities, where most undergraduates are educated—in particular, in state schools.

One thing that's unlikely to happen is a sudden increase in funding for higher education, along the lines of the post-World War II surge that made college possible for so many young people. The budgetary demands of swelling entitlements and military spending, the wariness of voters who perceive schools (sometimes rightly, usually wrongly) to be growing fat off their high tuition, and the cultural chasm between a Republican-controlled government and a lefter-than-thou academy—all this and more ensures that spending on higher education will not leap to the top of the nation's political agenda. Instead, schools and legislators must be willing to experiment.

The College Pipeline

Some of the most basic information can also be the hardest to come by—and data about who moves on to what level of education, and when, is a classic case in point. Official education statistics often omit students when they switch schools, or when they drop out and then re-enroll. As a result, there is disagreement over precise numbers. The chart below, derived from a study that followed 12,000 eighth-graders from 1988 through 2000, represents the Department of Education's best available snapshot of what percentage of young people make it through college within twelve years of leaving the eighth grade.

The good news is that there's no shortage of ideas. Bowen, for instance, points out that state schools might consider rethinking their relatively low tuition, which amounts to a subsidy for wealthy in-state parents. (Indeed, upper-income parents are increasingly choosing to send their children to state schools, presumably with just this advantage in mind.) These schools could keep their official tuition low while charging premiums for better-off applicants. Or they could follow the lead of Miami University, in Ohio, which recently raised in-state tuition to the same level as out-of-state tuition (from $9,150 to $19,730).

What should be done with the extra money? State governments might consider tying funding for schools more tightly to access—either directly, by rewarding those colleges that graduate larger numbers of low-income students, or indirectly, as Bowen and his co-authors suggest, by shifting funding from flagship universities to regional schools, which are more likely to enroll disadvantaged students.

More radically, states might ask how well they are serving their populations by funding public universities directly and allowing the universities to disburse the funds as they see fit. If the point of a public university is to hire superstar faculty members, build world-class research facilities, and compete

Out of Every 100 Eighth-Grade Students . . .

78 graduate from high school on time with a standard diploma . . .

Of these, 60 start college (35 in a four-year college, 25 in a two-year college or trade school) by age 26 or 27 . . .

Of these, 47 remain in the post-secondary system after their first year . . .

Twelve years after the eighth grade 29 have earned at least a bachelor's degree, five an associate's degree, and three a certificate . . .

Sources: National Center for Education Statistics; National Education Longitudinal Study of 1988/2000 Postsecondary Transcript Files

with Harvard and Yale, then perhaps this way of funding makes sense. (It's worth noting that since the 1970s public schools have spent an increasing share of their funds on research and administration rather than on instruction.) But if the point is to make higher education more accessible, it doesn't.

The Ohio University economist Richard Vedder has suggested that states might consider offering less money to schools and more money to students, in the form of tuition vouchers redeemable at any public institution in their home state. These could be distributed according to financial need: if the average tuition in a state university system were $15,000, a poor student might receive a voucher for $15,000 and a wealthy student one for $3,000. Schools would have less of a financial incentive to admit mostly rich students. Vouchers might also simplify filing for financial aid: the economist Thomas Kane has argued that the sheer complexity of this process deters many low-income students.

Like class-based affirmative action, a voucher program might be able to command support from both sides of the political aisle. The system's market-based efficiency would delight free marketeers (Vedder is affiliated with the conservative American Enterprise Institute), and its potential for increasing access might win the support of egalitarian liberals. And a voucher approach to funding state schools would mean less direct state involvement in higher education, which would please academics and administrators tired of having cost-conscious legislators looking over their shoulders.

A more egalitarian college-admissions system would run counter to the interests of upper-middle-class parents, who wield great influence in the politics of higher education.

Governments and public universities may also have lessons to learn from for-profit schools, which increasingly attract the students shut out of American higher education. Driven by bottom-line concerns, some of these schools enroll students who can't do the work, or promise job opportunities that never materialize. But many are oriented toward the needs of low-income populations. In New York State, for instance, some commercial schools set tuition at around $9,000—exactly the amount that a needy student can expect to receive from a Pell Grant combined with the state's tuition-assistance program. And they tend to serve the kind of students that traditional universities are failing—working adults, for instance, looking for the economic advantages that come with a college degree.

What gives the for-profit schools a leg up is their ability to "unbundle" a college education from its traditional (and costly) campus environment—something made possible in large part by the spread of the Internet. Some for-profit schools are entirely

Web-based. Many others have put their reading lists, class registration, and even advising online. This is obviously not a model that a flagship state university is likely to emulate. But it may no longer make sense to spend a vast amount to sustain a traditional campus experience for the few when the same amount can provide an education for the many.

All these experiments—and that's what they are—have drawbacks. Public universities that spend more to improve access and graduation rates could make up for the expense by cutting, say, faculty salaries. Public schools already have a hard time keeping sought-after teachers from jumping to private colleges; if more money were spent enrolling and graduating poorer students, the problem would only worsen.

And the more that market efficiency was brought to bear on higher education, and the more that degree-granting and graduation rates were emphasized over the traditional academic experience, the more the liberal arts would be likely to suffer. Computer classes would crowd out Shakespeare, management courses would replace musical instruction, everyone would learn Spanish and no one Greek. Who would speak up to save liberal education?

The most obvious drawback is that a more egalitarian system, in which a college degree is nearly universal and therefore a less exclusive pathway to later success, would run counter to the interests of upper-middle-class parents—the people who wield the most influence in the politics of higher education. It's elite Americans who would lose out in class-based affirmative action. It's elite Americans who would pay more if state schools raised their tuition and state governments handed out income-adjusted vouchers. And it's elite Americans who would lose some of their standing if educational opportunity were more widely distributed. Why should they give it up? *It's not as if our child doesn't deserve his advantages,* parents might say, after helping that child rack up not only high grades and SAT scores but also a sterling record of community service.

What, really, does an eighteen-year-old high achiever "deserve"? A good college education, certainly—but surely not the kind of advantage that college graduates now enjoy. As Nicholas Lemann put it in *The Big Test,* his history of the American meritocracy, "Let us say you wanted to design a system that would distribute opportunity in the most unfair possible way. A first choice would be one in which all roles were inherited . . . A second unfair system might be one that allowed for competition but insisted that it take place as early in life as possible and with school as the arena." Students should be rewarded for academic achievement. But twelve years of parentally subsidized achievement should not hand them an advantage for the next fifty years of their lives.

ROSS DOUTHAT is a reporter-researcher for *The Atlantic* and the author of *Privilege: Harvard and the Education of the Ruling Class.*

Test-Your-Knowledge Form

We encourage you to photocopy and use this page as a tool to assess how the articles in *Annual Editions* expand on the information in your textbook. By reflecting on the articles you will gain enhanced text information. You can also access this useful form on a product's book support Web site at *http://www.mhcls.com/online/*.

NAME: _____ DATE: _____

TITLE AND NUMBER OF ARTICLE: _____

BRIEFLY STATE THE MAIN IDEA OF THIS ARTICLE: _____

_____

LIST THREE IMPORTANT FACTS THAT THE AUTHOR USES TO SUPPORT THE MAIN IDEA:

_____

WHAT INFORMATION OR IDEAS DISCUSSED IN THIS ARTICLE ARE ALSO DISCUSSED IN YOUR TEXTBOOK OR OTHER READINGS THAT YOU HAVE DONE? LIST THE TEXTBOOK CHAPTERS AND PAGE NUMBERS:

_____

LIST ANY EXAMPLES OF BIAS OR FAULTY REASONING THAT YOU FOUND IN THE ARTICLE:

_____

LIST ANY NEW TERMS/CONCEPTS THAT WERE DISCUSSED IN THE ARTICLE, AND WRITE A SHORT DEFINITION:

We Want Your Advice

ANNUAL EDITIONS revisions depend on two major opinion sources: one is our Advisory Board, listed in the front of this volume, which works with us in scanning the thousands of articles published in the public press each year; the other is you—the person actually using the book. Please help us and the users of the next edition by completing the prepaid article rating form on this page and returning it to us. Thank you for your help!

ANNUAL EDITIONS: United States History, Volume 2, 20/e

ARTICLE RATING FORM

Here is an opportunity for you to have direct input into the next revision of this volume.
We would like you to rate each of the articles listed below, using the following scale:

1. **Excellent: should definitely be retained**
2. **Above average: should probably be retained**
3. **Below average: should probably be deleted**
4. **Poor: should definitely be deleted**

Your ratings will play a vital part in the next revision.
Please mail this prepaid form to us as soon as possible.
Thanks for your help!

RATING	ARTICLE	RATING	ARTICLE
_____	1. The American Civil War, Emancipation, and Reconstruction on the World Stage	_____	21. A Monumental Man
_____	2. 1871 War on Terror	_____	22. When America Sent Her Own Packing
_____	3. Little Bighorn Reborn	_____	23. Wings Over America
_____	4. Gifts of the "Robber Barons"	_____	24. Labor Strikes Back
_____	5. The Spark of Genius	_____	25. World War II: 1941 to 1945
_____	6. Global Cooling	_____	26. The Biggest Decision: Why We Had to Drop the Atomic Bomb
_____	7. Lockwood in '84	_____	27. Dollar Diplomacy
_____	8. A Day to Remember: December 29, 1890	_____	28. From Rosie the Riveter to the Global Assembly Line: American Women on the World Stage
_____	9. Where the Other Half Lived	_____	29. The Civil Rights Movement in World Perspective
_____	10. The Murder of Lucy Pollard	_____	30. The Rise of Conservatism Since World War II
_____	11. Joe Hill: 'I Never Died,' Said He	_____	31. The Spirit of '68
_____	12. Alice Roosevelt Longworth	_____	32. Soft Power
_____	13. A Day to Remember: March 25, 1911 Triangle Fire	_____	33. From Saigon to Desert Storm
_____	14. The Fate of Leo Frank	_____	34. The Tragedy of Bill Clinton
_____	15. The Ambiguous Legacies of Women's Progressivism	_____	35. The Rove Presidency
_____	16. The Enemy Within	_____	36. Refusing to Lose
_____	17. A Day to Remember: January 16, 1920	_____	37. A Legend's Soul Is Rested
_____	18. Evolution on Trial	_____	38. Ending the Fool's Game
_____	19. Rethinking Politics: Consumers and the Public Good During the Jazz Age	_____	39. Pssst . . . Nobody Loves a Torturer
_____	20. A Promise Denied	_____	40. Global Warming
		_____	41. Boomer Century
		_____	42. Does Meritocracy Work?

||||

BUSINESS REPLY MAIL
FIRST CLASS MAIL PERMIT NO. 551 DUBUQUE IA

POSTAGE WILL BE PAID BY ADDRESSEE

McGraw-Hill Contemporary Learning Series
501 BELL STREET
DUBUQUE, IA 52001

Լ․ Ն․Ս․․Ս․ԼՍ․․․Ս․․․․ՍՍ․Ս․Ս․Ս․․․Ս․Ս․Ս

ABOUT YOU

Name

Date

Are you a teacher? ☐ A student? ☐
Your school's name

Department

Address | City | State | Zip

School telephone #

YOUR COMMENTS ARE IMPORTANT TO US!

Please fill in the following information:
For which course did you use this book?

Did you use a text with this ANNUAL EDITION? ☐ yes ☐ no
What was the title of the text?

What are your general reactions to the Annual Editions concept?

Have you read any pertinent articles recently that you think should be included in the next edition? Explain.

Are there any articles that you feel should be replaced in the next edition? Why?

Are there any World Wide Web sites that you feel should be included in the next edition? Please annotate.

May we contact you for editorial input? ☐ yes ☐ no
May we quote your comments? ☐ yes ☐ no